Someone once said, "A man is helped to live by remembering he must die." Jim's new book investigating the meaning of life through the lens of a seasoned homicide detective is fascinatingly eye-opening and invigorating! Learn from felons, fugitives, and frauds through these true crime stories and discover who you really are and why you were created.

> **KIRK CAMERON,** actor, evangelist, host of *Takeaways with Kirk Cameron*, and author of *As You Grow*

Why are we here? How should I live? Who am I? Every worldview, directly or indirectly, offers answers to these questions, but, as J. Warner Wallace lays out, the answers offered in a Christian worldview are true. This book is a different kind of apologetic, pointing to how Christianity best explains life as we experience it.

> **JOHN STONESTREET,** host of *Breakpoint*, coauthor of *A Practical Guide to Culture*

God's truth is revealed everywhere, even in the stories of a former homicide investigator, and God's truth leads to human flourishing. Jim brilliantly weaves these truths together in practical real-world living for those interested in being a disciple of Jesus.

> **ZACH DASHER,** cohost of the *Unashamed* podcast, producer of *The Blind* movie

This book brings true crime and apologetics together in a way I've never witnessed before. Jim's approach is brilliant, extracting spiritual truth from true crime stories that every reader can apply in their daily Christian walk.

> **MATT HAMMITT,** Grammy-nominated singer (including as lead singer for Sanctus Real), songwriter, and author of *Lead Me*

Once again, J. Warner Wallace uses his longtime experience as a homicide detective and gives a one-of-a-kind approach to look at human nature, the struggles we face, and how each of us desires and seeks Truth. In *The Truth in True Crime*, Wallace invites you into the drama of the investigation only to find out what really matters in the end.

> **CISSIE GRAHAM LYNCH,** host of the *Fearless with Cissie Graham Lynch* podcast, Billy Graham Evangelistic Association and Samaritan's Purse

What can we learn from some of the darkest deeds humans commit? As a cold-case homicide detective, Jim undertook grisly cases and, in doing so, uncovered many truths about what makes us tick—and why we need a Savior. Join him on this eye-opening journey to discovering the truth about life through an exploration of life and death, morality, and, ultimately, the good news of Jesus Christ.

GREG LAURIE, senior pastor of Harvest Christian Fellowship

I am no stranger to homicides, but I never thought to look for the meaning of life in a homicide investigation or trial. Detective Wallace's cerebral and precise approach lays out the prima facie evidence to return a quick and confident verdict that the evidence for God is clear and all around you, even in homicides worthy of a true crime thriller.

DAVID STIDHAM, former assistant district attorney, current vice president of business affairs and general counsel of The Chosen, Inc.

As someone who often watches true crime, I am constantly reminded of the depths of human nature. Jim takes his unique experience as a homicide detective and offers valuable biblical insights into human nature, life, death, who life is really all about, and how the answer to pain and suffering is always found in the gospel.

MELISSA DOUGHERTY, author of *Happy Lies*, host of the Melissa Dougherty YouTube channel

It's amazing what you can learn from a crime scene. In this new book by J. Warner Wallace, you'll discover what a routine police investigation can reveal about human nature, the meaning of life, and our need for a Savior.

JIM DALY, president of Focus on the Family

What can you learn by tracking down murderers for a living? "Aha wisdom" that—if you follow it—will bring you direction, hope, and security, even in the worst of circumstances. This book takes the best lessons J. Warner has discovered and shows you how to apply them to transform your life.

FRANK TUREK, speaker, author, and president of CrossExamined.org Ministries

Sometimes death instructs us deeply about life, and vice schools us painfully in virtue. In *The Truth in True Crime*, Wallace shares fifteen critical insights about human flourishing that he learned from years of chasing criminals and convicting killers. This latest work is a storehouse of wisdom, both life wisdom and biblical wisdom—which turn out to be the same thing. You will be the wiser for feasting on it.

GREGORY KOUKL, president of Stand to Reason, author of *Street Smarts, Tactics,* and *The Story of Reality*

THE
TRUTH
IN
TRUE
CRIME

THE TRUTH IN TRUE CRIME

WHAT INVESTIGATING DEATH TEACHES US ABOUT THE MEANING OF LIFE

J. WARNER WALLACE

ZONDERVAN
REFLECTIVE

ZONDERVAN REFLECTIVE

The Truth in True Crime

Copyright © 2024 by J. Warner Wallace

Published in Grand Rapids, Michigan, by Zondervan. Zondervan is a registered trademark of The Zondervan Corporation, L.L.C., a wholly owned subsidiary of HarperCollins Christian Publishing, Inc.

Requests for information should be addressed to customercare@harpercollins.com.

Zondervan titles may be purchased in bulk for educational, business, fundraising, or sales promotional use. For information, please email SpecialMarkets@Zondervan.com.

ISBN 978-0-310-11137-5 (softcover)
ISBN 978-0-310-11141-2 (audio)
ISBN 978-0-310-11138-2 (ebook)

Published in association with the literary agency of Mark Sweeney & Associates, Chicago, Illinois 60611.

Cover design: Darren Welch Design
Cover photo: © Denis Tangney Jr. / Getty Images
Interior design: Kait Lamphere
Illustrated by J. Warner Wallace

Printed in the United States of America

24 25 26 27 28 LBC 5 4 3 2 1

To my grandchildren

CONTENTS

SPECIAL THANKS

Without my amazing wife I would never have taken the time to explore the truths in this book. Thanks Susie, for encouraging, inspiring, and partnering with me for over four decades.

Thanks also to Amy Hall for her steady, consistent commitment to truth and excellence. Her sage advice is reflected on every page of this book.

Thanks, finally, to my friend Frank Turek for his continued support and wisdom.

FOREWORD

My childhood neighbor was a smoker. My big sister and I went over to her house one afternoon, and I was desperate to impress her teenage daughter Tara, who I thought was the absolute coolest. I caught a glimpse of the amber-colored glass ashtray out of the corner of my eye and had the brilliant idea to pick a cigarette butt out of the soot and hold it to my lips. Just as I had fully embodied the elegant style of Audrey Hepburn with her long cigarette holder, my sister gasped and exclaimed, "Oooh, you are gonna be in so much trouble! I'm telling Mom." At this point, my sister and Tara ran out of the room, presumably to race next door and end my life as I knew it. I was left alone in my neighbor's bedroom with nothing but my pigtails, Spider-Man jeans, and crushing guilt. So I did what any sane seven-year-old would do and quickly dashed under the bed.

I must have fallen asleep because before I knew it, the sun had gone down and I overheard the muffled voice of my mom frantically talking with my neighbor. Then I heard them call the police. "Oh my goodness," I thought. "Now I've done it. I am definitely going to jail for this!" So I burrowed in and hid even longer until I worked up the courage to face the music. I finally came out from under the bed and turned myself in. To my surprise, the police officers were not mad at me. They didn't cuff me, drive me downtown, and book me for underage pretend tobacco use. My story did not turn into a true crime documentary on Netflix. Instead, the officers smiled warmly and took me outside to where my mom was surrounded by neighbors, police cars, blinking lights, and the chopping noise of a helicopter flying overhead. Of course, I could have saved the police the paperwork and trip out to my house and saved my mom the trauma of thinking her child had been kidnapped for several hours, had I known one thing. Truth. That's it. If I had known the truth of the situation, it all would have been resolved quickly, with almost no fuss. The truth is, there are no laws against fake smoking. Plus, my sister and Tara probably just ran over to my house, forgot about the whole thing, and started doing something else. Truth changes everything.

Truth is liberating. In the case of my smoking debacle, the truth set me free! I was not in trouble. However, it may seem counterintuitive to think of truth as beneficial when the truth is heartbreaking, such as a grim diagnosis or a life-altering phone call. Yet truth always provides a way of direction and healing. We often cannot appreciate good news until we know the bad news. A cancer patient will not be thankful for the benefits of chemotherapy, and be willing to endure its side effects, until he knows the truth about the diagnosis. Nor can we turn toward God until we know about our true fallen spiritual condition. Sadly, in our present world the truth is exchanged for happy false-hoods within the millions of self-help books that confidently advise you on how to live your life. They counsel you to trust your gut, follow your heart, and put yourself first. However, the truth is that you can dig into your own heart as deep as you want, but you will always find the sinner waiting for you there.

J. Warner Wallace, a Los Angeles homicide detective renowned for the cold cases he's broken, is uniquely qualified to talk about the worst of the human condition. Wallace also knows how humans flourish when they embrace biblical truth. If I could sum up *The Truth in True Crime* into one word, it would be in the word *wisdom*, which is truth applied to life.

Wisdom is what J. Warner Wallace is known for. You may know him as the homicide detective Keith Morrison referred to as "the evidence whis-perer" on *Dateline* NBC. Or you may know him as the former atheist who put the evidence for Christianity to the test and found it to be true. He is both those things. But for those who know him as a brother in Christ, Jim (J. Warner) is the one we go to when we have a major life decision to make. He always has thoughtful advice that is built on hard-won wisdom, common sense, and truth. That is why I am so thrilled he has written this book. In it, he recounts true crime stories from his real-life experience and provides readers with applicable life-changing truths. He demonstrates the superior wisdom of biblical principles, which is surprisingly supported by secular research. Want to know how to live a life that is fruitful, filled with joy, and aligned with truth? Want to glean from the wise advice Jim (J. Warner) has offered so many friends and loved ones? Read the words of this book. I did, and I walked away encouraged. And I think you will too. Truth is hard, but as Jesus promised, "You will know the truth, and the truth will set you free."

Alisa Childers, author of *The Deconstruction of Christianity*
and host of *The Alisa Childers Podcast*

PREFACE

Chasing Leads

Rick's dress shoes were getting wet as the snow fell with increasing intensity. I could read the expression on his face: *this better be the one.*

We were standing on a porch—the twenty-seventh in a long series of porches—waiting for a redhead to open the door. It was a bitterly cold December day, less than a mile from Temple Square in Salt Lake City.

Thirty-eight years earlier, Cathy Jacobsen had been stabbed to death in her bedroom, two states west of Utah. She was a junior in high school at the time and innocent enough to allow the killer into her home while her parents were at work.

He stabbed Cathy with a knitting needle she had been using to make a scarf for her mother's Christmas gift. The killer then left Cathy on the floor of her bedroom next to the scarf, a baseball cap, and several unwrapped gifts.

He must have panicked. Perhaps Cathy screamed, although no one in the neighborhood reported hearing her. In any case, the killer inadvertently left an important clue: his cap.

The original detectives recovered a single red hair from that baseball cap, but there was no DNA technology at the time to help identify the suspect. When we reopened the case nearly four decades later, the technology was sufficient to retrieve a partial DNA marker from the hair. Not enough to identify the murderer, but enough to match a redhead from whom we might obtain a larger sample.

And thus began our long porch-to-porch journey across America. You might not think a seventeen-year-old girl would know many redheads, but in this case you would be wrong. We identified thirty-four redheaded associates, friends, and relatives.

I turned on my small audio recorder, tucked it in my outer pocket, and knocked.

A man with red hair opened the door, and Rick presented him with a business card. I began my well-rehearsed introduction: "Hello, Mr. Carson, my name is Detective Wallace, and we are investigating the murder of Cathy Jacobsen."

"Oh my . . . yes, we were friends many years ago. What a nightmare. It was so shocking."

"Well, we were fortunate enough to obtain the killer's DNA from the crime scene, and we've been visiting her friends and family members to eliminate them as suspects." My opening statement was intentionally diagnostic. Who would refuse the opportunity to be eliminated as a killer? Rick and I knew the murderer would likely hesitate at such a request, so we carefully evaluated Mr. Carson's response.

"Of course, I'm happy to give a sample. Anything I can do to help. I've always hoped the police would eventually solve this murder." Rick and I exchanged knowing expressions. We'd seen this enthusiasm before. *Twenty-six times* before. We swabbed Carson, only to later find he, like the prior twenty-six candidates, failed to match the DNA profile from the cap.

We continued to chase leads for three more months, eventually locating, swabbing, and eliminating all thirty-four redheaded suspects. Eighteen months into our investigation, we realized we were no closer to solving the case. The murder of Cathy Jacobsen remains one of my open, unsolved mysteries.

While our inability to solve the Jacobsen case seemed an abject failure at the time, we later came to see it as much more. From murder cases like this one, we discovered a lot about people—and about ourselves—even when the cases remained unsolved. We learned a lot about life from investigating death, a lot about the nature of people from investigating victims and suspects.

Maybe that's why "true crime" stories are more popular than ever before, dominating fiction bookshelves, podcast queues, and streaming platforms. True *crime* reveals our true *nature*, and everyone enjoys plumbing the depths of humanity's deepest truths (and darkest secrets). Homicide investigations reveal more than the identity of the killer. They also reveal what's important to us, what threatens our well-being, and what causes us to flourish. Every murder investigation teaches two lessons: a *death* lesson and a *life* lesson. Some of the lessons Rick and I learned were cautionary tales. Others, guiding principles.

All, however, happened to confirm the truth of the Christian worldview.

I initially found this surprising. I wasn't a Christian when I started my career as a detective. But along the way, I began investigating the case for God's existence, the reliability of the Gospels, the resurrection of Jesus, and the divine impact of Jesus on human culture. I've written about my discoveries in other books. This book is different. It contains truths about *life* gleaned from investigations about *death*. It also includes the surprisingly accurate description of human nature found not in the latest scientific journals but in the ancient pages of the Bible.

The Truth in True Crime is intended to be a practical wisdom book (the kind of book one might pen for one's grandchildren) and a Christian evidence book (the kind of book one might write for those who still doubt the explanatory power of Christianity). While every chapter includes a real death investigation, I've exchanged details between cases to protect the identity of victims (and suspects), and I've altered storylines to protect ongoing investigations.

Join us as we chase a few leads and examine the truths we discovered in true crime. Along the way, you may pick up a guiding principle or two to help you thrive and flourish as a human created in the image of God. You may also recognize yourself in the unique descriptions that Christian Scripture offers.

These lessons and clues will be valuable even if you don't believe in God, but make no mistake about it, each lead affirms an aspect of "biblical anthropology," the description of human nature that our divine Creator offers in the pages of the Bible. Rick and I typically chase leads to determine the identity of a killer in true crime murder cases. This book will help you chase leads and investigate clues to better understand your own identity and the identity of your Creator.

A POOL OF BLOOD (UNDER MY FEET)

How to Make Age-Appropriate Mistakes

Wisdom is the daughter of experience.
—LEONARDO DA VINCI

Experience is merely the name men gave to their mistakes.
—OSCAR WILDE

A re you kidding me!" Alan yelled as I was completing a line in my notebook.

I was the new guy on the homicide team, still concerned about my image with the other five detectives who had been serving on the team for years. Alan was the senior member and a vocal source of praise or scorn. Tonight, he intended the latter.

"Look around, newbie," Alan barked. "There are six of us standing here. Does anything stand out to you?"

For a moment, I wondered if I missed an important bit of evidence in the crime scene. Kenny Riggs was murdered in the concrete side yard of his modest home. He'd been tied up and beaten severely before he was eventually shot in the head. His son discovered his body. In my effort to impress this seasoned team, I arrived early and began a quick assessment of the area. Looking up from my small notebook, I could see my partners had now arrived.

I glanced at Alan, then down at my notes, searching for what I may have missed.

"I'm talking about *you*, kid, not whatever's in your stupid notebook.

1

Look at the six of us." Alan began singing the song from Sesame Street: "One of these things is not like the others, one of these things just doesn't belong." Several of the seasoned detectives laughed. Rick tried to keep a straight face.

My partners were standing on one side of the yellow crime scene tape. I was standing on the other.

Eager to evaluate the scene, I had lifted the tape and walked toward the body. All this *prior* to the arrival of the crime scene technicians and prior to any photography of the scene. Looking back, I realize how ridiculous this sounds. But early in my career as a detective, and prior to attending my first homicide school, it never occurred to me to protect the crime scene from *everyone*, including me.

I began to sheepishly exit the scene when Alan added yet another insult to my injury.

"Stop, knucklehead! Look where you're standing!"

Poking out from under the right side of my shoe, I could see a darkened spot of concrete. Bloodred.

"The more you walk in that scene, the more you're going to track blood."

Rick couldn't contain himself any longer: "Yeah, if we arrest the killer based on the shoeprint evidence, Wallace is our guy!"

Now everyone was laughing.

I slipped out of my shoes and carried them from the crime scene, walking delicately like a man trying to avoid land mines. Fortunately, cell phone technology hadn't yet surpassed the flip phone, so no one was able to take a picture as I joined them on the other side of the tape with shoes in hand.

1   Defining What We Seek

Alan eventually became one of my closest friends. I turned to him often for knowledge *and* wisdom, and he taught me the difference between the two.

Everyone seems to value wisdom. Secular self-help manuals abound in the publishing industry, and the genre of "wisdom literature" dominates religious texts. Wisdom sells, for religious and nonreligious people alike. We flock to texts promising this coveted commodity.

But while most of us want to be "wise," we often fail to distinguish wisdom from knowledge. Wisdom is sometimes described as "accumulated philosophical or scientific learning" or "scholarly knowledge."[1] But if wisdom is nothing more than "learning" or "knowledge," why not use those words instead of "wisdom"? Wisdom appears to be something different, something more.

Some believe science can help us define the term. Igor Grossmann, an associate professor of psychology and director of the Wisdom and Culture Lab at the University of Waterloo in Canada, for example, invited behavioral and social scientists to "explore the possibility of a scientific consensus on the psychological characteristics of wisdom and best practices for its measurement."[2] They concluded that "moral aspiration" was one of two "pillars of wisdom." In other words, the scientists, "like many philosophers before them, considered wisdom to be *morally* grounded" (emphasis mine).

 **EVIDENCE: Humans Covet Wisdom**

Human beings have been wisdom-seekers across the ages and across the globe. The ancients (like Socrates, Confucius, and Ptahhotep) were known for their wise proclamations, and modern humans are no less interested in this sometimes-elusive commodity.

Why is this the case? Why are humans consistently interested in wisdom, even when applying this wisdom may not increase their comfort or gain?

For example, is there a wise way to commit a murder? Or is murder unwise—by definition—because of its immoral nature?

This moral dimension to wisdom complicates the definition of the term. How, for example, are we to determine what is morally virtuous or vile? If wise choices are defined by their moral "goodness," who gets to decide what is morally good (and, therefore, wise)? While science can establish "what is" (or what happened), it is incapable of determining what *ought* to be (or what *ought* to have happened). As David Hume observed centuries ago, it's not clear how science alone can move from physical *descriptions* to moral *prescriptions*.[3]

So where can we turn to establish a moral "ought" if science can only provide an observable "is"?

Can people simply decide what is morally "good" or "bad"? In a culture where truth is largely a subjective matter of "lived experience" and personal opinion, it's tempting to conclude that people might be the final authority when it comes to moral truths as well. But Kenny Riggs' killer could not make the murder morally virtuous with a simple personal proclamation. The act was immoral regardless of what the killer personally believed.

Was the murder morally wrong simply because the people of California passed a law against murder? Do groups of people decide what is morally vile? If California changed its laws, would the killing of Kenny Riggs suddenly become a virtuous act?

No. The moral nature of murder is not determined *subjectively* by people, neither individually nor collectively. The murder of Kenny Riggs was *objectively* immoral in a way that transcends individuals and groups.

 ## Better Wisdom

If objective, transcendent wisdom is "morally grounded" (as philosophers, theologians, and even scientists agree), then it requires an objective, transcendent source for moral truth. That kind of wisdom is unavailable if moral truths are simply personal (or collective) opinions. If wisdom is morally negotiable, Kenny's killer might have a case for the wisdom of his act.

Wisdom's need for an objective moral foundation explains why the ancient Christian worldview provides a better basis for wisdom than the relativism of our culture does.

Christianity recognized the value of wisdom long before self-help books led the other genres at internet bookstores. The Bible describes wisdom as supremely valuable and better than gold, silver, treasure, or jewels.[4] But more importantly, the Bible also recognizes that wisdom must include what scientists now describe as "moral aspiration." True, objective, transcendent wisdom is grounded in the one true, objective, transcendent source for moral truth: God. Wisdom doesn't change with the times or vary depending on human opinions or preferences. The "wisdom of the ages" is just that: wisdom spanning the ages, grounded in the unchanging moral nature of *the* ancient moral authority: God himself.

That's why the Bible authors declared, "The fear of the Lord, that is wisdom, and to turn away from evil is understanding."[5] True wisdom calls us to recognize God as the unchanging source of moral truth and to shun what God describes as evil. All wise choices are also morally virtuous choices, and their moral virtue is grounded in the wise, moral authority of God. "The wisdom that comes from heaven is first of all pure; then peace-loving, considerate, submissive, full of mercy and good fruit, impartial and sincere."[6]

Wisdom grounded in the nature of God is true, objective wisdom because God is both omniscient (all-knowing) *and* omnibenevolent (all-good). The Bible declares, "The foolishness of God is wiser than human wisdom, and the weakness of God is stronger than human strength."[7]

Christianity recognizes the value of wisdom and its dependence on moral virtue. But unlike human attempts to ground wisdom subjectively in popular, moral opinions, Christianity grounds wisdom in the unchanging, dependable nature of God.

Now, if you're not a Christian believer, before you flinch at the idea of a moral code based on the nature of the Christian God, keep in mind that atheists *also* recognize the value of the Christian moral code. One study of believers and nonbelievers found that "atheists and theists appear to align on moral values related to protecting vulnerable individuals, liberty versus oppression, and being epistemically rational."[8] When prominent atheists say they can be "good without God," they typically offer examples in which they embrace the values described in the Ten Commandments, the same moral virtues Christians uphold.

The question here is not whether nonbelievers can *know* or *learn* moral truth, but rather if nonbelievers can *ground* these truths in something other than God. Can true wisdom, the kind of transcendent wisdom most of us require as we navigate relationships, challenges, hardships (and murder investigations) best be found in the social science section of the library or on the theology shelves? Can we best determine what's virtuous or vile by surveying cultural opinion or by sitting at the feet of our Creator?

 Learning through Experience

I wiped the bottom of my shoes and followed along with the rest of our homicide team as the patrol sergeant briefed us about her observations prior to our arrival. I didn't say a word for the rest of the evening.

I was embarrassed, to say the least. Consumed by failure, I felt like the dumbest detective in history. Looking back, however, I understand the role this failure played in my journey toward wisdom. Definitions describing wisdom as mere knowledge are inadequate. A better definition would include the important role of *experience*:

> (Wisdom is) the ability to use your knowledge and experience to make good decisions and judgments.[9]

This definition recognizes our "moral aspirations" to make "good decisions and judgments" but also acknowledges the role of experience.

Experience is defined as "the conscious events that make up an individual life,"[10] and none of us lives more than a few years without encountering failure. In fact, we're more likely to experience failure than success. It's much easier to thoughtlessly mess things up than mindfully succeed. Just ask me—I've got a story about a crime scene to share with you.

EXAMPLE: Solomon Got It

Few people in history understood the value of wisdom as did Solomon, the ancient king of Israel. God told him, "Ask for whatever you want me to give you." Solomon could have asked for power, money, fame, or longevity. Instead, he asked for "a discerning heart to govern your people and to distinguish between right and wrong" (1 Kings 3:9 NIV).

Given everything you might pursue in life, how high is wisdom on your list?

But failure appears to be the *root* of wisdom and success. One study spanning over forty years and studying over one million pieces of data concluded that "every winner begins as a loser."[11] Why? Because failure often leads to honest self-examination, and honest self-examination to wisdom—*if* the failing party is willing to learn.

I entered a crime scene prematurely on *one* occasion. I never did it again. That single episode revealed my status as a novice. It humbled me. My response was not indignation but the realization that there was still a lot to learn. Mistakes were painfully common in my first weeks and months as an investigator, but those early miscues were critical to my later success.

Research confirms this truth, even for people who aren't standing in a pool of blood. The aforementioned study found that repeated failures (if suffered early) were actually the *key* to success. "In other words, the faster you fail, the better your chances of success, and the more time between attempts, the more likely you are to fail again."[12]

Even without this research data, the truth about early failures would be evident from the history of successful people. Jerry Seinfeld was booed off the stage when he froze during his first live appearance. Elvis Presley's first performance at the Grand Ole Opry was so terrible that talent manager Jim Denny fired him and reportedly told him to stop singing publicly. The Wright brothers failed *many times* before becoming the first to fly. Thomas Edison failed more than a *thousand times* before successfully inventing the world's first light bulb. James Dyson failed over *five thousand times* before successfully inventing his famous vacuum cleaner. Had they given up, all would have been considered failures. They understood, however, the power of making *age-appropriate mistakes.*

I was the youngest member of our homicide team when caught standing in a pool of blood, and while that mistake was clearly a failure, it was an age-appropriate mistake. If Alan had committed the same blunder, he would have received an even harsher scolding from the team. After all, he had over fifteen years of experience, so they would have said, "He should have known better."

KNOWLEDGE GAINED IN AN AREA

COURAGE TO MAKE AGE-APPROPRIATE MISTAKES

EXPERIENCE FROM MAKING MISTAKES

OBJECTIVE MORAL FOUNDATIONS

THE RECIPE FOR
BETTER WISDOM

Chase the Lead

If you're seeking wisdom, let the guy with blood on his shoes offer a few insights. I learned some of this from Alan but most of it from making bone-headed mistakes (some more public than others).

Embrace Your Age-Appropriate Mistakes

Everyone errs. Just do your best to fail in an age-appropriate manner. Don't sweat the blunders of your youth or the mistakes you make when you are new on the job. This is the time when you're *supposed* to make mistakes. The Bible recognizes that "we all stumble in many ways"[13]— some of us are just better at hiding it. It's been said that mistakes don't have to *define you* if you allow them to *refine you.* Embrace the inevitability of your early mistakes and move on. In each mistake, learn from it, rub some dirt on it, and shake it off. Try again.

Admit When You're the Fool

People who can't admit they made a mistake often refuse to change. (Why change? I didn't do anything wrong in the first place!) This is when our "moral aspirations" need to guide us. Biblical wisdom calls us to "do nothing out of selfish ambition or vain conceit," but rather, in humility, to value others above ourselves.[14] When Alan scolded me publicly, I was inclined to defend myself with equal vigor and sarcasm— maybe even try to justify my actions—but wisdom called me to take the higher, more honest, road. I was, after all, the fool standing in blood.

Let Others Fail for You

Oliver Wendell Holmes reportedly recommended, "Learn from the mistakes of others . . . You can't live long enough to make them all yourself!"[15] Wisdom comes from life experiences and failures, but they don't have to be *your* life experiences and failures. Become a careful "mistake watcher," and glean wisdom from the wise counsel of family and friends. Rethink the way you ask people for advice. Rather than just asking, "How did you do that?" ask also, "What mistakes did you make along the way?" Failure is a good teacher. Start learning from the failures of others, including the historical failures recorded on the pages of the Bible. Biblical history is replete with men and women who failed miserably yet were redeemed and restored through their failures.

Build a New Foundation

Once you've deconstructed a few *contemporary* failures (including your own), construct a foundation of ancient wisdom to limit your mistakes going forward. Start by consulting the Master Builder. According to the Bible, people who lack wisdom should ask God, who gives generously to all without finding fault.[16] King Solomon wrote, "By wisdom a house is built, and by understanding it is established; by knowledge the rooms are filled with all precious and pleasant riches."[17] If you want to build a house filled with knowledge leading to success, start with the wisdom of God. Jesus said everyone who heard his words and *did them* would be like a wise man who built his house on the rock.[18] Rock-solid decisions are built on the rock-solid wisdom of Jesus.

Listen to Old People

Why do most people value the insight of their grandparents? Because they've "been there and done that." The longer you've been around, the more likely you are to have made mistakes and learned something important. Studies reveal that "crystallized intelligence" (the accumulation of knowledge, facts, and skills acquired throughout life) is "a necessary condition for wisdom in all age-groups."[19] That may be why "wisdom belongs to the aged, and understanding to the old."[20] Wise *young* people typically spend time learning from wiser *old* people, including the ancients whose wisdom has been documented in Scripture. You're never too young to learn from the oldest in your family or the most ancient in the Bible. Get started.

Do Better
Make a commitment to better decision-making. Ask yourself, (1) Is what I'm about to do within the moral will of God? Is it permissible according to the Bible? (2) Is this action generally wise from a practical perspective? Will it help me reasonably, morally, and efficiently accomplish the goal God has for me in this setting? (3) Does the action utilize the gifts and talents God has given me? (4) Will this decision elevate or glorify God (rather than me)? Can I leverage the opportunity to share Jesus with others?[21] It's hard to make a bad decision if these four objectives are forefront in your mind.

Tell Someone
Wisdom is transferrable only if people are willing to *do the transferring*. Once you know something worth sharing, make sure you take your place in the long line of wisdom-sharers.

The Truth in True Crime: You Were Created to Learn

"Did they teach you to stand in blood at the homicide school?" Alan didn't really expect a response. I foolishly gave him one anyway.

"Last month's class was fully registered; I don't go until next month."

"Can't come soon enough," he replied. I was content to let Alan have the last word. *That's* one lesson I'd already learned.

I considered myself a learner prior to becoming a detective. As an atheist and a committed naturalist, I held education in high regard. I believed humans evolved because of our capacity to learn, and I saw education as the key to progress (including my progress as a detective).

Most humans see themselves as learners in need of an education. One global study of parents, for example, found 79 percent believed their kids needed some sort of advanced education to achieve their life goals.[22] Studies also confirm the ongoing value of learning. People with higher levels of education live longer,[23] are generally healthier,[24] and are even kinder to others.[25] Humans thrive and flourish when they exercise their ability to learn.

 EXPLANATION: We Seek What We Lack

Most people, on a global level, believe in God or a "higher power." We innately understand our comparative lack of wisdom relative to that of such a Being, and this is reflected in our desire for wisdom.

We also innately recognize the need for an objective "wisdom standard," beyond the personal preferences of individuals and societies.

Christianity explains our desire for wisdom and provides the objective, transcendent source for *true* wisdom, grounded in the omniscience and omnibenevolence of God.

As it turns out, the Bible described humans as learners and wisdom-seekers long before we proved it with scientific studies. God created us to learn. The Bible says our desire begins in our youth, when we are "trained up" in the way we should go, continues every day as we grow with our parents, and extends into our lives as disciples of Jesus.[26] We are called to be transformed by the renewal of our minds, with the Holy Spirit's promise to teach us all things.[27] The very word *disciple* comes from the Latin word *discipulus*, meaning "student" or "learner."[28]

According to the biblical worldview, humans were created as wisdom-seekers, designed to learn.

So if you're wondering why we value education and why learning is one of many keys to human flourishing, now you know: it's part of the Creator's design. God is an infinite Being with perfect knowledge. He is the source of all truth. As finite humans with limited knowledge, we find ourselves seeking what we don't yet possess. In fact, God's infinite wisdom exposes our naivete and creates in us a desire to know more. As C. S. Lewis once wrote, "Thirst was made for water; inquiry for truth."[29] We thirst because water exists; we seek wisdom because truth exists (as possessed in the mind of our Creator). We pursue wisdom *initially* because we know it's available; we pursue wisdom *continually* because we know there's always more to learn, especially when compared to the knowledge of God.

Wisdom matters to humans. It's why we continue to seek truth and read books, even a book like this one. *We were created to learn.*

LEAD #2

FAKE IDS AND A STOLEN IDENTITY

How to Write Better Bios

In the social jungle of human existence, there is no
feeling of being alive without a sense of identity.
—ERIK ERIKSON

We know what we are, but not what we may be.
—WILLIAM SHAKESPEARE

We stood near the sill of the large open window and peered down toward the street, three stories above the spot where Lincoln Templeton intended to die. There was blood all over the room, along with heroin syringes and miscellaneous drug paraphernalia. My partner and I got the call just minutes into our shift.

"It's certainly high enough to have killed him."

"Yup, but not today . . ."

Lincoln was on one side of the room behind us, restrained on a gurney as paramedics treated his injuries. On the other side of the room, an officer interviewed a man named Teddy.

Teddy saved Lincoln's life . . . if only barely.

After ascending to national prominence as a college football player, Lincoln suffered a career-ending knee injury. He struggled to reinvent himself and eventually turned to alcohol and then narcotics to ease the pain and the lost sense of direction. An ex-teammate introduced him to heroin. A year later, he found himself living in this seedy hotel, a fraction of the man he had once been and unable to face the reality of who he had become.

He'd already lost his identity and purpose, so on this night, he decided to lose his life as well.

Teddy, the tenant in the next room, simply wouldn't allow it.

A drug addict himself, Teddy had been raised Catholic. When he heard Lincoln rant about suicide through the thin hotel walls, Teddy decided to save him from what he believed to be "eternal damnation." He stepped through Lincoln's unlocked door, and a struggle ensued. Lincoln was determined to jump from the window. Teddy was determined to stop him. In trying to restrain Lincoln to save his life, Teddy nearly wrestled Lincoln to death. By the time we got there, Lincoln was bloody and bruised, and Teddy was exhausted. But both were alive.

In settings like this, it can be difficult to investigate the scene without getting blood on your suit, but on this call, I was wearing a uniform rather than my usual detective attire. It was the first time I had worked in a uniform in nearly fifteen years. This was a special day for me—*and* for my partner. It was one of his earliest crime scenes, and my very last.

As I approached retirement, I asked my supervisor for the opportunity to work my final day in a patrol car rather than behind a detective's desk. I also asked to be partnered with my son Jimmy (a two-year officer) for one of his regular patrol shifts.

So there we were, working together for the first and last time, standing in Lincoln's hotel room, wearing the same uniform, the same badge, and even the same nameplate: *J. Wallace.* We wrapped up the scene and spent the rest of the day patrolling our downtown beat, making a few traffic stops and handling routine calls for service.

At the end of the shift, we returned to the station, took pictures, and headed toward the locker room. As I was changing, I emptied my locker into Jimmy's. We were nearly the same size, and my patches already bore his name. It was a surreal experience, and something unexpected happened as I said goodbye to everyone and drove out through the gates of the police compound for the last time.

I broke down in tears.

That was unanticipated because I had been waiting for this moment for most of my career. Cops put up with a lot during two or three decades of employment, and most of us can't wait to retire. I was no exception. But as I drove from the station, I had the overwhelming sense that I was no longer me.

"I'm a *was*," I thought. "Jimmy is an *is*."

I couldn't be prouder of my kids, and I was honored to hand the reigns and legacy of our family profession over to Jimmy, but for the first time ever, I realized I was going to have an identity problem.

For years I had been known both locally and nationally as "The Evidence Whisperer" because of my work as a cold case detective.[1] When I met someone for the first time, my career was almost always the first part of my introduction.

But my career (and how I had been known to others) was about to end.

The "Identity Age"

Social media exposes our interest in (and our obsession with) identity. Every social media profile begins with a "handle," the name by which we want to be known. Some of us use our real names, and some select new "identifiers." These usernames reveal our values, interests, and desires, including how we desire to be known by others. Just below our username, we carefully craft our bio, the more extended description of who we believe we are and how we want the world to view us.

Even before social media, our names and bios were usually the first things we offered when introducing ourselves to strangers at a dinner party or gathering. But prior to the internet, we seldom had the opportunity to identify ourselves publicly. Social media is driven by repeated public proclamations of identity. We establish our profiles by thoughtfully creating an identity, then feed our profiles with posts and images that amplify the identity we've created.

Why would anyone be surprised, then, to find that the Information Age has now been eclipsed by the "identity age"? Most of the information we seek (or proclaim) is, after all, related to someone's identity, if not our own.

EVIDENCE: Humans Seek Identity

Family ancestry businesses are thriving today, capitalizing on our common human desire to know ourselves and be known by others. Ancient philosophers and sages wrote about the importance of identity, and modern sociologists now study it.

Why do humans care so much about identity? What are we seeking, and why do we seek it? Is our effort to be known by others simply a shadow of a deeper longing?

When I use the term *identity*, especially as a detective, I'm distinguishing between two notions of the word. If Teddy and Lincoln left the scene prior to the arrival of officers, for example, we could later identify both based on their DNA markers and the blood evidence. This evidence might tell us who they were in *one* sense (their species, biological sex, or race, for example) yet fail to identify them in *another* sense (for example, their values, beliefs, priorities, or associations). The DNA could confirm *who they were* but not *how they wanted to be known*.

It's this second definition of identity, the "the sense of self, providing sameness and continuity in personality over time,"[2] that troubled Lincoln enough to consider taking his own life. It also troubled me enough to reexamine my place and purpose in the world.

While that might seem a bit overdramatic, studies reveal the important role identity plays in mental health. A ten-year survey of research in the formation of adolescent identity confirmed that "certainty about oneself and the direction one is going in is closely related to better functioning in multiple domains" and also that "a stable and strong sense of identity is associated with better mental health of adolescents."[3]

Identity matters. It's a key factor in mental health. When our identity is "stable" and "continuous over time," we experience less depression, anxiety, and trauma. If you charted your life on a timeline and noted those periods when you struggled with some aspect of mental health, you would likely find that those same periods were when you were struggling with your identity: in adolescence, after a career change, when your kids grew up, or after a divorce. Whenever we find ourselves grappling emotionally, we're often facing some sort of identity crisis. That's why grounding our identity in something stable and continuous is so important.

Prior to his injury, Lincoln derived his value and identity from his unique physical excellence. He was known by his friends and family as the best football player on his team. After the injury, although he was still Lincoln Templeton, he was no longer the Lincoln Templeton he wanted to be. He became increasingly unstable as he lost his sense of "continuity," direction, and purpose.

As I began the long drive home, I realized Lincoln wasn't the only one whose identity was attached to his purpose.

Outside-In Identity

The oldest French and Latin derivations of the word *identity* are grounded in notions of "sameness," or "oneness" (as expressed in the term *identical*), reflecting a time when individuals were far more likely to base their identity on the communities in which they lived.

The ancients embraced the continuity and protection found in family, profession, ethnic group, and culture, seeking "sameness" or "oneness" with these *external* sources of identity. Rather than looking inwardly for definition and purpose, they took an outside-in approach and adopted the identity provided by the world around them.

Many of us still do this today. Lincoln first started playing football because his father and older brother excelled at the sport. They were known as a football family. I have a similar story. My son and I are part of a three-generation law enforcement family—three of us having served at the same agency, with the same name. Lincoln and I formed an outside-in view of ourselves.

While this ancient approach provides a sense of belonging and purpose, it suffers from some deficiencies.

Finding your identity in the family or group to which you were born may not be desirable if your family is the famous Gambino crime family or your group is a crime syndicate. If your identity is formed entirely from an external community, you may be confined to the history and identity of your group, even if that's not how you want to be known personally.

Worse yet, groups develop their moral codes subjectively, even if collectively. For this reason, an outside-in, community-based approach to identity lacks an objective moral foundation. Is it "good," for example, to be a Gambino? Is the "Gambino life" a "life well lived"? You'd probably think so *if you were a Gambino*.

Without an objective moral foundation, those of us who form our identities around affiliations (either familial, professional, political, or ideological) will sometimes, out of loyalty and self-protection, reject "inconvenient" truths considered offensive to the group. A community-based outside-in approach may limit our pursuit of truth. This is especially true if our associations have been publicly declared on social media. It's not always easy to publicly admit when we're wrong.

Lincoln and I had, in part, formed our identity based on our family and professional associations, just as people have done for centuries. But that wasn't the only way we sought identity and purpose. We also adopted a more contemporary approach.

Inside-Out Identity

According to philosopher Charles Taylor, we are now living in a culture in which "people come to see themselves more and more atomistically, otherwise put, as less and less bound to their fellow citizens in common projects and allegiances."[4]

This may be yet another by-product of the Information Age.

While social media innovators promised an interconnected world of new relational opportunities and increased connectivity, few seem to have anticipated another consequence of their technology: the amplification of our sense of autonomy and its power to shift our priorities.

The first form of social media autonomy is informational. Most of us now get personalized information and news from social networking sites. As users, we choose where and how we get this data, usually reflecting our own personal presuppositions, biases, and beliefs.

The second form of social media autonomy is moral. Most Americans believe "knowing what is right or wrong is a matter of personal experience."[5] Social media algorithms only strengthen our moral "echo chambers," separating us from people who have different experiences and moral beliefs.

EXAMPLE: Rahab's New Identity

Rahab, a woman of disrepute, was not raised as a Jew. When she heard about what God had done for the Israelites, however, she knew Yahweh was "God in heaven above and on the earth below" (Joshua 2:11 NIV). She adopted a new identity and became a citizen of Israel, eventually becoming the mother of Boaz, and the great-great-grandmother of King David, in the lineage of Jesus.

How might your life change if you adopted a new identity?

These two forms of autonomy encourage us to craft our identity based on what we believe personally rather than the shared beliefs of others. We root our identities in our personal experiences rather than our communal histories. We define ourselves through the lens of *me*, rather than the lens of *we*.

We shape our identities from the inside out, using the individual desires of our hearts. "Be yourself," "Live your truth," "Just be you," "Follow your heart." These are the contemporary mantras of inside-out identity formed around personal characteristics (physical appearance, abilities, disabilities, gender, or sexual attraction) or personal experiences (relationships, interests, hobbies, habits,[6] successes, failures, hurts, or disappointments).

Lincoln formed his inside-out identity based on his athletic abilities. I formed mine based on my professional achievements. Neither identity fully described the men we really were, and neither was now capable of providing us with a purpose or direction for the future.

Our inside-out approach was unreliable from the onset, largely because it failed to navigate the ever-changing desires of our hearts and the unpredictable nature of life. Rooted in our personal attributes and experiences, it simply could not survive when those attributes and experiences inevitably changed.

In addition, our inside-out identities still lacked an objective moral foundation. If my personal attributes, abilities, and experiences (either as a football player or a detective) determine my purpose in life (and the way I want to be known by others), how can I be sure my identity is "good," "noble," or "virtuous"? How can I be certain I've lived a "good life"?

Is a life well experienced the same as a life well lived? Can a serial killer live a good life if he simply celebrates his evil attributes and enjoys his murderous experiences? No. An inside-out approach to identity fails to guarantee an *objectively* virtuous life because it is, like the community-based outside-in approach, subjective by nature.

Lincoln and I both needed a better approach to identity, one that wasn't dependent on our personal desires or experiences or our social or professional affiliations.

 ## Topside-Down Identity

Rather than looking inward or outward, Lincoln and I should have been looking upward.

The Bible recognizes our innate human desire to be known, and it did so long before modern sociologists began studying the formation of identity. Biblical names were often given to people in recognition of their relationship to *God*, the objective standard for identity. Names reflected value, character, authority, or reputation, revealing the God-given role or purpose of the name-bearer. Simon, for example, was renamed Peter, from the Greek word *petros*, meaning "rock" or "stone." Jesus changed Simon's identity (and purpose) with a new name and told Peter his confession would be the "rock" on which the church would grow.[7]

The men and women of the Bible formed their identities "topside-down," based primarily on their connection and relationship with their Creator. As Joshua Hollmann rightly observes, "While for Socrates the *unexamined* life is not worth living, for Christians, the *unrelated* life is not worth living" (emphasis mine).[8] Our relationship to God can define our identity and provide purpose and direction as we relate to others.

A topside-down approach recognizes the intentionality of our lives. According to the Bible, we're not accidental products of evolution. Instead, we were created uniquely in the image of God for a special purpose.[9] Our identities are to be *discovered* based on what God has revealed, not *created* based on public conformity or personal introspection. Our identity isn't *achieved* through effort or reflection, it's *received* from our Creator.

That's why our topside-down identity doesn't suffer when our desires or circumstances change. God didn't see Lincoln any differently after his injury, and he didn't see me any differently after my retirement. Our topside-down identities were stable, even when our hearts and circumstances weren't.

If Lincoln and I had sought our identity in God, we would have found our place in God's overarching story. As Patrick Rothfuss's character Bass, says, "Everyone tells a story about themselves inside their own head. Always. All the time. That story makes you what you are. We build ourselves out of that story."[10] If Lincoln and I had "built ourselves" from God's story rather than our own, we would have understood who we *really* were rather than who we had *imagined* ourselves to be. Lincoln and I would have recognized our true value in God, as uniquely loved, chosen, adopted, forgiven, and redeemed, even if it was sometimes difficult to see ourselves that way.

A topside-down identity would also have protected us from *us*. Christ followers are called to adopt an attitude of humility, to consider others better than themselves, and to serve others selflessly, expecting nothing in return.[11] When people adopt this identity and purpose, they are far less likely to be self-focused, on one extreme, or self-loathing, on the other.

Lincoln wasn't a Christian when he tried to take his life. He had formed his identity from the outside in and the inside out. When his circumstances changed, he no longer recognized himself.

But I was already a Christian on the day I met Lincoln. I understood the importance of a topside-down identity and was known at my agency as a Christian, a pastor, and a defender of the faith. So why was I struggling like Lincoln?

I simply didn't want to submit my identity to God. As a fallen human, I still wanted control. I wanted to define my own version of "unique."

If that's your challenge as well, I have good news. God doesn't ask us to stop being *us* to be known as *his*. In fact, God is the source of our unique attributes. He gave us gifts and a distinctive personal history so we could find our place in his story. When we identify ourselves in Jesus, we become part of a global community in which there is neither Jew nor Greek, neither slave nor free, neither male nor female, for we are all one in Christ Jesus.[12] At the same time, God still recognizes our unique gifts, abilities, and attributes.[13]

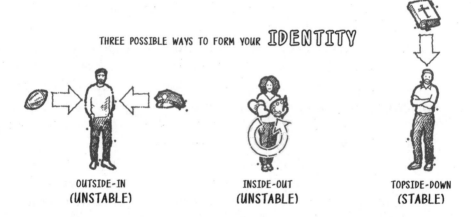

THREE POSSIBLE WAYS TO FORM YOUR IDENTITY

OUTSIDE-IN
(UNSTABLE)

INSIDE-OUT
(UNSTABLE)

TOPSIDE-DOWN
(STABLE)

A topside-down identity allows me to be me, but unlike the identity I created for myself, my God-centered identity recognizes my uniqueness without allowing it to separate me from others. I have been uniquely created by God to join people of all nations and races, unified in God's grand purpose.

Somehow, in my journey as a Christian detective, I lost my way and forgot who I really was. That wasn't age-appropriate foolishness, it was just flat stupid.

Chase the Lead

If you want to avoid being flat stupid, I have some advice. Rather than cobbling together a view of yourself from the bits and pieces you find in your heart or allowing other people—no matter how well-intentioned—to define who you are, turn to the fully informed mind of God for an accurate picture.

Assess the Mess

Ask yourself a few honest questions as you examine where and when you've "shown your ID." What did you say the last time you introduced yourself to a stranger? How do you describe yourself on your social media accounts or in your email signatures? Are you focused more on temporal traits than transcendent truths? Do your words give you away?

Become His Child

If you haven't yet done so, *join God's family*. God adopts all who receive him and believe in his name, giving them the right to become children of God.[14] If you already identify as a Christian, *renew your mind*. Throw off your old self and former way of life by letting God's Spirit renew your thoughts and attitudes. Put on a new self, created to be like God.[15] In either case, if you're a new or seasoned Christian, be intentional about embracing your family identity as a son or daughter of the King.

Listen to His Voice

If you've crafted your identity from the outside in or the inside out, you've probably been listening to the wrong voices. You'll never replace what you're thinking about yourself (or what others think about you) if you don't first know what God thinks of you. Start reading. According to the Bible, you are loved by God as his unique creation.[16] He chose and adopted you as his own, forgiving and redeeming you through the sacrifice of Jesus on the cross.[17] You're important. You're here for a reason. The Creator of the universe called you and equipped you for every good work.[18]

Live Accordingly

Once you discover what God has to say about you, exchange it for what you (or anyone else) have been saying. Allow your transcendent identity as a child of God to direct your steps and inform your actions. Epictetus, the Greek philosopher, once advised, "Know, first, who you are, and then adorn yourself accordingly."[19] Change the way you interact with others, rewrite your bios, and begin making decisions based on your new identity.

The Truth in True Crime: You Were Created to Be Known

"It looked like an amazing day!" Susie met me at the door when she heard my car in the driveway. I had been texting her selfies during my last shift with Jimmy.

"Did you actually *do* anything or just take pictures?"

I was ready for a laugh. Susie has known me most of my life; she knows how to make me smile and how to gently remind me about my identity in Christ. I counted on her to do the latter over the next several weeks.

Psychologist Gregg Henriques believes "the need to be known and valued by self and others" is humanity's *core need*.[20] He contends this desire is "the single most important variable in human development in terms of outcomes regarding character structure and well-being."

Psychologists like Henriques are simply affirming what ancient Christians described on the pages of the New Testament. According to the biblical worldview, humans were created to be known and find their identity in God.

The Christian story is an identity story from start to finish. It begins with God providing an identity to the first created human, who then assigns names and identities to every other living creature.[21] It ends when God gives his name to Jesus, who surrendered the privileges of his divine identity so he could identify with fallen humans like you and me.[22]

EXPLANATION: We Want His Attention

According to the Bible, humans were created in the image of God for the purpose of being known and loved by him.

People who reject the existence of God still experience this desire to be known in a significant way. That's why human alternatives for identity and purpose emerge in secular cultures.

Christianity explains our desire to be known and to identify ourselves with something (or someone) of utmost importance and provides an objective, transcendent source for true identity.

The Christian identity story addresses our "core need," and it did so before modern sociologists understood the importance of this primary desire. When we trust Jesus for our salvation, we change our identities as fallen imperfect creatures, destined for the grave, to redeemed children of God who "have life in his *name*" (emphasis mine).[23] According to the Bible, "There is no other *name* under heaven given among men by which we must be saved" (emphasis mine).[24]

Our "need to be known and valued by self and others," is simply a poor, temporal reflection of our need to be known by God. We seek identity and purpose because we were created for identity and purpose—in God.

We were created to be known, not simply by other created beings but by the Creator himself.

A TARGET, A BULL'S-EYE, AND A CIRCLE OF CONCERN

How to Protect Yourself from Stupid and Surround Yourself with Sensational

> Tell me with whom you associate,
> and I will tell you who you are.
> —JOHANN WOLFGANG VON GOETHE

> Be careful the environment you choose for
> it will shape you; be careful the friends you
> choose for you will become like them.
> —W. CLEMENT STONE

Maybe he just wanted to *make sure . . .*"

Rick tossed the large glossy 8" × 10" photo back on the table where it joined a dozen photographs taken nearly three decades earlier. If Rick had been a Christian, I would have considered "gallows humor" one of his spiritual gifts.

The photo in question depicted our victim, Cynthia Baynor, as officers discovered her in the doorway of her bedroom on a summer night in 1983. She had been bludgeoned with a wrench, and stabbed, and strangled. But that wasn't all. Before the killer left, he also shot her with a *crossbow*.

In all my years investigating murders, I'd never seen so many different injuries to one victim.

"At least we have a small suspect pool," I said as I opened the red cold-case notebook containing the original reports.

Rick and I decided to investigate this case because it was obviously a *targeted* murder. It wasn't a burglary gone wrong, nor was it a botched robbery. Nothing was taken from Cynthia's apartment, and the killing was far too aggressive and passionate to have been committed by a stranger.

Cynthia was murdered by someone who knew her, targeted her, and, for whatever reason, was angry enough to kill her *four times*. Although we hadn't yet identified Cynthia Baynor's friends or enemies, there probably weren't many who would fit this description.

While no one likes to hear this, most homicide victims put themselves in a position to be killed, either knowingly, unknowingly, willingly, or unwillingly. You can't be a victim if you're not at least in the vicinity of the killer, and victims usually put themselves within proximity. Maybe they're living with their killer, working with him, renting the apartment next door, or just walking past him in a parking lot. One way or another, victims become victims because killers have access to them.

I call this the "proximity principle."

Cynthia, for example, probably knew her killer personally, and since there were no signs of forced entry at her apartment, she most likely allowed the murderer to enter her home.

When investigating a crime like this, I begin by asking this question: "Who is in the victim's proximity?"

I usually start with *relational* proximity. Was the victim living with anyone? Did she have—or recently have—a boyfriend or husband? Were any of her friends or family members angry with her? Did she have a problem at work or with a professional rival? In a targeted murder like Cynthia's, the killer is usually in this first category: someone who knew the victim personally.

When relational proximity fails to provide a suspect, I turn next to *geographic* proximity. Who lives next door or down the street? Is a known offender living in the neighborhood? In Cynthia's case, however, there was no reason to look beyond her relationships.

When Cynthia was in grade school, she lived next door to her aunt and uncle. Her two cousins were her best friends. But by the time Cynthia was in high school, her family had moved away. She struggled with depression and sought new friendships at school. Unfortunately, she made several poor relational choices, and one of these poor choices became our primary suspect.

Herbert Finley was the most popular boy in Cynthia's senior class. Edgy, strikingly handsome, and a bit mysterious, he had the attention of all the girls. Cynthia considered herself lucky to land him as a boyfriend shortly after high school. She was intrigued by his popularity and rule-breaking spirit.

Rick and I were intrigued by Herbert's *mysterious* side.

Herbert introduced Cynthia to a large interconnected web of men and women who used drugs, stole from one another, and moved from place to place. A few years before, he had been arrested as a teenager after arguing with a boy who lived next door. In an unexpected outburst, Herbert bludgeoned the boy unconsciousness, then tried to strangle him. Sound a bit familiar?

Given the light sentencing common in the late 1970s, Herbert served just two years in a juvenile detention center. He was released in time for his senior year.

Just in time to meet Cynthia.

The Crucial Role of Community

Like many of the murders Rick and I investigated over the years, Cynthia's case was a story about relationships. Most people are remembered for their achievements or contributions, but everyone has an unwritten story involving hundreds of friendships and associations. This overlooked social narrative is often the true story of our lives. Our relationships, either good or bad, act as rudders guiding us toward success or destruction. Friends matter, and if we pick the right ones, our friends can help us flourish.

According to research, friendships impact our *mental* health. People who spend less time alone, for example, are happier. When asked in a survey "What makes people happy?" most respondents included friendships on the top of their list.[1] Conversely, lonely people with few friends often report feeling depressed: "Loneliness and depressive symptomatology can act in a synergistic effect to diminish well-being."[2] When important friendships are broken, our bodies experience "social pain" involving "some of the same neurobiological substrates that underlie experiences of *physical* pain" (emphasis mine).[3] Friendships affect our ability to flourish mentally.

Studies also reveal another reason our relationships matter: they impact our *physical* health. Believe it or not, people who enjoy "increased sociability" are less likely to catch a common cold, and one study even found that lonely people "mounted a weaker immune response to the flu shot."[4] Studies also reveal that people with "stronger social relationships" live longer, regardless of many other factors, and friendships also affect the quality of this longer life.[5] Lonely older adults suffer "poorer cognitive function," and one study found "loneliness was associated with a 40% increased risk of dementia."[6] Our friendships and social interactions aid our well-being. They help us flourish physically.

Why, then, wasn't this the case for Cynthia? She dramatically increased her circle of friends when she started dating Herbert yet enjoyed none of the benefits I've described here. Cynthia's story reveals another truth about the impact friendships have on human flourishing: *quality* is more important than *quantity*.

EVIDENCE: Humans Long for Friendship

Friendship has always been important to humans. Even the ancients (like Epicurus, Euripides, Plutarch, and Pythagoras) wrote extensively about the role friendships play in human flourishing. We view people who shun friends as "loners," "hermits," or "recluses."

Why do you think we describe unassociated people in this way? Why do you think we hold friendship in such high regard?

Our Desire for Deep Divers

In our social media age, it's tempting to think of friends in a contemporary, informal way, as when we are "friended" or "unfriended" on an internet platform. But online "friendships" are not the relationships social scientists measure when considering the impact friends have on human flourishing. Sociologists, instead, examine the impact of *close* social relationships as defined in a more traditional definition of the term:

Friend, noun
> One who is attached to another by affection; one who entertains for another sentiments of esteem, respect and affection, which lead him to desire his company, and to seek to promote his happiness and prosperity.[7]

True friendships involve meaningful relationships between people who "esteem" and "respect" one another and who, over the course of time spent in one another's company, seek to promote each other's well-being.

The *quality* of our relationships matters more than the *quantity* of our relationships. But what determines "quality" when it comes to friends? Three factors, according to the latest studies. The first characteristic of a quality friendship is *depth*.

In perhaps the longest study of this important truth, researchers at Harvard University started collecting information from over seven hundred people in 1939 and traced them for eighty years to discover which early social variables and biological processes predicted health and well-being in later life. The most important variable? The quality of their relationships.[8] This one attribute was more important than their achievements, financial position, social class, intelligence score, or genetic identity. Close, sincere friendships matter more than superficial, informal associations and more than any other variable studied.[9]

"Deep diving" friends are the ones who shape and direct us—people who know us genuinely and are willing to invest in our future. Cynthia found herself surrounded by people who called themselves friends but were more concerned with what Cynthia could do for *them* than what they could do for *her*. This is, by definition, the *opposite* of true friendship.

While Cynthia had more acquaintances than ever on the night she was murdered, none of these associates cared enough about her to warn her about the direction she had taken. Instead, one of them killed her in the most excessive manner Rick and I had ever seen.

Cynthia didn't need more informal acquaintances. She needed a few true friends.

 Drawing a Tighter Circle

The photographs from Cynthia's murder scene weren't the worst photos Rick and I had to endure in our careers. Some cases were more gruesome, and some (like those involving the murder of children) were more emotionally challenging.

I'm often asked how I could investigate grisly cases of this nature without experiencing trauma of one sort or another. Here's my secret: *I drew a tight circle around the people for whom I am willing to cry.*

That may sound callous, but it's not. It's *necessary*. How helpful would I be if an emotional connection to a victim immobilized me? When my agency called me to a murder scene, they expected me to do my job. I couldn't objectively investigate a murder if I was emotionally connected to the victim or the suspect. For that reason, *I drew a tight circle*. My immediate family was in that circle. My dog, Bailey, was in that circle. My cat, Simba, *was not* (sorry if you're a cat lover).

Before you judge me for my relationship circle, remember that everyone has a circle of one size or another. You also have a circle. I bet it's filled with people with whom you have close relationships. I also bet many of the people you've friended on social media are not in the circle.

Here's my point: you can't be close friends with everyone. And this reveals a second factor of friendship leading to human flourishing. If you examine your circle of friends, you'll find that your true friends, the ones with whom you have close relationships, are part of a very small group. That's not unusual. It's true for all of us. Deep friendships require time and commitment. That's why you have fewer close friends than you have acquaintances.

Studies demonstrate the difference, for example, between meaningful, close relationships and informal, social media acquaintances. Relational "quality" is more likely to produce happiness and contentment than the number of friends you have online, according to a study at the University of Edinburgh.[10] Another study found that people who had close confidants outlived people who didn't.[11] We flourish when we have *close friends* rather than when we have *many acquaintances*.[12]

 ## The Danger of Contagious Creatures

Cynthia grew up with a few close friends (her cousins) and eventually found herself in the company of many acquaintances. When we first started our investigation, Rick and I suspected Herbert killed Cynthia because of his prior history of violence and their romantic relationship. But the more we investigated Herbert, the more we realized he *wasn't* the killer.

Cynthia was killed, instead, by someone she considered her "best friend."

Herbert introduced Cynthia to Tabitha nearly two years prior to her murder. They connected instantly. Tabitha shared many of Cynthia's interests. They had a similar upbringing and even looked alike. They borrowed each other's clothes, and Tabitha spent nearly every day with Cynthia and Herbert. She considered them the sister and brother she never had.

Herbert's feelings toward Tabitha were more than familial, however.

He introduced her to cocaine and eventually used Tabitha's growing drug addiction to entice her into a secret affair. Tabitha began to see Cynthia as a foe rather than a friend. Herbert stoked Tabitha's growing jealousy and drug-induced paranoia as he tired of his relationship with Cynthia.

Tabitha eventually snapped.

We never discovered precisely what caused Tabitha to attack Cynthia with the passion we observed at the crime scene. Perhaps Cynthia confronted her violently about the relationship with Herbert. It's possible Tabitha was under the influence of cocaine. Maybe it was a combination of the two. While Herbert was the catalyst for the murder, we couldn't prove he was present at the time of the crime. Tabitha's ferocity led to Cynthia's death, but Herbert's "friendship" motivated the homicide.

Herbert had a deep, intimate relationship with Cynthia and Tabitha, but this relationship obviously didn't contribute to their well-being. Why not? Because it was missing the third characteristic of "quality" relationships: *virtue.*

Humans flourish when we have (1) *deep, meaningful relationships* with (2) a *small number* of (3) *virtuous friends.*

But what (or who) determines virtue in the context of a relationship? Once again, we find ourselves searching for the same elusive, objective foundation. Herbert saw nothing wrong in his relationship with Tabitha and Cynthia. In the years after Cynthia's murder, Herbert engaged in many similar relationships. According to Herbert's subjective moral standard, he did nothing wrong.

Establishing an objective standard for virtue in relationships is important because humans are *contagious creatures.* We are also *magnetic.* Relational virtue matters because our relationships can either lead us to something rewarding or something catastrophic.

One study, when examining the relationships of adolescents who had "disruptive behavior disorders" found that

EXAMPLE: Rehoboam Listened to His Friends

King Solomon's son, King Rehoboam, listened to the foolish advice of his friends ("the young men who had grown up with him" 1 Kings 12:10 ESV) rather than the wise counsel of his father's mentors. As a result, he frustrated and angered an entire nation until ten of Israel's tribes rebelled against him and became independent (1 Kings 12:1–15).

Have you ever listened to the foolish advice of a friend? What was the result?

teenagers were more likely to befriend others who shared their behavior patterns. The research concluded, "Disruptive behavior disorders may be socially rewarded . . . and socially clustered."[13] As magnetic beings, we attract friends who share our characteristics. As contagious creatures, we often conform to the image of those we find attractive.

Happy people, for example, often "catch" their happiness from other happy people. One study even found that "happiness *depends* on the happiness of others with whom [we] are connected" (emphasis mine).[14] Friends can contribute to our happiness or help us choose happiness. They also encourage other kinds of choices. The quality of our friendships can determine our likelihood of being depressed or suicidal.[15] Our friends also impact our probability of smoking, drinking alcohol, or using drugs.[16] One set of researchers found that friends can tempt us to do something we shouldn't or encourage us to *resist* destructive behavior.[17]

These studies reflect what we already know from our common experience: we catch many of our attitudes, perspectives, and behaviors from our infectious friends.[18] That's why your mom used to ask you, "If all of your friends jumped off a cliff, would you jump too?" She innately recognized the contagious nature of friendships. In Cynthia's case, this contagion eventually led her to jump into a world far from that of the family she knew as a child.

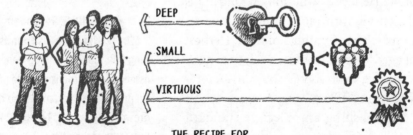

THE RECIPE FOR
QUALITY RELATIONSHIPS

Chase the Lead

What could Cynthia have done differently to change her proximity to danger? The answer is ancient and relies, unsurprisingly, on identifying virtue. Thinkers in antiquity understood the power of virtuous friendships and often connected virtue to true companionship. Cicero, for example, claimed virtue helped build and sustain lasting friendships.[19] Similarly, Aristotle identified three types of friendships but claimed *true* friends possessed noble character.[20]

The ancient biblical authors also identified virtue as a prerequisite for genuine friendship. If Cynthia had heeded the advice of the Bible authors, she would have left the presence of fools and unreliable friends, chosen her friends based on their righteousness, and walked with the wise.[21] If you want to change your proximity to danger, here are a few insights to help you set your circle:

 EXPLANATION: We Reflect God's Nature

Most people, when surveyed, view God as a loving deity who desires a relationship. Christianity agrees but raises the bar.

The apostle John declared, "God is love" (1 John 4:8 NIV). He didn't write, "God is *the source of* love," or, "God *showed us how to* love," but instead described God *as love*. This is reasonable given the triune nature of the Christian God. God has been in an intimate love relationship with the Son and the Holy Spirit *from all eternity*. We continue to seek these kinds of relationships because we were created in his image.

Reimagine the Role of Your Friends

Has anyone ever said, "Tell me about yourself"? It's tempting to respond to this query with a description of your identity or your life story, right? But what if you limited your response to a description of your relationships and the way your friends have impacted your life, for good or bad? Take a minute to reflect on your friendship choices so far. Your social media bios probably don't say much about your friendships, but your relationships influenced your "bio," even if you weren't paying attention. Rethink the role of your friends so you can make better choices (and chart a better course) moving forward.

Embrace Friends Who Hold an Objective View of Virtue

Cynthia's "friends" introduced her to drugs, stole from one another, cheated on her, and eventually committed murder. Their values were highly subjective and utilitarian. They lacked an objectively virtuous, unchanging moral code. Make sure your circle of friends is filled with people who recognize an objective view of virtue. Because objective moral truths are unchanging, they're also ancient. The biblical description of virtue, for example, is simply a reflection of the ancient, invariable, moral nature of God. Those who embrace this biblical standard sharpen one another as iron sharpens iron.[22]

Identify Friends Who Care about *All* of You

True friends care about you—*all* of you—as much as they care about themselves. Assess the people you identify as friends today (and any new candidates you consider in the future) by asking the following questions:

Do They Care about My *Spiritual* Well-Being?

True friends contribute to our spiritual growth by encouraging us daily, praying for us, and sharing their spiritual struggles with us.[23] They lead us to God by demonstrating the love, grace, and forgiveness of God.[24] Do any of your friends contribute to your spiritual well-being in this way?

Do They Care about My *Physical* Well-Being?

True friends respond when we have a physical need.[25] They step in to help us, providing for us when we can't provide for ourselves. They don't shun us or "close their ear" to us when we are destitute.[26] They care for us when we are sick or injured.[27] How many of your friends would truly do this for you?

Do They Care about My *Emotional* Well-Being?

True friends stand with us in suffering. They "bear our burdens" and encourage us when we are troubled or discouraged.[28] They are compassionate, kind, and patient, weeping when we weep and rejoicing when we rejoice.[29] Who in your circle of friends has exhibited this ability and desire to help you?

Do They Care about My *Ethical* Well-Being?

True friends are honest enough to tell us when we are wrong and help us chart a new course. They are gentle yet firm, unafraid to confront us directly and speak the truth.[30] Do you have someone like this in your life?

True friends are *complete* friends. They care about every aspect of your well-being. Some will be better equipped in one area than another. That's why your circle is so important. It encompasses a family of friends who care for one another in these important areas.

Initiate New Friendships

If you don't yet recognize any of your current friends in the descriptions I've offered so far, it's time to cultivate new friendships. Seriously. Sometimes the key to changing your *life* is simply changing your *friends*. As you examined the list in the prior section, did you feel convicted? Have you been this kind of friend to others? If not, start adopting these attributes in your own relationships. You just might become contagious.

Be on the Lookout

Close, committed friendships don't often happen by accident, and good candidates are sometimes hard to find. Are you paying attention to the people in your orbit? Have you identified people you would like to know better based on the traits I've described? Be as intentional about your friends as you are about your educational or professional goals.

Show You Care

Interesting people are *interested* people. Are you attentive to, engaged with, and concerned about the people you'd like to have as friends? Do you care in a holistic way? Do you seek what's best for people spiritually, emotionally, physically, and ethically? Are you kind, respectful, reliable, and supportive? When people know you care, they are more likely to return the gesture. Become the kind of friend you'd like to have.

Be Patient

Building the kinds of friendships I've described in this chapter takes effort, and time-tested friendships require . . . *time*. You can't rush the process. If a friendship is worth having, it's worth waiting for. Don't allow impatience to poison your pursuit.

Invest Your Time Accordingly

Once you've identified friends who possess the attributes I've described, reprioritize your calendar. It's been said, "You are the average of the five people you spend the most time with."[31] How (and with whom) are you spending your time? If you want to catch something from your contagious friends, spend more time with friends who possess something you want to catch.

The Truth in True Crime: You Were Created for Community

By the time we identified Tabitha as the killer, she had been dead for nearly five years. She was murdered by someone she also considered a "friend." Rick called it karma. I saw it as something much simpler. Tabitha, like Cynthia before her, didn't understand the power of her associations.

If Tabitha and Cynthia had held a biblical worldview, they would have known "bad company ruins good morals."[32] They would also have known what sociologists now confirm: humans flourish when we cultivate (1) deep, meaningful relationships with (2) a small number of (3) virtuous friends. This has been the claim of Christianity for thousands of years. Indeed, this truism about friendship is grounded in the nature of the Christian God.

The God of the Bible is triune—*one* God existing eternally as *three* distinct persons: the Father, Son, and Holy Spirit. These three persons of the Godhead have been in relationship forever. They experience a deep, meaningful bond between a small number of virtuous friends. That's why we flourish when we cultivate these kinds of relationships. As humans created in the image of God, we simply reflect this relational aspect of God's nature.

The Bible authors had it right all along.

They accurately described flourishing friendships, explained our nature as contagious creatures, and warned us about the importance of the "proximity principle." If Cynthia and Tabitha had followed the teaching of the Bible, they would have charted entirely different courses.

They would have known what to look for and what to avoid, who to exclude from their circle and who to draw near. They would have known they were created in the image of an intimate, virtuous, triune God. They would have known *they were created for community*.

TRAJECTORY DECISIONS (FOR BETTER OR WORSE)

How to Choose like a Champion

People are weird. When we find someone with
weirdness that is compatible with ours,
we team up and call it love.

—DR. SEUSS

Love is not weakness. It is strong. Only the
sacrament of marriage can contain it.

—BORIS PASTERNAK

The news cameras followed Paul Sanford as the bailiff handcuffed and walked him from the courtroom to lockup.

His facial expression was utterly unresponsive, just as it had been throughout the trial and the lengthy investigation. He unflinchingly accepted the guilty verdict, denying his children any satisfaction they might have experienced if he had shown the slightest remorse for brutally killing their mother. Instead, Paul remained icy and detached.

None of this should have surprised anyone, given Paul's thirty-year marriage to Nadia. As Rick and I investigated the case, twenty years after Nadia's murder, we never observed a single photograph in which Paul looked anything less than *chilling*.

He never seemed to smile, even in images memorializing birthdays, graduations, or weddings. His grown children consistently described him as undemonstrative and distant, and his grandchildren referred to him as

"Grumps." Even his closest friends wondered why Nadia had ever married him.

Rick and I knew the answer.

Paul was trained as a chemist and worked at one of the leading biochemistry laboratories in Southern California. He had been an excellent student, earning a PhD in organic chemistry. He was solely committed to his studies during his education and considered his position in this prestigious company to be his most important achievement.

Far more important than his marriage.

Nadia worked in the HR department, and they met when Paul first applied for the position. Nadia was similarly obsessed with her career while in her twenties, but now that she was in her thirties, her priorities were shifting. She had recently separated from her live-in boyfriend of four years and was concerned that the trajectory of her life might never lead to the commitment of marriage or the possibility of children. Nadia considered Paul her last opportunity in this regard and pursued him vigorously.

Nadia was the daughter of the company's owner, and Paul's first serious relationship. Had prenuptial agreements been common in those years, he most certainly would have wanted one. He was singularly focused on his career but agreed to marry Nadia about a year after he was hired. Their wedding photographs were consistent with other images we'd seen of Paul.

Paul and Nadia's marriage, according to their children, appeared loveless, a contractual agreement of sorts rather than a loving relationship. Their daughter, Roberta, could not recall a single expression of affection involving her father.

Nadia became a Christian early in their marriage, however, and although she never convinced Paul to attend church, her faith informed the way she navigated their relationship. She persevered for nearly *three decades* before her father died. The next day, Paul told her he wanted a divorce.

That's when the arc of Nadia's life took a turn toward tragedy.

 Trajectory Decisions

As Rick and I investigated Nadia's murder, we inevitably examined her marriage as well. What we learned made me sad. My personal experience of marriage as a life-giving relationship was very different. Paul and Nadia, had they made better decisions, could have experienced or cultivated an amazing marriage—one leading to a longer, more satisfying life rather than Nadia's murder.

Some decisions are more important than others, both in the *kind* of decision being made and in the *timing* of it. Imagine, for example, a rocket leaving earth on its way to the moon. If this rocket makes a one-degree error in its trajectory a mile before it lands, it will still reach the moon, given its proximity to the lunar surface. But if the rocket makes the same one-degree trajectory error just a mile after launch, it will miss the moon by thousands of miles. Important decisions, the ones that determine the direction of our lives, are *trajectory* decisions. They must be prioritized. They must be considered early.

Nadia's case demonstrates this important truth.

Nadia and Paul prioritized their commitments and trajectory decisions in the wrong order, like many of us living in a culture captivated by material success. As someone who now teaches regularly at the university level and mentors students at conferences and training programs, I've been asking young people to share what they believe are the most important decisions they will make in their early twenties. Most cite education and profession as their primary concerns. I suspect Nadia and Paul would have answered similarly. One was murdered, however, and the other died serving a life sentence.

Had Nadia and Paul understood the importance of making good trajectory decisions, their lives (and deaths) would have been very different. If they had prioritized the following three decisions, for example, Nadia's story probably wouldn't have been chronicled in a cold case file:

Trajectory Decision One: Choose the Right *Worldview*

A worldview is simply "a mental model of reality—a comprehensive framework of ideas and attitudes about the world, ourselves, and life."[1] Navigating our lives is much more difficult when we base our decisions and choices on *personal preferences* rather than *objective realities*. That's why it's so important to decide what's true "about the world, ourselves, and life" before we make other decisions. Our "mental model" of the world helps us answer the important questions we face as humans: "How did we get here?" "Why is the world so broken?" "How can we fix it?" and "What is the purpose of life?" Our worldview can also answer practical questions, like, "What should my priorities be?" "What is the purpose of marriage?" and "What kind of person should I marry?" Nadia became a Christian and adopted a Christian worldview *after* marrying Paul. While her faith helped her find peace and maintain her commitment in a troubled relationship, had she been a Christian *prior* to meeting Paul, her worldview might have informed her decision to marry him in the first place.

Trajectory Decision Two: Choose the Right *Spouse*

Not everyone wants to marry, but if you're like most people, marriage is probably in your future.[2] That's why the decision of who to marry should be prioritized. When we are young, we ought to be as intentional about a possible mate as we are about a possible education or career. I've known many educated, accomplished professionals who were derailed by bad spousal choices. On the other hand, I've known many contented, happily married couples who were not particularly well educated or professionally successful. As a homicide detective, I never heard anyone lying on their deathbed say they wished they had accomplished more at work or school. Instead, they often lamented poor relational choices or missed opportunities with their family. Relationships are more important than accomplishments.

Trajectory Decision Three: Choose the Right *Mission*

Neither Nadia nor Paul saw their work as their life mission. For Paul, his expertise as a chemist was a source of selfish pride and prestige within the company. For Nadia, her job was simply the result of her father's intervention and provision. Nadia and Paul failed to see their work as an opportunity to serve God or share him with others. Our decision about work is a trajectory decision, especially if we see it as a *missional calling* rather than merely a *professional choice*.

By the time Paul demanded a divorce, the opportunity to make the most important trajectory decisions—especially to choose the right spouse—had passed, and Nadia would eventually experience the terrible consequence.

Paul and Nadia married when both were already in their thirties. This is increasingly the norm rather than the exception. The average marriage age for men and women has been steadily increasing for decades.[3] And a growing number of people never marry at all.[4] The rate at which people wed is now less than half what it was in the 1970s, and nearly 50 percent of today's "first births" are to unmarried women.[5] Nadia lived with her first serious boyfriend, outside of marriage. Paul simply remained single during that time. Neither saw marriage as an important, early, trajectory decision.

Putting Marriage in Its Place

When their marriage ended, Paul wanted more than a divorce. He wanted a trajectory *reset*. He was never truly committed to Nadia. His dedication to his job was far greater. He was ready to restart his life as though he had never met her, content to give her the house, the furniture, and the family car.

But he drew the line at his pension.

His coworkers described Paul as the most serious, committed employee they had ever met. He was just as emotionless and socially detached at work as he was at home, but that peculiar attribute served him well as a chemist. He had a successful career and contributed to a substantial pension. He was now ready to enjoy his retirement, and he wasn't willing to share any of it with Nadia.

Paul thought he would be happier as an unmarried man, and he expected to live a long life alone with his sizable investments. He was apparently unaware of statistics gathered over several generations related to the value of a good marriage. According to sociologists and researchers, Paul would have been wiser prioritizing his marriage rather than his career, especially if he was concerned about wealth, happiness, or longevity.

On average, people who are married make more money than their unmarried counterparts.[6] Paul was married to Nadia while he was employed as a chemist, and his marital status likely contributed to his financial success. Married men typically work harder and are less likely to be fired.[7]

> **EVIDENCE: Humans Seek a "Significant Other"**
>
> Even though fewer people are getting married, our innate common desire for a commitment to a "significant other" remains constant. For every percentage *drop* in marriage rates, there is a percentage *rise* in cohabitation rates.
>
> Why are humans so consistently drawn to live-in unions? Why do we thrive best in marital unions? Is it simply a product of evolution or something more?

Married women are also less apt to be poor, and wedded couples accumulate more wealth.[8] Paul's success was not his own. He owed part of it to the fact he was married.

Paul's expectation of a long retirement would also have benefited from a good marriage. Married people live longer, and this is true across a wide variety of cultures.[9] Why? Perhaps because married people are typically healthier.[10] Married people have a better chance of surviving a heart attack and are even more likely to survive cancer.[11] Husbands and wives manage each other's illnesses more efficiently, monitor each other's health, and encourage better fitness and healthier lifestyles.[12] Married couples even fear death less than their unmarried counterparts.[13]

Rick and I failed to find a single witness who described Paul as "happy" (at work or at home), which may simply have been the result of his obsessive professional focus. People who prioritize their marriages have a lower risk of mental illness and are more likely to report happiness.[14] Married men and women report higher sexual satisfaction, experience more emotional support from each other, and experience less stress.[15] Married people also report better mental well-being than those who cohabitate outside of marriage.[16]

This spousal well-being rubs off on children. Studies continue to confirm that children thrive when raised by two biological parents in a low-conflict marriage.[17] Why? Because biological parents generate higher household income and are motivated to invest emotionally and financially at higher levels than cohabiting or single parents.[18] Married fathers are also typically more involved with their kids.[19] As a result, children raised this way do better on every level, including their education.

Children raised by their married, biological parents are less likely to cut or miss class and more likely to be prepared for school.[20] They get better grades, score higher on tests and other "progress indicators," and are more likely to graduate high school and attend college.[21] They also display less destructive behavior.[22] They show less aggression, for example, and are less likely to be expelled from school.[23] Kids raised in these kinds of households are less likely to suffer abuse, misuse alcohol or drugs, commit a crime, or find themselves in jail.[24]

Sara McLanahan, the William S. Tod Professor of Sociology and Public Affairs, Emeritus, at Princeton University, summarized the advantage of two-parent married households for children:

If we were asked to design a system for making sure that children's basic needs were met, we would probably come up with something quite similar to the two-parent ideal. Such a design, in theory, would not only ensure that children had access to the time and money of two adults, it also would provide a system of checks and balances that promoted quality parenting. The fact that both parents have a biological connection to the child would increase the likelihood that the parents would identify with the child and be willing to sacrifice for that child, and it would reduce the likelihood that either parent would abuse the child.[25]

Marriage is good for adults *and* for kids, aiding human flourishing on every measurable level and in every demonstrable way. Yet Nadia and Paul failed to experience any of the benefits of marriage. Why?

Neither made marriage an important, early, trajectory decision.

Worse yet, Paul considered his marriage—and eventually Nadia—entirely disposable. When her divorce attorney successfully negotiated a judgment against Paul and secured half his pension for Nadia, Paul drove to their old house, knocked on her door, asked to come in, and then shot her in the head. He then walked through the rear sliding glass door, jumped two fences, and walked to his car parked one block west of the house.

Their daughter, Roberta, discovered Nadia's body two days later.

 ## Making Matrimony a Priority

For Paul, marriage was an afterthought. He married the boss's daughter as an opportunistic, professional duty rather than an early priority decision. Like all of us, Paul was driven by his values, but he was far more committed to his educational and professional success than he was to the institution of marriage. If you listen to conventional wisdom today, you might find yourself agreeing with Paul's priorities. Why get married early? Isn't it better to wait until you know what you want, are more established professionally and financially, and are finished living the "single life"? Not according to the data.

Marriage helps us "grow up" in several significant ways, and the sooner we mature, the more likely we are to thrive. If we make it a priority, matrimony can be a training ground to help us be less selfish and to make the kind of mature, altruistic choices that are rare among young people who aren't yet married.[26] American satirist H. L. Mencken, once wrote, "A man may be a fool and not know it, but not if he is married."[27] Studies confirm this truth. Married people listen to the advice of their spouses and modify their behavior for the good of the marriage.[28] Men who marry work harder, attend fewer bars, increase their church attendance, and spend more time with family members.[29] This maturation begins once we commit to marrying our spouse, even *before* the wedding takes place.[30]

EXAMPLE: Joseph and Mary

Joseph and Mary, the parents of Jesus of Nazareth, were married when Mary was still very young. They exhibited many of the benefits of an early (and devout) marriage. Both trusted God and matured quickly as they overcame hardship. Joseph protected Mary and raised Jesus as a devoted father. Mary was a god-fearing, selfless mother and wife.

Their thriving marriage provided the foundation Jesus needed to flourish. (Matthew 1:18–2:23, Luke 1:1–2:52)

Women who wed early are more likely to marry a good "match" and experience a marriage "of the highest quality."[31] Young married couples become more financially stable, earn more money, and accumulate more net wealth.[32] Young married men are happier and less depressed, and couples who wed early are more satisfied, especially if they attend church regularly.[33] The children of young married couples are even healthier than the children of older parents.[34]

The benefits of an early marriage are dramatic. Sociologists Norval Glenn, Jeremy Uecker, and Robert Love Jr., after reviewing the data on early marriages, offered the following advice in a peer reviewed article:

> A 25-year-old person who meets an excellent marriage prospect would be ill-advised to pass up that opportunity only because he/she feels not yet at the ideal age for marriage. Furthermore, delaying marriage beyond the mid-twenties will lead to the loss during a portion of young adulthood of any emotional and health benefits that a good marriage would bring.[35]

That's why marriage needs to be an early trajectory decision. In the classic movie scene from *When Harry Met Sally*, Harry finds Sally on New Year's Eve and tells her, "When you realize you want to spend the rest of your life with somebody, you want the rest of your life to start as soon as possible."[36] When we enter a good marriage *early*, we benefit for the rest of our lives.

WEALTHIER

MORE EMPLOYED

LIVE LONGER

PHYSICALLY HEALTHIER

LESS DEATH ANXIETY

THE BENEFITS OF

MARRIAGE

MENTALLY HEALTHIER

HIGHER SATISFACTION

LESS STRESS / ANXIETY

MORE EMOTIONAL SUPPORT

HEALTHIER CHILDREN

Chase the Lead

What could Nadia have done differently to avoid the disaster that became her marriage? Dr. Laura Schlessinger, popular marriage counselor, radio host, and author, has a simple "mantra" for good marriages: "choose wisely and treat kindly."[37]

Here are a few words of advice to help you follow the first half of Dr. Laura's counsel:

Adopt a Biblical Worldview

There's a reason worldview choices ought to come before marital choices. A good decision in one category leads to a good decision in the other. Marriages built on a biblical foundation flourish. Religious married couples report better "marital quality" and are more faithful to one another.[38] Committed, praying, church-attending Christ followers divorce less, and because Christians are more likely to marry, they take advantage of the marriage benefits I've already described.[39] Worldview matters when it comes to marriage.

Be Purposeful and Intentional

If you're a conscientious person, you probably have a plan for your educational and professional goals. What degree or training will you need? What school will you attend? How will you pay for it? We usually have a plan to achieve our vocational goals but assume we'll simply get lucky and bump into a spouse along the way. *No* plan is not a plan. If you think marriage is part of your future, start thinking now about the kind of spouse you eventually want to marry. Where will you meet this kind of person? How can you increase your chances of finding him or her? Be as intentional and purposeful about marriage as you are about your career.

Make a List (and Check It Twice)

Researchers at the University of Pittsburgh and University of Iowa identified the traits most men and women say they want in a spouse.[40] "Mutual attraction" and "love" were on the top of both lists. What's on your list? Does it (or did it) include the following qualities?

A Spouse Who Loves God

A shared worldview provides the foundation for success. This was clear to Nadia once she became a Christian. Had Paul also given his life to Christ, his attitude toward his family would certainly have been different.

A Spouse Who Will Draw You Closer to God

According to the Christian worldview, marriage is a temporal picture of an eternal reality. The apostle Paul described the love of a husband for his wife as a picture of the love Jesus has for the church.[41] The finite relationship with our spouse is a small taste of what will be true for eternity. That's why spouses who know and love God want their spouses to know and love God. Nadia hoped to introduce Paul to Jesus. How much different would her fate have been if she had married someone who saw his relationship with God as a priority from the very beginning?

A Spouse Who Will Help You Become More Godly

The magnetic and contagious nature of humans can either draw us toward holiness or pull us toward destruction. Had Paul been in love with Nadia and been drawn to her as she became a follower of Christ, he would likely have adopted some of her attitudes, interests, and behaviors. In doing so, he would also have embraced the character of God, even if unknowingly. Godly spouses can help *us* become godly spouses—if we will let them.

Embrace an *Early* Marriage, Not a *Hurried* Marriage

The more you know about a potential spouse, the better your potential selection. According to the secular worldview, this usually means sampling every possible experience, including sexual experiences. How can anyone marry, the story goes, until they know if they're sexually compatible? Shouldn't we live together first, or at least sleep together? A biblical worldview argues for a different form of premarital sampling, however: a sampling of *character*. How does your potential spouse respond under stress? Under hardship or loss? Under pressure or failure? Discover the answers to these questions *before* you consider marriage, even if this takes time. Be a careful, honest observer and evaluator.

Ask Someone You Trust

Remember what I've already described about the nature and value of wisdom. Seek the wise counsel of people who *already* have what you *hope* to have. Talk to older, happily married people in your family, church, or community. Ask probing questions: What were your biggest challenges? How did you overcome them? What advice do you wish you could have given your younger selves, now that you've navigated marriage for so many years? While you're at it, ask one of these couples to mentor you in the years to come.

Seek More Than a Roommate

Finally, resist the cultural temptation to devalue marriage as an institution. Don't shack up. Don't move in. The positive benefits we've described related to marriage are simply not true of cohabitation. Couples who marry are more faithful than their unmarried, cohabiting counterparts and far less likely to separate if they have kids together.[42] When compared with cohabitating couples, married men and women are less likely to be depressed and less likely to abuse alcohol.[43] They also experience less violence in their homes, generally.[44] The children of married couples flourish at levels higher than children born to cohabitating couples.[45]

If you think it would be wiser to move in first and get married "down the road," think again. Cohabitating couples are less likely to marry later, less likely to spend time together if they do marry, and more likely to divorce if they marry after a period of cohabitation.[46] Their children are also less likely to marry in the future.[47] There's a difference between marriage and cohabitation. They are not interchangeable trajectory decisions because they lead to two very different destinations.

If you're already married, the second part of Dr. Laura's mantra will be more important to you than the first. Here's some advice to help married couples treat each other kindly:

Love Your Marriage More Than You Love Your Spouse

As unromantic as this may sound, a reverence for the institution of marriage—for the power it wields and the holy purpose it represents—is even *more* important to the success of your marriage than the love you have for your spouse. Studies confirm this truth. People who revere marriage experience "higher quality marriages," spend more time with each other, and sacrifice for each other more often.[48] On days when your feelings for your spouse are tested or found wanting, remember the importance of marriage as a goal and institution. If you love the union, you'll love the mate with whom you're united.

Preach the Right Message

Your marriage *preaches*. It's proclaiming something—something tragic or something holy—to your kids and to the world around you. As much as we might enjoy talking about marriage, our lives as husbands and wives are much better teachers. Our kids are learning how to treat their future spouses from watching us, after all. If you're a Christian, remember your marriage is also an image of Christ's love for the church. It's never too early (or too late) for your marriage to teach others. It can even preach the gospel.

Dump the Contract, Embrace the Covenant

Paul saw his marriage as a contract with Nadia rather than a covenant he and Nadia were making with God. While the secular definition of a covenant can sometimes sound a lot like a contract, the biblical definition is very different:

1. A covenant is based on trust between parties. A contract is based on distrust.
2. A covenant is based on unlimited responsibility. A contract is based on limited liability.
3. A covenant cannot be broken if new circumstances occur. A contract can be voided by mutual consent.[49]

Paul thought of his marriage in contractual terms. He never trusted Nadia, and when he ended the union, he expected to break the contract with "limited liability." When people view marriage in this way, their commitment clearly suffers. Why would someone who holds a contractual view of marriage take the decision to marry seriously in the first place? If it's just a contract, it can be easily undone. People who hold a covenantal view of marriage, however, make marriage an important trajectory decision. If marriage is a covenant agreement, it is based on unlimited responsibility and cannot be broken because of changing circumstances.

Love without Expectations

When you give your best to your spouse, expecting *nothing* in return, something magical happens. Joy and happiness are always tied to our expectations, so once we disconnect our expectations from our efforts, we unlock the door to satisfaction. Rather than doing something nice for your spouse because you expect something in return, try doing it because it's the right thing to do, whether or not he or she responds as you hoped.

Your responses to your spouse are between *you and God*. Your spouse's responses to you are between *your spouse and God*. Resist the temptation to expect your mate to act one way or another, either positively or negatively. Instead, follow God's instruction in your marriage, without an expectation of your spouse. When one of you starts behaving in this way, the other won't be able to resist the challenge to respond accordingly. Your daily competition to please God by unconditionally serving each other will transform your relationship.

Commit to Communication

Of all the abilities you can practice and improve, none is more important than the skill of communication. The ability to communicate is so important, it ought to be considered even before you get married. Nietzsche said it well: "When marrying, ask yourself this question: Do you believe that you will be able to converse well with this person into your old age? Everything else in marriage is transitory."[50] Develop your communication skills while you're still young, then practice these skills with your spouse. Learn how to speak *and listen*. Be sure to seek help if this is an area where you need to improve.

Focus on Forgiveness

Ruth Bell Graham once observed, "A good marriage is the union of two good forgivers."[51] If you've been happily married for any length of time, you know this is true. The elusive key to forgiveness—humility—is discussed in chapter 6. The most unforgiving people are simply those who think they have nothing for which they need forgiveness. Read that last sentence again. When we are honest about our failings and recognize the degree to which we personally need forgiveness, extending forgiveness to others is a lot easier. And when, as a Christ follower, I contemplate the degree of forgiveness Jesus offers me on the cross, I am immediately humbled. Leveraging that humility is the key to offering forgiveness to others.

The Truth in True Crime: You Were Created for Commitment

The day after killing Nadia, Paul told a friend his wife had been murdered by an unknown intruder. He then avoided his phone for the rest of the week. Paul mistakenly assumed someone would have discovered Nadia within a day of her murder, but their daughter didn't find Nadia's body for another *two* days. Paul's simple admission to knowing Nadia's fate—before anyone other than the killer would know she was dead—was one of several truths we eventually presented to a jury.

Like all our cases, Nadia's death was senseless and preventable. Paul convinced himself he would be happier without Nadia, when just the opposite would have been true if he had known what contemporary sociologists continue to affirm: humans flourish when a committed marriage is one of their trajectory decisions.

Studies reveal that we are hardwired for commitment. Even if you're single, you probably have a best friend, a close confidante, or a bosom buddy. The apostle Paul, as a single man, advocated for the kind of commitment common between spouses, even from those who never marry. If you prefer being single, you're called to harness your desire for relationship and commitment and apply it to your "undivided devotion to the Lord."[52]

The biblical authors recognized and affirmed the importance of commitment and marriage long before sociologists and researchers discovered it. Scripture begins and ends with a marriage. Adam and Eve become "one flesh" in the first book of the Old Testament, and the "marriage of the lamb" (where the church as the "bride" is presented to Jesus) is recorded in the last book of the New Testament.[53]

The Old Testament repeatedly refers to the importance of marriage. Three of the Ten Commandments involve the marital union (the fifth, seventh, and tenth commandments), and many additional passages describe rules related to marrying and being married.[54] One of the longest chapters in the Old Testament (Genesis 24) is a description of marriage: the union between Isaac and Rebekah.

EXPLANATION: We Seek Relational Commitment

We share a consistent, common desire for committed unions and the benefits they offer us. Humans thrive when married.

Christianity offers a robust explanation for the way the world really is, describing marriage as a divine *design feature*. Not everyone will marry, but marriage is God-ordained and designed to benefit all of us *as a species*—even those who remain single or may commit themselves more to the cause of Christ than to the cause of marriage.

In either case, Christianity explains the grounding for the institution of marriage and, once again, proves to be the wise way to live.

The New Testament also treats marriage with reverence, providing instruction related to the nature of marriage and the roles of husbands and wives.[55] Jesus showed an incredibly high regard for the sanctity of marriage and repeatedly used marriage as a metaphor, comparing himself to a bridegroom and his followers to wedding guests.[56] This metaphorical description is common throughout Scripture. Old Testament writers used the institution of marriage as a symbol of God and his people, and New Testament authors used marriage as a metaphor for Jesus and the church.[57]

Jesus and the biblical authors knew *then* what researchers are discovering *now*: humans thrive when they marry, conceive children with one another, and raise these children together in the context of a committed marriage. Jesus taught his followers: "Have you not read that he who created them from the beginning made them male and female, and said, 'Therefore a man shall leave his father and his mother and hold fast to his wife, and the two shall become one flesh'? So they are no longer two but one flesh. What therefore God has joined together, let not man separate."[58] When men and women unite in the bond of matrimony as "one flesh" and raise their children together, humans thrive. Why? Because God designed us for a deep, flourishing, dependent commitment.[59] This commitment changes and matures us, teaching us to be honorable and selfless.[60] When spouses raise their shared biological children in this kind of relationship, *everyone* flourishes.[61] Adults thrive, children are protected and nurtured, and societies succeed.[62] Virtually every benefit confirmed by modern research was first posited by Jesus and affirmed by the ancient biblical authors.

As a Christian, I believe the gospel is the single most important change agent in culture. Second only to the gospel, marriage does more to change the culture and improve human flourishing than any other institution on earth. Why? Because it is part of our God-given design. *We were created for commitment.*

SANTA CLAUS AND MISPLACED DEVOTION

How to Be More Careful about Your Object(s) of Worship

> What each one honors before all else, what before all
> things he admires and loves, this for him is God.
> —ORIGEN

> To glorify man in his natural and unmodified self is
> no less surely, even if less obviously, idolatry than
> actually to bow down before a graven image.
> —IRVING BABBITT

Santa Claus was lying on the ground, about twenty yards from his night-time residence: a surprisingly tidy porta-potty at a local construction site on the edge of town.

He was wearing several layers of clothing. These shirts, sweaters, and jackets kept him warm at night but made it much harder for first responders to determine why he was lying unconscious. Assuming he was simply drunk, they approached him without any sense of urgency.

As they peeled back each layer of clothing, they discovered the blood-saturated undershirts and eventually the fatal knife wounds. Jorge Santos, or Santa Claus as he was known locally, had been stabbed and left for dead. He did his best to stumble from the location of the attack to a liquor store but collapsed about fifteen feet from the business.

By the time I got there, the paramedics had already pronounced him dead. His long white hair and beard were stained red, and his clothes were partially removed, exposing the injuries he suffered earlier in the evening.

Rick and I spent the rest of the night talking with members of the homeless community who considered Santa Claus family.

No one could offer a motive for the crime. Everyone who knew Jorge considered him kind and jovial (just as you might expect for someone who resembled Saint Nick). He had always been harmless, even before he became an alcoholic and started living on the street. Jorge's biological family hadn't seen him in years, but they described him as "angelic."

What, then, would cause someone to murder him in this way? What was the killer's motive?

Even prior to these questions asked by Santa Claus's friends and family, I knew the answer. Not because I knew anything about Jorge or the killer but because I knew the motive for *every* murder. Santa Claus was killed over money, sex, or the pursuit of power. It was as simple as that. These are the only three reasons *anyone* commits a crime—any crime—including murder. If you think there's a fourth motive, you're wrong. What about jealousy? Ask yourself, "What were they jealous about?" What about envy? Ask, "What were they envious of?" The answer to these questions will always involve something related to money, sex, or power.

That's what made the Santos case so puzzling.

What motivated the killer? Santa Claus owned almost nothing. He lived on the street during the day and slept in the porta-potty at night. His daily routine involved the meticulous collection of cans from neighboring trash bins, followed by noontime visits to the recycling center where he redeemed his findings. By the afternoon, Santos had just enough money to buy a hamburger and the beer or wine he needed to make it to the end of the day.

He was a nearly invisible member of the community. What motive related to money, sex, or power could have driven someone to kill a man who seemed to offer nothing in any of these three categories?

Rick and I found the answer to this question, but only after interviewing other people who lived on the streets.

 The Allure of Adoration

Humans share similar priorities and seek the same pleasures, regardless of social status.

When asked about what is important, meaningful, or worth pursuing, people provide like-minded responses. Aside from relationships with family, respondents value—unsurprisingly—endeavors involving money, sex, or power.[1]

Sometimes these drives and desires are hidden within other more visible pursuits. When respondents report, for example, their yearnings related to comfort, material objects, leisure, or technology, they are exposing their interest in *money*. When studies reveal priorities related to personal appearance, marriage, family, or relationships, they are often highlighting our interest in *sex*. When researchers identify our cravings for security, free time, control, identity, status, fame, or celebrity, they are measuring our interest in *power*. We pursue these interests with passion, consistently assigning them the highest value. Why?

> **EVIDENCE: Humans Worship**
> Religious believers aren't the only people who worship. Everyone considers someone or something more important than anything else, and we are inclined to create our own objects of worship. When we offer love, honor, adoration, extravagant respect, or devotion to something or someone, we demonstrate our propensity to worship. Why are people so uniformly wired for this form of devotion? Why are humans—by our nature—worshipers?

Because we are, by nature, worshipers, and not just those of us who identify as "religious." Worship is the ultimate destination of a joyous heart. We form objects of worship because, as A. W. Tozer observed, "without worship, we go about miserable."[2]

The word *worship* finds its root in the Old English term *weorð* ("worthy") and the suffix *-scipe* ("-ship"),[3] and since everyone adores or assigns worth to *something*, everyone is involved in the act of worship. When we worship something other than God, we "love, respect, and admire someone or something very much, often without noticing the bad qualities of that person or thing."[4] This definition is accurate, especially when considering the motives for murder.

The pursuit of money, sex, and power can be noble. But these desires can also bring out the worst in us, especially if we assign them too much value and fail to "notice the bad qualities" they often provoke.

Rick and I made a career investigating suspects who allowed their desires to motivate them toward bad choices. The Santos case was no exception, even though it took us a little longer to discover how the pursuit of money, sex, or power could motivate someone to kill Santa Claus.

We discovered an entire hidden society of "canners" living in the back alleys and construction sites in our city. They shared the same collection routine, searching for recyclables in the morning, cashing them in, and drinking all afternoon. One of these "canners," Petey Caldwell, became our primary suspect.

 ## Choosing What We Worship

Like the rest of us, Petey was a worshiper. As David Foster Wallace observes, "There is no such thing as not worshiping. Everybody worships. The only choice we get is what to worship."[5] Petey chose to focus on money and power.

About two weeks prior to the murder, Santos inadvertently started collecting cans in an area Petey had been harvesting for months. This threatened Petey's revenue stream, so he confronted Santos one day at the collection center in front of several other canners. Santos listened calmly to Petey's rant, shrugged it off, and went about his business. Petey felt ignored and disrespected.

This verbal quarrel became a catalyst for Petey. He began to form his purpose based on the confrontation at the collection center. What started as a simple dispute over cans became a matter of street respect and honor. Two of the three motives for murder had been activated in a single afternoon.

We often craft purpose and meaning around our interests and objects of worship. That's why it's so dangerous to assign value to the wrong pursuits. When properly placed, our devotion can create a positive sense of value and direction. People with a focused and elevated sense of purpose are generally happier and more satisfied.[6] They are healthier, live longer, and thrive when they are older.[7] Purpose, when properly grounded, helps us survive hardship with better mental health and less drug and alcohol use.[8] People who adopt a healthy sense of purpose are also less likely to commit crimes.[9]

That's why Petey needed to be more careful about his objects of worship. His life became an object lesson in misplaced devotion. He obsessed over his desire for vengeance, driven by the pursuit of money (his lost revenue) and power (his lost status within the community of canners).

When money, sex, or power become the object of our worship, we are destined for failure. David Foster Wallace captures the futility:

If you worship money and things, if they are where you tap real meaning in life, then you will never have enough, never feel you have enough . . .

Worship your body and beauty and sexual allure and you will always feel ugly. And when time and age start showing, you will die a million deaths before they finally grieve you . . .

Worship power, you will end up feeling weak and afraid, and you will need ever more power over others to numb you to your fear.[10]

Our desire to worship is an undeniable feature of our human nature, but we flourish only when our objects of worship are truly worthy. Why? Because what we adore and esteem defines us. It's not just true for Petey and others who have misplaced their devotion. It's true for all of us.

 ## Our True Object of Obsession

None one can escape the relationship between worship and identity. If you worship material possessions, you will eventually *become a materialist* and the fleeting value of your possessions will drive you to gather more. If you worship sex, you will eventually *become an addict* and the temporary satisfaction of each encounter will motivate you to collect more experiences. If you worship power, you will eventually *become a tyrant* and the finite, earthly power available in this life will leave you abusing those you hope to control.

This is precisely what happened to Petey.

His fixation on power, status, and "street cred" changed his personality. He became a bully, not just toward Santa Claus but toward everyone he encountered on the street. He started threatening anyone who wandered into his canning territory. He also began to boast about his desire to eliminate Jorge Santos.

Petey allowed his worship to *ruin* him rather than to *lead him to restoration*. That's what happens when we place our misguided adoration on temporary, worldly pursuits. If only there was a more lasting, meaningful, and satisfying object of worship . . .

But, of course, there is.

Our desire to worship something of greatest value is yet another evidence that we were created for more than what's available in this world.

Unfortunately, our search for a greatest object of worship often results in what the Bible calls "idolatry." As John Calvin observed, "Every one of us is, even from his mother's womb, a master craftsman of idols."[11] This is, of course, true. Theodore Parker described it this way: "Yet, if he would, man cannot live all to this world. If not religious, he will be superstitious. If he worship not the true God, he will have his idols."[12]

The power of idolatry is much more alluring than you might suspect. Even people who claim to know and worship God fall into idolatry. One survey of Protestant pastors, for example, found that Christian church members are lured and distracted by the idols of comfort, control, security, money, and approval.[13] Another study found that fewer than 43 percent of Christian believers (depending on the denomination) listed any form of spirituality as their top source of "meaning." Instead, they often listed family, career, or finances.[14]

We take the adoration appropriate for what we cannot see—the eternal, all-powerful Creator of the universe—and mistakenly place it on what we can observe more readily: the temporary, compromised pleasures of the world around us. One has the potential to delight and restore, the others only to distract and ruin.

Some of us, when we come to the end of this ruinous distraction of "good things," begin the search for the "greatest thing." As Charles Spurgeon put it, "Nothing teaches us about the preciousness of the Creator as much as when we learn the emptiness of everything else."[15]

Petey also eventually discovered the "emptiness of everything else," but not until he tracked Santa Claus to his nighttime residence at the porta-potty.

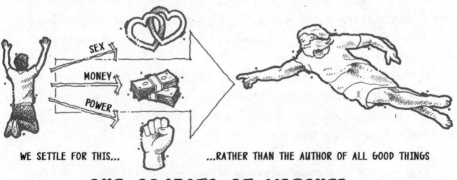

WE SETTLE FOR THIS...   ...RATHER THAN THE AUTHOR OF ALL GOOD THINGS

OUR OBJECTS OF WORSHIP

Chase the Lead

If you're a believer, a skeptic, or somewhere in between, you're a worshiper. Your objects of worship may be obvious or hidden, but one thing is certain: *your worship decides your destiny.* That's why it's important to be honest about your priorities and obsessions.

Here's a test to assess your own idolatry. Ask yourself these questions and be honest about your answers:

Where Do I Spend My Money?
We typically trade one thing of value for another, so your bank account is likely one of the best windows into your world of worship. If you make a detailed list of how you're spending your *discretionary income,* you'll soon discover your *extraordinary interests.*

On What Do I Spend My Time?
Your financial statement isn't the only place to find evidence of your obsessions. Your calendar is an equally evidential document. What do you prioritize? What appears most frequently on your schedule? For what are you willing to carve out time? If it made it to your calendar, it's likely something you value.

EXAMPLE: The Rich Young Man
The gospel of Mark records an occasion when a wealthy young man came to Jesus asking, "Good Teacher, what must I do to inherit eternal life?" (10:17 ESV) Jesus knew what the man considered most valuable. He challenged him, saying, "Sell all that you have and give to the poor, and you will have treasure in heaven; and come, follow me" (v. 21 ESV). The pursuit of money was the young man's greatest interest, his object of worship. "Disheartened by the saying, he went away sorrowful, for he had great possessions" (v. 22 ESV).

What is distracting you from God, the true, greatest object of worship?

On What Do I Spend My Talents and Abilities?
Sometimes our abilities emerge from the persistent exploration of our interests, and sometimes our abilities determine what we are willing to explore in the first place. Where are you most talented? How are you using those talents? The answer will probably reveal an object or area of worship.

What Captivates My Thoughts and Attention?

What do you think about most? What do you ponder when you're falling asleep or first waking up? Our thoughts are typically devoted to our objects of worship. As the ancient theologian Origen, observed, "What each one honors before all else, what before all things he admires and loves, this for him is God."[16]

Where Do I Get My Joy?

Ever find yourself smiling for no apparent reason? What are you thinking about? Our objects of worship have the power to please. If you worship a celebrity, you'll find joy in reading about him or her. If you worship politics, you're probably happiest when listening to your favorite political pundit. Follow your joy and see where it leads.

What Do I Most Eagerly Anticipate?

Have you ever been distracted by a future event or opportunity? Ever think, "I can hardly wait," or "The anticipation is killing me"? Eager, expectant thoughts like these often point to an object of worship. Albert Simpson described it this way: "As long as you want anything very much, especially more than you want God, it is an idol."[17]

What Music Do I Listen To?

Music is the primary vehicle of worship. We sing about our obsessions. Music instinctively flows from the desires of our hearts. Next time you're listening to music, ask yourself, What are the subjects of my favorite songs? What themes dominate my favorite playlist?

What Do I Trust?

Everyone trusts something (or someone) as their safety net in times of trouble. We place our trust in our abilities, savings, insurance, or friends. What do you trust? On what do you rely? Whatever you believe has the power to save you, that is your God. What do you trust to save you when times get tough?

With What (or Whom) Do I Identify?

Inside-out and outside-in identities (as we discussed in chapter 2) often reveal our objects of worship. If, for example, you seldom introduce yourself as a Christ follower, it may be because you revere your achievements, family position, or occupation to a greater degree. What does your stated identity reveal about your devotion?

What Do I Publicly Proclaim?
In our contemporary social media environment, most of our friends, family members, or followers already know what we worship; they've been reading about it in our posts. Look at your last twenty posts. Your idols are probably listed in your feed.

What Do I Wear or Display?
Fans wear the jerseys of their favorite sports teams for a reason. *Fan* is simply an abbreviation of *fanatic*: "a person with an extreme and uncritical enthusiasm or zeal, as in religion or politics."[18] Fans display their fandom on their clothing, jewelry, and automobiles. What does your clothing tell the world about what's important to you?

How Do I Behave?
Our interests and obsessions eventually shape our values and actions. Louie Giglio captures the relationship perfectly: "Worship is simply about value. . . . We may say we value this thing or that thing more than any other, but the volume of our actions speaks louder than our words."[19] What do your actions reveal about your values and their source?

To What (or Whom) Do I Submit My Freedom?
It's been wisely observed: "Whatever controls us is our lord. The person who seeks power is controlled by power. The person who seeks acceptance is controlled by acceptance. We do not control ourselves. We are controlled by the lord of our lives."[20] We willingly surrender our freedoms to our objects of worship. To whom (or what) are you willing to submit?

What Am I Unwilling to Question?
When we idolize something or someone, we surrender our willingness to *question our loyalty*. We are typically blind to criticisms of our objects of worship, so one way to identify them is simply to ask, To what am I unquestioningly loyal? What am I unwilling to examine critically?

What Makes Me Angry?

Because our idols are usually beyond criticism, we get angry when someone says something disparaging. When was the last time your wrath was provoked? It was probably because someone bruised one of your objects of worship.

Asking questions and examining these areas of your life helps you assess your idols. Giglio agrees: "It's easy: You simply follow the trail of your time, your affection, your energy, your money, and your allegiance. At the end of that trail you'll find a throne; and whatever, or whoever, is on that throne is what's of highest value to you. On that throne is what you worship."[21]

What emerged in your personal investigation? If it was something other than God himself, it is an insufficient idol. The gods we create from our pursuits of money, sex, or power are finite and fleeting. That's why they fail to satisfy in any deep, meaningful, or lasting way. They can be *good* things, but they aren't the *greatest* thing. They can be *appreciated* but shouldn't be *revered*.

True reverence is reserved for God.

Petey eventually came to understand this truth, but it wasn't until he did the unthinkable. When our interviews led us to him, he was already a broken man. It's one thing to obsess over your festering desire for power and vengeance, another to act on it. Petey bullied the local canners and boasted of his intention to put Santa Claus "in his place," but after killing Santos, Petey came to a sober realization.

On the night of the murder, he drank even more than he normally did. Under the influence of this additional liquid courage, he walked to the construction site and tried to quietly open the door to the porta-potty. It was locked. He could hear Santos snoring inside, so he tiptoed to the rear of the structure and pushed it enough to wake his victim. The movement confused Santos, so he exited the porta-potty. He looked around but didn't find the cause of the disruption. He took a few steps from the cubicle to better examine the area. That's when Petey jumped out and stabbed him.

Petey looked Santos in the eyes when he plunged the knife, and he held Santos upright briefly as the older man struggled to retain his balance. Petey wasn't prepared for the impact his proximity to Santos would have. By the time I located Petey, he was ready to confess everything he did that night. He cried through the entire interview.

Because he hid behind the porta-potty, lured Santos out, and then surprised him with the attack, Petey's crime was considered a "special circumstance" homicide. In California, murders like this, where the killer was "lying in wait," warrant the *death penalty*. The district attorney settled for life in prison without the possibility of parole, however.

This merciful sentencing decision provided Petey with the opportunity to reconsider his objects of worship. He eventually became a Christian while in state prison.

Petey's case is much more dramatic than anything most of us will experience, but it reveals something true for everyone: we thrive and flourish when we place our worship appropriately, and God is the truest, most appropriate object of worship. We can embrace this truth now, or like Petey, wait until our lesser objects of worship fail to satisfy us. Dr. Dan Wickert explains: "God is too good to allow His children to worship something or someone that will not satisfy. He is so good that He either wrenches our idols from our hands or makes us miserable as long as we clench and grasp."[22]

The Truth in True Crime: You Were Created to Worship

I discovered the common motives for misbehavior and our shared inclination toward worship as an atheist investigator. Contemporary research only strengthened my anecdotal observations. Years later, when I began to read the New Testament, I found that the Bible authors also described this attribute of human nature—thousands of years before sociologists started studying the phenomenon.

Our inclination to create idols based on our desire for money, sex, or power was described accurately by the apostle John when he warned his readers not to "love the world or the things in the world" and cautioned them against the temptations of "the desires of the flesh" (sex), "the desires of the eyes" (money), and the "pride of life" (power).[23] Paul also cautioned his readers to avoid being seduced by bodily desires, earthly possessions, and self-adoration.[24] The church fathers and Reformers acknowledged the danger of these forms of idolatry as well. Martin Luther, for example, recognized that "the god of the world is riches, pleasure, and pride, wherewith they abuse all the creatures and gifts of God."[25]

Christianity accurately describes our misguided obsession with *good things* and our attempt to make them the *greatest thing*. It also explains why this effort eventually leaves us empty and unsatisfied.[26] We are "master craftsmen of idols" because we were created in the image of God. As we longingly await our reunion with him, we substitute deficient deities of one kind or another.

Petey is waiting along with the rest of us, but he no longer settles for the substitutes.

His sister paid me an unexpected visit about two years after his arrest. We sat and talked in one of our interview rooms for nearly an hour. She became a believer after learning about God in her brother's jailhouse letters. After several months of self-reflection (and the gift of a Bible from a prison chaplain), Petey realigned his devotion. He came to understand what John Ruskin described over one hundred years ago: "God will put up with a great many things in the human heart, but there is one thing that He will not put up with in it—a second place. He who offers God a second place, offers Him no place."[27] Petey is now singularly devoted and patiently waiting to meet the True Object of Worship.

We chase what's good *in the world* because we long for what's great *in the universe*. Our desire to worship is a feature of our design, and it was given to us to point us back to the Designer, just like it did Petey. *We were created to worship.*

EXPLANATION: We Seek Substitutes

When kittens or puppies are separated from their mothers too early, they often seek comfort in a surrogate, snuggling, cuddling, or even suckling a stuffed animal or blanket.

Humans also seek comfort in surrogates, offering our devotion to *good things* because we feel separated from the *greatest thing*. We focus on what's immediately visible rather than what's infinitely valuable.

Our common desire to worship is a design feature that ultimately points us to the one true, worthy object of worship.

LEGENDS, LIARS, AND LIABILITIES

How to Moderate Your Celebrity

Fame is poison, so we must take it in small doses.
—HONORÉ DE BALZAC

Love of glory can only create a great hero;
contempt of glory creates a great man.
—CHARLES-MAURICE DE TALLEYRAND

This is your lucky day. You're about to meet a legend."

Danny Higgins peered carefully through the passenger window of my patrol car, scanning the sidewalk, trying to spot the local icon. Several ominous looking young men glared back in our direction. They recognized us immediately from the car we were driving, a marked black and white police car, modified with a lower profile and missing the typical rooftop lightbar.

Danny was a seasoned Los Angeles County Sherriff's deputy assigned to the gang unit. I met him shortly after I was transferred to a similar unit at our agency. Today he was helping me locate a suspect in a murder. Danny knew most of the gangsters in this area of South Central Los Angeles, but Pelon seemed to be the most intriguing.

"Right there. See him?" Danny pointed to a group of three gang members standing to the rear of a lowered 1980 Chevy Monte Carlo. They were nearly invisible from the street, tucked discreetly between the car and the house. I pulled to the curb.

The men barely looked in our direction as we approached them, but the one in the middle stood out immediately. Jaime Munoz was known as Pelon by everyone in this part of the city. He was a famous, recognizable influencer, long before social media coined the term. He was also deadly.

Pelon's fame was due, in large part, to his family connection, his status as a drug dealer, and his reportedly murderous nature. Pelon's two older brothers were notorious OGs ("original gangsters"), both serving life sentences for murder. While in jail, they became important members of one of our state's most vicious prison gangs. Their influence extended well beyond the prison walls, and Pelon was an early beneficiary.

Even as a young teenager, he embraced his legendary family reputation. Local gang members feared him, not because he was physically intimidating but because his brothers were protective and connected. Pelon was *untouchable*.

He was suspected in several murders, including one in our city. But unlike his older brothers, Pelon was still a free man, cleverly and deviously navigating his reputed criminal life without evidential detection. At times it seemed Pelon was more reputation than reality. Local gangsters rehashed his famous exploits, but none could (or would) offer firsthand verification. Pelon was a legend in the truest sense, the subject of extraordinary, albeit unauthenticated, tales and stories.

"Jaime, we've been looking for you. This is Officer Wallace." Danny introduced me to Pelon with a sense of intentionality, referencing his birth name and giving him time to see I was wearing the uniform of my agency. I was hoping Pelon's reaction would tip his involvement in the shooting I was investigating.

"What you mean you been 'lookin' for me'? You know where to find me. I ain't been hiding from *no one*." Pelon was uniquely cocky, especially for his age. But that wasn't the only thing unique about him. From the time Pelon was very young, he had *Alopecia universalis*, a medical condition resulting in the loss of all his body hair, including his eyebrows and head hair.

Pelon considered the condition an opportunity.

In all my years as a detective, I've never encountered anyone with tattoos like the ones I observed that day. Pelon tattooed the entirety of his head with profanity. Vile sentences, words, and expressions covered every available inch of his face, neck, and scalp. It was distracting, to say the least. But it was also *legendary*.

Pelon would have been famous enough because of his family identity.

He also would have been notable for his small stature and medical condition. Add his reputation as a clever, elusive killer and you can understand his growing celebrity among gangsters. But throw in the bold profanity of his tattoos and, presto, you've created a street legend.

Pelon leveraged his celebrity in several important ways. He was never alone or without protection. Girls clamored for his attention, and gang members defended him at all costs. Pelon seldom had to pay for anything and was almost always the center of attention. He lived the kind of life you'd expect of a legend.

Although I suspected him in the murder I was assigned, I never confirmed his involvement. The case I was investigating when Danny first introduced me to Pelon remains open to this day. It seemed like yet another chapter in the long narrative of Pelon's legendary reputation. Once again, he appeared untouchable, just outside the reach of the criminal justice system.

Until Pelon's reputation and local celebrity provoked a different form of justice.

Legend and Its Ability to Lure

Pelon surrounded himself with celebrity-seekers. It wasn't hard to find fans, given his connections and reputation and the innate inclination his groupies had as "master craftsmen of idols." There would be no celebrities if there weren't celebrity-seekers, and Pelon had no trouble finding his share.

The two young men standing next to Pelon would have given anything to be Pelon. They idolized him and did their best to mimic his mannerisms, language, and appearance. Both were well on their way to collecting their own outlandish set of tattoos.

Most of us are interested in celebrities to one degree or another, and many of us seek celebrity personally. That's unsurprising given the idolatrous motivations we've already discussed in chapter 5. Our desire for celebrity is simply an aspect of our pursuit of power. This desire is only amplified in the internet age.

Only a generation ago, the path to celebrity had gatekeepers. Publishers provided opportunities for authors, record labels elevated musicians, television and movie producers turned actors into stars, and expensive publicists made some people famous. All of that changed when do-it-yourself social media platforms emerged.

According to teenagers, the biggest celebrities in America jumped the gatekeepers entirely: social media stars are now more popular than film, television, or music celebrities.[1] These social media icons became influencers without the help of traditional media professionals, and young people are watching. It used to be nearly impossible to grab the attention of the gate-keepers. Not anymore. Now everyone possesses the power to be their own gatekeeper. The resulting temptation of celebrity, in a world where everyone has a potential pathway, is simply too strong for many of us to resist. Talent agent Jane Bulseco observes, "There's no doubt that social media is making fame more desirable than ever before for today's generation. Social media platforms have democratized the talent discovery process. . . . No longer do celebrities solely live on stages and movie screens, but they are born in their homes and are accessible to us in ours."[2]

Younger people are more likely to value fame, largely because of the allure of social media.[3] One study from the Pew Research Center found that fortune and fame were the first and second goals of millennials.[4] Another study from an online talent company found that one in four millennials would quit their jobs to become famous.[5] One in six preferred fame to having children. One in ten said they would forego their college education for fame, and sadly, one in twelve admitted they would disown their family for the opportunity to be famous.

Pelon became a local legend *before* the invention of social media, and like other contemporary celebrities, he was more than willing to forego work, children, and education to be "the man." He garnered the respect of people he thought were his friends, and he believed his fame would last forever.

Neither were true in the end.

 ## Fame, Fake Friendships, and Forever

Why are power, authority, respect, fame, and celebrity so enticing? One explanation is rooted in our desire for relationship and community. Fame offers an imaginary version of lopsided relationships in which fans, masquerading as friends, are expected to delight in our mere presence. Philosopher

Alain de Botton described the pursuit of celebrity as "the intimate desire to be liked and treated with justice and kindness by people [we] don't know."[6] This desire is stronger in some of us depending on how we grew up, especially if we experienced difficulty in our relationships or suffered neglect. De Botton even theorized, "No one would want to be famous who hadn't also, somewhere in the past, been made to feel extremely insignificant."[7]

This was, in fact, Pelon's story. During his childhood, his peers rejected him because of his size and medical condition. As his brothers' fame grew, he leveraged his family identity to develop his own version of celebrity, eventually turning the tables on those who had ignored him as a boy. Pelon then imagined himself to be accepted and loved, settling for a false version of true relationships.

Pelon also displayed another tempting aspect of celebrity: *the desire to survive beyond the grave*. A *legend* is typically defined as "a story coming down from the past."[8] Ancient legends live on in the present, so it's reasonable to assume current legends will live on in the future. Pelon's desire, like many other celebrities today, was to attain what some sociologists call "symbolic immortality," living into the future by virtue of his reputation.[9]

One researcher of celebrity described it this way: "Marilyn Monroe may have died on August 5, 1962, but her image is still very much alive today. Because the celebrities have 'entered the language of the culture,' they have the opportunity to create something that will outlive them."[10] This pursuit of "symbolic immortality" was appealing to Pelon, especially given the dangerously fleeting nature of his gang culture.

Sociologists and researchers who study the motives behind our desire for celebrity often cite acceptance and immortality as the aspirations. Fame, however, seldom provides either of these.

Friendship—true friendship—requires a level of familiarity unavailable to fans or onlookers. As Katelyn Beaty observes, "The very nature of celebrity, especially in a digital era, is that it hides its power behind the illusion of intimacy."[11] Friends care enough to tell you

EVIDENCE: Humans Seek Fame

Humans have always coveted fame. Achilles, the Greek hero of Homer's *Iliad*, chose to die in battle, attaining what the Greeks called *kleos*, the immortality that comes from a glorious reputation. Even though we seek fame, we flourish when we embrace the opposite. The importance of humility is just as ancient as our pursuit of celebrity.

Why do humans seek such a debilitating goal while simultaneously struggling to embrace this virtue?

when you are wrong, and they know you well enough to have earned the right. According to King Solomon, "Better is open rebuke than hidden love. Faithful are the wounds of a friend."[12] Fans and admirers simply haven't earned the right to do what friends need to do.

This was certainly true for Pelon. His associates were afraid to correct or admonish him.

"Symbolic immortality" is also a poor substitute for eternal life, and this lesser counterfeit comes with a price. People who hope their celebrity persona will survive their death are forever committed to the perception they have created. They become, in many ways, larger-than-life characters, carefully crafting their public image and protecting (or eliminating) any part of themselves contradicting this persona. As G. S. Bhogal writes, "This is the ultimate trapdoor in the hall of fame; to become a prisoner of one's own persona. The desire for recognition in an increasingly atomized world lures us to be who strangers wish us to be."[13]

Those of us active on social media have already experienced this phenomenon, even if we aren't yet bona fide celebrities. We select and reveal only the choicest moments of our lives, meticulously selecting what's appropriate for our online personas. We are one kind of person on social media, another in reality. The version that lives on in posterity (if we become famous), is the false description rather than the real person.

Fame fails to satisfy our desires for acceptance and immortality. Worse yet, it opens the doors to even more precarious cravings.

In my years investigating murders and other lesser crimes, I've seldom encountered someone who, in their unrestricted pursuit of power, didn't also succumb to the unrestricted pursuit of money or sex. I've seen it time and time again: if you scratch one itch, you'll eventually scratch the other two.

When our status grows, so do our opportunities, and some of these opportunities are dangerous. One celebrity described it this way: "I live in Hollywood and I'm a middle-aged man, and Miss September keeps throwing herself at me. That wouldn't happen if I wasn't famous. Believe me . . . the average guy turning down Miss September is a tough day. That would show intestinal fortitude that I don't know that I have."[14]

Researchers have noted this "dark side of fame" as well, finding that "the lure of life's temptations may be the most secret side of celebrity experience," with some study participants referring to the "perks" of fame as an "unexpected side benefit and also a danger."[15]

Notoriety promises acceptance and immortality it cannot deliver while introducing temptation it often cannot control. Along the way, celebrities also report demanding expectations, a loss of privacy, mistrust, and isolation.[16] This phenomenon is no longer unique to a select few of us. Because the gatekeepers of celebrity are gone, everyone has the opportunity to pursue celebrity at the risk of opening the door to other dangerous pursuits.

That's precisely what happened to Pelon.

His notoriety as the younger brother of dangerous gangsters established his authority on the street. But this power and influence eventually embroiled him in a dangerous sexual relationship.

 ## The Remedy for Celebrity

Pelon's pursuit of power and fame (like his eventual pursuit of sex and money) was driven by his pride, or as a dictionary might describe it, his "high or inordinate opinion of (his) own dignity, importance, merit, or superiority."[17] Pelon became the center of his own world, leveraging his power to get everything else he wanted.

Girls began presenting themselves to Pelon regularly. Some just wanted his attention. Others wanted to brag about their liaisons with him. Some wanted to have his baby. Their motive didn't matter to Pelon. His power and reputation made him more attractive than he ever imagined as a young teenager, and he intended to take advantage of every opportunity.

One of these prospects, Lucia, misrepresented herself to Pelon. He had no idea she was the younger sister of a fearless rival. After just a few visits, she considered Pelon the love of her life. He didn't feel the same way, dismissing Lucia as just another opportunity.

That dismissal would eventually prove costly.

All of this could have been avoided, of course, had Pelon resisted his own selfish desire for power and fame. Celebrity, because it is driven by pride, has a simple remedy, and Pelon missed it.

Humility is the antidote for celebrity because humility is, by definition, "freedom from pride or arrogance: the quality or state of being humble."[18] It is the opposite of pride, and people who possess this characteristic understand the difference between *personas* and *persons*. As Thomas Merton once observed, "Pride makes us artificial, and humility makes us real."[19]

People who possess humility flourish compared with those who don't. It is the secret weapon most of us are too self-focused to wield. But those who adopt a humble heart thrive, just as Augustine observed long ago: "There is something in humility which, strangely enough, exalts the heart, and something in pride which debases it."[20]

EXAMPLE: Joseph, the Son of Jacob

The Jewish patriarch Joseph was sold into slavery by his brothers but eventually found himself in a position of power and celebrity, second only to the Egyptian pharaoh (Genesis 37–41). At every point of his ascent, Joseph demonstrated humility. Even when accused of something he didn't do (in Potiphar's house), Joseph revealed his humble heart. Joseph was an excellent example of someone who leveraged humility to moderate his celebrity.

How can you employ humility to moderate your pursuit of notoriety on social media?

Research into the effect that humility has on human flourishing is a relatively modern endeavor, but the benefits of a humble heart are now clear. People with humility "experience better physiological responses to stress" and are physically and mentally healthier.[21]

Humble people are also better learners and problem solvers. They earn higher grades, score better on tests, and are "better able to differentiate between strong and weak arguments."[22] Employees who possess humility are more creative and perform at higher levels, and "humble leaders are more satisfied and productive at work."[23]

While fame tends to isolate celebrities, limiting their ability to cultivate deep friendships, humble people have closer, more satisfying relationships.[24] People who possess humility are kinder, more tolerant, more forgiving, and more likely to sacrifice for others.[25]

Humble people thrive on nearly every metric studied by sociologists, psychologists, and researchers as they measure human flourishing. People possessing humility are more helpful, more generous, and even more concerned about justice.[26]

Pelon displayed none of these virtuous attributes. He lived a selfish life, devoid of deep friendships or satisfying employment.

Just as he was preparing to dismiss Lucia, gang loyalties changed in the state prisons where his brothers were housed. Both his siblings were stabbed to death—in the same week—along with several of their associates in each prison. Pelon no longer had the protection of his brothers' reputations and was on the wrong end of a sexual relationship with the sister of a rival. He slipped from *legend* to *liability*.

Mother Teresa once wrote, "If you are humble nothing will touch you, neither praise nor disgrace, because you know what you are."[27] Pelon never truly knew his real self, and with his reputation weakened, he was no longer an untouchable icon. He had allowed his pursuit of power and celebrity to spark the pursuit of sexual conquest. But his notoriety shifted.

He was now famous for having taken advantage of the wrong girl.

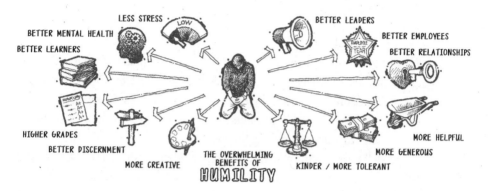

LESS STRESS
BETTER MENTAL HEALTH
BETTER LEARNERS
BETTER LEADERS
BETTER EMPLOYEES
BETTER RELATIONSHIPS
HIGHER GRADES
BETTER DISCERNMENT
MORE CREATIVE
THE OVERWHELMING BENEFITS OF HUMILITY
KINDER / MORE TOLERANT
MORE GENEROUS
MORE HELPFUL

Chase the Lead

Few of us will ever experience the kind of temptations Pelon's fame brought him, but it's still wise to be cautious about the allure of celebrity. We're all becoming addicted to fame, even if it's only the notoriety we experience within our circle of social media friends. Who doesn't want more likes, shares, or comments on a social media post? What else explains why "many teens and young adults learn to think of themselves as 'brands'" and experience depression when they don't receive the attention they were hoping for on social media?[28] Our growing technological access to fame and celebrity tempts us to pursue notoriety, even as every study demonstrates we flourish best when we pursue the opposite.

It's one thing to recognize the value of humility, however, and another to embrace it in a meaningful, transformational way. If you want to wield the "secret weapon" researchers revere, here are a few suggestions:

Know Yourself

Humility isn't achieved, it's *realized*. Charles Spurgeon once wrote, "Humility is the proper estimate of oneself."[29] This aspect of humility is key. Being honest about our shortcomings, failures, and limitations changes the way we see ourselves *and* others. It's the personification of humility. Even the definition of *humility* includes this form of self-awareness, describing it as "the quality of not being proud because you are aware of your bad qualities."[30] Take a minute to confess your "bad qualities" the next time you're inclined to think yourself worthy of celebrity.

Weigh the Risk

Acceptance and "symbolic immortality" may be what we're looking for as we pursue celebrity, but fame seldom satisfies either of these desires. More importantly, it introduces significant dangers. Take a minute to examine the shattered lives of celebrities who coveted their fame more than their families or leveraged their notoriety only to be caught in a scandal. There are many examples. One celebrity described the danger this way: "You try to put [fame] in its place because otherwise it will swallow up everything else. It will be totally out of control. It could destroy everything you have or it could make you into a monster."[31] One way to protect yourself from the temptation is simply to remember the cost.

Celebrate Others

If you ever listen to a humble, professional quarterback at a press conference after a win, you'll hear him credit his teammates with the victory. After a loss, he'll take the blame. Humility celebrates *others*, pride celebrates *self*. The world would be a very different place if we exercised our desire for notoriety by making others famous. We can do this by congratulating, celebrating, and helping those around us. Humility *serves*, pride simply *takes the credit*. Margaret Thatcher noticed this decades ago when she commented on the changing nature of politics in her own country: "It used to be about trying to do something. Now it's about trying to be someone."[32] Seek to serve and celebrate others.

Be Grateful

Legendary basketball coach John Wooden once said, "Talent is God given. Be humble. Fame is man-given. Be grateful. Conceit is self-given. Be careful."[33] Humble people are thankful people. They focus not on the celebrity or fame they *hope* to have but on the blessings they've *already received*. This attitude of gratitude is much easier to cultivate if, like Wooden, you recognize the *source* of your talent. When we shift from seeing ourselves as self-made to recognizing ourselves as God-blessed, we begin to focus our gratitude on someone other than ourselves.

Be United

Celebrity separates us from others; humility unites us. If everyone were famous, none of us would be famous. That's why notoriety seeks to divide us from those who don't possess it. Resist this divisive impulse by practicing unity. Be teachable, offer forgiveness, exercise patience, and exhibit tolerance. Seek to *fit in* rather than *stand out*. If we act like humble people, we just might become humble people.

Pull Back

At some point, if we hope to harness our pursuit of celebrity, we have to rein in our social media addiction. That means using it less often and paying less attention to the numbers. It's as simple as that. Instead of seeking higher levels of attention and interaction, follow the advice of Craig Bartholomew and "pursue obscurity."[34] Famous people want to be known *superficially* by *many*; humble people want to be known *deeply* by a *few*. Instead of posting every detail of your day to draw attention, pursue the "virtue of privacy" to increase intimacy. Save the *private* you for people who care about the *real* you.

Look Up

The best way to remain humble is to stand in the presence of the only One who is worthy of our fandom. Celebrity is rooted in comparison, and when we focus on the glory of God, our notoriety dims by contrast. C. S. Lewis observed, "A proud man is always looking down on things and people: and, of course, as long as you are looking down you cannot see something that is above you."[35] Conversely, if our focus is upward, we're less likely to think too highly of ourselves and look down on others.

Pelon eventually realized the futility of seeking acceptance and "symbolic immortality" through his reputation and local celebrity status.

When Danny first introduced me to Pelon, he was in the presence of two fellow gang members known as Creeper and Wicked. Although Pelon considered these men friends, they weren't. They *feared Pelon*, but they didn't really *know Jaime Munoz*, the person behind the persona. By the time Lucia's brother confronted him, Pelon's celebrity status and the untouchable immortality it promised had waned. Creeper and Wicked were nowhere to be found when Pelon was gunned down—right beside his Monte Carlo. After the murder, Creeper happily inherited Pelon's drug business.

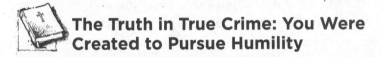

The Truth in True Crime: You Were Created to Pursue Humility

Pelon's story exposes the importance of humility and the futility of fame. Pelon missed the opportunity to flourish and thrive. His pride didn't allow him to see what researchers are now discovering: humans prosper when they adopt an attitude of humility and resist the desire for celebrity.

This wisdom about our human nature was available to Pelon years before any of the sociological studies were conducted. Had Pelon been a Bible reader, he would have known the importance of a humble heart.

Christianity dawned at a time and place in history when humility was not considered a virtue. The ancient Greeks excluded it from their list of worthy attributes (known as the "Delphic Maxims"), and the Romans saw it as a sign of weakness. Both cultures favored reputation and honor (celebrity) over humility.

Jesus changed all that.

When his disciples asked, "Who is the greatest in the kingdom of heaven?" Jesus turned their notions of power and notoriety on their head, proclaiming, "Truly, I say to you, unless you turn and become like children, you will never enter the kingdom of heaven. Whoever humbles himself like this child is the greatest in the kingdom of heaven."[36]

Jesus came to serve rather than be served. Though he existed in the form of God, he did not consider equality with God a thing to be grasped. Instead, he emptied himself, took the form of a servant, and humbled himself by becoming obedient to the point of death on a cross.[37] His sacrifice shifted our notions of humility, returning it to its rightful place as a design feature of our Creator.

The New Testament authors repeatedly wrote about the value of humility, and Christians have historically endeavored to embrace what modern researchers now revere as a mechanism for flourishing. John Newton, the Anglican minister who penned "Amazing Grace," once wrote, "I am persuaded that love and humility are the highest attainments in the school of Christ and the brightest evidence that He is indeed our Master."[38]

The Old Testament writers warned their readers not to think too highly of themselves, instructing them instead to embrace humility and walk humbly with God.[39] The reward for those who adopted an attitude of humility was the promise of wisdom, success, peace, and immortality.[40]

Jesus amplified this teaching, citing negative examples of people who thought they had celebrity status and warning his disciples against elevating and separating themselves from others on the basis of their reputation.[41] When minor debates broke out among his disciples related to their relative notoriety, Jesus admonished them to humble themselves like children.[42]

Jesus's followers paid close attention to this teaching. Peter later told his readers to clothe themselves in humility and humble themselves under the "mighty hand of God."[43] James encouraged humility to facilitate learning and gain eternal life.[44] Paul encouraged his readers to live quietly, mind their own affairs, and work simply with their hands.[45]

EXPLANATION: We Seek Acceptance and Eternity

Created in the image of God, we innately yearn for something only God can satisfy.

Humans will never offer us the acceptance and approval we seek. As humans who have been separated from God by our sin, we innately yearn to be accepted and approved by *him*, and only he loved us enough to remove our unacceptable sin through Jesus's death and resurrection so we can be united to him forever.

The acceptance and immortality God offers require us to humbly acknowledge him as the source of our desires. This is why humility is the key to human flourishing.

The Bible authors identified humility as the secret weapon of human flourishing. The authors of both the Old and New Testaments described the benefits of humility related to health, learning, employment, and relationships.

But there's something even more surprising if you're not familiar with the teaching of the Bible.

Our desire for acceptance and immortality, left wanting by the limitations of contemporary celebrity, is satisfied completely in the ancient Christian worldview. According to the Bible, God knew you before you were born, created you, and delights in you.[46] He knows everything about you and considers you "fearfully and wonderfully made," even if you've been ignoring him.[47] The acceptance you and I crave has been available all along, not on the social media platforms we frequent but in the love God offers.

And there's more.

Our obsession with immortality isn't just selfish, wishful thinking. Our hearts are inclined toward eternity because we were made in the image of an eternal God. He promises what celebrity cannot deliver: true eternal life. According to the Bible, God loves us and offers us eternal life as a gift.[48] Not "symbolic immortality" but *true eternal life*.

These two common yearnings—our desire for acceptance and our longing for immortality—cannot be met by celebrity. Fame, instead, is simply a secular placeholder, a surrogate distraction from what only God can offer. Our pride keeps us focused on this inferior substitute, but if we can manage to embrace humility, we just might free ourselves long enough to find the true satisfaction of our desires.

That's why a humble heart is so important and why *you were created to pursue humility*.

FELONS, FUGITIVES, AND FINANCIAL FREEDOM

How to Get Everything You Want and Get It Today

> How many people do you know who are spending
> money they have not yet earned for things they
> don't need to impress people they don't like?
> —EDGAR ALLAN MOSS

> It is not the man who has too little, but the
> man who craves more, that is poor.
> —SENECA

Jackson Kelcher finished wiping his hands as Pati, our forensic identification specialist, put away her gunshot residue kit. Jackson was seated in our jail interview room, just a few steps from where we would complete his booking process.

He had been in jail many times, but this was probably going to be his last.

I arrested him for a street robbery nearly ten years earlier. This time it would be for murder, although that wasn't what he intended in his latest crime.

Jackson was the suspect in a series of nearly fifty liquor store robberies in our county. Although the suspect descriptions were sometimes slightly different, the MO was always the same: the robber entered each business wielding a pistol and told the clerk to empty the cash register and then the safe (if they had one).

Jackson supported himself well with the profits from these robberies, spending his money on girls, hotel rooms, drugs, and fast food. He was enjoying himself, although his tastes were becoming more extravagant.

Until tonight.

Pati left the room, so Rick and I closed the door, pulled up two chairs, and started filling out the forms we needed to complete the booking. I still remembered Jackson's younger self; he was one of the many gang members I investigated when I was assigned to the gang detail. He looked much older tonight, and *weary*.

Rick read him his Miranda rights, but we didn't need him to admit any wrongdoing. The case was open and shut. Instead, I wanted to talk to the younger man I once knew.

"How did you end up here, Jackson?" I asked quietly.

No response. Jackson sat at an angle with one elbow on the interview table, the other hand in his lap. His head was down. His facial expression was one of resignation and disbelief. I thought this would likely be the last time I would talk to him, so I got right to the point.

"You know, Jackson, we met once before. Do you remember? It was a long time ago."

He looked up for a moment but remained silent.

"I recall if you don't. Here's what I said back then—see if this jogs your memory . . ."

Jackson was now staring at me and clearly trying to remember our prior conversation.

"You and I aren't that different. We want the same things. Meaning and purpose, a safe place to sleep, a woman who cares about us, a car to get us around, food to eat. We're the same guy, really, with the same desires and goals."

Jackson continued to stare.

"But it's not always easy to get what we want, and there aren't any true shortcuts. It takes time, steady effort . . . work. It means you gotta spend a bunch of hours at a job to slowly earn the money you need to achieve your goals. There's no quick way to get what we want, and robberies are just a cheat, so to speak. You get the money immediately but end up spending more time in jail than just working a nine-to-five. You and I are chasing the same goals, but shortcuts seldom work . . . and look where they've landed you."

"So what's your point?" He was expressionless.

"No point, really . . . Just wish you would have listened to me when you were younger."

When Is Enough, Enough?

Jackson discovered what Charles Spurgeon once described: "You say, 'If I had a little more, I should be very satisfied.' You make a mistake. If you are not content with what you have, you would not be satisfied if it were doubled."[1] With every robbery, Jackson steadily increased his spending, renting better hotel rooms and eating better meals. Enough was never enough.

He began his series of crimes just a month after being released from prison on a burglary charge. It's not easy to find work when you've got a record, but Jackson never even tried. He skipped meetings with his parole agent and failed to seek employment placement assistance. He was still the young man I knew years earlier.

Although Jackson didn't remember our first conversation, I did. Jackson understood there were no shortcuts but told me a job would deprive him of his freedom:

"I don't need to be tied up like that every day. Life is too short. I don't want to waste my time. When I want something, I want it now," he said in our first conversation.

The irony was palpable, given that he forfeited his freedom to serve several years in jail for that first purse-snatch robbery. But I understood his point about independence. Our common human desire for freedom is an offshoot of our yearning for power. One study directly linked our desire for "autonomy" to this pursuit.[2] Jackson wanted to live what he considered a "good life" without the associated obligations. He wanted financial independence. So I gave him the same advice I often give others: "Look, Jackson, financial independence is not the ability to buy *anything*, it's the ability to buy anything *you want*. I have that kind of freedom right now. You know why? Because I don't want anything."

I was simply trying to express what others have also learned. Epictetus once wrote, "Wealth consists not in having great possessions, but in having few wants."[3]

EVIDENCE: Humans Flourish When They Work

Employment is more than a financial necessity. It is an important safeguard against envy and discontentment. We thrive when we participate in meaningful and purposeful work, even though most of us daydream about our vacations and time off. Leisure, however, fails to provide the benefits that employment offers.

Why is work such an important feature of human flourishing?

More recently, Oscar Wilde mused, "True contentment is not having every-thing, but in being satisfied with everything you have."[4]

Jackson remained unimpressed in that first interview. So I tried to restate the idea:

"Jackson, you mentioned wanting things now. Well, there are two ways to get what you want. You can decide what will make you happy and go get it . . . or decide that what you've already got will make you happy. Get what you want or want what you got. The second way is a lot easier, my friend, and it will keep you out of jail."

Jackson was obviously unmoved by my wisdom, given that he didn't remember our first conversation and had now been arrested for robbery *and* murder.

 ## The Key to Contentment

Jackson wanted the life he'd seen others live. There was a reason why some of the victims in the robbery series described the suspect in a slightly different way. Jackson committed less than half the crimes we were investigating. His friend, Stephen Poole, committed the rest.

Discontented with his own life and envious of Stephen's success, Jackson carefully mimicked his friend's MO as he began a robbery series of his own. He also imitated Stephen's lifestyle. If Stephen had it, Jackson wanted it, and their lives became eerily similar.

Except for the part about murder.

Contentment finds its history in the early to mid-fifteenth century. It is rooted in the Latin word *contentus*, the past participle of *continere*. Those historic terms express the notion of being "contained," "enclosed," or "held together."[5] An apt etymology, given that *discontentment*, including the kind Jackson experienced, begins when you start looking outside the "container" of your own "enclosed" life.

The current definition of contentment, described as being "satisfied with your life or the situation you are in,"[6] exposes what Jackson lacked: a sense of inner peace and satisfaction. When Jackson started looking outside the "container" and comparing himself to Stephen, he became increasingly discontented and envious.

Contentment is possible for all of us now, rather than later, because it is a decision we make *internally*, not a pursuit of things we seek *externally*. Spurgeon observed, "It is not how much we have, but how much we enjoy, that makes happiness."[7] Contentment is a decision made from the inside out, and it's a decision worth making, especially when you consider the alternative.

Psychologists, sociologists, and researchers continue to identify contentedness with human flourishing. Studies find that contented people report higher well-being, describing contentment as "'unconditional wholeness,' regardless of what is happening externally."[8] Contentment is also connected to a greater sense of fulfillment and life satisfaction.[9]

This form of satisfaction is critical to human flourishing, and not just because it will help you resist the impulse to start a robbery series. Contentment requires us to rid ourselves of a poisonous human emotion: envy.

The Bible refers to envy as "covetousness," an ungodly human impulse so offensive to human flourishing, God prohibited it as part of the Ten Commandments.[10] *Envy* is derived from the Latin term *invidus* (to be "envious," or have "hatred or ill-will") and *invidere* (to "hate," "look at with malice," or "cast an evil eye upon").[11] The idiom "She's giving him the 'evil eye'," expresses the belief "an eye or glance" is "capable of inflicting harm."[12] This notion is rooted in the definition of envy. We look disparagingly at what others have, desiring these things for ourselves and wishing ill will on those who presently possess them.

Some contemporary researchers seek to soften the destructive nature of envy by distinguishing between "benign envy" and "malicious envy," but make no mistake about it, the corrosive impact of envy cannot be minimized.[13]

Envy emerges when we find ourselves comparing, and research continues to reveal the impact our envious comparisons have on human flourishing. People who envy experience poorer mental and physical health.[14] The more we envy, the more likely we are to feel depressed, view ourselves as inferior, become angry, or experience resentment.[15] Envious people are even "less likely to feel grateful about their *positive* traits and their circumstances" (emphasis mine).[16]

Envy brings out the worst in us, corrupting even the way we treat others.

Envious people are more likely to deceive their friends and talk maliciously about them behind their backs.[17] Envy also motivates more than its fair share of murders.[18]

Studies reveal that young people are *more* susceptible to the corrosive power of envy.[19] One reason for this may be their use of social media, the technological "petri dish" for discovering what threatens well-being. Social media encourages malicious envy, and consistent users experience higher levels of depression "based on the upward social comparison" they make with others.[20] These envious "social comparisons" leave users feeling inadequate, jealous, and unattractive.[21] They become more dissatisfied with themselves and more likely to experience a decline in "affective well-being."[22]

Envy impacts our well-being and causes us to think things, say things, and do things we shouldn't. Envy led Jackson to a life of crime. It was exciting at first but devastating in the end. Author Joseph Epstein once penned, "Of the seven deadly sins, only envy is no fun at all."[23]

Jackson experienced this truth firsthand.

 ## Work and Well-Being

"Boy, your 'sage' advice all those years ago really changed Mr. Kelcher's life, didn't it?" Rick's sarcastic tone matched the wry smile he displayed as we left the jail and returned to our office.

"Not everyone recognizes my superior wisdom," I replied. "You know, I don't think Jackson has ever worked at a legitimate job."

"Why would he, when this is working so well for him?"

Rick's sarcasm aside, Jackson missed more than the opportunity to stay out of jail when he avoided his parole officer and shunned employment. As Thomas Edison once said, "Opportunity is missed by most people because it is dressed in overalls and looks like work."[24] Jackson, in rejecting a chance to earn something (rather than steal it), missed the possibility of flourishing. As connected as human well-being is to contentment, it is even more connected to purposeful work.

Meaningful employment improves our physical and mental health. It reduces depression, lowers anxiety, and increases resiliency.[25] Researchers find purposeful work has a larger impact on our well-being than "leisure and other life domains," and its impact extends far beyond our place of employment or the time in which we were employed.[26] When we work with purpose, we are happier, more satisfied with our lives, more confident in our identity and role within society, and more connected to the people we love.[27]

Work matters, not just because it keeps us out of trouble but because it contributes to our flourishing.

If only Jackson had embraced the longer path to financial success rather than the expedient shortcut. When he entered the last liquor store, he encountered a victim who was prepared for him. Victor Sanchez was aware of the robbery series.

EXAMPLE: Cain's Deadly Envy
Adam's son Cain was envious of his younger brother, Abel (Genesis 4:1–16). Both made sacrificial offerings, but God favored Abel's. Cain's envy took an inevitable turn toward anger. This malicious aspect of envy turned Cain's heart against Abel and eventually motivated him to kill his brother. When God confronted Cain, his first reaction was to lie, a response commonly observed by researchers studying envy today. What does the example of Cain tell us about our human nature?

He read about the crimes in the newspaper and heard about them from his friends who worked locally as clerks. Victor started carrying a pistol to his store every day, but unlike Jackson's, Victor's gun was the "real McCoy."

Jackson had been using a *toy* pistol in his robberies, painted black to give it the appearance of authenticity.

On the night of his final robbery, Jackson entered the business, jumped the counter, and produced his "gun." Victor drew his own. Jackson was stunned for a moment as he considered his options. Knowing his pistol was nothing more than a toy, he dropped it and immediately wrestled Victor for the one true weapon.

The shot was deafening.

Jackson managed to pry the gun from Victor's hands, but not until Victor's finger, wedged in the trigger guard, discharged the fatal bullet. Victor fell to the ground, and Jackson stood there with the murder weapon dangling from his fingertips. He felt paralyzed by what he had just done.

He was prepared to commit a robbery, but not a murder. He froze, thought about trying to assist Victor in some way, but ran instead. Patrol officers captured Jackson just a block away, ten yards from where he parked his getaway car.

The gun shot residue still covered his hands.

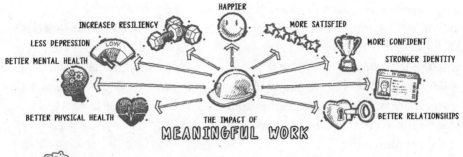

HAPPIER

INCREASED RESILIENCY   MORE SATISFIED

LESS DEPRESSION   LOW   MORE CONFIDENT

BETTER MENTAL HEALTH   STRONGER IDENTITY

BETTER PHYSICAL HEALTH   THE IMPACT OF   BETTER RELATIONSHIPS

MEANINGFUL WORK

Chase the Lead

Jackson remains in jail to this day. He never experienced the transformational impact of meaningful employment, succumbing instead to the destructive power of envy. His continual discontent informed his every decision, and the results were disastrous.

Benjamin Franklin wrote, "Content makes poor men rich; discontent makes rich men poor."[28] If only Jackson had known the relationship between contentment, wealth, and poverty. Perhaps he would have been more patient and given himself the opportunity to thrive. His story is an object lesson for the rest of us. If we want to cultivate contentment and leverage meaningful work so we can flourish, we should consider taking the following steps:

Stop Comparing

Epicurus warned, "Do not spoil what you have by desiring what you have not; remember that what you now have was once among the things you only hoped for."[29] Contentment is the product of looking inwardly at what we *already possess*, rather than outwardly at what we *wish we possessed*. So, as difficult as this may seem, it's time to stop paying attention to the envy-inducing social media world. We need to resist the temptation to focus on the activities, achievements, or appearances of others. Comparison is the seedbed of discontent. If we reduce one, we can shrink the other.

Be Grateful

A classic study found Olympic bronze medal winners were happier than silver medal winners. Why? Because many silver medalists coveted the gold medal, while many bronze medalists were happy to have earned a medal at all.[30] Gratitude can turn a seeming failure into success *if* we choose to be grateful for what we have rather than envious of what we don't. Henry Ward Beecher observed, "The art of being happy lies in the power of extracting happiness from common things."[31] When we are grateful—even for "common things"—we reduce the power that envy and discontentment have on our lives.

Resist Debt

Gratitude for "common things" also helps us resist the temptation to overspend, a behavior often connected to credit cards. Studies find we spend more than we should when using credit rather than cash.[32] Many of us also fail to pay our debt completely at the end of the month, and as our debt increases, our quality of life decreases.[33] Debt also changes the way we look at our work, causing us to see our employment as primarily a way to satisfy our financial obligations rather than the opportunity to exercise our gifts for a purpose beyond the paycheck. Henry David Thoreau noted, "That man is richest whose pleasures are cheapest."[34] When we seek the "cheaper pleasures," we guard ourselves from debt, allowing the opportunity to experience the power of purposeful employment.

Want Less

It's difficult to find joy in "cheaper pleasures" if we continue to covet the more expensive ones. Jackson certainly experienced this phenomenon. With each additional "score," he increased his spending. He imagined himself eating at more expensive restaurants, using more cocaine, and sleeping in fancier hotels. The frequency of his robberies quickened accordingly. Sir Walter Scott once advised, "Teach self-denial and make its practice pleasure, and you can create for the world a destiny more sublime than ever issued from the brain of the wildest dreamer."[35] If Jackson had taken this approach—dreaming and yearning for less—he might never have started robbing liquor stores in the first place. When we find pleasure in what we already possess, we find it more often.

Give More

Charitable people are cheerier people. Studies confirm that people who spend money on others are happier than those who spend money on themselves.[36] "Giving to others makes us feel good about ourselves."[37] Generosity is also an important safeguard against envy and discontentment because it is rooted in benevolence rather than ill will. When we want the best for others, we cease seeking their misfortune (an attribute of envy). The more we give, the more content we become.

Work Well

Balance is the key to working well. "Idle hands are the devil's workshop," but "all work and no play make Jack a dull boy." Neither extreme contributes to human flourishing. When we understand the role work plays in our lives and the opportunity it provides to care for ourselves and others, we begin to leverage our labor for a grander purpose. People who thrive at work are interested in more than just the money it provides. They understand working is an essential part of living. It's far easier to be a committed, reliable, and diligent employee when you understand the importance of work *as well as* the importance of the financial reward it provides.

Trust God

Researchers also find that people who see work as a "higher calling" are more content than those who don't. "People who feel called to their careers are likely to find their work deeply meaningful."[38] "Callings" require "callers," however, and the more transcendent the "caller," the more rewarding the "call." That's why people who trust God for the direction and purpose of their career are happier employees.[39] When God is our priority, we assess what we have (and what we hope for) through the lens of God's transcendent plan for our lives. We also have the benefit of God's wisdom about work and contentment as it is offered in Scripture. Rather than *try harder*, we simply *trust more*.

Jackson trusted only himself. He certainly didn't accept the advice I gave him years earlier. But his short career as a liquor store robber demonstrated how dangerous it is to reject the truth, especially when it's the truth about what makes us flourish. Jackson would have been far better served working as a store clerk than robbing one, and if Jackson had been content, Victor Sanchez would be alive today.

The Truth in True Crime: You Were Created to Work

Jackson's robbery spree occurred before much of the modern research on the value of contentedness and productive work was conducted. If Jackson had read a Bible, however, he would have known what these studies would eventually find. When Paul wrote to the church in Ephesus, for example, he declared, "Thieves must give up stealing; rather let them labor and work honestly with their own hands, so as to have something to share with the needy."[40]

Had Jackson embraced this ancient wisdom, he might have guarded himself from thievery and discovered the power of purposeful work.

God has always held work in high regard. The Old Testament begins with a record of God's activity creating the universe and everything in it, and God repeatedly describes this "work" as "good."[41] Jesus identified both himself and God the Father as workers who are continually working, and both revealed themselves to the world through their miraculous work.[42]

As humans created in the image of God, we were created with work in mind. Our first jobs were to "work" and "keep" the garden, and this purposeful task became laborious only after we rebelled against God and suffered the consequences of our crime.[43] God intended (and continues to offer) work as a gift that can provide pleasure and enjoyment, both now and forever.[44] Like the angels, we will also serve and work in heaven, and our efforts there will contribute to our *eternal flourishing*.[45]

In the meantime, God's call to contentment can protect us from envy.

The Bible encourages us to be happy with what we have and joyous in our employment, regardless of our circumstances.[46] Contentment is connected to godliness, and it offers great

 EXPLANATION: We Were Created in the Image of a Working God

Purposeful work is the antidote for envy and discontentment because we were created by a God who works.

Many of us (like Jackson) are driven to near destruction by our envious thoughts. When those human responses eventually fail, we turn to seek a solution. That's why envy and discontent often lead us to the throne of God, the one source of true contentment.

God created us to work in all things as though we are working for him. This is the biblical remedy for envy and a key ingredient of flourishing.

benefits to those who find their joy in God rather than being envious of others.[47] The authors of Scripture encouraged their readers to refocus their attention on God instead of wallowing in the futility of envious thoughts.[48] In fact, envy is a mechanism God can use to draw us to himself.[49]

Scripture predated and predicted what modern studies would eventually tell us about work, contentment, and envy. It accurately describes how to navigate these aspects of our human condition. The Bible advises us to stop comparing, be grateful, resist debt, want less, give more, work well, and trust God.[50]

Every truth modern researchers have discovered was already known to the authors of the Bible. While they didn't have access to the current data, they did have access to the mind of God. That's why they knew the danger of envy and understood *we were created to work*.

SENSE AND SUFFERING

How to Surprise Yourself by Flourishing after a Trauma

> If there is meaning in life at all, then there must be
> a meaning in suffering. Suffering is an ineradicable
> part of life, even as fate and death. Without suffering
> and death human life cannot be complete.
> —VIKTOR E. FRANKL

> To give life a meaning, one must have
> a purpose larger than self.
> —WILL DURANT

From across the courtyard, I could already read the expression on Kelly Winston's face. Pensive and serious, she glanced at her watch as I approached.

"Hello, Kelly, I'm Detective Wallace." Even her smile was reserved as she extended her hand.

Rick and I were investigating the murder of Kelly's sister, Andrea, a crime unsolved for nearly twenty-five years. The suspect in this case, Kevin Turner, had been confirmed for several weeks, and much of the preliminary work was completed. An arrest was imminent.

Up to this point, we hadn't notified the family about the investigation. We didn't want to get their hopes up or allow an opportunity for information about Turner's identity to make its way to the public. But with our case about to culminate, all that changed.

It was time to write our final reports. It was also time to break some good news to Andrea's family.

These first meetings are often joyous, given how long some families wait for justice. But this one seemed different. Within minutes we realized Kelly—and the entire Winston family—were still actively suffering in a way we hadn't seen before.

"I feel like I haven't been able to breathe after losing Andrea," Kelly said as she relived the day she learned her sister was murdered. Her words were measured and emotional. She leaned toward us tearfully and earnestly tried to express the pain her family still experienced, more than two decades later.

"We just kind of stopped living. I mean we went on, of course, and I know it's been a long time, but everything changed, and we can't seem to get in a normal rhythm. It's like there's a heavy cloud over us. We stopped really celebrating anything. When my dad died a few years later, I knew he died of a broken heart. He never recovered from the pain of losing Andrea. None of us has. It was so senseless. We all still wonder, how could something like this happen to Andrea?"

That last question is always difficult to answer, but for the Winston family, it seemed impossible. As we investigated Andrea's short life, we found her to be the least likely victim we had ever studied. She was young, innocent, and unsuspecting. Barely in her twenties, she didn't put herself in danger, hang out with the wrong people, or date anyone troubling. Instead, she volunteered dutifully at her church, served her community, and worked tirelessly at her job.

That last part contributed to her death.

She happened to stay late one night when Turner, an ex-employee, entered the business to steal some money. He killed Andrea, only to discover the money had already been deposited at a local bank. Andrea was simply in the wrong place at the wrong time. Nothing else connected Andrea to Kevin Turner, and for the next two decades, the Winston family wrestled with the senselessness of the murder. Unable to move forward with their lives, they waited hopelessly for what might eventually free them from the trauma.

We arrested Kevin a week after our first interview with Kelly. A year later, we convicted him in a Los Angeles criminal courtroom. Rick and I were there, of course, eager to see how the verdict would impact the Winston family. Everyone seemed to be present: Andrea's aunts and uncles, siblings and cousins. Their response was akin to resigned relief rather than joy. For the Winston family, the verdict seemed surprisingly . . . *insufficient*.

Except for Kelly.

Kelly discovered true freedom and joy, although it ultimately came from a different kind of conviction.

The Trouble with Trauma

Few of us will ever face the kind of trauma the Winstons experienced, but everyone encounters some form of suffering or hardship. It is part of the human condition, although most of us don't factor unavoidable hardships into our plans. Undefeated heavyweight boxing champion Mike Tyson was once asked if he was worried about the prefight strategy of one of his opponents. He replied, "Everyone has a plan until they get punched in the mouth."[1] He expected to win every fight, only to eventually suffer a knockout in shocking fashion. After that first defeat, he lost another five times before his career was over. Most of us, like Tyson, experience defeat as well as victory, hardship together with prosperity, calamity in addition to blessing.

These defeats, hardships, and calamities may cause trauma, an "emotional response that often results from living through a distressing event."[2] This is particularly true if the event is severe, sudden, or unpredictable.[3] Distress of this kind can have a lasting negative impact, just as it did for the Winston family. Traumatic events cause people to fear for their safety, lose their identity, wrestle with their emotions, and struggle in their relationships. Over time, we can begin to feel helpless, powerless, or fearful.[4] Many experience flashbacks, nausea, or headaches.[5]

Why does this happen when we suffer traumatic experiences? The answer lies in our expectations and presuppositions.

Trauma occurs when our perceptions of the world and our role in it (our "global" beliefs and goals) are disrupted, especially if we assumed nothing bad would ever happen to us. Traumatized people find themselves "reappraising the traumatic event to perceive it as more consistent with their pre-trauma global beliefs and goals . . . or revising their global beliefs and goals to accommodate their experience."[6]

The Winston family simply didn't think it possible someone like Andrea could be killed so senselessly. When it happened, their view of the world—and their expectations about how they would live in it—were shattered. They struggled to "revise their global beliefs." Their present reality was not as they had once hoped.

My courtyard meeting with Kelly was followed by dozens of phone conversations over the next year as I arranged interviews with her family members and collected information about Andrea. As the criminal trial neared, I could see Kelly's demeanor changing.

Kelly and Andrea were both Christians, and after meeting me, Kelly learned more about my background as a Christ follower and part-time youth pastor. On one phone call, she shared something about her faith.

EVIDENCE: Humans Are Meaning-Makers

We suffer trauma when something shocking disrupts our expectation and view of the world. In essence, we construct a personal narrative about the nature of life, then struggle when an unexpected event challenges the story we've created for ourselves.

Why do humans create these personal narratives in the first place? Why do we resist reinterpreting our stories when we experience crisis?

"Andrea was the first Christian in our family. I was her younger sister, and I wanted to be just like her. But when she was killed, it shook me. I mean it shook my faith in God. I couldn't understand why he would let that happen to Andrea when she loved and served him so."

Even as she described her doubt, I could sense something different in her tone.

"I don't think it's a coincidence that you are the detective who reopened Andrea's case. Now I'm starting to think maybe God had a larger plan in all this."

I remained silent. Anything could happen at trial, and I didn't want to set Kelly up for another disappointment.

When people experience trauma, they often reconsider their spiritual beliefs, just like Kelly. Studies confirm this, even for people who didn't previously believe in God. Trauma survivors begin asking religious questions and are more sensitive to spiritual realities. Faith in God (or a higher power) often increases, even for previously nonreligious people.[7]

Kelly experienced this firsthand as she reassessed her beliefs about the world and how God might work in it. She also wondered if she could finally begin to live the life she had placed on pause for so many years.

The Resiliency Rebound

When Andrea was murdered, the quality of Kelly's life plummeted. She found a way to survive but failed to thrive. She completed her education and accepted a position at a local accounting firm. As a dutiful daughter, she lived at home and took care of her parents. Then her father died of a heart attack and her mother's health started to deteriorate. The dark cloud of the murder continued to define their identity as a family. Kelly lived in the darkened present without any anticipation of a bright future. She didn't date, seldom spent time with friends, and feared dying alone.

Kelly was trapped in the valley her life had become.

Although many trauma victims find themselves in a similar position, not everyone remains in a dark valley. Some experience restoration. When this happens, counselors and psychologists call the recovery "resilience," describing it as the ability to bounce back and return relatively quickly "to one's pre-trauma levels of mental health."[8]

As much as Mike Tyson knew about getting punched, the fictional boxer Rocky Balboa seemed to know more about resiliency: "It's not about how hard you can hit; it's about how hard you can get hit and keep moving forward."[9] Resilient people aren't permanently paralyzed by the stress of their trauma. Instead, they rebound and continue moving forward until they return to their old form.[10] They find a way to take the "hit," then find the strength to stay in the fight.

Some trauma survivors do even better than that.

Some find a way to *flourish* after a trauma, rebounding to levels far *above* where they were prior to the traumatic event. This degree of flourishing is known as "post-traumatic growth," a phenomenon first studied at length in the mid-1990s. Survivors who experience post-traumatic growth "develop new understandings of themselves, the world they live in, how to relate to other people, the kind of future they might have and a better understanding of how to live life."[11]

They thrive.

According to researchers, those who learn how to grow after a trauma flourish in five ways: they develop stronger personal relationships, learn how to explore new possibilities, discover their personal strengths, grow or initiate a spiritual journey, and appreciate life more robustly.[12] This happens not despite the trauma but as a direct consequence of the trauma. People who flourish and grow in this way do so *because* they suffered.

Not everyone thrives in this way, of course. Some simply cannot move out from under the "dark cloud" Kelly described. I knew, however, Kelly was an excellent candidate for post-traumatic growth, even though it had been years since she lived what she called a "normal" life.

Kelly was about to discover the difference between surviving and thriving.

From Meaning-Making to Meaning-Finding

"I don't think it's a coincidence that you are the detective who re-opened Andrea's case . . ."

I remember Kelly's words to this day. Holocaust survivor Viktor Emil Frankl, observed, "To live is to suffer, to survive is to find some meaning in the suffering."[13] This is precisely what Kelly was starting to do.

". . . Now I'm starting to think maybe God had a larger plan in all this."

Researchers call the effort to make sense of trauma and to incorporate one's experience of suffering into a larger framework "meaning-making."[14] Kelly was trying to integrate the traumatic experience of her sister's death into her preexisting Christian worldview. She began to see the reopened case as evidence that Andrea's story—and God's involvement in it—was not yet over.

According to researchers, this is what meaning-making is all about. Kelly had three choices after Andrea's murder: She could (1) abandon her Christian worldview, finding it incompatible with Andrea's murder, (2) minimize Andrea's murder to preserve her idyllic notions of Christianity, or (3) make sense of the murder by better understanding the teachings of Christianity.

Kelly chose the third option.

This was a wise decision because people who make sense of their trauma thrive. While secular researchers call this process meaning-making, Frankl's description of the effort is far more accurate.

> **EXAMPLE: Ruth**
>
> Ruth and her mother-in-law, Naomi, suffered the loss of their husbands and, as widows, were virtually destitute. Ruth seemed ready to resign herself to a life of caretaking and followed Naomi back to her native land. With Naomi's encouragement, however, she slowly rewrote her own story, diligently working and drawing the attention of her future husband, Boaz.
>
> Ruth overcame the trauma of her first husband's death and flourished, ultimately taking her place in the family line of the Messiah.

rate. People thrive after suffering trauma when they *find* meaning in their *objective worldview* rather than when they *make* arbitrary meaning based on their *personal preferences*. Kelly was striving to make sense of her pain by finding meaning in her suffering. For this reason, meaning-finding is a more accurate description of what secular researchers currently describe as meaning-making.

People who make sense of and find meaning in their suffering experience better psychological and physical well-being and are less likely to be depressed, mentally ill, or experience post-traumatic stress disorder (PTSD).[15] They are also less inclined to overdrink or become addicted to medication and less apt to commit suicide.[16]

Meaning-finding helps people learn how to cope with traumatic events and other challenges they may encounter.[17] They find significance, purpose, and coherence in their lives and are driven to set and achieve new goals, both personally and professionally.[18] They even make more money, accumulate more wealth, volunteer more, and give more to charities.[19]

People who make sense of and find meaning in their suffering are "more likely to engage in physical exercise and to exercise for longer intervals, even if they were previously physically inactive."[20] As a result, they have a higher quality of life as they age, are "at peace with their own mortality," and are likely to live longer.[21]

Kelly was beginning a meaning-finding journey as she pondered whether "God had a larger plan in all this." But how could an all-powerful, all-loving God allow this to happen to someone as innocent and devoted as Andrea in the first place?

This became the critical question Kelly sought to answer.

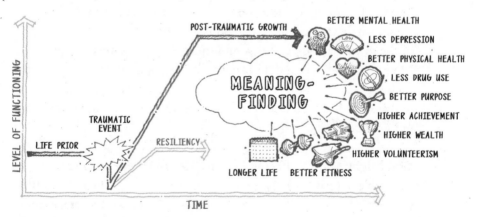

Making Sense of Suffering

I had been a Christian for nearly five years when I shook hands with Kelly in that courtyard. Her question was one I had to answer for myself when I first investigated the evidence for Christianity.[22] I had been a detective for many years by then, and I was fully aware of the horrific presence of evil in the world. Was God just too weak to stop the crimes I had been investigating? Was he too busy? Why do we consider God all-powerful and all-loving if he allows these horrific crimes to occur? I asked and answered these questions on the path to becoming a Christian.

I was ready to share what I had learned with Kelly.

Our intermittent phone conversations provided the perfect opportunity. Kelly repeatedly circled back to questions about Andrea's death, the existence of God, and the "problem of evil," especially once she discovered I was a Christian.[23] On those occasions, I did my best to help Kelly reconcile her sister's murder with the existence of a loving God:[24]

God Might Allow Suffering Because He Offers Eternity
Like the rest of us, Andrea hoped to live a long life without unnecessary pain or hardship. Christianity offers this kind of life for everyone, including Andrea. How? According to the Bible, our lives are not "line segments," short personal timelines connecting our point of birth to our point of death. Instead, our lives are "rays" beginning at birth, extending through the point we call death, and continuing infinitely into the future. If God offers life beyond the short "line segment," this would surely change the way we look at pain and suffering on this side of the grave, wouldn't it? It would mean Andrea is alive today, on the "ray," beyond the second point of the line segment. If there is an eternal, divine Creator, Andrea is in his presence, free of pain, and waiting for Kelly to join her. As eternal creatures, we must consider all forms of evil in light of eternity.

God Might Allow Suffering Because He Offers Free Agency
The Bible describes God as "love,"[25] but this cherished emotion, along with many other attributes and activities we value and revere, requires a dangerous prerequisite: free agency. Love requires freedom because no true expression of love has ever been coerced. Even those who deny the existence of a divine Creator must first have the personal freedom to do so. Without free agency, we would be enslaved robots, unable to love, hate, reason, or rebel. If the divine Creator of the universe respects freedom as much as we do, it seems reasonable he would create a world

in which Andrea would have the freedom to love genuinely, but Kevin Turner would also have the freedom to do great harm. C. S. Lewis understood the connection between free agency and suffering when he wrote, "Try to exclude the possibility of suffering which the order of nature and the existence of free-wills involve, and you find that you have excluded life itself."[26]

God Might Allow Suffering Because He Wants to Draw Us to Himself
In desperate situations, many people consider eternity for the very first time.[27] If there is a loving God who designed us for an existence beyond the grave, it might not be unreasonable for this Creator to use hardship to refocus those of us who haven't been paying attention. According to Lewis, "God whispers to us in our pleasures, speaks in our conscience, but shouts in our pains: It is His megaphone to rouse a deaf world."[28] The divine Creator of the universe can use a tragedy like Andrea's murder to awaken others, including Kelly.

God Might Allow Suffering Because He Cares about Our Character and Our Future
Loving parents are usually more concerned with their children's character than their comfort, and character is more likely developed through *adversity* than *advantage*. Trauma (if we can begin to understand why God would allow it) has the capacity to shape our character for the better. Suffering offers an opportunity for reflection, endurance, compassion, and resolve. It also provides us with a chance to share what we've learned with others who are hurting. A divine Creator might allow us to suffer trauma to renew our sense of purpose and calling and to chart a course toward a meaningful future.

God Might Allow Suffering Because He Knows Better
But even with these prior explanations in mind, there are times (as in Andrea's murder) when suffering still seems inexplicable. As I did my best to respond to Kelly's questions, I reminded her I've never investigated a case in which I was able to answer *every* possible question a juror might ask. If there is a vastly superior divine Creator, we shouldn't expect to understand every motive, thought, or set of concerns in the Creator's mind. Joni Eareckson Tada, who suffered a life-changing

spinal cord injury, encourages us to trust what we *can't* know on the basis of what we *can*: "Real satisfaction comes not in understanding God's motives, but in understanding His character, in trusting in His promises, and in leaning on Him and resting in Him as the Sovereign who knows what He is doing and does all things well."[29]

By the time the criminal trial began, Kelly sat confidently in the front row of the gallery, listening intently to every word of testimony and processing how God might use this terrible tragedy for something unexpected. Her questions were shifting from "Why would God allow this?" to "What is God trying to achieve in my life?"

 ## Chase the Lead

That shift in thinking is common for religious thinkers who've suffered trauma, and it contributes to post-traumatic growth. People who search for spiritual answers related to the purpose and meaning of suffering are more resilient after a trauma and report higher life satisfaction.[30] Trauma survivors who are religious experience less stress, depression, and anxiety. They are better able to negotiate adversity and have an increased sense of purpose after trauma.[31] This is true for adults *and* teenagers.[32] Religious believers feel less helpless, have better community support, and are better able to process the prospect of dying.[33]

Psychologist Richard G. Tedeschi, an originator in the field of post-traumatic growth, says this kind of flourishing is facilitated through "education, emotional regulation, disclosure, narrative development, and service."[34] As Kelly reflected on her life during the trial, she interacted with each of these steps of recovery. If *you* want to flourish after a trauma, you might consider following her lead:

Learn about It
Kelly realized Andrea's murder was far more than a tragic loss; it was also a shocking event that disrupted her understanding of life, her sense of self, and her view of God. This realization was pivotal because no one moves from trauma to growth unless they first understand *why* the event was so traumatizing. When Kelly recognized the impact

the murder had on her notion of "global meaning," she set a course to rethink her beliefs.

Manage It

Kelly also realized she had allowed herself to wallow in pity and negativity. The dark cloud had become part of her identity. She decided it was time for a new frame of mind. Rather than dwelling on the obvious loss and despair she experienced after the murder, she focused on the many blessings she could count in her life and how God might use the trauma for an unexpected good. She decided to move forward by looking through her windshield rather than her rearview mirror.

Talk about It

Kelly used the trial as a catalyst to begin talking honestly and transparently about the murder and her family's reaction to it. The few friends she had were, of course, aware of Andrea's murder, but it became something they were afraid to discuss. Kelly accommodated that preference and seldom shared anything personal about her struggles. All that changed when the trial began. Kelly used the monthlong event to finally empty her thoughts and emotions to anyone willing to listen, including the national news media. When we talk openly about our struggles, we begin to "make sense of the trauma and turn debilitating thoughts into more-productive reflections."[35]

Find Its Place

Kelly then started to rethink her Christian worldview to reconsider why God might allow Andrea's murder and how he might use it in the future. In essence, she rewrote her story, from a young woman paralyzed by her sister's murder and faltering in her faith, to a daughter of God, confident in her purpose and catalyzed by her sister's death. When we "produce an authentic narrative about the trauma and our lives afterward,"[36] we begin to write new chapters in our story.

Let It Motivate You

Kelly started imagining her next chapter. She knew one thing for sure: it would involve helping other families who had been traumatized by murder. Kelly learned how to become "an expert companion for others," looking for opportunities to encourage, listen, and love people who have experienced similar trauma.[37] Kelly started serving others, and trauma survivors who do this are far more likely to thrive.[38]

Psychiatrist David Viscott believed "the purpose of life is to discover your gift. The work of life is to develop it. The meaning of life is to give your gift away."[39] Kelly discovered her gift after Kevin Turner was convicted and sentenced to life in jail without the possibility of parole. Kelly found her voice and is now an articulate advocate for victim rights, testifying at hearings, lecturing at legal conventions, and appearing on a variety of media outlets. She made sense of her suffering, recognized her gift for helping others, and continues to share what she's learned. Kelly has renewed purpose.

She let the conviction of a murderer convict her to take action.

The Truth in True Crime: You Were Created to Overcome

During all this, Kelly was completely unaware of the contemporary research related to post-traumatic growth. She learned how to flourish, instead, by embracing something ancient: the unparalleled meaning-finding capacity of Christianity.

The Bible describes the world the way it really is, including the inevitability of trauma and the path to victory. Jesus told his disciples they would have tribulation and may even suffer unjustly.[40] Jesus also knew this trauma did not have to be without purpose or blessing. Trauma can change our character for the better as we grow in compassion for others and are slowly conformed to the image of Christ, the God-man who knew suffering well.

Jesus understood what it was like to undergo a "fiery trial"; he suffered an unjust, murderous death on a cross.[41] That's why Jesus doesn't simply watch us suffer from a distance. He is, instead, present in every excruciating moment, crying when we cry and listening when we pray. Jesus sympathizes with our suffering.[42] He's been there in the past, and he's with us now. He knows what it's like. He's felt the pain, experienced the sadness, and suffered the loss.

He's also *overcome*.

Kelly took steps toward flourishing by tapping into the wisdom and power of the Overcomer. The Bible commends those who try to understand their traumatic event by "learning" and seeking "guidance."[43] Jesus and the biblical authors also encourage us to control our negative emotions, focus on our blessings, and learn how to "rejoice" by changing the way we think.[44] The authors of the Bible encourage us to talk about our trauma with one another *and* with God.[45] They also help us understand the trauma in the overarching story of our lives so we can recognize it as the catalyst for endurance, character, and hope.[46] Finally, the writers of Scripture encourage us to share everything we've learned with others who are hurting.[47]

But make no mistake about it. This thorough guidance from the biblical authors would be insufficient without the robust power of the author of life.[48] Jesus died yet rose from the grave, demonstrating power as never before.

EXPLANATION: Trauma Points Us to the True Story

We yearn to make sense of our lives and the inevitable traumas we face. We often begin by crafting a personal narrative to explain why we suffer.

When this explanation fails, trauma often initiates a journey toward a better, less subjective, explanation.

Christianity offers that better, objective explanation, providing an accurate description of why we are here, why we experience trauma, and how God can use this trauma for our good.

Trauma can point us to the truth, just as the Bible describes.

When we place our faith and trust in Jesus, he guides us and empowers us through the Holy Spirit. Jesus is more than a powerful role model. He is the *source of real power.*

When we're united to Christ, our trauma cannot hold us any more than the grave could hold Jesus.

We long to overcome because we were created in the image of the God of life. He suffered as part of the overarching story of our salvation, demonstrated his power in the resurrection, and promised this power to those whom he is conforming to his image.[49] Jesus provides us with the power to flourish, even after suffering, and the power to thrive, even after a trauma because *we were created to overcome.*

PREJUDICE, INJUSTICE, AND THE FATHER OF ALL "ISMS"

How to Identify What's Separating Us

> Reasoning against a prejudice is like fighting against a shadow; it exhausts the reasoner, without visibly affecting the prejudice; argument cannot do the work of instruction any more than blows can take the place of sunlight.
> —WALTER MILDMAY

> By death prejudice is annihilated.
> —GEORGE BANCROFT

The tow truck driver slipped into neutral for a moment and revved his engine before backing up toward Tito Serrano's pristine Camaro. He throttled the tow truck again, just as we had instructed.

"A light came on toward the rear of the house . . ." I could hear Rick's voice in my radio headset. "We've got movement. Get ready. Someone just parted the curtains to look outside . . ."

Rick and I were working together, but not as partners on the homicide team. On this morning, years before being officially assigned to the detective division, we were working on our special weapons and tactics (SWAT) team, preparing to arrest a homicide suspect. Rick was our team sniper, watching the residence through a scope from the roof of an apartment building across the street. I was staged with four other SWAT entry team members, just to the west of the Camaro.

We had no idea if Tito was living alone or if he was armed. So rather than knock on the door to serve the warrant and risk a dangerous encounter at the point of entry, we decided to coax Tito out in a safer way: with a noisy tow truck.

"... the front door is opening ..."

Tito stepped out into the cold in his T-shirt and boxers. His car had been repossessed in the past, and he was determined to prevent that from happening again. Our entry team met him on the lawn before he discovered it was a ruse. The arrest was uneventful. We cleared the house and transported another suspected killer to jail.

Tito's crime was relatively common in Los Angeles County in those days. He killed a rival gang member. Tito belonged to a multigenerational Hispanic gang, and years earlier, when he was in middle school, his membership in this group landed him in a juvenile detention facility. Too young to drive at that time, he sat in the back as one older brother drove and another loaded a pistol in the front passenger seat. Tito watched excitedly as they murdered a member of a local Black gang.

When Tito was arrested and questioned after that drive-by, he exaggerated his involvement in the crime to make a name for himself. He also confessed their motive: they didn't like sharing this part of town with other gangs, but they *especially* didn't like sharing territory with Black people.

Tito was underaged at the time, and he wasn't the shooter or the driver. He remained in custody for less than a month before he was released from the juvenile facility. Now, several years later, he was in custody again, standing in his front yard, surrounded by SWAT members.

This time Tito *was* the shooter, and his latest victim was somewhat surprising.

 ## Our Predisposition to Exclude

When Tito was questioned after his arrest at the age of thirteen, he celebrated his prejudicial motive for murder. At one point in the interview, the detective simply asked Tito if he was a racist. Tito eagerly embraced the identity and used several words to demonstrate his prejudice against anyone who didn't share his ethnicity. Rick and I watched the video of this interview the night before we served the warrant with the SWAT team. We were trying to understand the man we were about to encounter.

Tito was like no other thirteen-year-old we had ever observed. His language was shocking, even to two seasoned cops who thought we'd heard everything.

Police officers and detectives are familiar with prejudice. It's often the motive for murder and sometimes the impetus for police misconduct. Prejudice is an equal opportunity influencer. It divides us as a community, dominates our news headlines, and catalyzes violence.

When five police officers were killed in a racially motivated murder spree in Dallas, Texas,[1] the president of the United States offered this observation:

> Faced with this violence, we wonder if the divides of race in America can ever be bridged. We wonder if an African-American community that feels unfairly targeted by police, and police departments that feel unfairly maligned for doing their jobs, can ever understand each other's experience.[2]

Prejudice, unfortunately, doesn't seek to "understand each other's experience." It is, by definition, irrational. It begins even *before* we know anything about one another. As the American Psychological Association defines it, prejudice is "a negative attitude toward another person or group formed in *advance* of any experience with that person or group" (emphasis mine).[3] It's one thing to have an unpleasant encounter with someone and then shun him or her based on your experience, another to exclude or reject entire categories of people before you have any experience at all. The latter is the nature of prejudice.

It doesn't wait for a reason.

Most definitions include the illogical nature of prejudice, describing it as "an unreasonable dislike of a particular group"[4] or an "irrational attitude of hostility directed against an individual, a group, [or] race."[5]

Tito demonstrated prejudice as it is

EVIDENCE: Humans Are "Otherists" Who Seek Justice

We are selfish creatures, inclined toward self-adoration and "otherism." We favor people who are like us in one way or another and shun those who are different. Despite this truth, we recognize the harmful nature of prejudice when we see it in others, and we long for justice and unity.

Why are humans so commonly inclined toward otherism? Why do we revere justice, despite our innate predisposition?

described in these definitions. As a middle schooler, he lived in a Hispanic neighborhood and had little interaction with people of other races. His first experience with a Black person was from a distance, through a window, sitting in the back seat of his brother's car. Tito's disdain wasn't based on anything other than his unwarranted presuppositions.

According to psychologists who study and describe it, unjustified prejudice is *not* ineffectual. It starts as an emotional impulse, twists our reasoning, then compels us to act. The "affective component" of prejudice resides in emotions ranging from "mild nervousness to hatred." The "cognitive component" then emerges as a series of "assumptions and beliefs about groups, including stereotypes." As a result, the "behavioral component" can materialize as "discrimination and violence."[6]

Prejudice inevitably drives us to *action*, even if not to the extent it did Tito.

When I watched his teenage interview video, I came away with a better understanding of Tito and—if I'm honest—a higher view of myself. "I'm not a racist *like him*," I thought. But while I may not be a murderous killer, I'm sure I hold many unexamined biases of one nature or another. All of us do. Racism may not be *our* "ism," but a different form of favoritism is likely lurking in our minds and peeking through in our actions.

The list of potential isms is staggering.

Ableism, adultism, ageism, anti-Semitism, classism, colorism, lookism, nativism, racism, saneism, sexism, shadeism, sizeism—if you can define a group or a behavior, you can coin a term for people who hold a bias. Given how many groups and behaviors some of us may dislike, *all* of us hold a prejudice of one kind or another. If you're honest with yourself, you know this is true. Our biases may not be as extreme as Tito's, but they exist, nonetheless.

The seventeenth-century poet Fulke Greville observed, "A fish will sometimes with pleasure rise out of his element, and spring into ours: so a man will sometimes with pleasure rise from prejudice and falsehood, into the sphere of reason and truth. But the fish will most naturally and joyfully dive again into his element of water; and the man as joyfully and naturally into his element of prejudice and falsehood."[7] Humans are inevitably predisposed to return to our innate prejudices.

This truth is more than the speculation of a poet. Modern research has confirmed it.

The Ism of All Isms

Nearly every modern definition of prejudice describes it as an attitude toward or against *others*. It is a "dislike of a particular group of people or things," a "thought that prevents objective consideration of an idea, individual, group, or thing."[8] These descriptions of prejudice focus on who we might exclude or reject.

But the flip side of our innate desire to *shun* is our common inclination to *include*. When we prejudicially reject somebody, we inadvertently expose our preferences for whom we might embrace. A substantial body of research now helps us understand the nature of our prejudice and the depth of our preference, and these studies identify what I call "the father of all isms": otherism.

Humans are "otherists." We uniformly favor people with whom we are similar in any number of ways, rejecting anyone we view as "otherly." We select our friends and associates based on how closely they resemble us, seeking relationships with people who share our "political views, religion, sports-team loyalty . . . music preferences, . . . television-viewing habits, dress type preferences, birth order, body type, socioeconomic status and gender."[9] We pursue friends, associates, partners, and spouses based on how much we have in common. Dissimilar people and groups are relegated to the status of "others."

The depth of our self-absorption is astonishing.

According to studies, we react positively to people who look like us, especially if they share our facial features or resemble our parents or family members.[10] As visual beings, we focus on physical appearances and gravitate toward people of the same age, height, weight, eye, and hair color.[11] We also favor those who share our skin color. This is true for light-skinned *and* dark-skinned people. We build our social networks primarily around people of the same race, but we also favor subtle variations of skin pigmentation *within* our race.[12]

So consumed are we with physical familiarity, we even prefer strangers who display facial expressions we recognize from members of our own family. The more someone's responses resemble those of our family, the more positively we react. This isn't just a learned behavior; researchers have identified the innate neural pathways involved in this preference.[13]

Even if we are unable to assess each other's physical appearance (as is often the case in online social media groups), we *still* find a way to embrace people who are similar to us while shunning those who aren't.[14] We are much more likely, for example, to associate with people who share our religious background or political affiliation.[15]

Our inclination to seek similar people is even more apparent in our romantic relationships. The age-old belief that "opposites attract" has now been disproven by sociologists and researchers. Similarity is the strongest predictor of attraction in the early stages of a relationship, and the stronger the similarity, the more likely the relationship will be satisfying.[16] Like-minded couples and spouses are far more likely to communicate well, experience closeness and intimacy, and stay together.[17]

For this reason, we are more likely to marry someone who looks like us, believes like us, and behaves like us.[18] Our future spouses generally share our intelligence and educational level, socioeconomic status, occupational interests, and religious beliefs.[19] We are also likely to smoke or drink at the same level.[20] Our future spouses even share our language preferences, using similar cultural expressions.[21]

If you've noticed the similarity between spouses who have been married for many years, it's not simply an example of mutual *adaptation*, it's also a product of mindful *selection*. We choose spouses who look, think, and act like us. DNA studies even reveal that spouses are more likely to share similar genetic code than two non-spouses chosen at random.[22]

EXAMPLE: Jonah

When God called the prophet Jonah to warn the Assyrians in the city of Nineveh of his coming judgment and their need to repent, Jonah's "otheristic" tendencies got the better of him. He tried to run, but God wouldn't let him.

Later, when the Ninevites repented because of his preaching, Jonah complained about God forgiving them. God had to remind Jonah that the 120,000 Ninevites were *also* created in the image of God. Jonah had much more in common with these people than he first imagined.

Our prejudice is grounded in "otherism," our innate inclination to seek and affirm those who are *like* us while shunning those who are otherly. Otherism isn't unique to any particular group, race, sex, or ethnicity. If you're a human, you've experienced and demonstrated this predisposition. Sexism, ableism, racism, classism—studies now confirm why the list of isms is endless. They are grounded in our interest of self.

Otherism is the ism of all isms.

Racism, sexism, colorism, and other isms based purely on physical appearance are simply lazy versions of otherism. We can typically spot these attributes from across the room with little or no effort. If we're inclined to act on our innate otherism, we can distance ourselves from visually different strangers without knowing anything more about them.

Anti-Semitism, classism, and other less visible isms take a little more effort. We may have to ask a few questions or get to know someone before we can identify our differences. But one thing is certain: our prejudicial inclination toward otherism will likely encourage distancing. Otherism isn't static. It moves from the heart, to the mind, to action. Sometimes a single difference is enough to motivate our prejudice.

Tito's murderous history demonstrated this truth.

Years earlier, his brothers killed a man based on obvious otherism. Their victim was another race and was wearing clothing identifying him with a rival Los Angeles gang. Tito could see the physical differences from a block away. He and his brothers knew nothing more about their victim than the fact he was a Black man from a different gang. They didn't know his name or his personal history. But he appeared otherly, and that was enough.

The difference between Tito and his latest victim, a man named Hector, was much less obvious. Hector was *also* Hispanic; he didn't appear otherly from across the street. Rather, he looked a lot like the Serrano brothers. Some might even say he bore a family resemblance.

 ## Prejudice, Pride, and Otherism

That didn't stop Tito from committing a second murder. Instead of focusing on what he had in common with Hector, he looked for what differentiated them.

Tito isn't the only one to *seek what separates*. Social media facilitates otherism in everyone. We now separate over single beliefs, affiliations, or statements, even if we share everything else in common. You've probably experienced this online. A solitary post often separates the best of friends and the closest family members. Why is this the case?

The answer is another common human attribute: pride.

When defining *pride*, secular dictionaries generally highlight its *positive* qualities first, describing it as a "pleasure that comes from some relationship, association, achievement, or possession that is seen as a source of honor, respect, etc." or "a feeling of pleasure and satisfaction that you get because you or people connected with you have done or gotten something good." The *dark* side of pride is usually hidden at the bottom of the definition and described as "exaggerated self-esteem" or "the belief that you are better or more important than other people."[23]

Biblical dictionaries, on the other hand, typically define *pride* by prioritizing its *dangers* first, describing it as "inordinate self-esteem; an unreasonable conceit of one's own superiority in talents, beauty, wealth, accomplishments, rank or elevation in office, which manifests itself in lofty airs, distance, reserve, and often in contempt of others."[24]

This "contempt of others" is the inevitable outcome of otherism. It's also the reason why pride is the catalyst for prejudice. Our "exaggerated self-esteem" and "unreasonable conceit" motivate us to befriend, hire, include, promote, protect, and favor those who are like us, unjustly excluding those who *aren't*. Prejudice, according to science fiction screenwriter Rod Serling, is the "the singular evil of our time . . . It is from this evil that all other evils grow and multiply. In almost everything I've written there is a thread of this: a man's seemingly palpable need to dislike someone other than himself."[25]

The biblical authors understood this truth about prideful otherism and its role in catalyzing prejudice. Rather than celebrating pride as a source of "pleasure and satisfaction," the Bible warns us about the relationship between pride and prejudice. The authors of Scripture knew, millennia earlier, what self-improvement guru Dale Carnegie later observed: "When dealing with people, remember you are not dealing with creatures of logic, but with creatures bristling with prejudice and motivated by pride and vanity."[26]

The Greek word in the New Testament used to describe prejudice is πρόκριμα, a term capturing the notion of an unfair "prejudgment."[27] Our modern word *prejudice* has its root in a Latin term, *praejudicium*, most directly translated as "injustice."[28] This etymology accurately captures the nature of unjust isms and their solution. Think about an act of injustice you can recall in the last calendar year. The incident likely involved an act of prejudice in which someone pridefully prejudged another.

Since pride is the root cause of otherism (and often the cause of injustice), the solution is now painfully clear: If we're truly concerned about resisting otherism and injustice, we don't need to start a nonprofit, build a website, or join a march. We should simply begin by addressing our own selfish pride. If we yearn to be "justice warriors," the "battlefield" is closer than we think.

Prideful otherism is a universal human condition. Everyone struggles with prejudice and contributes to injustice, and because we share culpability, everyone can be part of the solution. It begins when we identify the problem with *us* before we identify the problem with *others*. It culminates when we seek and celebrate what we have in common rather than focusing on what might separate us.

Tito did just the opposite.

He knew Hector his entire life. They grew up together, and for a season, they even shared a bedroom. They were the same age, with a comparable personal history, common interests, and the *same last name.* Despite these similarities, Tito obsessed over the one thing they no longer had in common.

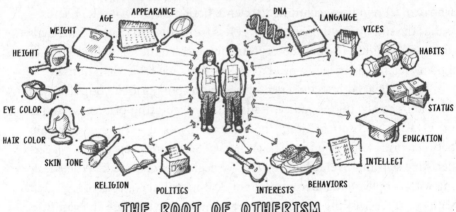

WE ARE ATTRACTED TO PEOPLE WITH SIMILAR:

APPEARANCE · AGE · WEIGHT · HEIGHT · EYE COLOR · HAIR COLOR · SKIN TONE · RELIGION · POLITICS · INTERESTS · BEHAVIORS · INTELLECT · EDUCATION · STATUS · HABITS · VICES · LANGAUGE · DNA

THE ROOT OF OTHERISM

Chase the Lead

Hector Serrano was Tito's *cousin* and his best friend growing up. They were inseparable as children. When Hector met the girl of his dreams, Angela, he was still living with Tito's family. But when Angela became pregnant during Hector's senior year, he moved across town and started living with Angela's family. The longer he resided there, the more his identity shifted. Hector was living in rival gang territory, and as his commitment to Angela grew, so did his allegiance to her neighborhood.

Tito refused to accept this change in identity. He now saw Hector as otherly.

This inclination toward otherism is engrained in our nature, just as it was in Tito's, and its roots run deep. After many years investigating murders, observing the culture, and honestly assessing my own fallen nature, I'm not sure we can completely eliminate otherism. It's that powerful. But I do know this: succeed or fail, *we need to make the effort.* Humans thrive and flourish when we resist bigotry and seek the best in each other, despite our differences. The alternative is a world where pride, prejudice, and injustice reign. Given that challenge, these steps may help us temper our otheristic tendencies:

Learn the Difference between *Pre*judgment and *Good* Judgment
Injustice results when we unfairly prejudge others *before* we know who they are. Justice results when we rightly assess others *after* they reveal themselves. The first is called *prejudice*; the second is called *discernment*. There are some people we *ought* to shun because of their character and behavior. Only a fool treats evil as though it is virtue. It's one thing to allow our otherism to exclude people simply because they are different, another to embrace everyone—regardless of their behavior—without sound discernment. Don't confuse the two.

This might be more difficult than it sounds. Discernment requires a judgment about good and evil, virtue and malice, righteousness and iniquity. But if moral truths are simply a matter of personal opinion or cultural consensus, discernment is nothing more than an expression of preference. According to Tito's personal moral code, for example, Hector did something reprehensible. Tito believed he had a *duty* to shun and punish Hector for his actions. This is the danger of trying to discern good and evil without an objective standard beyond one's personal power of discernment.

While we can encourage one another to avoid *pre*judgment and to embrace *good* judgment, we must remember both still involve *judgment*, an act made meaningless without the existence of an objective, transcendent standard of good and evil.

Celebrate Our Morally Neutral Differences and Seek Unity
Most otherism occurs when we shun someone because of a morally
neutral attribute. It's not evil or immoral to possess a particular skin
tone, for example, so this ought not be the criteria by which we exclude
someone from our lives. Our innate attributes, the anatomical features
we possess from birth, are uncontrollable and morally irrelevant. Rather
than separate from one another over physical traits we did not choose
for ourselves, we should seek unity and celebrate the differences that
define the human family. As Martin Luther King Jr. so wisely observed,
"We must learn to live together as brothers or perish together as fools."[29]

Focus on What We Have in Common
Humans are surprisingly similar. Despite the cultural differences
between people groups, we share the same innate desires, concerns, and
inclinations. For example, we seek community, revere wisdom, yearn
to worship, and struggle with humility, just as this book describes. Our
shared humanity provides an opportunity for empathy and compassion
if we can focus on what we have in common.

Alien invasion movies illustrate this truth. Scenes from these kinds
of movies typically depict councils of humans from every nation, meeting to decide how they can defend themselves from an alien massacre.
Humans of every color, ethnicity, shape, and size are seen laboring in
a unified fashion, acting in harmony, and focusing on their shared
humanity. It's almost as if they've discovered what they have in common
for the very first time. We don't have to wait for an alien invasion to
make this discovery. We could choose today to identify what we have in
common.

This also might be harder than it sounds. What overarching com-
monality can unify us as a species? Our common biology? Our shared
planet? A global cause of one kind or another? Whatever our focus,
otherism will continue to motivate our choices until we discover and
commit to a unifying identity transcending our individuality.

Reject the Idea, Not the Individual
Tito had a long history with gang members from Angela's neighborhood. He hated what they represented, what they stood for, and what
they believed. When Hector showed up with a tattoo representing that

neighborhood, Tito immediately redirected this hatred toward his cousin. He no longer saw Hector as a person. He saw him, instead, as a representative of a competing ideology.

It's often difficult to separate how we treat people from what we think of their beliefs. But this is the definition of tolerance, an important antidote for otherism. *Tolerance*, as classically defined, is the "fair, objective, and permissive attitude toward those whose opinions, beliefs, practices, racial or ethnic origins, etc., differ from one's own."[30] We can reasonably shun a *belief or concept* without shunning the *people* who hold these beliefs or concepts.

When we practice tolerance, we learn how to embrace others based on their human dignity while maintaining our own beliefs and practices. Tolerance provides a pathway from otherism to relationship, despite what might otherwise separate us.

Forbearance was not one of Tito's gifts. Hector's murder was very different from the one Tito's brothers committed years earlier. Tito acted on his own this time, parking his car in front of Angela's house. When Hector saw Tito's Camaro through the screen door, he came outside to greet him. As Tito approached, Hector leaned forward to embrace his cousin. Tito responded by shooting Hector in the chest.

In that moment, two Serranos were on Angela's porch. They could have been unified if Tito hadn't been so focused on what made them different.

The Truth in True Crime: You Were Created to Seek Justice and Unity

Our shared inclination toward otherism is an obstacle to human flourishing. We've all seen it, experienced it, and participated in it. Yet, as the research demonstrates, we seem unable (or unwilling) to control our otheristic tendencies.

The ancient authors of the Bible described this aspect of human nature and offered a solution still available in our modern world.

The Bible accurately describes the impact pride and otherism have on our relationships, identifying our tendency to be "haughty," a term capturing our arrogant and presumptuous nature.[31] Arrogance catalyzes our attraction to people with whom we are similar, and presumptuousness motivates us to unfairly prejudge those with whom we aren't. The authors of Scripture understood this and repeatedly warned us not to allow self-absorption to separate us from those who are different.[32] Instead, they instructed us to seek the good of people who are *unlike* us by lavishing them with the same adoration we typically offer ourselves.[33]

God cares about justice, and he calls us to act accordingly.[34] We are called to recognize and honor the dignity of our fellow humans, to resist our otheristic tendencies, and to stop treating people unfairly on the basis of morally neutral characteristics. God wants us to stop looking in the mirror and start looking out the window.

EXPLANATION: We Long for What Is Yet to Come

As humans possessing free agency, we pridefully select that with which we are most familiar. We favor those like us, while simultaneously despising the injustice that inevitably results from our prejudice.

We value justice and unity because we were created in the image of a just, unified, triune God.

We struggle with otherism because we are rebellious humans living in a fallen world.

Christianity explains both realities and offers a pathway to unity, justice, and restoration. Our present desire for fairness and harmony points us to a future kingdom in which these lofty goals will be realized.

As Kevin DeYoung describes, "Doing justice means following the rule of law, showing impartiality, paying what you promised, not stealing, not swindling, not taking bribes, and not taking advantage of the weak because they are too uninformed or unconnected to stop you."[35]

God also calls us to remember what we have in common.

According to the Bible, we were created in the image of God and descended from one couple.[36] We are from the same family, sharing similar desires, hopes, struggles, and expectations regardless of our race, color, shape, or size.[37] These differences are simply the product of pride, time, and regional isolation.[38] We are children separated from one another in a fallen world, waiting to be restored to the family of God. A day is coming when God's people from every tribe, nation, and language will live together in perfect harmony with God as their father.[39]

That's why God "shows no partiality," regardless of what we look like or where we live.[40] He doesn't judge us by our appearance, race, sex, or national origin because he knows how the story began *and* how it ends.[41] God has a plan "for the fullness of time, to unite all things in him, things in heaven and things on earth."[42] A day is coming when peace and justice will reign forever.[43]

In the interim, he's calling us to focus on our common lineage. Far more unites us as a family than separates us as a species. If we can remember where we came from and where we are headed, we can live in peace and unity along the way.[44] We can thrive.

If you're wondering why you crave *justice*, it's because we were created by a God who is *just*. If you're wondering why you yearn for *unity*, it's because you were created by a God who is *unified* in his triune nature. He's calling you to resist otherism so you can flourish until he rights every wrong and restores his people to perfect fellowship.

You were created to seek justice and unity.

TOUGH LOVE AND A TALE OF TWO BROTHERS

How to Balance Your Two Polar Inclinations

> Rats and roaches live by competition under the laws
> of supply and demand; it is the privilege of human
> beings to live under the laws of justice and mercy.
> —WENDELL BERRY

> Every act, every deed of justice and mercy and
> benevolence, makes heavenly music in Heaven.
> —ELLEN G. WHITE

W here is Jeremy now?" Angela's voice trembled. Even over the phone I could tell she was trying to suppress her emotions.

"He's here in lockup until his arraignment tomorrow—" I tried to provide a few extra details, but Angela cut me off.

"It's my fault . . . I could see this coming. It's all my fault."

Jeremy Buckhanon was in jail for the seventh time, and for the *third* on charges related to murder. He had previously tried to kill an uncle, then a roommate. His uncle left the country without testifying, and his roommate changed his story to avoid trial. Jeremy escaped jail in both situations, returning to live with his mother, Angela.

The remainder of Jeremy's arrests were for drug and theft charges. His sentences were never lengthy. Jeremy committed his crimes prior to 1993, the year California and many other states adopted three-strikes laws in response to the murder of twelve-year-old Polly Klaas.[1] Polly was killed by a man who was a paroled felon. Before the three-strikes laws, convicted felons were often released relatively quickly, only to commit increasingly violent crimes.

Jeremy was one of those ex-felons.

On the day of my conversation with Angela, he had beat a man to death in an aging apartment building on the east side of our city. Jeremy was there to purchase rock cocaine with money his mother had given him as an "allowance" of sorts. At the end of the transaction, he was convinced the dealer had cheated him. Jeremy was used to getting what he wanted—and hurting those who stood in his way.

A resident in the next apartment reported the beating, and officers responded quickly. Jeremy was pulling his mother's car from the curb when officers arrived. He led them on a high-speed pursuit, eventually crashing on the 91 freeway at Avalon. Angela's car was totaled. Jeremy came away unscratched.

"I should have been stricter on that boy." Angela's voice was calmer. "I let him get away with murd—" She stopped abruptly as if she realized the ironic gravity of her statement. She quickly changed direction.

"He's my youngest. He has two older sisters and an older brother. His sisters never gave me any trouble, but Jason, his brother . . . that boy was a *rebel*. I was so strict with Jason. Maybe *too* strict. I put so many rules on him because he was the oldest. Lots of boundaries so he could learn the truth about what's right and wrong. Seemed like I was always disciplining him."

Our records showed that Jason was murdered in a shooting at a local party several years prior to my conversation with Angela. She never mentioned this detail, and I didn't press it.

"I didn't want to do that with Jeremy. Maybe I was too soft. He's my baby, you know. Didn't want to lose him like I lost Jason. I knew he was using coke, but I only saw him bring it home one time. I didn't know what to say . . . He's always been good to me, you know? He's really a loving boy. Really . . . he *is*. I just made life too easy for him. I gave Jeremy everything. Too much . . . I don't know . . . Do you have children, Detective Wallace?"

"Yes."

"Do *you* think I was too soft with Jeremy?" Angela waited for my response.

My conversation with Angela wasn't unusual. Even before I became a Christian I was interested in my arrestees as *people*. Every story seemed a cautionary tale, another example of what to do—or not to do—as a parent, husband, or son.

"My kids are still young, Mrs. Buckhanon. I have a lot to learn, so I am listening to everything you're telling me. I just want you to know . . . I am interested in what you have to say."

"Am I going to lose my baby, Detective Wallace? Is he going to jail forever this time?"

"Yes, I think there's a good chance this crime will be his last." Angela ran out of things to say. I could hear her sobbing on the other end of the line, crying about the fate of her youngest child.

Jeremy may have been her baby, but he wasn't a boy. Jeremy was nearly fifty years old.

The Tenacity of Truth and Justice

Jeremy Buckhanon was convicted of murder nine months later. Angela was present every day in the courtroom. After the trial was over, she told Jeremy's defense attorney she wanted to speak at the sentencing hearing.

EVIDENCE: Humans Desire Justice and Mercy

We live in a justice-seeking world. Social justice. Racial justice. Gender justice. Nearly every form of human identity and interaction is now being examined through the lens of justice and mercy. When we hold these two inclinations in perfect balance, we thrive as a species, yet we almost *never* achieve the equilibrium we are looking for.

Why are these two characteristics of human interaction the key to well-being? Why would something so essential to human flourishing be so difficult to achieve?

The attorney assumed Angela would attempt to "humanize" Jeremy before the judge declared the sentence. Angela had something else in mind.

"Your Honor, I am Jeremy Buckhanon's mother." Angela was wearing a tailored dress and hat. She stood sharply and confidently at the podium. "I love my son, but I want you to know you have my permission to sentence him to whatever the law requires. He knows what he did. Now he must pay for it."

She returned calmly to her seat in the gallery. Jeremy sat at the defendant's table in a county jumpsuit. His head remained down for the entire hearing.

Angela was a churchgoing single parent. She understood the importance of truth and justice, and not just because she learned about it in the Bible. Like the rest of us, Angela had an innate understanding of the value of justice, given her nature as a human being. Even ancient philosophers considered justice an instinctive characteristic of humans. Socrates, for example, claimed justice was a "virtue of the soul." Plato also believed justice resided innately in humans.[2]

The youngest among us have a sense of justice even before they're formally taught the concept. Kids are the first to complain when something seems unfair, especially if they suffer an injustice personally. Perhaps this is because they don't yet understand how unjust the world can be, and therefore hold an unreasonably high expectation. As G. K. Chesterton observed, "Children are innocent and love justice, while most of us are wicked and naturally prefer mercy."[3] Children expect fairness, and when it doesn't happen, they are properly outraged.

When psychologists and sociologists study infants and toddlers, they find that "young children, have strong feelings about what counts as a wrongful action and how much punishment a wrongdoer deserves."[4] Justice is a universal human expectation, innate concern, and common yearning.[5] Regardless of where they are located geographically or historically, humans share intuitions about justice and law. Studies now confirm that the origin of justice and criminal law is in our commonly held "cognitively sophisticated human nature."[6]

Researchers believe justice is a left-brain activity rooted in "higher-order cognition" because they observe increased brain activity in people who are more concerned about matters of fairness.[7] Our interest in truth and justice is, according to research, motivated *rationally* rather than *emotionally.*

Angela loved both of her sons, but she admitted taking what might be called a left-brain approach with her oldest, Jason. She was concerned he might get into trouble without a father in their home, so she set firm rules and punished him when he violated them. She was fair and consistent even though she was seldom present or available. She worked two jobs and was usually exhausted by the time she got home.

Jason grew wearier of his mother's rules with each passing year. By the time he was a teenager, he decided to leave home. He was dead within two years.

"I was so strict with Jason. Maybe *too* strict."

Rules, when disconnected from relationship, often result in rebellion.[8] Angela learned this the hard way.

The Magnitude of Mercy and Grace

Jeremy was only ten years old when Jason was killed. Jeremy was already his mother's favorite, but the murder only caused her to cling more tightly. She pampered him, forgave him after every act of rebellion, and chose to see the best in him, regardless of his behavior. Angela took an emotionally driven, right-brain approach with Jeremy, suffering through six arrests and embracing him unconditionally upon every release.

Jeremy never changed his behavior in response to his mother's unreserved love, but at least he stayed home.

Abraham Lincoln once told a friend, "I have always found that mercy bears richer fruits than strict justice."[9] Angela hoped this would be true with Jeremy. Rather than restrict him in any way, she took the opposite approach.

Grace and kindness matter to human well-being, but in this case, the unconditional love Angela offered may have benefited her more than it did her son. Researchers find that people who extend grace and kindness to others "enjoy better health due to the biological changes that occur while being kind." Those who extend grace and kindness also live longer.[10]

Mercy is powerful. So powerful, it can improve our well-being even when we don't offer or experience it directly. Studies reveal health benefits for people who simply *observe* the kindness of others, even when they aren't personally involved. Kindness and mercy, when offered, received, or simply observed, have the power to change us for the better, increasing our positive emotions, reducing our stress levels, and improving our physical health.[11]

The impact of mercy is not simply a cultural phenomenon. We didn't learn it from one another as a species. Instead, we are born to respond favorably to kindness. It is part of our innate human nature. Secular researchers observe this attribute in infants and consider the benefits of grace to be a "feature of human behavior" seen universally in "diverse societies" with "surprising ubiquity in humanity compared with our closest evolutionary cousins."[12] Humans uniquely yearn for—and respond favorably to—mercy, grace, and kindness, and this simple truth is obvious even to atheist researchers.

But this didn't seem to be the case for Jeremy.

Angela babied him like none of her other children, and Jeremy was usually kind in return. But the power of his mother's love couldn't overcome the addictive control cocaine had on his life.

"I knew he was using coke, but I only saw him bring it home one time. I didn't know what to say . . ."

Angela's uncertainty acknowledges a dilemma common to *all* humans. We yearn for and understand the power of justice, truth, and law on the one hand, while longing for mercy, grace, and love on the other. Angela exercised justice with Jason, mercy with Jeremy. Neither produced the result she was hoping for.

 ## The Battle of Balance

This "tug of war" between our two polar longings defines what it means to be human. It is our common struggle, and its resolution is yet another key to human flourishing. We experience the "pull" between grace and truth, mercy and justice, in nearly every aspect of our lives. When we engage the struggle for equilibrium, we learn what it means to be human. It's a battle of balance.

When we pull too hard in one direction, our lives become uncentered. As Thomas Aquinas wrote, "Mercy without justice is the mother of dissolution; justice without mercy is cruelty."[13] If we're overly focused on matters of justice, as Angela was with Jason, indifference, detachment, and rebellion result. When we're overly focused on mercy, as Angela was with Jeremy, sentimentality, disorder, and instability rule the day.

Angela failed to strike the balance we call "tough love."

This term is sometimes confused in popular media as simply a focus on justice, but, by definition, "tough love" incorporates both ends of the "tug of war" rope. The "tough" side of the term describes the emphasis on truth and justice, the "love" side of the term describes the importance of mercy and grace. When a parent practices tough love, for example, they express an "affectionate concern" in an "unsentimental manner" to "promote responsible behavior."[14]

EXAMPLE: Jesus, the God-Man

Jesus possessed the attributes of God, exhibiting the fullness of grace and truth (John 1:14). Jesus expressed grace repeatedly, healing the sick, welcoming children, feeding the hungry, and sharing a meal with sinners and tax collectors. He also boldly proclaimed truth as he predicted judgment on Jerusalem, criticized religious leaders, and called his followers to a higher standard of commitment.

How can we follow the example of Jesus and hold grace and truth in proper balance?

Angela practiced toughness and justice with Jason, permissiveness and mercy with Jeremy.

Parents who balance mercy and justice typically fare much better. They are more likely to raise children who develop empathy, resiliency, willpower, and self-control.[15] Children raised in a balanced environment also perform better at school and are more "cooperative, self-regulating and socially responsible."[16] They have better self-esteem and confidence, cope well with stress and failure, manage their aggression, and develop stronger relationships.[17]

Parenting isn't the only area of human interaction benefiting from a balanced approach. Educators and coaches also succeed when they balance justice and mercy. When teachers cultivate empathetic and caring relationships with their students and exercise "compassionate discipline," students thrive.[18] When coaches challenge players from a position of caring, supportive involvement, their players flourish.[19]

Effective rehabilitation and reform efforts also require a balance between justice and mercy. Confrontational drug rehabilitation strategies, for example, have been effective with recovering addicts, but they are far more effective when employed by family members who have deep relationships with the subject of the addiction.[20] This is also true in long-term recovery programs. More broadly, rehabilitation efforts in correctional facilities experience the best results when attempting to balance justice and mercy. Researchers now believe offenders in programs "characterized by 'tough love' perform better than those with only 'hard' or 'soft' features by themselves."[21]

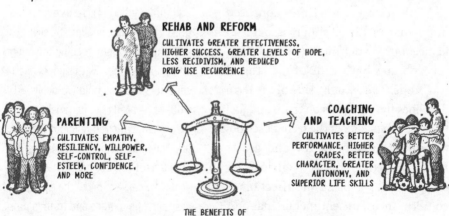

REHAB AND REFORM
CULTIVATES GREATER EFFECTIVENESS, HIGHER SUCCESS, GREATER LEVELS OF HOPE, LESS RECIDIVISM, AND REDUCED DRUG USE RECURRENCE

PARENTING
CULTIVATES EMPATHY, RESILIENCY, WILLPOWER, SELF-CONTROL, SELF-ESTEEM, CONFIDENCE, AND MORE

COACHING AND TEACHING
CULTIVATES BETTER PERFORMANCE, HIGHER GRADES, BETTER CHARACTER, GREATER AUTONOMY, AND SUPERIOR LIFE SKILLS

THE BENEFITS OF
BALANCING JUSTICE AND MERCY

In every area of interaction, humans flourish when achieving a balance between justice and mercy. Yet, as simple as this may sound, none of us consistently achieve this elusive equilibrium. Angela succumbed to the extremes with her two sons, and sadly, both are dead today.

 ## Chase the Lead

Martin Luther wrote, "Human nature is like a drunk peasant. Lift him into the saddle on one side, over he topples on the other side."[22] Author Randy Alcorn, citing Luther in this regard, described our common struggle to "mount the horse with one foot in the stirrup of truth, the other in the stirrup of grace."[23] Humans *always* favor one stirrup or the other, yet we flourish when we sit squarely "in the saddle." If you want to thrive in this way, here are a few suggestions:

Rethink Justice and Mercy

According to researchers, our decisions are guided by reason *and* emotion, resulting in expressions of justice or mercy.[24] Instead of viewing these expressions as distant, polar extremes, recognize them as two sides of the same coin, wedded, inseparable, and interdependent. Thomas Aquinas noted, "Justice and mercy are so united, that the one ought to be mingled with the other; justice without mercy is cruelty; mercy without justice, profusion."[25] The next time you are inclined to react from a standpoint of justice or truth, remember their interdependence on mercy and grace. One side cannot exist without the other.

Rethink the Nature of "Balance"

It's tempting to think of balance as the process of removing something from one side of a scale until both sides are equally weighted. By this definition, the effort to balance justice and mercy might require us to be less just or merciful (depending on the situation) to achieve an equilibrium. But this is not the nature of balance as described in Scripture. God calls us to exhibit justice and mercy in their *fullness*. The scale is in balance when both sides are *filled to the brim*. Resist the temptation to be less merciful or less just to achieve equilibrium. Strive instead to express the fullness of justice and mercy.

Check Your Pride

Whenever you catch yourself leaning too heavily on the truth and justice stirrup, ask yourself, "Whose stirrup is this anyway? Am I upset because an injustice occurred, or simply because *I* don't like what happened?" We sometimes pridefully judge people using *our* standard of what "ought to be," and we usually think more highly of ourselves than we ought.

Ground Your Justice

How can we limit the impact pride has on our sense of justice and truth? The best way to take yourself out of the equation is to adopt a view of truth that's independent of your personal preferences and desires. Voddie Baucham, for example, describes justice as "the righteous application of the law of *God*" (emphasis mine).[26] When we recognize *God* as the transcendent, objective source of truth and justice, our responses are less likely to be motivated by personal beliefs or popular cultural notions. Recognize the *source* of justice before you *exercise* justice.

Love More Than the Person

The iconic coach of the Dallas Cowboys, Tom Landry, once described a coach as "someone who tells you what you don't want to hear, [and] who has you see what you don't want to see."[27] Landry knew it was important to love *more* than just his players. He also loved what was *best* for his players. Angela discovered this truth the hard way. Jason needed a mother who would love *Jason* as much as she loved *what was right for Jason*, Jeremy needed a mother who loved *what was right for Jeremy* as much as she loved *Jeremy*. When you find yourself leaning too heavily on the mercy and grace stirrup, remember love involves more than making someone feel good. It also involves doing what's right and seeking the best for the person you love.

Distance Your Responses

Research reveals our inclination to act emotionally before we act rationally. Human beings "are first and foremost emotional creatures."[28] We seldom balance our emotional and rational sides when we act too quickly. Thoughtful balance occurs when we create space between our reactions and our responses. When we *slow down*, we are more likely to show restraint, reigning in our inclination to lean on one stirrup over the other. Take a minute to assess your reaction before you regret your response.

Consider the Cost

Richard Carlson is known for writing, "There are two rules for living in harmony. #1) Don't sweat the small stuff and #2) It's all small stuff."[29] Carlson's rules are hyperbolic, but his point is still important: when everything's a big deal, we inevitably overreact in one direction or the other. Before you respond, ask yourself, "Do I really need to act at all? Does my opinion really matter here?" Pick your battles to balance your response.

Stay Out of the Way

If you're looking for examples of imbalanced behavior, look no further than your social media network. Online platforms seem to exacerbate our polarization and amplify our extremes. Research reveals we are more likely to respond irrationally on social media platforms as "users conform their outrage expressions to the expressive norms of their social networks."[30] This kind of expressive conformity isn't unique to social media, of course. It also happens at work, school, and even at family gatherings. Some environments (either physical or digital) *encourage* imbalance, and we contribute to the problem when we willingly enter these arenas. If you want to reduce your sugar intake, you probably shouldn't work at a candy store. Similarly, if you want to achieve better equilibrium, avoid those places where justice or mercy are leveraged to the extreme.

Pretend It's You

We don't like it when people treat us unjustly or unmercifully. Instead, we bristle at the imbalance. It's an ancient notion: when we treat others as we want to be treated, we are more thoughtful, intentional, and balanced.[31] Before you react or respond, imagine yourself the transgressor. How would you want to be treated?

Draw Rather Than Drive

Coaches who inspire are more effective than those who simply demand. Why? Because in our prideful state, we resist being *driven* against our will. Instead, we respond favorably to people who *draw* us toward a better destination. Do the people you're disciplining know you love them and have their best in mind? Are punishments dispensed in the context of a caring relationship? When they know you love them, your discipline can *inspire* rather than *destroy*.

Angela called me two weeks after the sentencing hearing. I could barely make out her words. I waited patiently for her to calm down enough to tell me the news. Jeremy was transported from county jail to state prison about a week after receiving his sentence: life without the possibility of parole. Once he got to prison, he refused the opportunity to make a phone call, settled into his cell, and managed to find a way to hang himself with a bedsheet. He never spoke to Angela after the hearing.

She now regretted her sentencing statement.

"Angela, the judge sentenced Jeremy based on the state's sentencing guidelines. I'm certain he would have given him the same sentence even if you hadn't testified." Angela didn't respond to my effort to comfort her. Instead, she simply shifted her sense of guilt.

"I gave him everything. That's my fault. I let him live at my house without any rules . . . I guess he wasn't gonna survive in prison without that kind of freedom."

Balance matters. It's an important contributor to human flourishing. Without it, Jason and Jeremy became cautionary tales rather than thriving role models.

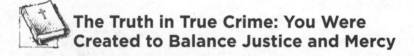

The Truth in True Crime: You Were Created to Balance Justice and Mercy

Angela described herself as a Christ follower, but she was admittedly unfamiliar with the teaching of the Bible. Had she been a student of Scripture, she would have recognized the importance of wisely reflecting—and balancing—God's justice *and* his mercy.

Christianity uniquely predicts the discoveries of modern researchers, accurately describing the relationship between justice and mercy and the role they play in human flourishing. Unlike many theistic worldviews in which deities dispense justice at the expense of grace (or mercy at the expense of truth), the full arc of the biblical narrative describes God as a being who exemplifies both attributes in perfect fullness and balance.

The Bible starts with a description of justice and mercy. When Adam and Eve disobeyed God, he dispensed his judgment *and* his mercy, promising evil would be vanquished through Jesus, a descendent of Eve.[32] In this first book of Scripture, Yahweh is described as a God of "lovingkindness" and "truth,"[33] and throughout the Old Testament, this balanced aspect of God's nature distinguishes him from the competing idols of antiquity.

As theologian R. C. Sproul observed, "A god who is all love, all grace, all mercy, no sovereignty, no justice, no holiness, and no wrath is an idol."[34] Yahweh is not simply an ancient idol. He exhibits the perfect fullness of justice, truth, and righteousness on the one side, mercy, grace, and faithfulness on the other.[35] He is described as the place where "steadfast love and faithfulness meet," where "righteousness and peace kiss each other."[36]

When the coming Savior was prophesied in the Old Testament, he was described as someone who would sit on a

EXPLANATION: We Yearn for Divine Equilibrium

Our continual desire to balance justice and mercy, and our modern interest in studying the benefit this balance has on well-being, are the product of design.

We long for equilibrium between grace and truth because we were created in the image of a God who personified justice and mercy. We innately and uniformly recognize their value because the fingerprints of God can be found on our souls.

Christianity explains our yearning in both the Old and New Testaments. Yahweh demonstrated loving-kindness and justice; Jesus came in grace and truth. We are drawn to the Divine when we yearn for the equilibrium only God can achieve.

throne "established in steadfast love" and someone who "seeks justice and is swift to do righteousness."[37] The promised Messiah would possess the divine fullness and balance of grace and truth.

Jesus uniquely embodied this prophetic description. The New Testament introduces him as the Savior who "made his dwelling among us" and came "full of grace and truth."[38] He called his followers to balance these aspects of his nature in similar fullness, even though this is incredibly difficult.

God created us in his image with justice and mercy at our core, but in our fallen state as prideful creatures, we struggle to return to the balance for which we were designed. You know this is true, even if you're not a believer. Think about it. If you've ever struggled in a relationship at home, work, or school, it's probably because you failed to balance justice and mercy in their fullness, and contemporary research has corroborated our anecdotal experiences.

Jesus understood our struggle long before modern sociologists did. That's why the New Testament writers continually call us to rebalance our lives by seeking the fullness of God's nature. As theologian Lesslie Newbigin described, "The living God is a God of justice and mercy and He will be satisfied with nothing less than a people in whom his justice and mercy are alive."[39] Nearly every admonition for believers in the New Testament is either a call to be more merciful in our judgments or more just in our relationships.[40] These writers simply echo the words of the Old Testament prophets who recognized the steadfast love of God and called us to hate evil, love good, and establish justice.[41]

The gospel message itself is God's clearest expression of truth and grace.

God created us as creatures capable of justice and mercy. We are rebellious, however, and continually resist God's design for our lives, violating his rules for living as well as our own. Worse yet, we often reject God as the divine source of the transcendent moral laws we innately recognize. The Bible calls this consistent rebellion "sin," and the just penalty for sin is death.[42] But God crafted a merciful way to satisfy the demands of justice while still expressing his grace in love. He paid a price we wouldn't want to pay to provide the reward we couldn't hope to earn. While we were still sinners who were ignoring God entirely, Jesus died for us on the cross.[43] If we simply admit and turn from our sin, confess Jesus as Lord, and believe what the New Testament authors said about his power to conquer death, the requirements of justice are satisfied and we experience the love of God.[44]

That, my friend, is the finest example of justice and mercy ever offered.

As Anglican pastor John Stott observed, "It is not easy to decide which is the most luminously revealed, whether the justice of God in judging sin, or the love of God in bearing the judgment in our place."[45] When humans designed in the image of God experience his love in this way, we are changed forever. This transformation is both spiritual *and* physical, just as researchers are now discovering.

People who experience the grace of God flourish, now and forever. In this life, they experience better mental health, closer relationships, stronger resiliency after trauma, and better character.[46] In the next life, they experience a better eternity. God seeks to show his grace and justice to every one of us, reaching down from heaven to save us, demonstrating "His loving-kindness and His truth."[47]

Our interests in justice and mercy are not simply an artifact of human evolution. If they were, we would also have evolved the ability to hold these two inclinations in balance. Instead, none of us experiences this equilibrium, because we are limited, finite beings created in the image of an unlimited, infinite God. We yearn for what we can't experience fully in our temporal lives and long for (either consciously or unconsciously) the *source* of objective truth and grace.

We press on, however, striving to express the fullness of God's nature as we seek the equilibrium for which we were designed. *We were created to balance justice and mercy.*

THE KILLER INSIDE

How to Be Honest about You So You Can
Give and Receive Forgiveness

Everyone is a moon, and has a dark side
which he never shows to anybody.
—MARK TWAIN

You can learn more about human nature by
reading the Bible than by living in New York.
—WILLIAM LYON PHELPS

N
o way. You've got the wrong guy . . . it's impossible."

Lieutenant Colonel Herman Dominguez pushed back from his broad desk and stared at us like we had lost our minds. Rick and I sat in two small chairs on the opposite side of his desk, attempting to notify Lt. Col. Dominguez that one of his closest friends was a killer.

Dominguez had the appearance of someone cast in a military movie. He possessed chiseled, sun-worn features and a stern expression, even when he smiled. He was an executive commander and battalion leader at the Marine Corps Base Camp Pendleton, about an hour south of our agency. He'd seen his share of action and was deployed several times in Fallujah, Iraq, and Afghanistan before being stationed here.

Our arrestee, Retired Master Gunnery Sergeant Randall King, served with Lt. Col. Dominguez at Camp Pendleton. They became *very* close friends. We arrested King earlier in the week and were now wrapping up our interviews to make sure we hadn't missed anything.

"I've supervised many Master Guns in my time, and I've never had one as capable as Randy. You must have the wrong guy." Lt. Col. Dominguez remained unconvinced. He stood up, walked to our side of the desk, and sat on its edge, directly in front of us. He was a huge man dressed sharply in a spotless uniform. Rick and I pretended to be unintimidated.

"Randy isn't just anyone, gentlemen. He earned a Silver Star and a DM . . . that's a Distinguished Service Medal. That puts him in rarified air. He had an outstanding career here for twenty-five years. And it's not just that . . . He's a genuinely good man. I know him personally. I can vouch for him."

"But did you know him thirty-two years ago?"

"No, of course not . . . we met right here at Camp Pendleton." Lt. Col. Dominguez folded his arms. He understood the implications of Rick's question.

"Look, we get it," Rick replied. "No one wants to believe their friends are capable of murder, but we see this all the time. People do the unthinkable, then spend the rest of their lives as though they didn't."

"That's true in almost every case we work," I added. "It's the nature of cold cases."

Our interview didn't last much longer. We left without any additional useful information and without convincing Lt. Col. Dominguez.

Rick and I were convinced, however. We spent nearly three years investigating Randall prior to his arrest, and the case against him was as solid as any we had ever assembled. He killed a coworker, Bruce Tapia, thirty-two years earlier, and although Randall was interviewed at the time of the murder, the first detectives didn't consider him a suspect. He appeared to be a good man, even then.

Despite appearances, however, Randall was the man who brutally stabbed Bruce in an alley behind a bar. For almost no reason at all.

EVIDENCE: Humans Are Paradoxical

Our increasingly humanistic culture highlights human altruism and compassion while minimizing human depravity and selfishness. From this perspective, humans are born innocent but may be corrupted by their environment. But our collective human experiences seem to tell a different story. Philosophers and thinkers have observed our propensity for evil (even at a very early age) in every culture and location on the globe.

How can we explain our enigmatic nature? Why does our explanation matter?

The Hard Truth about Our Dark Side

Rick and I conducted hundreds of cold case interviews over the years involving friends and family members of our arrestees. Seldom did anyone describe the killer in an unflattering way. This makes sense when you think about it. Killers who manage to stay undetected for decades are good at concealing their true nature. Randall was no exception.

In our first interview, prior to his arrest, Randall remained calm and confident. He was also incredibly gracious and warm. Rick and I met in the briefing room afterward, and Rick was clearly impressed.

"I actually *like* the guy."

"Yeah, me too, but that's how he *wants* us to feel," I replied. "He sounds like every other cold case suspect we've arrested, doesn't he?"

The more we investigated unsolved murders, the more suspicious Rick and I became, not just of murder suspects but of people generally. If killers can look and act like good people, how many other good people are capable of murder?

The answer? *All of us.*

Throughout human history, philosophers, theologians, psychologists, and casual observers have been trying to answer a fundamental question: Are humans innately good or bad? Are we born as noble beings or evil brutes? Most thinkers over the centuries believed we are innately selfish and inclined toward misbehavior. Famed philosopher Arthur Schopenhauer described it this way:

> "Man is at bottom a dreadful wild animal. We know this wild animal only in the tamed state called civilization and we are therefore shocked by occasional outbreaks of its true nature; but if and when the bolts and bars of the legal order once fall apart and anarchy supervenes it reveals itself for what it is. For enlightenment on this matter, though, you have no need to wait until that happens; there exist hundreds of reports, recent and less recent, which will suffice to convince you that man is in no way inferior to the tiger or the hyena in pitilessness and cruelty."[1]

Psychiatrist Carl Jung agreed with the sentiments of Schopenhauer, describing the dark side of human nature as an undeniable "shadow": "It's a frightening thought that man also has a shadow side to him, consisting not just of little weaknesses and foibles, but of a positively demonic dynamism. . . . Everyone carries a shadow, and the less it is embodied in the individual conscious life, the blacker and denser it is. . . . If it is repressed and isolated from consciousness, it never gets corrected."[2]

Psychiatrist Thomas Anthony Harris observed, "Sin, or badness, or evil, or 'human nature,' whatever we call the flaw in our species, is apparent in every person."[3] Similarly, philosopher Thomas Hobbes believed that humans, when left to "their own strength and their own invention," are destined to live "solitary, poor, nasty, brutish, and short" lives.[4]

You might think our innate inclination toward evil is rather self-evident, especially if you've raised children or remember your own early predispositions. Parents needn't teach their kids to be selfish, impatient, or rash. These are features of our *default* nature, and early studies into our propensity for evil confirmed just how "nasty" and "brutish" we can become.

In the 1960s, for example, psychologist Stanley Milgram conducted an experiment in which participants were told to administer electric shocks of increasing severity to another individual. The participants were unaware the shocks were counterfeit and the individual was an actor. Most of the participants obeyed the instructions and continued to apply the "electrical charges," even when the individual screamed in "pain."[5] Although this experiment came under intense scrutiny, its findings have since been replicated. Our capacity for cruelty remained the same in the replication, performed over forty years later.[6]

In 1971, Stanley Milgram's classmate, psychology professor Philip Zimbardo, conducted what is now known as the Stanford Prison Experiment. Zimbardo wanted to examine the behavior of people in a simulated prison environment. After building a mock prison with hidden microphones and cameras, he selected twenty-four undergraduate students, making sure none had any prior record of violence or mental illness. He then flipped a coin to see who would play the role of prisoner or guard. Although the experiment was supposed to last fourteen days, Zimbardo canceled it after only six. The students playing the role of guard became abusive and dehumanizing. The students playing the role of prisoner became submissive and displayed signs of excessive stress and anxiety.[7]

In both experiments, researchers confirmed our capacity for evil, even in students and volunteers who hadn't previously shown a propensity for violence. Their dark inclinations, like ours, lay hidden in the "shadows."

Modern studies continue to reveal that we are innately selfish creatures, even when cooperation and kindness could contribute to our well-being. Researchers find that when stress increases, resources are limited, and money is tight, our true nature emerges. In a pandemic, for example, we become hoarders of limited resources. We cheat others and serve ourselves, especially if no one is looking. "In highly stressful, resource-poor environments, we'll step on whoever is in front of us if it helps us survive."[8]

The more we believe we can exist without help from others, the more likely we are to return to our innately selfish nature. We isolate ourselves and become less caring, less involved, and less helpful.[9] Our inclination toward otherism (as described in chapter 9), leads us to dehumanize people who are different from us,[10] and this occurs early in our development.

One study discovered children as young as five years old are inclined to see some people as less than human, and that's not our only early predisposition.[11] According to clinical psychologist and psychoanalyst Jennifer Kunst, "We do not start out in innocence. We do not come into the world as blank slates, even when it comes to our capacity for goodness. . . . There is an urge in all of us to be naughty, to fight, to punish, to spoil, to take our revenge."[12]

This urge toward "naughtiness" can also be seen in our propensity to judge others more harshly than we judge ourselves. We are moral hypocrites, typically viewing our own misbehavior as less objectionable than the same misbehavior in others.[13] When *we* make a mistake, we blame it on a situation we couldn't control. When *others* make the same mistake, we attribute it to bad character.[14] Maybe that's why we typically assign some level of blame to people suffering misfortune, even before we know the relevant details of their situation.[15]

We quickly form bad impressions and stereotypes and then resist revising our views.[16] We stubbornly cling to our prideful beliefs and refuse to consider evidence to the contrary. Along the way, we usually think too highly of ourselves and overestimate our level of understanding.[17]

Our dark side is evident even in our attractions. If you're raising teenagers (or remember when you were a teenager), you've probably observed the popularity of "bad boys" (or "bad girls"). Studies confirm our attraction to people who possess the "dark triad" of traits: narcissism, psychopathy, and Machiavellianism. Rather than repel us, these traits often lay the foundation for "short-term mating success."[18] Men who display these traits are considered more attractive to women. We even favor *leaders* who demonstrate "psychopathic traits."[19] This data is revealing, given our innate self-interest and attraction toward people with whom we are similar (as described in chapter 9).

Our dark-side selfishness is obvious to those who lead us. Governmental leaders recognize "well-designed laws and public policies" as regulations that "harness *self-interest* for the common good" (emphasis mine).[20] Laws are necessary, precisely because of our innate predisposition toward evil. Governments *assume* we are selfish, for example, when they tax our incomes rather than trusting us to donate generously.

Religious systems also assume we are more concerned with ourselves than others. Jesus, for example, told his listeners, "As you wish that others would do to you, do so to them."[21] Jesus knew we think most highly of ourselves, and he harnessed our self-interest as an example of how to treat others. Scripture often encourages us to be patient, kind, and compassionate with others because these attributes are *not* part of our innate nature.

They weren't part of Randall's nature either, although Rick and I would never have guessed that from our first interview with him.

Randall denied harboring any animosity toward Bruce, even when we confronted him with statements from coworkers. Randall and Bruce were employed as warehouse stockers for a large furniture store in our city. On their first shift together, Bruce teased Randall about the size of his arms and his inability to lift a large box from the truck to the receiving dock. This occurred just prior to lunchtime and in the presence of many coworkers. Although Bruce apologized, his coworkers continued to tease Randall through the lunch period and for weeks afterward. Randall never spoke to Bruce again, even though they worked together often. Randall eventually quit and joined the Marine Corps.

Bruce was murdered a week before Randall signed his commitment papers.

The Motivation for Altruism

You might think someone capable of murder, especially over such a small matter as being publicly teased, would be hard pressed to conceal his angry impulses for the rest of his life. But Randall, according to everyone who knew him in the years that followed, did just that. For over thirty years, Randall displayed a sense of sacrifice, service, and compassion both on duty and off.

Our ability to elevate ourselves toward nobility (just as Randall did for many years) has also been the subject of much study. Modern researchers recognize "empathy-induced altruism [as] part of human nature."[22] For as many acts of evil we might observe in the news, just as many acts of bravery, sacrifice, and service are apparent in our daily lives.[23] Humans are capable of *both* extremes.

The real question, however, is this: Do we learn how to be good (because we are innately evil), or learn how to be evil (because we are innately good)? We certainly seem to have the capacity for decency and compassion, but researchers find we are "fickle about goodness."[24] Altruism seems rare, yet it is clearly an aspect of our nature, despite our propensity toward evil. How can this be the case?

Some historic philosophers and thinkers believed altruism was simply the product of self-interest. In Plato's *Republic*, for example, Socrates's older brother, Glaucon, claimed people acted nobly only when they selfishly feared being caught or punished for misbehavior.[25] Adam Smith, the father of economics, also believed many human efforts were connected to self-interest, writing, "It is not the benevolence of the butcher, the brewer, or the baker, that we expect our dinner, but from their regard to their own interest."[26]

EXAMPLE: King David

David, the boy who defeated the giant, Goliath, eventually became king of Israel. He was courageous, loyal, faithful, and successful in the eyes of God. The Bible describes him as "a man after [God's] own heart" (1 Samuel 13:14 ESV). Despite his capacity for good, David also committed adultery with Bathsheba, the wife of Uriah. When Bathsheba became pregnant, David tried to hide his sin by arranging for Uriah to be killed in battle (2 Samuel 11). The Bible is filled with paradoxical men and women capable of greatness but predisposed to evil.

Why do you think this is true? How can this truth help you effectively interact with others?

Many scientists also believe our selfish predisposition is the true cause of altruistic behavior. Famed atheist and evolutionary biologist Richard Dawkins, for example, believes "we are survival machines—robot vehicles blindly programmed to preserve the selfish molecules known as genes."[27] According to Dawkins, the "predominant quality" in our genetic code is "ruthless selfishness," and "this gene selfishness will usually give rise to selfishness in individual behavior."[28]

Despite this genetic inclination, Dawkins believes selfishness can be the catalyst for altruism: "Gene selfishness will usually give rise to selfishness in individual behaviour. However . . . there are special circumstances in which a gene can achieve its own selfish goals best by fostering a limited form of altruism at the level of individual animals."[29] Scientists who embrace the theory of psychological egoism concur. According to this theory, self-interest motivates all human behaviors such that "if [people] sometimes act for others, it is only because they think that it is in their own best interests to do so."[30]

Like many other scientists, Dawkins believes humans must *learn* to act altruistically in opposition to their genetic predispositions: "Be warned if you wish, as I do, to build a society in which individuals cooperate generously and unselfishly towards a common good, you can expect little help from biological nature. Let us try to teach generosity and altruism, because we are born selfish."[31]

Research confirms Dawkins's premise. Even though "self-interested behavior is alive and well," and we think of ourselves before others, we can still act altruistically.[32] Unselfishness is a learned behavior based on the fear of punishment or the desire for reward.[33] The more time we spend in community with others and the more we recognize the personal benefits of collaboration, the more we move from innate baseline selfishness toward *learned* cooperation.[34]

As a young man, Randall acted on his impulses, but as he lived in community as a Marine, he learned the benefit of altruism, sacrifice, and service. He was repeatedly rewarded for this behavior. He earned a Silver Star, was awarded a Distinguished Service Medal, and escaped the scrutiny of homicide detectives.

Until we served a search warrant.

 ## The Enigma of Man

After our interview with Randall, Rick and I developed enough probable cause to write a search warrant for his home. Randall had been retired from the military for several years and was living alone in the foothills of San Bernardino. His cottage residence was small but tidy. It also reflected the struggle he was having with the two sides of his nature.

Randall's kitchen looked like a drinker's laboratory. Three alcohol carousels sat on the longest counter. Each dispenser contained six bottles (varieties of whiskey, rum, and vodka), perched upside down with "pouring faucets" for each one. The rest of the counter was populated with cocktail syrups, mixers, shakers, and a variety of bar tools. The adjacent surface was covered in unwashed utensils and glasses.

The room was well stocked as a place to make drinks but poorly stocked as a place to prepare food. Randall's refrigerator was nearly empty, except for two frozen dinners. His cupboards were similarly bare. Randall's regular calorie consumption appeared to be little more than alcohol.

His living room was a stark contrast. Filled with bookshelves, it had barely enough room for a single recliner and an end table. No television, no music center, no radio. It looked more like a library than a living room. His collection caught my eye immediately: hundreds of Bible studies and personal journals filled each shelf. Randall also collected biblical commentaries and books on systematic theology. His Bible library was immediately next to the drinker's laboratory. One was pristine and orderly, the other sullied and chaotic, displaying Randall's Jekyll and Hyde nature.

And their secrets helped prove he was the killer.

Our propensity for evil and our capacity for altruism have been the subject of novelists over the centuries. The famous Robert Louis Stevenson novella, *The Strange Case of Dr. Jekyll and Mr. Hyde*, captures in fiction what researchers observe in reality. Stevenson's story describes the work of Dr. Jekyll, a kind scientist who experiments in the laboratory to expose his "second" nature, transforming himself into an evil alter ego named Mr. Hyde. The story probes the dualistic nature of humans, leading Dr. Jekyll to conclude, "I learned to recognise the thorough and primitive duality of man; I saw that, of the two natures that contended in the field of my consciousness, even if I could rightly be said to be either, it was only because I was radically both."[35]

This duality is classically referred to as the "enigma of man." The paradoxical nature of human behavior was described perfectly by Plato, who compared the human soul to a chariot pulled by two opposing horses, one representing the noble side of our nature, the other the evil.[36]

Randall successfully reined in his evil horse and kept it under control, at least publicly. But his strategy to harness the noble horse eventually gave him away as Bruce's killer.

Randall was interested in the Bible, even if he struggled to adhere to its teaching. His collection of biblical journals and Scripture studies was extensive. He kept years' worth of notes, carefully dating and cataloging them for future reference. He even had a study dated to the month of Bruce's murder. It examined Psalm 51, and Randall journaled several pages regarding the first two verses:

> Have mercy on me, O God,
>   according to your steadfast love;
> according to your abundant mercy
>   blot out my transgressions.
> Wash me thoroughly from my iniquity,
>   and cleanse me from my sin![37]

King David wrote this psalm after unjustly killing Uriah, one of his own elite soldiers. Randall underlined these two verses and included his personal notes and prayers in an accompanying journal. Related to this passage, Randall noted the passage in which David killed Uriah and wrote:

> 2 Samuel 11—murder murder murder
>   Please God, forgive me the way you did David

Not exactly a confession, but these simple sentences became part of our cumulative case at trial.

WE OFTEN BEHAVE VIRTUOUSLY

WE ARE INNATELY SELFISH, HOARDING, CHEATING, VENGEFUL, JUDGMENTAL, HYPOCRITICAL, STUBBORN, AND PRIDEFUL OTHERISTS WHO ARE QUICK TO BLAME OTHERS AS WE OVERESTIMATE OURSELVES. WE ARE ALSO ATTRACTED TO PEOPLE WITH EVIL TRAITS AND ARE MOTIVATED TO ABUSE THE PURSUIT OF SEX, MONEY, AND POWER

THE ENIGMA OF MAN

Chase the Lead

Randall's defense attorney, Sidney Arlington, was a conscientious public defender and someone I had known for several years. We liked each other.

During a break in the trial one day, he made an interesting statement in the hallway.

"I think I've represented hundreds of defendants over the years, and many of them were not good people. But this guy is different. He's a really great guy . . . super mild mannered . . . and honorable at the same time. I'm telling you, Jim, you got the wrong guy. He *couldn't* have done this."

Sidney reminded me of Lt. Col. Dominguez. Neither understood the enigma of man. But both changed their opinion of Randall within a month of the trial. After his conviction, Randall thought it pointless to continue the charade. He confessed first to Sidney, then to the judge. Randall's *noble horse* finally took the lead.

Adam Smith believed that "to feel much for others and little for ourselves . . . to restrain our selfish, and to indulge our benevolent affections, constitutes the perfection of human nature."[38] If you're ready to restrain your evil horse and indulge the one that's noble, consider taking these steps:

Devote Yourself to the Painful Truth

Sometimes the truth hurts, especially when it runs counter to the popular opinions of culture. In societies dominated by secular humanism, you can expect a collective effort to describe humans in the most flattering way possible. Many contemporary studies take this approach, highlighting humanity's capacity for good while concealing our propensity for evil. When evaluating the truth of our nature, consider the breadth of wisdom, both ancient and modern, demonstrating our evil predispositions. Become a good student, as did author Fyodor Dostoevsky, who in a letter to his brother observed, "Man is an enigma. This enigma must be solved, and if you spend all your life at it, don't say you have wasted your time; I occupy myself with this enigma because I wish to be a man."[39] Careful, truthful observation isn't a waste of time. You'll find many examples of our fallen proclivities if you simply devote yourself to searching for the truth.

Hope for the Best, Prepare for the Worst

During our interviews with Randall, we hoped he would simply tell us the truth. But given what I knew about human nature, I didn't count on it. Instead, Rick and I prepared for trial. Once you accept the enigma of man, holding your optimism and pessimism in balance is easier. I'm never surprised when "bad people" do the right thing, and I'm never disappointed when "good people" mess up. By adopting a brutally clear view of our innate nature, you'll begin to see the potential good in people who have disappointed you and the potential bad in people you were previously inclined to trust. A popular expression warns, "When you're wearing rose-colored glasses, all the red flags just look like flags."[40] Your glasses are less likely to be tinted if you embrace the truth about humans.

Resist an Overreliance on "Systems"

Political and social pundits often describe our cultural problems as "systemic," claiming issues such as racism, inequality, and bigotry are a product of corrupt *systems*. These kinds of claims pose an important question: Do wicked structures and systems corrupt humans who would otherwise be innately inclined toward virtue, or do wicked humans corrupt structures and systems because we are innately inclined toward evil? The answer is clear. Yes, systems can be designed to aid altruism, tolerance, and cooperation, but it would be foolish to believe we can eliminate human evil by simply exchanging a system. Governments, organizations, and structures recognizing the enigma of man and providing the strongest mechanisms by which to check, balance, and restrain the human propensity for evil will always be more successful than those that don't. In the end, however, humans will find a way to exploit *any* system for their own benefit. It's the consistent narrative of history.

Feed the Right Wolf

In most horse races, proper nourishment, training, and exercise determine the winner. The same is true of the noble and evil horses of human nature. A well-known Cherokee folk tale describes this truth with a different pair of animals. According to the story, a grandfather once told his grandson, "A fight is going on inside me. It is a terrible fight, and it is between two wolves. One is evil—he is anger, envy, sorrow, regret, greed, arrogance, self-pity, guilt, resentment, inferiority, lies, false pride, superiority, and ego. The other is good—he is joy, peace, love, hope, serenity, humility, kindness, benevolence, empathy, generosity, truth, compassion, and faith. The same fight is going on inside you—and inside every other person, too." When his grandson asked, "Which wolf will win?" his grandfather replied, "The one you feed."[41] It's important to exercise your *noble* horse. The right thing is often hard to do. That's why it's important to practice doing hard things.

Become a Better Forgiver

Understanding the truth about human nature is the key to becoming a more forgiving person. Wholly good people have no need for forgiveness. Unfortunately, there are no wholly good people. Instead, everyone requires forgiveness, not just for the things we might have done in the past but also for the things we will most certainly do in the future. As I described in chapter 6, the more you understand your own fallen nature, the more forgiving you will become of others. If you're strong enough to seek and offer forgiveness, you just may be able to restore the broken relationships in your life. As Gandhi observed, "The weak can never forgive. Forgiveness is the attribute of the strong."[42]

Seek an Explanation *and* a Solution

Philosophers, scientists, thinkers, and poets have correctly articulated the enigma of man, but their descriptions are merely diagnostic. They've *described* the problem without *prescribing* a solution. In fact, secular scientists and thinkers *can't* offer a solution, given the nature of their worldview. Dawkins, for example, illustrates the futility of trying to explain evil in a universe governed only by physics: "In a universe of electrons and selfish genes, blind physical forces and genetic replication, some people are going to get hurt, other people are going to get lucky, and you won't find any rhyme or reason in it, nor any justice. The universe that we observe has precisely the properties we should expect if there is, at bottom, no design, no purpose, no evil, no good, nothing but pitiless indifference."[43]

While atheism of this sort fails to offer a solution, Christianity both explains and resolves the problem we face as intrinsically fallen human beings. It would be foolish to seek *de*scriptions without appropriate *pre*scriptions. Seek an explanation *and* a solution so you can rise above "pitiless indifference."

The Truth in True Crime: We Were Created for Redemption

Christianity offers a unique solution, accounting for the nature of our past and present, even as it offers hope for our future. Dutch theologian Herman Bavinck described it well:

> Science cannot explain this contradiction in man. It reckons only with his greatness and not with his misery, or only with his misery and not with his greatness. It exalts him too high, or it depresses him too far, for science does not know of his Divine origin, nor of his profound fall. But the scriptures know of both, and they shed their light over man and over mankind; and the contradictions are reconciled, and the mists are cleared, and the hidden things are revealed. Man is an enigma, whose only solution can be found in God.[44]

The Scriptures "shed their light" on our problem long before it was discovered through research, and better yet, they offer a divine solution.

According to the Bible, God's original design for our planet was perfect. God declared his creation "good" no fewer than seven times in the first chapter of the Old Testament, and after creating humans, God declared his handiwork "*very* good" (emphasis mine).[45] As humans in the image of God, we were "fearfully and wonderfully made" with the capacity for altruism, compassion, and honor.[46]

Yet the first humans chose to rebel against God, and as a result, "sin came into the world through one man, and death through sin, and so death spread to all men because all sinned."[47] This "sin nature" is now our default position as we inherited it from Adam. Our hearts are "deceitful above all things and desperately sick," "for out of the heart . . . come evil thoughts, murder, adultery, sexual immorality, theft, false witness, [and] slander."[48] No one is exempt from this heart condition. No one.[49] Careful observation and contemporary research confirm this truth.

Christianity provides an ancient—and better—explanation for our enigmatic nature. It also provides a better solution.

Randall understood the Christian solution but hesitated to embrace it fully because any meaningful admission of guilt would result in his incarceration. Instead, he lived a continual lie and attempted to redeem himself after the murder. He entered the Marine Corps, served nobly, and became the kind of man no one would suspect of a homicide. His redemptive efforts were much like our own. We measure each other, trying to convince ourselves we're more virtuous than vile. We settle for "mostly good" and compare ourselves favorably to serial killers and habitual thieves. But we all know the truth. We are just as fallen as the Bible describes. We need redemption, and we can't redeem ourselves.

EXPLANATION: We Pervert God's Perfection

We recognize the nature of moral perfection because we were created in the image of an infinite, all-powerful, morally perfect God. But as finite creatures, we simply cannot consistently approach (much less achieve) this perfection.

In our limited, fallen nature, we fail more than we succeed, perverting the law of God to serve our selfish desires. We know this (either consciously or unconsciously) and recognize our need for forgiveness and redemption.

That's why Christians who read their Bible aren't surprised by human duplicity. We understand it, *expect* it, and embrace the solution for it. We know that rather than living in a "pitiless, indifferent" universe, as Dawkins described, we were created in the image of a God who sympathizes with our struggles and desires to redeem us. The salvation Jesus offered through his payment for our sins on the cross is a "free gift of God," and it includes forgiveness, redemption, and eternal life.[50]

The gospel is good news because as humans, we innately seek the restoration offered by a Creator whose fingerprints are on our soul. That's why—even as nonbelievers—we often seek temporal redemption by devoting ourselves to virtuous causes, committing to well-intended change, or promising to do better. We innately understand our need for forgiveness because we were created by the *source* of forgiveness. We long for restoration because *we were created for redemption.*

A GOOD GUILT TRIP

How to Harness the Force of Remorse

Guilt is a universal experience. . . . Even people who
deny that there is any such thing as right and wrong are
trapped by the law of God written on their hearts.
—JOHN PIPER

Guilt comes from within. Shame comes from without.
—VODDIE BAUCHAM

Wesley Myers confessed without changing his expression in the slightest. He never raised his voice, changed his tone, or altered his inflection. He calmly answered our questions while sitting next to Chad Mitchell, his seasoned defense attorney. Even Chad winced at several points during the interview, despite his vast experience with guilty killers.

Wesley, on the other hand, remained emotionless.

He described the way he murdered his neighbor like a math teacher explaining how to find a common denominator—impassive, detached, and factual. His description was even more disturbing given the way he killed Teresa Hodgkins. Rick and I will never forget the crime scene.

Wesley lived next door to Teresa, a friendly woman nearly twice his age. We interviewed Wesley after the murder, just as we routinely interviewed all of Teresa's neighbors. He was relaxed and emotionless during our conversation, so we were somewhat surprised when the DNA at the crime scene matched his profile. After we arrested Wesley, he continued to coolly deny any involvement, confidently claiming someone planted his DNA at the scene. We suspected otherwise, however, even though we still weren't sure how he got into Teresa's apartment or why he wanted to kill her in the first place.

Eleven months later, we were preparing to take the case to a jury. Given the nature of the murder, Wesley was facing the death penalty.

Chad Mitchell called my office just prior to the start of the trial with a proposition. Wesley was willing to plead guilty to first degree murder and accept a sentence of life in jail without the possibility of parole if we would drop the death penalty enhancement. Rick and I talked with the prosecutor to evaluate our options. We agreed to the plea deal but required Wesley to give us a final interview in which he would tell us the truth about how—and why—he murdered Teresa.

Twenty minutes into the confession, our questions were answered. Wesley's description of the murder was *shameless*. He was the first true psychopath Rick and I had ever encountered.

"That was the most chilling monster we've interviewed," Rick said as we packed up the camera and digital recorder.

Wesley's wife, Rachel, was waiting for us in the hall. When Wesley was first arrested, Rachel hoped the DNA evidence would prove inaccurate, but because of his detached personality, she feared otherwise. Once she heard about his confession, she broke down in tears.

"It's scary. I feel like I should be shocked he did this . . . but, but, I'm not really."

The contrast between Wesley and Rachel was striking. Rachel appeared more ashamed she had been *married* to a killer than Wesley did for *being* a killer.

"I'm so sorry. I'm so, so . . . sorry."

"Why? Did he tell you he killed Teresa?" I asked.

"No, no, never. He doesn't tell me much about anything, really."

"Then why are you sorry?"

Rachel struggled to answer. "I, I don't know. I just feel so . . . *stupid* . . . embarrassed, I guess."

Rick and I did our best to console Rachel, but we both wondered how she had ever been attracted to her husband.

Back at the station, we watched the confession a second time. Then a third. Neither of us had ever encountered a killer with less remorse nor felt better about locking someone up for the rest of his life. Wesley was dangerously indifferent.

Rick and I still talk about this case. Sometimes it's about the confession. But most of the time, it's about what Wesley did *two years later*.

Conflating Shame and Guilt

Wesley displayed one of the classic attributes of psychopathy: shamelessness.[1] The value of shame is often debated. Is it good or bad? As an experience, shame is certainly unpleasant. But was Wesley's lack of shame a *good* thing?

Part of the confusion about shame is its relationship to guilt. These two terms are frequently mistaken for one another. Compare, for example, these dictionary definitions:

> a feeling of worry or unhappiness that you have because you have done something wrong, such as causing harm to another person[2]

> an uncomfortable feeling that you get when you have done something wrong or embarrassing, or when someone close to you has.[3]

They sound like definitions for the same feeling, but the first is a definition of guilt, the second of shame. If you didn't know better, you might think there was no important distinction between guilt and shame. But that's not true. Shame is related to guilt, but from the perspective of psychology, there is a critical difference.

While both guilt and shame are self-conscious emotions, guilt is "characterized by a painful appraisal of having done (or thought) something that is wrong and often by a readiness to take action designed to undo or mitigate this wrong."[4] Shame, on the other hand, is described as "a highly unpleasant self-conscious emotion arising from the sense of there being something dishonorable, immodest, or indecorous in one's own conduct *or circumstances*" (emphasis mine).[5] Shame often involves a concern over how one is *perceived*, rather than what one has *done*.[6] As psychologist Paul Ekman describes, "No audience is needed for feelings of

EVIDENCE: Humans Struggle with Guilt and Shame

Shame and guilt are unpleasant "self-conscious" emotions. We struggle when we experience them and wonder if the human species wouldn't be better off without such debilitating feelings. Worse yet, we sometimes feel shame even when we haven't done anything *worthy* of shame.

Why haven't humans progressed past these negative, self-destructive emotions? Is it possible these emotions might benefit us, and if so, how?

guilt, no one else need know, for the guilty person is his own judge. Not so for shame. The humiliation of shame requires disapproval or ridicule by others. If no one ever learns of a misdeed there will be no shame, but there still might be guilt."[7]

It's possible to feel shame and guilt at the same time, but this isn't always the case. Wesley, for example, admitted his guilt in Teresa's murder, even though he felt no shame. Rachel felt shame, even though she wasn't guilty of anything. Shame and guilt are clearly different, and you can feel one without feeling the other.

Guilt is *action* focused. Shame is *person* focused. Researchers who study the two emotions believe "shame is about the self" while "guilt is about things in the real world—acts or failures to act, events for which one bears responsibility."[8] As counselor John Bradshaw observed, "Guilt says I've *done* something wrong; shame says there *is* something wrong with me. Guilt says I've *made* a mistake; shame says I *am* a mistake. Guilt says what I *did* was not good; shame says I *am* no good."[9]

Guilt and shame are not just different by definition, they are also neurologically distinct. Researchers find that "guilt and shame share certain neural networks, but their patterns are very different. When your actions collide with your conscience, you feel guilty. When we believe we have harmed our reputation, shame is triggered."[10] Because guilt and shame are part of human nature and are processed biologically, researchers have found they're part of the universal human experience, regardless of race, ethnicity, or sex.[11]

Guilty people struggle with what *they've done*, shameful people struggle with *who they are* (or how they are perceived). The distinction is important because our response to guilt or shame matters. These emotions can destroy or restore us, depending on our ability to recognize the difference and react appropriately.

Rachel is a good example.

 ## The Shame about Shame

Between Wesley's arrest and plea agreement, the local news media contacted Rachel. They hounded her for several weeks until they caught her coming home from the grocery store. She reluctantly gave them a brief interview on the sidewalk in front of her apartment. She regretted it immediately.

By the time she was interviewed, the media had already constructed an unbecoming (albeit true) profile of Wesley. They were now interested in Rachel and suspicious that she either helped Wesley conceal the crime or failed to alert police about his dangerous nature. Their report sounded more like an accusatory opinion piece than a neutral interview.

Rachel spiraled. Growing up, she made several poor choices, dabbled with drugs and shoplifting, and eventually severed relationships with her family when she married. Rachel now realized Wesley was yet another poor decision. The massive, negative public attention she received only compounded her guilt and shame.

When people enter a state of *shame*, they often view themselves as habitual, fundamentally flawed, unredeemable mess-ups rather than simply feeling *guilty* for having made a mistake. Rachel adopted this shame-based perspective and considered herself defective. She retreated from her friends and family members, and when she did interact with people, she hid her true feelings and opinions for fear of further humiliation. Rachel became a different person entirely.

Researchers refer to shame as a maladaptive emotion, and studies reveal the way in which it changes us. People who feel shame, for example, are more likely to avoid eye contact than people who feel guilt.[12] Like Rachel, they struggle with self-esteem, conceal what they consider to be "personal flaws," and drink or medicate more often to hide from or escape their self-perception.[13] People who experience shame often avoid interaction with others due to their perception of "diminished social standing."[14]

Shame often drives people to experience deep depression, anxiety, and difficulty sleeping.[15] It can cause us to spiral into destructive behaviors like eating disorders, substance abuse, physical aggression, and forms of self-injury.[16] Shame can even lead us to sabotage our own efforts. One study found that shame motivated people to avoid studying for a test so that when they failed, they could avoid feeling like a failure by telling themselves it was simply because they failed to study (rather than because they were intrinsic failures).[17]

These negative consequences of shame have an even more detrimental impact on young people. A longitudinal study involving fifth graders found that kids who experience shame will eventually have more sexual partners, use more drugs, and get in more trouble with the law.[18]

Shame often accompanies lawbreaking. People who commit crimes usually carry a sense of guilt and shame, fearing that their criminal activity now defines them as criminals. That's why the Teresa Hodgkins case seemed so paradoxical. Wesley was guilty of the criminal act but felt no shame as a criminal. Rachel wasn't guilty of anything yet felt the shame of being associated with a criminal.

Shame is clearly destructive, especially when it isn't earned. It's possible to experience shame when you haven't done something *worthy* of shame. Some of us are ashamed of our appearance, our weight, our neighborhood, or our economic status. Some people even feel shame based on the way they were raised, especially if shamed by their parents. Others experience shame for things completely beyond their control.

Carl Jung is famously quoted as saying, "Shame is a soul eating emotion."[19] Rachel understood this firsthand. Shame devoured her and separated her from friends and family.

Two years after his confession, Wesley contacted Chad Mitchell and asked him to call us. He told Chad he had additional information involving a potential accomplice. He was willing to tell us who helped him kill Teresa in exchange for a visit with Rachel. Rick and I discussed it with the district attorney and decided to hear what Wesley had to offer.

Three of us drove to the California Correctional Institution in Tehachapi. The third person in our car wasn't Rachel, however. Instead, the deputy district attorney came along, as Rachel refused to make the trip. In the two years since Wesley was imprisoned, Rachel found a remedy for her shame. Her new life didn't include Wesley, and she wasn't going to make an exception for this visit.

Her decision was a wise one. It ended up saving her life.

 ## The Good Thing about Guilt

Wesley's case manager met us when we arrived at Tehachapi. He told us this was Wesley's second prison assignment since his conviction. In his first placement, he murdered a cell mate. He was immediately transferred to Tehachapi, a maximum-security facility.

We entered the prison interview room to find Wesley waiting calmly, seated at a table with three empty chairs. He was shackled loosely with a belly chain. His cuff chains were long enough to shake our hands if he so desired. He didn't. And although his expression was emotionless at first, it changed quickly when he saw the deputy district attorney.

"Where's Rachel?"

"She wasn't able to come.. . ." Rick tried to respond calmly.

"You said you were going to bring her!" Wesley showed an anger we hadn't yet seen. His facial expression twisted, and he immediately stood up from his chair.

"You lied to me!" I could hear the door opening behind me as Wesley lunged toward us from the opposite side of the table. The guards ran into the room and restrained him as the three of us stepped back from the table. Wesley was ushered back to his cell.

As we were escorted out, one of the guard supervisors showed us what they discovered in Wesley's sock. Three wooden pencils taped firmly together and sharpened as a single object—crude but potentially effective.

"I think he was hoping to kill one of you guys," said the supervisor.

Rick and I looked at each other. We were thinking the same thing.

"No, he was hoping to kill *Rachel*."

Wesley learned about Rachel's remedy for her shame when she served him with divorce papers shortly after he was incarcerated. Prior to his arrest, Rachel and Wesley lived next door to a local church. She visited it for the first time the Sunday after her interview with the media. Rachel was at her lowest and ready to hear the truth about her identity and the difference between guilt and shame.

She had been confusing the two emotions for years, just like many contemporary thinkers and authors. Consider, for example, the following popular descriptions of guilt:

Guilt is the worst enemy of true happiness and self-esteem. It is indeed the worst thing you can ever do to your soul.[20]

Guilt is a destructive and ultimately pointless emotion.[21]

Guilt steals our joy, hinders our productivity, interrupts our peace, harms our relationships, and worst of all, makes us self-focused.[22]

Guilt is a useless feeling. It's never enough to make you change direction— only enough to make you useless.[23]

While some of these quotes effectively describe *shame*, they don't confirm the findings of psychologists and researchers who study *guilt*. Guilt is considered a "moral and adaptive emotion," while shame has been described as the "darker side of moral effect."[24] Why the difference?

According to psychologists, guilt appears when we break our personal or societal moral codes. Unlike shame, which focuses on the *person*, guilt allows us to identify and modify problematic *behaviors*. Author Gretchen Rubin says, "Emotions like loneliness, envy, and guilt have an important role to play in a happy life; they're big, flashing signs that something needs to change."[25] Researchers continue to find that guilt benefits us, especially when compared with shame.

The advantages of guilt are seen early in human development. Guilt, rather than shame, motivates children to correct a wrong or restore a broken relationship. Guilt plays "a mechanistic role in the development of prosocial behavior in becoming a key aspect of children's conscience."[26] Some researchers have even described guilt as "the guardian of our goodness."[27] Adolescents raised to feel guilt without shame show less delinquency and depression as older teens.[28]

When we feel guilty about our behavior, we are more likely to correct it.[29] Guilt prompts us to manage our anger and think more deeply about our actions, especially as they impact others.[30] For this reason, guilt "functions as a relationship enhancer," leveraging "repair-oriented behaviors" that can help us *restore* our relationships rather than *withdraw* in shame.[31] This is particularly true between close friends or family members.[32]

According to researchers, there is also a surprising connection between guilt and empathy. Though shame disrupts empathy, "feelings of guilt go hand in hand with other-oriented empathy."[33] Studies reveal that guilt and empathy provide pathways to cooperation and sharing. For example,

EXAMPLE: The Woman of the City

Jesus once attended a dinner party at the home of a Pharisee (Luke 7:36–50). A "woman of the city," known to be a "sinner," gained entry when she heard Jesus would be present. Because she recognized all she had done wrong, her guilt drove her to seek forgiveness from the one through whom "all things were made" (John 1:3). She wept and anointed Jesus's feet. Jesus understood her need for restoration and said to her, "Your sins are forgiven."

Guilt drives us to repair relationships and our standing within the community. The "woman of the city" is another excellent example of this truth.

"kids who are low in sympathy (or empathy) may make up for that shortfall by experiencing more guilt, which can rein in their nastier impulses." This observation led one researcher to say, "Schools and programs have almost exclusively focused on empathy promotion. I think it's incredibly important to nurture empathy, but I think it's equally important to promote guilt."[34] When kids feel *appropriate* guilt for things they've *done*, rather than *inappropriate* shame for who they *are*, they propel themselves toward better behavior.

This is true for all of us, regardless of age. When humans leverage guilt to acknowledge wrongdoing, correct bad behavior, and restore relationships, we flourish.

Rachel embraced the remedy for shame and harnessed the power of guilt while attending the church next to her apartment. She stopped responding to Wesley's letters and demands. As she grew stronger and more confident, Wesley grew more desperate. His lie about an accomplice was simply another shameless effort.

A MALADAPTIVE EMOTION THAT LOWERS SELF-ESTEEM, TRANSPARENCY, AND SELF-CONTROL, CAUSING PEOPLE TO DRINK AND MEDICATE MORE, EXPERIENCE MORE DEPRESSION, ENGAGE IN MORE EATING DISORDERS, SUBSTANCE ABUSE, SELF-INJURY, AGGRESSION, AND RISKY BEHAVIOR

AN ADAPTIVE EMOTION THAT HELPS IDENTIFY BAD BEHAVIOR, PROMPTS CORRECTION, ENCOURAGES PRO-SOCIAL BEHAVIOR, RESTORATION, EMPATHY, AND BETTER RELATIONSHIPS WHILE REDUCING DELINQUENCY AND DEPRESSION

SHAME   GUILT

Chase the Lead

Rachel called our office a week after the trip to Tehachapi to report a threatening letter from Wesley. I assured her Wesley would never be released from custody, but Rachel wasn't seeking reassurance. She simply wanted to document and add the threat to Wesley's growing file. Rachel had a renewed sense of peace about her past and her future. Rachel was flourishing.

Her new life reflected an accurate understanding of shame and guilt. If you've ever struggled to navigate these two emotions or to overcome the challenges they present, here are a few suggestions:

Separate the Individual from the Indiscretion

If you're struggling with shame or guilt, take the time to determine which emotion you're experiencing. "Do I feel bad about *what I've done*, or do I feel bad about *me*?" Remember, people who do bad things aren't automatically unredeemable. Identify your struggle so you can *embrace your guilt* and *reject your shame*.

Embrace Guilt's Accountability

Guilt can be incredibly productive if you leverage it to restore relationships and become a better person. Connect your feelings of guilt to the specific actions causing these emotions. Rather than denying what you've done, excusing your actions, or blaming others, allow your feelings of guilt to motivate you to admit wrongdoing. Gandhi once correctly observed, "It is wrong and immoral to seek to escape the consequences of one's acts."[35] When we acknowledge our errors, we allow guilt to work its magic on our character.

Reject Shame's Identity

Shame results from how we perceive *ourselves* or what we believe about how *others* perceive us. If we're not careful, perceptions can define our identity. That's another reason why it's important to resist outside-in or inside-out identity formation (as described in chapter 2). When we embrace a topside-down identity, we stop listening to temporal, fallen voices and listen, instead, to the One who created us and has the power and authority to forgive us.

Embrace Guilt's Response

When Wesley was convicted of Teresa's murder, he received something in addition to a life sentence. He was also ordered to pay a restitution fine to the State Restitution Fund. The judge did this, even without considering Wesley's ability (or inability) to pay the fine. Why? Because restitution is a critical aspect of restorative justice. Guilt should drive all of us to seek restoration through restitution, regardless of the level of our offense. Once you've admitted your error, do everything you can to right the wrong. Sometimes this is as simple as asking, "What can I do to make it right?" "How can I make amends?" or "What can I do to fix this?"

Reject Shame's Arrogance

Pride is at the root of shame because shame is inextricably connected to our perception and reputation. Dutch philosopher Bernard Mandeville understood the relationship when he wrote, "Do but increase a man's pride, and his fear of shame will ever be proportioned to it; for the greater value a man sets upon himself, the more pains he will take, and the greater hardships he will undergo to avoid shame."[36] When we humbly adopt and accept a realistic view of our own limited nature, we diminish the power shame has to destroy us.

Embrace Guilt's Guidance

Guilt for *past behavior* can often guide us to better *future conduct*. If you've touched a hot frying pan, you're likely to be more careful the next time you use one. Guilt can serve as a cautionary emotion as we evaluate poor past choices and a catalyst when we evaluate better future choices. Leadership author John C. Maxwell describes it this way: "Life is a matter of choices, and every choice you make makes you."[37] Allow guilt to guide you to better choices and a better you.

Reject Shame's Trajectory

Shame and guilt are described as self-conscious emotions that share certain neural networks even though they eventually follow distinct neurological pathways.[38] When we reconsider our feelings of shame and redeem our feelings of guilt, we effectively change the path of our emotions. Instead of landing on *who we are*, they land on *what we've done*. When we refocus from shame to guilt, we adopt a better trajectory. We point our emotions toward restoration.

When Rachel heard the gospel for the first time, she finally understood the relationship between guilt and shame. She realized she was feeling appropriate guilt for the mistakes of her past but inappropriate shame for her relationship with Wesley. The gospel addressed both issues. In seeking the forgiveness of God through the work of Jesus on the cross, she allowed her guilt to guide her to a new life. By embracing a new identity in Christ, she exchanged shame for righteousness and reconciliation.

Rachel flourished as she became a new creation.[39] She restored her relationships with her family and started a new life in Christ.

The Truth in True Crime: You Were Created for Restoration

Modern researchers no longer consider guilt an obsolete, destructive, religious concept. Instead, they now concur completely with the ancient authors of the Bible. Guilt *aids* human flourishing, just as the Christian worldview has always claimed.

The Bible recognizes the power of guilt and our universal need for restoration. According to Scripture, all humans are morally guilty because of our fallen, innate propensity for evil, and this is especially obvious when compared with God's perfect moral standard.[40] "All have sinned and fall short of the glory of God."[41] We sin without even trying, sometimes by simply failing to do what we ought.[42] Voltaire, the French writer and philosopher, captured this truth: "Every man is guilty of all the good he did not do."[43] That's why guilt and shame are such common human emotions. Our shared fallenness leads to a shared need for forgiveness and restoration.

The Bible recognizes this need, the role of guilt, and the terrible cost of shame.[44] According to the authors of Scripture, Satan, the father of lies, accuses and reminds us of our sin to shame us until we feel utterly unredeemable. He leverages our shame to keep us from experiencing the restorative power of guilt.[45] Guilt and shame, without remedy, are described as a soul-crushing experience.[46]

But God offers a plan of restoration to relieve our pain and leverage our guilt.[47]

Rather than chide or shun us in disgust, he "is merciful and gracious, slow to anger and abounding in steadfast love."[48] God will eventually eliminate Satan and the shame he creates.[49] In the meantime, as the highest moral authority in the universe, God offers to remove our guilt, forgive our mistakes, and restore us from the destructive effects of shame. His promise of salvation "blots out [our] transgressions"[50] as he "remember[s] [our] sins and [our] lawless deeds no more."[51]

All we have to do is accept his offer.

Modern researchers now believe guilt becomes a catalyst for restoration and human flourishing *if* we admit what we've done, ask for forgiveness, and seek a remedy. This truth is also on the ancient pages of Scripture. According to the Bible, our guilty consciences draw us to the forgiveness of God, and his forgiveness restores our joy.[52] If we confess our sin, God faithfully and justly forgives and cleanses us from guilt, shame, and unrighteousness.[53]

Our new identity in Christ then frees us from shame as we are delivered from the domain of darkness and transferred to the kingdom of God's beloved Son.[54] There is no condemnation for those who are in Christ Jesus, because anyone who believes in him embraces and adopts the identity of Jesus, the perfect, blameless Son of God.[55]

Forgiven people, once freed from shame, are also free to seek remedy and restoration, just as researchers describe. This is especially true for those who seek the forgiveness of God. According to the Bible, if anyone is in Christ, he is a new creation; the old has passed away, and the new has come.[56] Forgiven Christians become part of a holy nation, a people for God's own possession, empowered by the Holy Spirit to love others, seek restoration, and live a new life.[57]

Our common human experiences of guilt and shame are not evolutionary accidents. They are restorative *design features*. Our guilt leads us to the transcendent, just, and merciful *source* of forgiveness. Our shame guides us to the true, defining, and loving source of our identity. Guilt and shame are simply symptoms in search of a cure, clues in need of an investigation. They call us to be good detectives because *we were created for restoration.*

EXPLANATION: Guilt and Shame Drive Us to Restoration

We experience guilt and shame because we were created in the image of God, with knowledge of his perfect moral character. We know what we ought to do, even when we fail to do it. As a result, we experience shame or guilt—or both.

We were designed to experience these emotions because they find their resolution in our Creator. These emotions are clues planted in our nature by a God who knows they will eventually lead us home.

Guilt and shame sound an alarm when we stray from our Maker. He uses them to call us back into relationship.

WHAT GANGSTERS HAVE IN COMMON

How to Know Your Father, Even If You Don't Know Your Father

Noble fathers have noble children.

—EURIPIDES

The rights of a father are sacred rights
because his duties are sacred duties.

—M. R. BRETT

O fficer Mike Stovall rolled down the passenger window as we approached a group of teenage gangsters sitting in lawn chairs in a front yard on the north side of town. Neighbors called to report the group, although these young men weren't really causing a disturbance. Unless, of course, you considered their *appearance* disturbing.

Each member was heavily tattooed and wearing attire popularized by Hispanic gangs in Los Angeles County. But the residents in this quiet, law-abiding neighborhood weren't used to this display of gang identity. They were afraid something bad was about to happen.

As members of the gang detail, Mike and I didn't need the address. We already knew it was Oso's grandmother's house.

Javier Maldonado was a large, seventeen-year-old member of one of East Los Angeles's oldest Hispanic gangs. They called him Oso (Bear) from an early age, and by the time he was fifteen, he'd been in and out of trouble many times. His mother was at her wit's end, and without a father in the home, she decided to send Oso to his grandmother's house in a neighbor-hood far from his gang.

He'd been living here for almost two years, and Mike and I knew him *very* well.

Mike was the senior member of our gang detail, and I had been his partner for the past two years. He was younger and single. I was married with two young boys.

Mike understood gang culture. He was experienced and closer to the age of these gang members. Mike was also raised in a part of the county where gang activity was common. And he had relatives involved in gangs. Mike spoke their language, shared many of their interests, and listened to their music.

When we drove up to the front yard, he casually hopped out of the unit, walked through the cluster of gang members, and approached the large young man standing on the porch.

"Oso, how's it hangin', homeboy?"

I cringed. Mike and I were about as different as two partners could be. As members of this detail, we responded to every call for service involving a gang member, investigated the reports involving gang activity, and made the lion's share of gang-related arrests. We knew the local gangsters by name, and we were familiar with their backstories.

Mike built relationships by talking to them as one would talk to a famil-iar friend. He often sounded like a gangster himself. My approach was very different. I knew from the start I could never blend in as Mike had. I didn't look the part, and I felt foolish trying to pretend.

My relationships with these young men were paternal.

"Hey, Javier," I said, once Mike was done greeting him. "You can only imagine what the neighbors are thinking with everyone on the lawn like this."

"Yeah, I get it . . ."

"How's Grandma doing?" I visited Carmela nearly every time I stopped to see Javier. She was getting on in years and seldom came outside. I knew she was incredibly important to Javier. Carmela's love for him mattered even more than the admiration of his peers.

"She's doing good, Wallace . . . doing good. You wanna talk to her?"

"No, I don't want to bother her, and I don't really want your grandma to know her neighbors are concerned." I gestured to the young men sitting in the yard. "Let's take this party to the back yard, OK?"

Javier paused. He looked back toward the open door to his grand-mother's house.

"You know, they didn't tell me they were comin'." I knew this was true, based on my past interaction with Javier. He wasn't the same boy he was two years ago. He was surprisingly reflective for his age. He was also *teachable*.

"I'll ask 'em to leave," he said in a whisper. "But I'm gonna blame it on you guys."

"No problem, son. I appreciate you. Everything else OK with you?"

"Yeah, but I'm broke."

"What's up with the GED?"

"Almost done."

Mike entered the contact in our log as we waited for Javier's crew to disperse. We handled four or five other calls that day, and although they all involved gang members, the groups were very different. Our city was diverse, and our gang problem transcended racial, cultural, and socioeconomic boundaries. The gang members we investigated were white, Black, Hispanic, and Korean. Some came from wealthy neighborhoods, some from impoverished segments of our community.

But they shared one thing in common with Javier.

 ## The Common Denominator

As a father myself, I wanted to understand what caused young men like Javier to become gang members. Considering my experience with these diverse groups, the cause didn't seem entirely attributable to race, culture, or economic status. The answer crystallized when Mike told me about a movie he watched.

"Dude, you need to see this. It's called Boyz in the Hood."

"Really? Like we don't get to see gangsters every day?"

"No, this is different. You might learn something."

Mike was my senior officer, so I interpreted his polite recommendation as a partner requirement. Susie and I watched the movie on VHS tape the following weekend.

Boyz n the Hood traces the lives of three young men as they grow up in the Crenshaw district of Los Angeles.[1] The movie engages many important issues related to race, justice, poverty, and violence, but the scenes between the lead character, Tre Styles, and his father, Furious Styles, are particularly poignant.

In one of the early scenes, Tre's mother, Reva, drives Tre to his father's house. Reva is frustrated with Tre's increasingly rebellious behavior and her inability, as a single mother, to reign him in. Reva tells Furious it's *his* turn to raise Tre: "I can't teach him how to be a man."[2] Furious accepts the responsibility and welcomes Tre into his home in the Crenshaw district, an area saturated with gang activity.

Tre's father personifies tough love, immediately assigning Tre numerous chores designed to teach him discipline, structure, and responsibility. Tre's new friends aren't quite sure what to think. One tells Tre, "D——, your Daddy mean. He worse than the bogeyman himself. You got to do all these chores. Who do he think you is?"[3]

Although Furious may appear authoritarian to Tre's friends, there's a method to his "madness." One day, when Tre is frustrated with his father's demands and expectations, Furious points to the gang members across the street. "You may think I'm being hard on you right now, but I'm not. What I'm doing is I'm trying to teach you how to be responsible. Like your little friends across the street, they don't have anybody to show them how to do that. They don't. And you're gonna see how they end up too."[4]

I watched that scene and the lightbulb came on. Every gangster I'd met so far, and every gang member I encountered afterward, suffered from the same malady:

Lack of dad.

It was as simple as that. "Lack of dad" looked different, depending on the gang member I encountered. Some never knew their fathers because their mothers weren't sure who got them pregnant. Others had fathers who committed crimes and were sentenced to long prison terms. Several gangsters had fathers who were uninvolved alcoholics or drug addicts. Some had immigrant fathers who worked incredibly long hours, never learned English, and seldom monitored their kids.

The *reason* didn't matter. The *results* appeared the same. The fathers were absent, and their kids seemed rudderless.

This should be concerning to us, especially in America where we have the "world's highest rate of children living in single-parent households."[5] According to the US Census Bureau, 18.4 million children (that's one in four, nationally) live without a biological, step-, or adoptive father in their home.[6] Nearly 80 percent of the approximately 11 million single-parent homes are headed by single mothers.[7] Around half of these single mothers have never been married, almost a third are divorced, and just under a fifth are separated or widowed.[8]

When polled, Americans understand the growing dilemma, citing fatherlessness as the most significant problem facing our country.[9]

"Lack of dad" has been an increasingly disturbing phenomenon for several generations now. Many years ago, the president of the United States addressed the issue in a speech at a church in Chicago, saying,

> Of all the rocks upon which we build our lives, we are reminded today that family is the most important. And we are called to recognize and honor how critical every father is to that foundation. They are teachers and coaches. They are mentors and role models. They are examples of success and the men who constantly push us toward it. But if we are honest with ourselves, we'll admit that too many fathers also are missing—missing from too many lives and too many homes. They have abandoned their responsibilities, acting like boys instead of men. And the foundations of our families are weaker because of it.[10]

Boyz n the Hood captured this reality for an entire generation of moviegoers, and it's only gotten statistically worse. Men are less interested in children than ever before. According to one study, "A growing share of childless men do not want children and increasingly, a lack of children would not bother them at all."[11] Many of the gang members I encountered had fathers who were entirely uninterested in kids, even though *they already had them.*

Javier was an excellent example of what happens when dads aren't available for their kids. His father was incarcerated on a life sentence when he was three years old, and by the time his mother sent him to live with Carmela, his grandfather had passed. Javier's male role models were the older boys in his neighborhood.

And one of those boys would eventually put Javier in a tight spot.

EVIDENCE: Fathers Aid Human Flourishing

Fathers are essential to human flourishing in every culture and every region of the world. While many of us were raised without the presence of an interactive, loving father, it can hardly be argued we wouldn't have benefited from such a paternal influence.

Given the relationship between fathers and human flourishing, why do you think fatherlessness seems to be increasing?

Fathers Matter (Even Today)

Modern views of parenting often minimize the distinctions between mothers and fathers, arguing that family structure doesn't really matter if kids are loved and cared for. Some modern researchers deny the extraordinary importance of fathers altogether. But no matter how researchers structure, collect, or study the data, "lack of dad" *does* account for much of what ails us as a society.[12]

Why, then, does the scholarly debate remain? Does family structure really matter, or can *any* form of family accomplish what mothers and fathers achieve *together*? One major study, when examining this question, found that most scholars still believe family structure matters and efforts to claim otherwise are based on "arguments, rhetorical devices, and modes of data interpretation . . . so unconventional and contrary to accepted 'best practices' that ideological bias is the only reasonable explanation for them."[13] Fathers matter, even though some scholars, for ideological reasons, may try to deny this truth.

Dads and moms parent differently, and many of these differences are driven by our biochemistry. Parents influenced by testosterone interact one way, parents influenced by estrogen, another.[14] "Involved fathers—especially biological fathers—bring positive benefits to their children that no other person is as likely to bring."[15]

When fathers live with their children, the kids flourish. Why? Because fathers who live in the home spend much more time in the presence of their kids, and more time means more opportunities for involvement.[16] Most fathers understand this yet confess they are less involved than they should be. When polled, dads are much more likely than moms to say they don't spend enough time with their kids, and even when they *are* present, fathers don't believe they're doing enough as a parent.[17]

I felt the same way, especially after watching *Boyz n the Hood*.

"Lack of dad" became my primary concern. In my assignment to the gang detail, then later as a member of our SWAT, surveillance, and homicide teams, I was away from home far more than I care to admit. Murderers have no respect for holidays, birthdays, or special occasions. I was often investigating a homicide on my family's most important days. "Lack of dad" has many causes and *none of them matter*. A workaholic father can be just as absent as an alcoholic father, and both forms of absenteeism can lead to the same result.[18]

Javier longed for a relationship with his father, just like other members of his gang did.

I made it a point to visit him at least once a week, stopping to say hello to Carmela and see what Javier was up to. We would sit on his porch and talk for over an hour if there were no other calls holding. About three months into my routine, I noticed Javier had more questions for me than I did for him.

Javier had fallen in love with a girl, Margarite. She lived four doors down, and her parents were not happy about her new love interest. But Margarite saw something in Javier: a sense of unexpected, thoughtful maturity. Margarite was not raised like Javier. She was an only child. Her parents expected her to graduate at the top of her class and pursue a nursing degree, and she was not about to compromise her plans or her expectations for a boyfriend. Javier had a choice to make.

"So, Wallace, what would you do if you were me?"

I was the parent of elementary aged boys, so Javier's teenage question stretched my paternal wisdom.

"Margarite is a pretty amazing girl," I replied. "She deserves a good man . . ." Javier nodded. "So become a good man."

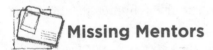 **Missing Mentors**

When I was nearly at the end of my rotation in the gang detail, a shooting occurred, just a hundred yards from Javier's house. Two men in a tan Chevy Impala shot a teenage boy walking on the street. When Mike and I heard the call, I feared Javier was the victim. He was, after all, the only gang member who lived within a mile of the shooting, and I recognized the description of the Impala from one we had seen parked in front of his house.

We were the third unit on scene, and as we approached the end of the block, we could see Javier standing on Carmela's porch. I pulled up and hopped out as additional units arrived in the area.

"Son, I have a bad feeling you know what happened here, don't you?"

Javier was quiet at first. "Wallace, do me a favor and get off my porch, OK?" He looked around nervously, even though we appeared to be alone on the property. "Just leave, OK? . . . Then call me."

We talked for an hour on the phone that evening. The shooters were two senior members of his gang. They had been visiting earlier in the evening and confronted a young man as they were driving away. Javier wasn't sure why they shot him, but he did know the identity of the killers. This knowledge provided a defining opportunity for Javier, a chance to exercise what we'd talked about for months—take a step toward a new life and explore what it meant to be a good man.

Javier knew I had high expectations for him, and he didn't want to let me down.

Paternal mentorship is largely missing for young men and women who find themselves in gangs or in trouble with the law. When children are raised without a father, they are more likely to associate with "delinquent peers" or join a gang.[19] Some studies indicate that young fatherless teens "find a sense of community and acceptance" in gangs whose leaders "may fill the role of [a] father."[20] Whatever the motivation, one thing is certain: when fathers are absent, the likelihood that a young person will become part of a gang, commit a crime, or interact with the juvenile justice system increases dramatically.[21]

One researcher found that children from father-absent homes were more likely to shoplift.[22] Another study of 835 juvenile male inmates found that young men from fatherless homes were 279 percent more likely to carry guns and deal drugs than those who had been raised with fathers.[23] Children raised in father-absent households face "elevated incarceration risks" (emphasis mine) and the highest incarceration rates.[24]

This behavior isn't limited to those, like Javier, who eventually find themselves in street gangs. Children raised without a father display more behavioral problems and higher degrees of delinquency in any form. Father absenteeism is more responsible for juvenile delinquency than peer influence or a child's socioeconomic status.[25] Kids raised without fathers are also more aggressive. One study found there are more acts of teen violence in neighborhoods where fathers are most absent.[26]

In some ways, Javier was set up for failure. Raised initially without a father and in a community with a dominant gang presence, Javier fell unsurprisingly into the pattern of many other fatherless young men.

But things were different now. He had been living in a much safer community for several years, separated from the gangsters he grew up with by many miles. He was also under new mentorship.

He decided to identify the killers, knowing full well the incredible risk this presented. He did the right thing.

Now it was my turn.

 ## The Overwhelming Truth about Dads

The more I came to know Javier, the more I recognized my limits as a mentor. I could build a relationship, offer advice, and set an example, but I couldn't offer the kind of fatherly discipline he needed.

Javier was a *big* teenager, and his size, even as a child, intimidated his mother and grandmother at times. Had Javier been raised by an engaged father, this would not have been the case. Several studies demonstrate the important disciplinary role men play in their families. With their size, strength, and vocal tone, fathers have a disciplinary advantage, especially with boys.[27]

Fathers also play differently than mothers, and their style of interaction helps boys and girls develop character. Dads play more aggressively and respond more slowly to their kids' frustration. For this reason, a father's rough-and-tumble play promotes problem-solving, independence, emotional intelligence, ethical understanding, and self-regulation in boys *and* girls. Children who play with their fathers in this way learn to fight fairly, "explore, take chances, overcome obstacles, be braver in the presence of strangers, and stand up for themselves."[28]

Dads hold high expectations for their children and are "more likely than mothers to encourage their children to tackle difficult tasks, endure hardship without yielding, and seek out novel experiences."[29] Fathers also tend to be more realistic. One meta-analysis of thirty-two studies found that engaged dads were better able to predict the problematic behaviors their children would eventually exhibit. According to the analysis, dads tended to be more involved in "preparing children to deal with life."[30]

And lest you think dads are valuable only in developing attributes typically associated with masculinity, a twenty-six-year study found that the number one factor in developing empathy in children was father involvement. When dads regularly spend time alone with their kids, their children become compassionate adults.[31] In addition, fathers greatly influence their children's spiritual formation, both in the way young people view God and in their level of commitment to spiritual communities.[32]

When fathers are engaged, children also enjoy and perform better at school, are more likely to participate in extracurricular activities, and are less likely to be truant from school or to be suspended, expelled, or required to repeat a grade.[33] Most high school dropouts, on the other hand, come from fatherless homes. When kids enjoy a close relationship with their father, they're twice as likely to enter college or find lasting employment after high school.[34]

Kids raised with fathers are also less likely to be poor and more likely to have paternal "networking connections to aid them in the working world."[35]

Fathers also have a "substantial influence on both their children's and their families' health and development."[36] When dads are involved in their kids' upbringing, for example, pre-term infants experience improved weight and breast-feeding rates. Infant mortality is lower, and pregnant mothers "experience a lower prevalence of pregnancy loss."[37]

Older children also experience a health benefit when their fathers are present and engaged. The fitness level of a father, for example, serves as the best indicator of fitness and body-fat levels in his adolescent children. Fathers who exercise tough love have kids who are more physically fit.[38] Conversely, "children with higher body mass indices (BMI) are more likely to come from father-absent homes."[39] Kids are physically healthier when raised in households with engaged fathers.[40] They experience fewer accidents and have a lower rate of chronic asthma, headaches, and speech defects.[41]

Fathers also contribute uniquely to the mental well-being of their kids.[42] Children raised with loving, involved fathers experience greater emotional security, higher self-esteem, and lower psychological distress as children, teens, and adults.[43] They are also much less likely to experience mental health issues, such as developing a mood disorder, experiencing depression, or committing suicide.[44]

Sadly, kids raised in fatherless homes are more likely to suffer physical,

EXAMPLE: The Prodigal Son's Father

Jesus told a parable about a young son who asked for his father's inheritance then promptly spent it on worldly pleasures. He was eventually reduced to working in a pigpen before deciding to return to his father's estate. Prepared to work as a servant, he was instead welcomed back into the family (Luke 15:11–32). The father displayed grace *and* justice, celebrating his son's return without unfairly restoring his inheritance. Why do you think Jesus used this example of a father with his disciples?

sexual, or emotional abuse.[45] They also use drugs or alcohol more frequently.[46] The less fathers engage their *kids*, the more their kids engage in *risk*. Researchers find that boys and girls raised without their fathers have a weaker sense of right and wrong. They are less likely to delay gratification or control their impulses related to anger or sex.[47] Teenage girls engage in riskier sexual behavior and are more likely to get pregnant or have an abortion.[48] Teenage boys are similarly less self-controlled and sexually active.[49]

Fathers also help set the pattern for their kids' successful marriages. Children raised with loving dads learn how to *love* and *be loved*. Their early friendships and relationships thrive at a higher level, and they become more companionable and responsible as adults.[50] Boys who have a close relationship with their father develop a more favorable attitude about intimacy and the prospect of marriage.[51] They also usually grow up to be involved fathers themselves.[52]

I was thinking about Javier's potential as a husband and father as I hung up the phone.

My lieutenant, Tom Hurley, was eager to make an arrest. He impatiently paced back and forth during my conversation with Javier, and once I hung up, he gave me an hour to write the warrant and get it signed by a judge. I knew the danger in using Javier as an informant, however, and I wasn't willing to put him at risk. So I asked for three additional hours to find another way to accomplish the same goal.

Tom was livid and considered my request an act of insubordination. But he also knew I was the only one who had the information necessary to solve the case.

Mike and I spent the next two hours scouring the neighborhood to identify additional witnesses. One told us he had seen the suspect vehicle parked on the street earlier in the week, and because he thought it looked suspicious, he scribbled the license plate on a notepad and tucked it in a drawer. According to our records, a car with that plate had been stopped in Norwalk a week prior. The local police department there had information about who was in the car at the time: the two men Javier had already identified in our case. Once we obtained local booking photos, we showed a "six pack photo lineup" to our witnesses, and they confirmed the identification. Our SWAT team made the arrests several hours later.

There was no need to include Javier's involvement in my arrest warrant.

I visited him the next day. We didn't say much, but we didn't have to. Javier was getting ready to turn an important corner. I was preparing to be reassigned. Our days talking on the porch were about to come to an end.

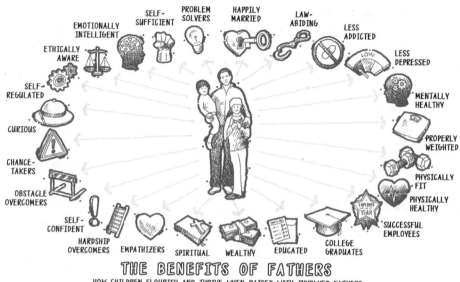

THE BENEFITS OF FATHERS
HOW CHILDREN FLOURISH AND THRIVE WHEN RAISED WITH INVOLVED FATHERS

Chase the Lead

As my own kids grew up over the years, I reflected on my assignment to the gang detail. Those critical years catalyzed my views on the importance of fathers and male mentors. Billy Graham once said, "A good father is one of the most unsung, unpraised, unnoticed, and yet one of the most valuable assets in our society."[53] My time with gang members certainly proved this to be the case. If you're a father, grandfather, future father, or plan on being married to any of these, here are a few suggestions for you or your spouse:

Love Your Wife First
Your marriage is the vehicle through which you teach and influence your kids. Your children are watching you, and they learn about marriage (and parenting) from your example. Boys learn what it means to be brave, protective, and compassionate providers. Girls learn what to look for in a good husband. Boys often follow the example of their fathers,

and girls "who enjoy good childhood relationships with their fathers are more likely to select partners who resemble their dads."[54] Before you focus on your kids, make sure you focus on your spouse.

Lean on Mentors

Author John Green observed, "The nature of impending fatherhood is that you are doing something that you're unqualified to do, and then you become qualified while doing it."[55] Like any other learned skill, the more you thoughtfully engage the role of *father*, the more you will learn about *fatherhood*. You may not have been raised by a great father role model, but your future as a father isn't solely dependent on the way you were fathered. Apply yourself, read, listen to the wisdom of others, and find good mentors in your extended family, collection of friends, or church.

Seek More Than Quality

When struggling to give our kids the time they deserve, some may console themselves by embracing *quality* over *quantity*. Quality time is, of course, incredibly important, but fathering isn't an "either/or" proposition. Instead, it's a "both/and" promise. If you find yourself feeling bad you haven't been spending enough time with your kids, let that appropriate response motivate you to change your schedule. Your best ability as a father is your *avail*ability. Time matters because it's in the unplanned, spontaneous moments when we impart the most to our kids. As author Umberto Eco wrote, "What we become depends on what our fathers teach us at odd moments when they aren't trying to teach us. We are formed by little scraps of wisdom."[56] Allow yourself *large portions of time* so you can impart these *little scraps of wisdom*.

Provide Every S

Biology often determined the historic role fathers played as protectors and providers. Sigmund Freud wrote, "I cannot think of any need in childhood as strong as the need for a father's protection."[57] But fatherhood involves more than salary, safety, and shelter. Dads also provide smarts, solace, and stability. Good dads spend time with their kids, imparting wisdom and addressing their physical, emotional, and spiritual needs. They are consistent, stable, and dependable. Fathers are the steady launch pads from which kids can skyrocket.

Model Your Role

Children pay attention to their fathers, even when they aren't teaching or admonishing. Kids listen, watch, and then become. Javier and I were similar in this regard. Javier knew very little about his father, as most of his interaction growing up was over the phone or in jail visits. But when I first met him, he was on the road to becoming his father. My father was a police officer for my entire life, and although I pursued a bachelor's degree in the arts and then a master's degree in architecture, at the age of twenty-seven I entered the police academy and started to become my father, just like Javier. That's the power of fathers as role models. Take your modeling responsibility seriously.

Cultivate Communication

As my boys were growing up, I remember telling them, "In every profession, there are two kinds of workers: those who master their craft and those who master their craft and learn how to communicate. The second group are also known as bosses, supervisors, or employers." Practice the art of communication with your kids, even if you don't consider yourself a great communicator. Rope your children into adult conversations whenever possible, and raise your expectations. Good communicators become good leaders.

Relish Acceptable Risk

Hall of Fame baseball player Harmon Killebrew once recalled this story from his youth: "My father used to play with my brother and me in the yard. Mother would come out and say, 'You're tearing up the grass.' 'We're not raising grass,' Dad would reply. 'We're raising boys.'"[58] Risk is part of life. As fathers, we can't provide a risk-free environment. Instead, we can help our kids identify *acceptable* risk so they can tackle and leverage it for success. Teach your kids to distinguish between acceptable and reckless, then encourage the former.

Think beyond Your Own

I have several good friends who never married and never had children of their own. They "fathered," nonetheless. They became mentors for kids suffering from "lack of dad." As it turns out, "lack of dad" is often remedied by "presence of mentor." Studies reveal the importance of such mentors to fatherless children.[59] That's why all men must learn how to father well. Every one of us may have the opportunity to change a life.

When Javier earned his GED, he moved from his grandmother's home and found an entry-level factory position as he started earning an associate of arts degree at a junior college. I didn't hear from him for another *fifteen years.*

One morning as I walked into my office, I discovered a voicemail message on my desk phone. Javier just wanted me to know how much he appreciated the conversations we had many years earlier. He also wanted to tell me he was married with two kids—just like the gang officer he met on his grandmother's porch.

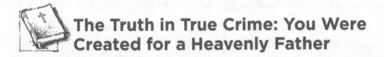

The Truth in True Crime: You Were Created for a Heavenly Father

Javier and I learned something ancient about fatherhood long before I embraced the ancient Christian worldview. Fathers matter, just as modern researchers and the biblical authors claim.

The Bible recognizes the importance of marriage and the impact fatherly commitment has on family structures.[60] The Old Testament proverb writers described how committed fathers are far more likely to have wise children who bring honor to their family.[61] Jesus used parables describing fathers and the impact of paternal patience, loyalty, and responsibility.[62]

The biblical authors admonish men to protect, provide, and carve out time for their children and families.[63] Fathers are to walk in a manner worthy of God, become their children's *first teacher*, and share the wisdom they have stored in their hearts.[64]

Fathers are also instructed to reprove, discipline, teach, and rebuke, but to do so without discouraging or provoking their children.[65] Instead, they are to turn their hearts to their kids and show them mercy.[66]

If you're familiar with the text of the Bible, you're probably not surprised that humans flourish and thrive when their fathers are present and engaged. Our need for a father is not a vestigial, evolutionary relic. It is, yet again, what the biblical authors described: a design feature.

We were created by a loving heavenly Father who promises to mentor and care for us in every way. Our temporal, fatherly yearnings are simply a shadow of this eternal reality. That's one reason why the biblical authors repeatedly analogize the role of fathers to the work of God. We thrive when we are protected, loved, and disciplined by our earthly dads. How much more would we thrive if we were protected, loved, and disciplined by a heavenly Father?[67]

Here's the good news: we *are* loved by a God who yearns to guide us as a Father, if we simply come to him as children.

Dads are essential to human flourishing because the fingerprints of our eternal Father are etched on our souls. We thrive under the influence of earthly fathers because we long to restore the broken relationship between rebellious humans and a righteous God. We seek a relationship with our earthly dads because *we were created for a heavenly Father.*

EXPLANATION: We Long for Our Heavenly Father

We miss people from whom we have been separated, and we long to restore broken relationships. This is especially true of our parental relationships. That's why adopted children often want to meet their biological parents.

Genesis describes how we were created in the image of God so we could interact with him as a child interacts with a father. Adam and Eve enjoyed the presence of God until their rebellion led to expulsion.

Humans continue to long for the restoration of this relationship with our heavenly Father, and we thrive when we experience an earthly surrogate. Our innate yearning for a father is designed to lead us back to God.

DEATH SENTENCES AND LIFE WITHOUT PAROLE

How to Rethink the Nature of Death
So You Can Live a Better Life

For the majority of people, though they do
not know what to do with this life, long for
another that shall have no end.
—ANATOLE FRANCE

I don't believe in an afterlife, so I don't have to spend
my whole life fearing hell, or fearing heaven even
more. For whatever the tortures of hell, I think the
boredom of heaven would be even worse.
—ISAAC ASIMOV

Dan Howard was one of the first killers we arrested after forming the cold case team. He looked very different today than he did on the day he was convicted of killing his ex-wife. Dan murdered Karen three decades before his arrest. They were both in their late twenties at the time, but Dan was nearly sixty when justice finally caught up with him. Now, fifteen years later, Dan looked much older than his age.

At least, that's what the deputy district attorney, Jerry Sheldon, told us. Jerry attended Dan's parole hearing, and Rick and I were anxious to hear the details the next day. Jerry recalled the scene in vivid detail.

The parole suitability hearing took place in a long, sparsely furnished room. The commissioner and deputy commissioners sat at a table at one end, Dan at a table on the other side. Jerry sat behind him.

Dan made an impassioned plea to be released from his fifteen-to-life sentence. He had been a model prisoner and was now what he described as a "weak old man" who just wanted to live his last few years in freedom. Dan was thin, shaky, and emotional. He broke down and cried during the hearing.

"Life is so short." Dan spoke slowly in a frail voice between sobs. He occasionally used the sleeve of his prison uniform to wipe his tears. "I'm afraid of dying . . . and of dying alone in here . . . I just want to spend my last days . . . with my family . . . before I'm back in the dirt forever."

Dan's plea appeared heartfelt, and he certainly didn't look like a man who would present a threat to anyone. The commissioner seemed genuinely moved and asked Dan where he would live when released.

Jerry couldn't believe it.

As the prosecutor in the case, Jerry'd had an opportunity to represent the victim's family and make a statement at the hearing. He could barely control himself.

"Mr. Commissioner, I certainly understand Dan Howard's fear of death and his desire to die with his friends and family, but he didn't seem to care about *Karen's* opportunity to die that way. Instead, he brutally murdered her and then has the unmitigated gall to sit here and talk about how short life is! You know whose life was short? Karen Howard!"

"Prosecutor Sheldon, please calm down."

"I am calm! But it's absurd for you to consider releasing this man when he was essentially paroled for thirty years before he ever served a day in jail. Karen never got to experience those thirty years. This killer enjoyed his life while Karen was lying cold in the grave—"

"Mr. Sheldon, lower your voice."

"If you parole this killer—a murderer who viciously stabbed his wife and then lied about it for thirty years—you are a disgrace to the parole commission. You simply cannot do this."

Two weeks later, we learned how wrong Jerry could be. The board paroled Dan Howard. They set a date for his release, and although Rick and I assumed the drama was over, nothing could have been further from the truth.

The Focus of Our Fear

After listening to Jerry's description of the hearing, I wondered why the commissioner responded so favorably to Dan's plea. It's incredibly rare for convicted killers to be paroled, even in California. What was so persuasive about Dan's statement? Jerry was convinced he knew the answer.

EVIDENCE: Humans Fear Death

While death is an ever-present reality for all of us, not everyone is aware of their mortality to the same degree. But according to researchers, our "mortality salience" has a larger impact than we might think. The data reveals that our awareness of death guides many of our decisions and attitudes.

Is death anxiety simply a product of evolution, as some might suggest? If so, how does this fear of death benefit the species, especially if it has the negative consequences researchers describe?

"I'm telling you, the commissioner's face changed completely when Dan started talking about *death* and being *afraid to die*." Jerry was still upset. "Hey, we're all afraid to die—*I'm* afraid to die—but that doesn't justify paroling a killer. I'm not done yet; I'm writing up a response."

Researchers confirm Jerry's observation about our fear of death. Psychologists define "mortality salience" as an *awareness* of death, "death anxiety" as the *extent* to which each of us fears dying, and "death depression" as the degree to which we become *depressed* about this inevitable reality.[1] Studies reveal that "death anxiety is a common human experience," even among the young, and some psychologists even believe it to be a "universal psychological response."[2] Death anxiety is widespread among humans because, unlike other species of animals, we have the ability to contemplate, anticipate, and predict the future.[3] We are aware of what might happen as we age, and this awareness changes the way we think, feel, and act.

One study, for example, found that we use words, expressions, and language to draw attention *away* from our own mortality.[4] Humans avoid talking about death because we fear it, either consciously or unconsciously. Some of us fear the pain that may accompany the process of dying. Others dread the prospect of being separated from the people they love. Some fear the unknown. Many fear the "permanent end of existence after death."[5]

The underlying awareness and fear of death is more than merely common. Some believe it is the central driving force behind our actions.

A growing field of study, terror management theory, proposes, "Control of death anxiety is the primary function of society and the main motivation in human behavior." According to this theory, our unique awareness of the future and our impending death (our mortality salience) motivates us to embrace beliefs and values buffering us "against the frightening recognition of [our] own mortality."[6]

Proponents of this theory have designed studies to confirm the concept as first described by anthropologist Ernest Becker in his book *The Denial of Death*.[7] According to Becker, human value systems based on moral philosophy, politics, culture, or science are constructed to deny the finite nature of our lives. We embrace these worldviews and strategies because we are afraid of dying, and in doing so, we hope to achieve some form of symbolic immortality.

Dan and Karen Howard held two different views of the world, and their belief systems offered different responses to human mortality. Although they met in church and attended services when they were first married, Dan's interest in Christianity waned. He eventually told Karen he wasn't interested in church anymore. Months later, he confessed he no longer believed in God. Dan's values and views about life changed.

So did his views about death.

 ## Death and Its Downside

Dan distanced himself from Karen. She suspected he was having an affair, but he denied it when confronted. Karen no longer recognized the man she married. With each passing year, they became more polarized and independent. Karen was increasingly committed to her Christian worldview, Dan to his newfound atheism. In their fifth year of marriage, he demanded a divorce.

Neither Dan nor Karen had openly expressed a fear of death at this point in their relationship. But studies find that *underlying* mortality salience and death anxiety also have the capacity to polarize us and entrench our views. According to terror management theorists, "When people are reminded of their own mortality, they become especially punitive toward those who violate their standards and especially benevolent toward those who uphold them."[8] We dig in our heels, defending our view of the world and distancing ourselves from people who disagree, just as Dan and Karen seemed to do at the end of their marriage.[9]

Our awareness and concerns about death have other consequences as well, according to researchers. Death anxiety decreases our quality of life generally, and people who fear death typically have lower self-esteem.[10] They experience deeper, prolonged grief after losing a loved one, are more likely to lose sleep, suffer depression, and experience greater post-traumatic stress.[11] Death anxiety can also lead to a number of mental challenges, including a variety of anxiety disorders, phobias, and eating behaviors.[12] Our fear of death even causes some of us to withdraw emotionally and become less compassionate or intimate.[13]

Data from current research shows that death anxiety clearly inhibits human flourishing. If terror management theorists are correct, fear of death is a "universal psychological response," and everyone must find a way to cope with the "frightening recognition of their own mortality."

Prior to his arrest, Dan seemed like a man determined to live the fullest life possible. Was mortality salience the motivation? Perhaps. If Dan was like other killers I've encountered, he must have been painfully aware of the reality of death. He was, after all, the last person to see Karen alive and the man who *caused* her death.

After the murder, Dan became a successful investor. He owned several homes in desirable Southern California resort locations. He took expensive vacations, dated many women, and owned expensive cars. Dan was living what most would consider the "high life." The stark contrast to his prison existence must have been shocking. Maybe that's why he so desperately wanted to be paroled. Dan still had plenty of money, and he appeared eager to return to the life he had constructed for himself prior to his arrest—a life he may have crafted as a coping mechanism.

 ## Coping, Consolation, and Comfort

Death anxiety is a strong motivator, especially as we grapple with "the tension between our actual conditions as temporal, restricted beings and human aspirations to be unlimited, immortal beings."[14] Dan wrestled with this tension just like everyone else, applying one of many coping devices researchers have identified. Here's how people manage their fear of death, according to the findings:

Consumerism

Some pursue money, possessions, and experiences as a coping response to death anxiety. If life is short, why not live the most luxurious life possible? Material wealth offers a mechanism by which we can "buffer existential anxiety."[15] If this was Dan's approach, we certainly disrupted it when we arrested him.

Distraction

French mathematician and philosopher Blaise Pascal understood the power of distraction: "Those . . . who think men unreasonable for spending a whole day in chasing a hare . . . scarce know our nature. The hare in itself would not screen us from the sight of death and calamities; but the chase, which turns away our attention from these, does screen us."[16] Diversion and distraction were common death avoidance strategies long before Pascal wrote about them in the seventeenth century.

Meaning Construction

Some of us lack the financial means to distract ourselves through material pleasures, so we seek an affordable alternative. If life feels short and meaningless, why not assign a meaning of our own? Many accomplish this by creating achievable goals and purposes increasing our self-esteem and softening the inevitability of death.[17]

Children

If my life is limited to a single generation, why not extend my influence by birthing or fathering an additional generation? According to studies, when we think about death, our desire for kids increases, as does our desire to name our children after ourselves "to symbolically extend [our] life."[18] Although this coping mechanism is common, research also reveals that our efforts to live through our kids have a "generally negative effect" on children.[19]

Fame

Most people are forgotten within a generation or two, so generation-spanning fame may seem a reasonable strategy to overcome our fear of death. Studies confirm that people with mortality salience have a greater interest in fame, "based in part on the desire for symbolic continuance beyond death."[20]

Risk-Taking

Risky or dangerous challenges provide an opportunity to test our mortality, strengthen our confidence, and decrease our anxiety, but researchers find they have limited ability to allay our fear of death. In fact, the more experience you have taking dangerous risks, the more fearful you become. On study found that avid risk-takers eventually realized they "can't cheat death after all."[21]

Denial

Pascal described man's propensity to deny the reality of death in the following way: "To be happy he would have to make himself immortal; but, not being able to do so, it has occurred to him to prevent himself from thinking of death."[22] This form of denial encourages avoidance strategies, however, as we attempt to limit our mortality salience. One study, for example, found that young adults embraced a form of *ageism* in their effort to "distance themselves from their future older selves and from an awareness of their mortality."[23] Denial comes with a cost.

Immediacy Strategies

Researchers describe mindfulness as being singularly focused on the present rather than the future. This strategy is most effective when intentional and repeated. One researcher described the effort this way: "Like little kids who nearly suffocate under blanket protection to fend off the monster in the closet, the first thing we try to do is purge any death-related thoughts or feelings from our mind."[24] This may work for fictional monsters, but it's less effective for real concerns about death and dying.

Philosophical Endeavors

Many of history's great thinkers adopted philosophical constructs to alleviate their death anxiety. Epicurus, for example, declared, "When we exist, death is not yet present, and when death is present, then we do not exist."[25] According to Epicurus's argument, there was no reason to fear death since it affects neither the living nor the dead. The Stoic philosopher Seneca argued a slightly different philosophical construct: "Would you not think him an utter fool who wept because he was not alive a thousand years ago? And is he not just as much a fool who weeps because he will not be alive a thousand years from now? It is all the same; you will not be and you were not. Neither of these periods of time belongs to you."[26] Even today, many people allay their fears by thinking about life and death in a more philosophical way.[27] Humanist Leon Kass, for example, attempted to argue death as a *necessary* evil: "Could life be serious or meaningful without the limits of mortality? Is not the limit on our time the ground of our taking life seriously and living it passionately?"[28] Philosophical efforts to overcome the fear of death are both abundant and creative.

Science

Death anxiety leads some people to consider scientific proposals aimed at immortality. "Mind uploading," for example, is a futuristic theory of using brain scans to meticulously map each candidate's mental state. This data would then be transferred to a computer so it could run intricate processing simulations to duplicate the candidate's consciousness.[29] Although this technology isn't yet available, some people with death anxiety are considering cryonics (the low temperature freezing of bodies and brains) as an option to extend their bodies until more expertise is available. Studies reveal, however, that people who favor technologies like cryonics "experience more fear of death" than those who don't. Researchers speculate this might be "due to the lack of providing their ego with psychological ways of coping with the reality of ultimate dissolution."[30]

EXAMPLE: The Disciples of Jesus

At their last meal together, Jesus reminded his disciples of the death he was to face. The disciples were appropriately "troubled" and asked Jesus where he was going. Jesus recognized their distress and responded by saying, "Let not your hearts be troubled," then described the afterlife waiting for them: "In my Father's house are many rooms. If it were not so, would I have told you that I go to prepare a place for you? And if I go and prepare a place for you, I will come again and will take you to myself, that where I am you may be also" (John 14:1–3 ESV).

Why do you think Jesus responded to their fear with a promise to bring them to where he would be for eternity?

Some of these coping mechanisms are more effective than others. Dan's mechanism of choice was interrupted by his incarceration, and Jerry wanted to make sure it stayed that way. He wrote a formal response and filed it with the Parole Commission. He then conducted several public interviews with Los Angeles radio stations and print media. The well-publicized case landed on the governor's desk during an election year. Dan's parole was eventually denied. Because of Dan's advanced age, Rick and I thought that would be the last we would hear from him.

Once again, we were wrong.

 ## Faith and the Fear of Death

Coping mechanisms fail because they provide relief from a reality they cannot eliminate, just as a painkiller might offer relief from the pain of a cancerous tumor. You may feel better, but the cancer is still waiting for you. In a similar way, these popular coping devices cannot eradicate death, the very object of their concern. Most of these approaches strive for *symbolic* immortality rather than the *real* immortality we all desire.

Agnostic astronomer Carl Sagan wrote, "I would love to believe that when I die I will live again, that some thinking, feeling, remembering part of me will continue. But as much as I want to believe that, and despite the ancient and worldwide cultural traditions that assert an afterlife, I know of nothing to suggest that it is more than wishful thinking."[31] Sagan's views about immortality and life after death are relatively rare, however, according to global surveys.

Humans are a surprisingly religious species. Most people believe in a "Supreme Being" and life after death.[32] Most Americans (young and old alike) also believe in an afterlife, and our belief levels have remained unchanged over several decades.[33] In fact, more people believe in an afterlife than believe in the existence of God.[34] For example, deceased Nirvana lead singer Kurt Cobain, the pop icon who described religion as a "sedative for the masses," still believed in life after death, saying, "As far as I'm concerned, [life's] just a pitstop for the afterlife. It's just a little test to see how you can handle reality."[35]

Unlike coping mechanisms offering symbolic immortality, theism (the belief in God) offers *true* immortality—if theistic claims are accurate.

People who believe religious claims about an afterlife flourish, suffering far less death anxiety (and its resultant trauma) than those who don't.[36] This is also true for people who hold spiritual or religious beliefs in general. Studies repeatedly find that "religions provide a platform to expand individuals' self-awareness, address existential crises of life and death, contemplate the mystery of existence, and face their emotional pain."[37] Spiritual beliefs related to an afterlife "act as a preventive factor against feelings of existential despair."[38] The more committed one is to these beliefs, the less likely one is to experience death anxiety.[39]

Belief in an afterlife matters, but not just *any* afterlife will do.

Studies find that Christians, for example, have less death anxiety than other religious believers, such as Hindus or Buddhists.[40] Why? According to one study, the answer lies in a notion described as the "persisting self."[41] Researchers examined the way theistic systems make claims about who (and what) we are as humans. Our identity, according to the study, "is something that persists from childhood through old age. [We] exist to the extent that [our] self exists."[42] Unsurprisingly, if you believe your "self" has the capacity to transcend your mortal existence, you're far less likely to experience death anxiety.

That's where Christianity offers an advantage. Religious worldviews offer differing descriptions of the afterlife, and these descriptions impact the way we perceive our "persisting self":

Buddhism argues *against the existence of self*. According to Buddhism, your sense of self is only an illusion, and for this reason, it will not extend beyond your mortal existence.

Hinduism argues for the *reincarnation of self*. While your self may continue into the next life, its reincarnated characteristics, attributes, traits, and memories will be very different.

Atheism argues for an entirely *materialistic version of self*. As a purely material being, you are nothing more than your body. As a result, your self ceases to exist once your body stops functioning.

Christianity argues for a *dualistic sense of self*. According to this view, you are more than a physical, material being. You have a soul. This "soulish" self transcends your mortal experience and carries your characteristics, attributes, traits, and memories into eternity where you'll be made whole again when your physical body is resurrected and redeemed.

When compared with these other worldviews, Christianity offers the most powerful notion of "persisting self." For Christians, death is little more than a new chapter in our continuing existence. Christians suffer less death anxiety because we expect *true* immortality rather than the empty promise of *symbolic* immortality.

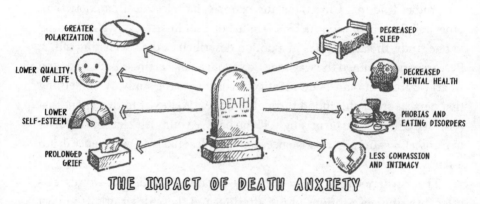

THE IMPACT OF DEATH ANXIETY

Dan's atheistic worldview offered no such hope. His next parole hearing was years away, and without access to the coping mechanism he desired, he slipped into depression. He decided to adopt a new strategy. Dan now found meaning and purpose in what he considered an achievable goal: vengeance.

 ## Chase the Lead

Rick received a phone call from a prison supervisor about a month after Dan's parole was denied. Dan's cellmate, Ike Hauser, approached one of the guards. Ike was anticipating a parole hearing of his own later in the year. He wanted to divulge some information about Dan, hoping his cooperation would aid his next opportunity for parole.

Ike told the guard Dan had secured the help of one of the prison's most notorious inmates, a gang leader with connections to local gang members in our community. Ike said Dan arranged to pay this inmate $40,000 to deploy a hit man. Dan's target?

Jerry Sheldon.

Dan's desperation clearly worsened as his death anxiety increased. His coping mechanisms failed because, as a committed atheist, he rejected the idea of an afterlife. Dan was convinced he would die in custody and end up "back in the dirt forever." Had he remained a Christian, he would have suffered less death anxiety in the first place. *Perhaps.*

Not *every* Christian responds the same way. Self-identified Christians who are doubtful and less committed to their faith fear death at approximately the same level as nonbelievers.[43] Committed believers who are convinced Christianity is true (rather than simply useful or familiar) live with less death anxiety. Certainty is the key. If you want to overcome the hidden influence of mortality salience or the obvious impact of death anxiety, develop certainty in the afterlife by considering the evidential case for Christianity:

Examine the Evidence for God

The existence of an infinitely powerful, purposeful, creative, and personal God is the best explanation for our finite, fine-tuned universe, the information found in DNA, the appearance of design in biology, and the existence of transcendent, objective moral laws. Even the presence of evil requires the existence of God as the objective standard of righteousness by which we measure something and declare it amiss. There is more than enough reason to believe God exists. Even the "world's most notorious atheist," Antony Flew, eventually acknowledged the existence of God, saying his "discovery of the Divine [was] a pilgrimage of reason not of faith."[44] For an in-depth look at the evidence for God, read *God's Crime Scene: A Cold-Case Detective Examines the Evidence for a Divinely Created Universe.*[45]

Examine the Evidence for the Soul

There are also many good reasons to believe humans are more than physical beings. For example, our immaterial minds are not the same as our material brains, yet both exist. Your brain can be publicly accessed, but your thoughts are only privately known. Your brain can be weighed and measured, but your thoughts cannot.[46] If minds exist in addition to brains, there is sufficient reason to believe that immaterial souls exist in addition to bodies. Scholars like Mark C. Baker and Stewart Goetz have also reached this conclusion: "Among people who think seriously about such things, there simply is no agreement about how one can explain human beings without a soul."[47] If we are living souls, the death of our physical bodies would not necessitate the death of our souls.

Examine the Evidence for the Bible

The New Testament authors made many claims about the life, miracles, and resurrection of Jesus. These claims can be tested using the criteria we employ to test eyewitnesses in criminal trials. Were the eyewitnesses present to see what they said they saw? Can their claims be corroborated in some way? Have they changed their story over time? And finally, do the eyewitnesses have something to gain by lying to us? When assessed in this way, the gospel authors pass the test. As Duke University scholar E. P. Sanders observed, "After [Jesus's] death his followers experienced what they described as the 'resurrection': the appearance of a living but transformed person who had actually died. They believed this, they lived it, and they died for it."[48] Their testimony about Jesus is reliable, including what Jesus said about our souls and the afterlife. Jesus told his disciples, for example, "Do not fear those who kill the body but cannot kill the soul."[49] More importantly, Jesus appeared to the disciples after his resurrection, demonstrating he was raised from the dead as "the firstfruits of those who have fallen asleep."[50] His resurrection is evidence we will *also* be resurrected.[51] If Christianity is true, souls exist and the promise of a resurrection body is real. For a complete investigation of the New Testament Gospels, read, *Cold-Case Christianity: A Homicide Detective Investigates the Claims of the Gospels* and *Person of Interest: Why Jesus Still Matters in a World That Rejects the Bible.*[52]

Live with Certainty

The more certain you are of the evidence, the more likely you are to act decisively, stand confidently, and remain committed. This is true for jurors, and it's also true for believers. If you want to flourish, avoiding the damage that death anxiety causes, embrace a committed faith based on the evidence. Allow the overwhelming case for Christianity to close the gap between your unanswered questions and certainty.

The Christian claims about the afterlife are evidentially reliable. As we grow in confidence, our fear of death wanes and we begin to flourish. For more on developing a confident, committed, and evidential faith, please read *Forensic Faith: A Homicide Detective Makes the Case for a More Reasonable, Evidential Christian Faith.*[53]

Rethink the Future *and* the Present

The afterlife we experience in the future can change the way we live today. Imagine working long hours in terrible conditions for the promise of receiving one dollar at the end of the day. Now imagine working in the *very same job* but for the promise of one *million* dollars at the end of the day. Which job offer would be easier to endure? Your future expectations are the key to your present well-being. If an *afterlife* is waiting for us beyond the grave, our *present life* will be transformed. Billy Graham once said, "I trust Jesus with all my tomorrows, knowing that He will solve the mystery of life beyond the grave."[54] Allow the promise of eternity to change the way you interpret the present.

Prison authorities acted quickly to isolate Dan and prevent his payment to the hit man. To be safe, Jerry applied for a concealed carry permit and purchased a gun. He carried the pistol everywhere he went, and continued to carry it, even after Dan died in custody. Jerry found himself grappling with his own death anxiety.

Like Dan, he had never truly examined the evidence for Christianity or the promise of eternity it offered.

The Truth in True Crime: You Were Created for Eternity

Augustine understood the relationship between immortality and well-being: "The true life is one that is both everlasting and happy," and "since all men want to be happy, they want also to be immortal if they know what they want; for otherwise they could not be happy."[55]

The Bible described this truth about human desire long before modern researchers confirmed it.

The authors of the New Testament understood the debilitating power of death anxiety. The first human couple had no personal experience with the nature of mortality, and as such, they had no anxiety about death. Their sin, however, introduced death to humans, and we've been aware of our mortality ever since.[56] God had a plan to conquer the grave. Just as death entered the world through Adam, the opportunity for eternal life entered the world though Jesus.[57] This promise of eternity is made possible by the penalty Jesus paid for our sin.[58] His death destroyed our death. His resurrection assured our resurrection. As C. S. Lewis wrote, "Death is, in fact, what some modern people call 'ambivalent.' It is Satan's great weapon and also God's great weapon: it is holy and unholy; our supreme disgrace and our only hope; the thing Christ came to conquer and the means by which He conquered."[59]

EXPLANATION: Our Fear of Death Points Us to God

Human flourishing is inversely related to our fear of death. Yet according to researchers, everyone experiences this destructive concern. If we are the product of naturalistic, evolutionary forces, why haven't we evolved past this harmful emotion?

The answer is clear. Our death anxiety serves us well because it points us to the one reasonable solution: life beyond the grave.

If our belief in an afterlife is based on reason and evidence rather than wishful thinking, our confidence will reduce our death anxiety and open the door to human flourishing. Our fear of death should point us to our Creator and his offer of eternal life.

The biblical authors, therefore, encouraged us not to be anxious about the future, reminding us that life is more than what we eat, wear, or experience on this side of the grave.[60] They acknowledged the promise of our future resurrection, describing death as the "last enemy to be destroyed," assuring eternal life as citizens of heaven, and promising that our *next* life will be far greater than our *present* reality.[61]

For those who accept the gift Jesus offered, the afterlife will be a place without tears, remorse, or pain.[62] Every injustice will be righted, every evil vanquished, every desire met, and every expectation exceeded as we experience "the immeasurable riches of his grace in kindness toward us in Christ Jesus."[63]

The authors of Scripture also knew the *future* reality of heaven would change our lives *today*. They called us to remain steadfast when facing trials or hardships by setting our mind on "things that are above."[64] Like the worker who expects a huge reward at the end of the day, we are to rejoice and be glad, remembering that "the sufferings of this present time are not worth comparing with the glory that is to be revealed to us."[65]

Jesus came so "that through death he might destroy the one who has the power of death, that is, the devil, and deliver all those who through fear of death were subject to lifelong slavery."[66] Those who aren't yet aware of the eternal life available through Jesus will continue to suffer death anxiety and its negative consequences. Those who overcome their fear of death by accepting Jesus as Savior will thrive. The fear of death can cripple us or guide us to our Creator. He didn't create us to dwell on our mortality. He didn't create us to die at all. He created us instead for a relationship with him. *He created us for eternity.*

EVERY KIND OF STUPID

How to Employ the Ultimate Solution to Every Situation

No problem can be solved from the same
level of consciousness that created it.
—ATTRIBUTED TO ALBERT EINSTEIN

I think we have to look much deeper . . . if we are to find
the real cause of man's problems and the real cause of
the world's ills today. If we are to really find it I think
we will have to look in the hearts and souls of men.
—MARTIN LUTHER KING JR.

Sandra Springwell's modest home was a museum of 1980s relics and artifacts. Her furniture, wallpaper, and drapes needed updating and repair, but Rick was complimentary as we settled in on her well-worn couch.

"Sandra, thank you for seeing us today." He pointed to several photographs perched on the coffee table. "I can see how much Nicole means to you."

Nicole was Sandra's only child, and her images were neatly distributed in a semicircle. They represented an altar, of sorts. The photographs depicted Nicole at many points in her young life, but in none of them was Nicole older than seventeen. The images of her smiles were the only optimistic features of the room.

Sandra looked older than her seventy-four years, and her eyes seemed sad and discouraged. Her husband died years earlier, but only her niece still lived in California. Sandra seemed frail, quiet, and *resigned*.

"I was surprised to get your phone call." Sandra's voice was delicate and pensive. "Are they closing the case?"

"No," I replied. "The case won't close unless it's solved. We still don't know who killed Nicole, but we are officially reactivating the case, and we have several important questions to ask you."

Sandra's expression changed immediately.

"Really? Oh, thank you both so, so much. I thought everyone had forgotten Nicole."

"We have been working on the case off and on for about a year." Sandra looked surprised as Rick opened his notebook. "But Nicole's murder now has our full attention. That's why we're here."

"You have no idea how much it means to me that someone still cares about Nicole." Sandra seemed to transform before our eyes. "I've been waiting over twenty-five years. I lost hope a long time ago . . . I've been sick a lot lately, and I thought I would die without knowing who killed Nicole." She smiled and leaned forward, brightening an otherwise dark living room. "I'm so grateful to get this news."

We spent the rest of the afternoon sitting with Sandra, even though we planned to stay for only a short time. She pulled back the drapes, made coffee, and answered every question. She even provided new information we hadn't anticipated. Sandra seemed to genuinely relish the company. The more we talked, the more optimistic she became.

"With you two on the case, I *know* we'll catch the murderer."

I glanced at Rick, and his expression confirmed my thoughts: it was time for us to leave. As much as we wanted to encourage Sandra, we were still a long way from solving this case, and we knew—better than anyone—the challenges ahead. We also knew the difference between *hope* and *false hope*.

And we weren't yet sure which we were offering.

 ## The Heavy Weight of Hopelessness

Years earlier, Sandra's despair changed the course of her life, just as it has many others who've lost hope. Everyone experiences hopelessness at one time or another. Sometimes we become hopeless about a personal situation, other times, a global concern. If you've ever found yourself thinking, "That'll never change," "Good luck with that," or "No one can help me," you've experienced hopelessness. We lose hope when there seems no possibility a situation will improve or resolve itself with a "happy ending."[1]

Hopelessness and depression are often connected. There is scarcely a clinical description of depression that doesn't include *some* form of hopelessness. The data on depression, therefore, reveals that many of us struggle to retain hope.

According to global statistics collected over the past ten years, approximately 300 million people live with some form of depression or hopelessness.[2] Here in the US, depression affects over 18 million adults in any given year (one in ten) and is now considered the leading cause of disability.[3]

Kids and teens are not immune to depression and hopelessness. In one lengthy national study of children three to seventeen years of age, researchers found that over 2.7 million had experienced depression.[4] Teen hopelessness remains high, with depression increasing fastest among this age group.[5] In one study, nearly 30 percent of boys and 60 percent of girls reported "persistent feelings of sadness or hopelessness."[6]

Hopelessness often expresses itself when we lose interest in watching the news, give up on learning new things, or stop participating in previously meaningful activities.[7] Like Sandra, we settle into a rhythm and reality of despair. Why does this happen?

Some researchers believe our use of social media has exacerbated the problem in recent years. Our "negative emotional state" *increases* the longer we use social media, especially if we are simply scrolling "passively."[8] The more time we spend online, the more convinced we become of the fallen nature of the world, our increasing polarization, and the futility of "happy endings." One study revealed that nearly 70 percent of us are no longer optimistic that *anything* will change or improve.[9] This kind of hopelessness is more common than ever before.

Sandra lived with similar despair for over twenty-five years. She was convinced nothing would ever change, the case would never be solved, and Nicole's murderer would never be punished.

She was only *half* right.

> **EVIDENCE: Humans Experience Hopelessness**
>
> Hopelessness is easy to describe because everyone has experienced it at one time or another. It is yet another attribute of our universal human condition. It is demonstrably destructive, however. Human beings *need* hope to thrive, but if naturalism is true, life is ultimately meaningless and destined for death. What then, from this perspective, can be the basis of our hope? Why do humans require something a materialistic universe can't provide?
>
> If theism is true (and Christian theism specifically), how can hopelessness *benefit* humans and aid in human flourishing?

The Hard Truth about Hopelessness

Rick and I always worked with urgency as we investigated unsolved murders, but after meeting Sandra, we felt additional pressure. We saw firsthand how the hope of resolution changed Sandra's disposition, and we knew her health was poor. We wanted to catch Nicole's killer while Sandra was still alive to see it.

The kind of despair Sandra experienced is persistently destructive. Researchers now understand the impact of hopelessness on our mental well-being.[10] Hopelessness increases our sense of loneliness and isolation.[11] People who feel hopeless are more likely to become depressed and struggle to overcome difficulty or trauma.[12] They're also more likely to seek antidepressants and psychotherapy.[13] The deadly nature of hopelessness is well documented. Hopelessness is "significantly related to eventual suicide."[14]

Lost hope also impacts our physical health. People who feel hopeless are more likely to experience fatigue, lack of energy, dizziness, and other somatic symptoms.[15] Studies repeatedly find a strong connection between hopelessness and many cardiovascular diseases, including hypertension, atherosclerosis, and coronary artery disease.[16] According to researchers, hopelessness also leads to lower levels of vitality and higher levels of pain and higher likelihood of cancer and chronic illness.[17]

Hopeless despair even inhibits our ability to recover from illness. Cancer patients, for example, suffer a lower quality of life and higher awareness of symptoms when they experience hopelessness. Indeed, the level of hope one has "may predict probability of survival in advanced cancer."[18] Hopelessness also predicts the degree to which we will survive intensive care recovery, postoperative recovery, or an organ transplant.[19] It even predicts the degree to which diabetes patients will adhere to a healthy lifestyle.[20]

Hope is the key to improved health outcomes in patients of any age and is a "significant predictor of mortality."[21] Hopeless people live shorter, unhealthier lives.

Philosopher Hans-Georg Gadamer rightly observed, "People cannot live without hope; this is one of the statements I can defend without any reservations."[22] Sandra's life confirmed Gadamer's claim. She suffered several heart issues in the years after Nicole's murder and nearly died as she slowly succumbed to despair.

That began to change when she became hopeful after our visit, just as researchers might have anticipated.

Hope drives us to act, persevere, and flourish. Hopeful people identify and communicate their feelings, blossom in their relationships, and thrive in the workplace.[23] Hopeful people make better parents, and hopeful children are less likely to engage in risky relationships or dangerous behaviors.[24] As Helen Keller, a woman who had more than her share of struggles, wrote, "Optimism is the faith that leads to achievement; nothing can be done without hope."[25] Hope drives achievement, resiliency, and growth. Hopelessness, on the other hand, leads to despair, illness, and harm.

We saw this transformation in Sandra when we reactivated the case. With her hope renewed, she found something to live for. She called us often and encouraged us with renewed confidence and optimism. She modeled this newfound hopefulness for nearly a decade, surpassing the expectations of her doctors.

She almost lived long enough to see the resolution of Nicole's case.

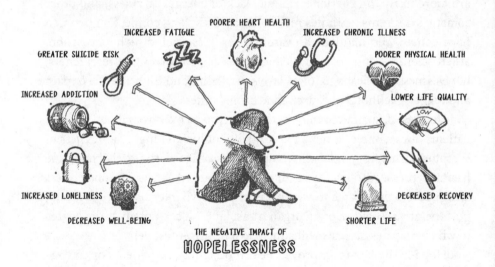

THE NEGATIVE IMPACT OF
HOPELESSNESS

Hope for "Every Kind of Stupid"

Long before I partnered with Rick on our cold case team, we worked together in a patrol car. I was a rookie; he was my field training officer. Rick was known for his sarcasm and humor, and he never failed to deliver. On our first night together, we arrested a drunk driver who unwisely decided to drive home from a bar and nearly killed himself along the way.

"Yet another foolish decision," Rick said as we finished the booking forms. "If you do this job long enough, Wallace, you're gonna see *every kind of stupid you can imagine.*"

I've never forgotten that statement. *Every kind of stupid.*

Rick was right. Police officers and detectives have a unique perspective on the world. Working with Rick, I eventually *did* see every kind of stupid you can imagine. The stupid things humans do to one another, the stupid plans we make to get away with murder, and the sad consequences of . . . *stupid.*

Anyone who's been paying attention to the news is probably making similar observations. There are plenty of reasons to worry or lose hope, and many of those reasons are the result of foolish actions or thoughtless responses.

Americans, for example, are worried about the economy, unemployment, crime, violence, climate change, poverty, racism, moral decline, social polarization, political corruption, education, and inequality.[26] People in other nations worry about these things as well, in addition to concerns about war, terrorism, threats to global health, hunger, and housing.[27]

Some of these concerns seem beyond our control, others the result of unwise behavior. Why do people commit murder? Why are we racist, violent, and corrupt? Why are poverty, homelessness, and polarization still problems? These questions often seem hopelessly unanswerable. Management consultant Peter Drucker once noted, "The most serious mistakes are not being made as a result of wrong *answers.* The truly dangerous thing is asking the wrong *questions*" (emphasis mine).[28]

Before we lose hope, maybe it's time to ask the *right* questions: "Were we created in the image of a God from whom we have strayed?" "Might this God offer hope and power to save us from ourselves?" If we can answer these questions, a hopeful solution to every kind of stupid may be within our grasp.

Researchers have confirmed the power of religious belief to—at the very least—alleviate our sense of hopelessness. People who find meaning in life and explore their spirituality are more optimistic.[29] Religious people experience lower levels of depression, and their belief in God provides "a protective factor against the development of suicide ideation."[30] Religious belief helps people survive *and* thrive, even providing hope for those recovering from serious illness.[31]

Some forms of religious belief are more effective than others, however.

Religious people who believe in a God who cares about their personal welfare (a "concerned God"), for example, are more hopeful and respond more favorably to treatment for depression.[32] In addition, people who pray are also more optimistic and react in a similarly favorable manner.[33] Finally, people who believe God has the power to save and offers everlasting life are more hopeful, even when diagnosed with PTSD or a terminal disease.[34] Not every form of religious belief offers the same capacity to dispel hopelessness. Those who believe in a caring, attentive, life-offering God thrive at the highest level.

Christians believe in just this kind of God.

Jesus cares about us and knows us personally. He listens to our prayers, has the power and desire to save, and offers eternal life. It's this salvation power of Jesus that has the unique ability to fix every kind of stupid.

Rick and I investigated more suspects in the Springwell case than I care to remember in the ten years after we met with Sandra, and *none* of them was Nicole's killer. Somehow, Sandra stayed optimistic right up to her death, even though we hadn't yet solved the case and were privately frustrated with our progress. She never complained.

She had been inexplicably transformed into a hopeful person, and her transformation didn't appear to be dependent on our progress.

 ## The Gospel as the Cure

A week after Sandra died, our criminalist called with news. DNA from Nicole's crime scene had been processed through ancestry databases, and a profile emerged from someone who appeared to be our killer's daughter. Within a month, we traced the genetic marker back and confirmed the identity of the murderer, a wandering recluse named Scott Harden.

Scott wasn't a family friend or relative of the Springwells. He wasn't one of the many suspects we had considered as part of our investigation. He wasn't even a resident of our city. He was just a stranger who drove through town and, for reasons we'll never understand, did the unthinkable. The DNA technology ultimately solved the case. Too late to tell Sandra, and too late to seek justice.

We never arrested Scott Harden.

He died in his sleep about a year prior to being identified as Nicole's killer. The mystery was solved, but Scott got away with murder, at least in *this* life. Sandra died without resolution but was hopeful to the end.

It would be another four years before I would learn the secret to Sandra's optimism.

Hope was pivotal to Sandra's joy, just as it is to ours. Famed English poet and playwright Samuel Johnson described it this way: "Hope is itself a species of happiness, and, perhaps, the chief happiness which this world affords."[35]

The gospel is unique in its ability to provide this "species of happiness." The good news of salvation in Jesus provides joy for today and hope for the future. It offers a cure for *every kind of stupid.* Why? Because it answers the right question: "Might God offer hope and power to save us from ourselves?"

God cares about crime, violence, the environment, poverty, hunger, housing, racism, social polarization, political corruption, and oppression. He loves us and is concerned about our moral decline, our education, and our well-being. He created a righteous world where all our needs were perfectly met, and if we were still living in the garden of Eden, there would be no need for hope.

But we're not in the garden anymore.

We are instead in the world our sin created. Sin separated the first couple from the garden, and our prideful rebellion continues to cause *every kind of stupid you can imagine.* That's why the gospel is the only cure. It accurately describes the problem *and* offers the solution.

The Bible proclaims, "All have sinned and fall short of the glory of God."[36] No one is exempt, and our wickedness has a consequence. It's the reason we die and the reason we treat others poorly. The Bible describes this

EXAMPLE: Abraham

Abraham, the first Old Testament patriarch, is the father of the Jewish nation. Christian believers are also called "children of Abraham" (Galatians 3:7 NIV). When Abraham was *ninety-nine years old*, God told him he would be the "father of a multitude of nations" (Genesis 17:4 ESV). Abraham's wife Sarah was ninety and had been unable to conceive a child. God's promise vanquished their despair and provided hope. Abraham "did not weaken in faith when he considered his own body, which was as good as dead (since he was about a hundred years old), or when he considered the barrenness of Sarah's womb" (Romans 4:19 ESV).

Why do you think Abraham's hope was so transformational?

truth and immediately offers a remedy: "The wages of sin is death, but the free gift of God is eternal life in Jesus Christ our Lord."[37] Even though we are innately prone to prideful foolishness, "God shows his love for us in that while we were still sinners, Christ died for us."[38]

Jesus came to pay the penalty for our sin, even though he, as the Son of God, lived a *sinless* life. He paid the price we can't afford for crimes he didn't commit. When we admit our rebellion, turn from our sin, and acknowledge Jesus as our Savior, he forgives our sin and empowers us to live a new life.

Hope is only a decision away. "If you confess with your mouth that Jesus is Lord and believe in your heart that God raised him from the dead, you will be saved. For with the heart one believes and is justified, and with the mouth one confesses and is saved."[39]

When we place our trust in Jesus, hope is visible on every horizon. Our *difficulties* may remain, but our *destination* is secured. We'll still encounter trouble in this life, but "since we have been justified by faith, we have peace with God through our Lord Jesus Christ."[40] This peace is the key to a hopeful future, both personally and collectively.

The sin separating us from God and each other is the cause of crime, violence, poverty, hunger, racism, social polarization, political corruption, and oppression. The gospel is the cure for every kind of stupid because it is the cure for sin. The gospel is the solution for *every problem* because it is the solution for our *greatest problem*. It's as simple as that.

 ## Chase the Lead

In one of his most quoted books, C. S. Lewis wrote, "I believe in Christianity as I believe that the sun has risen: not only because I see it, but because by it I see everything else."[41] The gospel fixes every kind of stupid because it changes the way we see ourselves and others. It is eye-opening.

First, the gospel changes the way we see the future. If Christianity is true, God has written a story and he's already revealed how it ends. While it's tempting to wallow in the hopelessness of any given chapter, the gospel calls us to focus on the postscript. A day is coming when our questions will be answered, justice will be measured, and our illnesses will be cured. The saved will live forever in the blissful presence of our Creator. This is the hope the gospel offers.

Second, the gospel changes the way we view the primacy and power of God. The message of salvation is more than a human proposition, philosophical principle, or useful contrivance. The gospel is "the power of God for salvation."[42] It is *God's* solution. *He's* the authority and the source of power behind the remedy for every kind of stupid. Jesus said, "Those who are well have no need of a physician, but those who are sick. I came not to call the righteous, but sinners."[43] God is the Great Physician and the author of the cure. He is fully able to fill his prescription. The gospel leverages the power of God.

Third, the gospel changes the way we envision the sickness *and* the cure. Sinful pride is our common illness, destroying relationships, corrupting governments, and dividing societies. Every worrisome, seemingly hopeless dilemma we face as a species is rooted in this form of selfishness. The gospel offers a simple remedy: humility. Personal salvation *begins* as we humbly admit our need for a Savior. It *continues* as we allow God's Spirit to transform us into "a new creation."[44] It *finishes* when we move from despair to hope.

Finally, the gospel provides the *power* to apply the cure. The authors of Scripture described the role our humility plays in our marriages, families, and communities. As new creations indwelled by the Holy Spirit, we now have the power to put our pride to death and live humbly as we navigate every kind of stupid, including the following:

Crime and Violence

The Bible recognizes the fallen nature of humans and the crimes we commit against one another. Moses, for example, chronicled God's law in the Ten Commandments and recorded additional regulations to address criminal behavior. Jesus also condemned crime and violence, inspiring early Christians to humbly follow the example of their Master. Second-century Christian philosopher and defender Justin Martyr wrote, "We who formerly treasured money and possessions more than anything else now hand everything we have to a treasury for all and share it with everyone who needs it. We who formerly hated and murdered one another . . . now live together and share the same table. Now we pray for our enemies and try to win those who hate us."[45]

Poverty and Hunger

The poor and needy are of special concern to those who have embraced the gospel. The Bible authors called for believers to humble themselves as they care for needy family members, friends, strangers, and sojourn-ers.[46] The earliest Christians embraced this teaching. Lactantius, a fourth-century Christian author who became an advisor to Roman emperor Constantine I, warned, "If you esteem justice so highly, lay aside the burdens [of wealth] that oppress you and follow justice. Free yourself from bondage and chains, so that you can run to God without any hindrance."[47] Once converted to Christianity, Constantine followed the discipleship of Lactantius and "distributed money largely to those who were in need . . . and even for the beggars in the forum, miserable and shiftless, he provided, not with money only, or necessary food, but also decent clothing."[48]

Greed and Injustice

The Bible also addresses issues of greed, partiality, and justice. The rich and poor are described as brothers created by the same Maker, and believers are instructed to act without partiality when engaging people who may have less money, status, or influence.[49] God also spoke through the biblical authors to warn against cheating others in the marketplace.[50] The earliest Christians took these admonitions seriously. The fourth-century theologian, statesman, and bishop Ambrose of Milan observed the degree to which citizens of the Roman Empire took advantage of one another and warned, "Who then is so unjust and so greedy as he who uses the livelihood of many other people not merely to satisfy his own needs, but to have an abundance and ingratiate his delights?"[51]

These few examples illustrate only a fraction of the gospel's power. The gospel proposes a solution and provides hope for the concerns we report in polls, surveys, and studies. If you're feeling hopeless, embrace the gospel. If you know someone consumed by despair, share the gospel. If you want to change the world, preach the gospel.

Several years after we closed the Springwell case, Sandra's niece, Ashley, found my social media profile and messaged me. It was the anniversary of Sandra's passing. I called her as soon as I got the note.

"Detective Wallace, I just wanted you to know something. My aunt was such a private person, especially after Nicole died. She withdrew from everyone except her doctors. But I saw an incredible change when you visited her and reopened the case. She called me out of the blue and asked me to visit her the next Sunday. When I got there, she told me we were going to church. I don't think she had been in *years*. So we went. Keep in mind now, I was not a Christian. I just went to make her happy. But the pastor preached the gospel, and I saw God do something in my aunt. Something powerful."

Before I could respond, Ashley added more.

"I became a Christian later that year. I'm sorry it took so long for me to reach out to you. I just wanted you to know the impact the investigation had on my aunt. I think God used it to bring her back home. He also used it to reach me. My aunt was *sure* Nicole's case would eventually be solved, but she told me it would be OK with her if it didn't happen during her lifetime. I just wanted you to know my aunt Sandra is waiting for us in heaven."

 ## The Truth in True Crime: You Were Created to Be Saved

Sandra found peace, even *before* we found Nicole's killer. As the apostle Paul might have written, the God of hope filled Sandra with all joy and peace in believing, so that by the power of the Holy Spirit she would abound in hope.[52] Sandra was certain that divine justice would eventually be served. More importantly, she was confident she would spend eternity with God because she heard the gospel message and accepted Jesus as her Savior.

Her confidence was perfectly suited to the New Testament definition of hope.

Today, hope is often synonymous with wishful thinking. If I asked, for example, "Do you think the Dodgers will win the World Series this year?" You might respond, "I sure hope so," as if to say, "I don't know, but I would really like that to happen!" The New Testament authors never used *hope* in this way. They consistently employed the Greek verb *elpizō* (ἐλπίζω) and the noun *elpis* (ἐλπίς) to describe hope as a sense of certainty and full confidence.

When Paul wrote, "Faith is the assurance of things hoped for, the conviction of things not seen,"[53] he didn't mean, "Faith is the assurance of things *wished* for." Instead, he meant, "Now faith is the assurance of things for which I am certain and fully confident, the conviction of things not seen."

That kind of hope changes everything.

We live with renewed optimism when we are certain about our eternal life "which God, who never lies, promised before the ages began."[54] We "rejoice in hope of the glory of God" when we are *fully confident* that Jesus has secured our salvation.[55] We let our hearts "take courage" and "wait for the Lord" when we are *convinced* God will act.[56] We "rejoice in hope," are "patient in tribulation," and "constant in prayer" when we are *assured* God is present, even in our suffering.[57]

EXPLANATION: Hopelessness Finds Its Remedy in God

Hopelessness is a destructive emotion requiring a remedy. That's why people who experience hopelessness usually find themselves searching for a cure. The gospel is the purest source of hope ever offered, providing real solutions for our past, present, and future.

Despair fuels our search for hope, a pursuit leading ultimately to the Greatest Physician, the source of hope, and the author of the gospel.

Our universal experiences of hopelessness are designed to introduce us to a certain and fully confident hope available only in the promises of God.

That's why the gospel is the purest expression of hope ever declared. When we confidently place our trust in Jesus for our salvation, he redeems our past, renews our present, and redirects our future. He restores our hope.

Victor Hugo, in his famous book *Les Misérables*, described hope as "the word which God has written on the brow of every man."[58] Humans thrive when we find hope because we were created by the *author of hope*. Humans flourish when we embrace salvation because we were created by the *author of salvation*. Hopelessness is a temporal illness God uses to guide us to his eternal remedy: salvation. Hope is "written on our brows" because *we were created to be saved*.

POSTSCRIPT

The Bible Describes You the Way You Really Are

Josh Henderson stood at the edge of a pristine lake, marveling at the distant Alaskan mountain range. He held Samantha's hand as she anticipated her baptism.

Susie and I reflected on what God had done in the past few days. When Josh and Samantha arrived at this law enforcement marriage resiliency retreat, they were on the verge of divorce. Now, a week later, they seemed like newlyweds.

Josh was a twelve-year police detective at a major East Coast city. One night when serving a search warrant, he was shot by a suspect hiding in the back bedroom of the house. Josh suffered two gunshot wounds to his right arm, hindering his ability to pull his pistol and return fire. He retreated from the house as the rest of the search team engaged the shooter.

The responding paramedics barely transported Josh to the hospital in time. His arm was broken, his brachial artery was severed, and his radial nerve was damaged. Josh's doctors said the injury would likely end his career.

The next year was the worst of Josh and Samantha's marriage. The rehabilitation was excruciating, and Josh became bitter and hopeless. He couldn't fathom himself as anything other than a police officer. The injury threatened his identity *and* his marriage. He became a different person, one his wife could hardly recognize.

Samantha heard about the marriage retreat for wounded officers. A month later, she and Josh were in Alaska where Susie and I were serving as the chaplains.

We talked about the nature of marriage, trauma, forgiveness, and growth. We also talked about the evidence for Christianity. Three days into the retreat, Samantha wanted to know how she could become a Christian. She gave her life to Christ that afternoon.

Josh remained quiet over the next two days. He witnessed a transformation in his marriage and watched Samantha blossom. He seemed on the verge of a decision.

"Samantha, you're next," Susie said from the edge of the water.

Josh kissed his wife and watched her enter the lake. He was *beaming*.

"Dude, what are you waiting for?" I asked as we watched Samantha prepare for her baptism. He looked at me and paused. He shook his head briefly as if lost in thought. "Well, I *know* Christianity is true . . ."

"Then why aren't you in the water?"

Josh paused again. He stared at me, then looked in the direction of his wife, then back at me.

"You're right!"

Josh put his faith in Jesus at the edge of that Alaskan lake, just before we baptized him with Samantha.

Josh chased leads as a detective, but until this retreat, he never applied his investigative prowess to the claims of Christianity. The more Josh and Samantha learned about themselves, their marriage, and their journey through trauma, the more they understood the surprising explanatory power of the Christian worldview.

The Bible describes the world the way it really is: the good, the bad, the beautiful, and the ugly. It also describes the world the way it *could* be if we adopted the ancient, divine truths of Christianity.

Like Josh and Samantha, Susie and I had no idea what the Bible taught about human flourishing when we started our relationship. We weren't Christians for the first eighteen years together. We turned instead to scientists and researchers for the information we hoped would help us raise our kids and thrive in our marriage. I also leaned on the truth I discovered in true crime investigations, sifting through my cases to identify the nature of humans and the path to human flourishing.

But after becoming believers, we realized modern research and my discoveries as a detective failed to reveal anything new about human nature. These independent findings simply reflected the collective wisdom of the biblical authors. Compare, for example, modern discoveries (and my true crime observations) to the ancient claims of Christianity:

Secular Studies Find That Humans Thrive . . .
1. When we revere wisdom
2. When we ground our identity in something bigger than ourselves
3. When we engage in virtuous friendships
4. When we commit to marriage
5. When we devote ourselves to something worthy
6. When we exercise humility
7. When we find contentment and purpose in our work
8. When we make sense of our trauma
9. When we seek and revere justice
10. When we balance truth and grace
11. When we admit our fallen nature
12. When we embrace guilt and resolve shame
13. When we experience the love of a father
14. When we conquer our fear of death
15. When we find hope in every difficult situation

The Bible Claims That Humans Thrive . . .
1. When we revere wisdom (Proverbs 4:5–9)
2. When we ground our identity in an unchanging, all-powerful God (2 Corinthians 5:17)
3. When we engage in virtuous friendships (Proverbs 27:17)
4. When we commit to marriage (Proverbs 18:22)
5. When we devote ourselves to God, the one who is most worthy (Hebrews 12:28)
6. When we exercise humility (Proverbs 22:4)
7. When we find contentment and purpose in our work (1 Thessalonians 4:11)
8. When we make sense of our trauma (1 Peter 1:3–9)
9. When we seek and revere justice (Isaiah 1:17)
10. When we balance truth and grace (Luke 6:31)
11. When we admit our fallen nature (Romans 3:23)
12. When we embrace guilt and resolve shame (1 John 1:9)
13. When we experience the love of an earthly and heavenly Father (Galatians 4:6)
14. When we conquer our fear of death (Hebrews 2:14–15)
15. When we trust God in every difficult situation (Psalm 9:10)

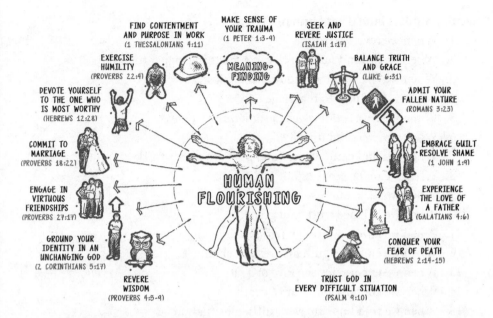

The ancient authors of the Bible accurately predicted the discoveries of modern researchers because humans were created in the image of the God of the Bible. Additional studies won't change these findings about our nature because they are rooted in our God-given design. Societies, trends, and preferences may change over time, but our human nature will remain the same, just as the Bible describes.

When we embrace these fifteen ancient *biblical* attributes of human flourishing, we thrive according to every accepted *secular* metric. When we reject them, we do so at our own peril. You may have noticed that our national depression and suicide rates are rising. We are also more divided and polarized than ever before as violence and crime rates skyrocket, all while self-reported Christian belief is declining. Why? Because the more we reject the instruction of our *Designer*, the more we fail to function properly *as designed*. Our future, therefore, is dependent on our willingness to embrace the teaching of Christianity.

Cultures that aim at human flourishing hit the bull's-eye called Christianity every time.

Before I ever chased a lead or investigated a true crime, I chased Susie. When I met her, I knew she was the woman I wanted to marry. She was beautiful, intelligent, and yearned to be good. When I began chasing leads in the Bible, I recognized those same characteristics in Christianity.

Christianity is *beautiful*. Jesus has inspired more authors, writers, artists, and musicians than any other figure in history. Christianity is *intelligent*. Christ followers have contributed more to the history of education, theology, and philosophy than any other group.[1] Christianity is *good*. The Bible recognizes our human nature, identifies our inclinations, and inspires us to godliness.

The Bible provides the outline for human flourishing because it contains the wisdom of our Creator. And because it comes from God, its truths can be discovered in every corner of God's creation, including modern research and true crime stories.

We cheered and applauded as Josh and Samantha emerged from the Alaskan lake. From the looks on their faces, you'd never know the water temperature was near freezing. They didn't seem to care in the least. They chased leads in Alaska and found something beautiful, intelligent, and good. They were now prepared to let the truth of the gospel change their lives forever.

The gospel can change *your* life as well—if you're willing to chase a few leads and embrace the truth in true crime.

NOTES

For quotes, commentary, and more information see the full Case Notes file at https://coldcasechristianity.com/case-notes-for-the-truth-in-true-crime.

Lead #1: A Pool of Blood (Under My Feet)

1. *Merriam-Webster*, s.v. "knowledge," https://www.merriam-webster.com/dictionary/wisdom, accessed 11-28-22; Dictionary.com, s.v. "wisdom," "scholarly knowledge or learning; wise sayings or teachings; precepts; a wise act or saying." https://www.dictionary.com/browse/wisdom, accessed 11-28-22.
2. Grossmann, Igor. (2020, October 15). The science of wisdom. Aeon.com. https://aeon.co/essays/how-psychological-scientists-found-the-empirical-path-to-wisdom, accessed 11-30-22.
3. For a brief evaluation of the "is-ought problem," visit https://en.wikipedia.org/wiki/Is%E2%80%93ought_problem, accessed 12-01-22, or read Hudson, W. D. (Ed.). (1969). *The is/ought question: A collection of papers on the central problem in moral philosophy.* Macmillan.
4. Proverbs 4:6–7; Proverbs 16:16; Proverbs 21:20; Proverbs 3:13–17.
5. Job 28:28 ESV. See also Ecclesiastes 2:13, Proverbs 3:7.
6. James 3:17 NIV.
7. 1 Corinthians 1:25 NIV. See also Isaiah 28:29; Daniel 2:20.
8. Stahl, Tomas. (2021, February 24). The amoral atheist? A cross-national examination of cultural, motivational, and cognitive antecedents of disbelief, and their implications for morality. *PLOS ONE*, 16(2): e0246593. https://journals.plos.org/plosone/article?id=10.1371/journal.pone.0246593, accessed 12-02-22.
9. *Cambridge Dictionary*, s.v. "wisdom." "The ability to make good judgments based on what you have learned from your experience, or the knowledge and understanding that gives you this ability." https://dictionary.cambridge.org/us/dictionary/english/wisdom, accessed 11-28-22.
10. *Merriam-Webster*, s.v. "experience." https://www.merriam-webster.com/dictionary/experience, accessed 12-01-22.
11. Noonan, David. (2019, October 30). Failure found to be an "essential prerequisite" for success. *Scientific American*. https://www.scientificamerican.com/article/failure-found-to-be-an-essential-prerequisite-for-success/, accessed 12-01-22.
12. More data from this study can be accessed here: Wang, Yang, Jones, Benjamin F., & Wang, Dashun. (2019, October 1). *Nature Communications*, 10(4331). https://www.nature.com/articles/s41467-019-12189-3, accessed 12-01-22.
13. James 3:2 ESV.
14. Philippians 2:3 NIV.
15. There is some debate about the origin of this quote; it's also been credited to Hyman Rickover, Martin Vanbee, Eleanor Roosevelt, Harry Myers, Laurence J. Peter, and Sam Levenson. https://navyreads.blogspot.com/2012/11/navy-reads-conversation-with-creator-ii.html. Referenced in the *Honolulu Star-Advertiser*. (2012, November 30). Quote page A6, column 3. Newspapers.com.

16. James 1:5.
17. Proverbs 24:3–4 ESV.
18. Matthew 7:24.
19. Glück, J., & Scherpf, A. (2022, August). Intelligence and wisdom: Age-related differences and non-linear relationships. *Psychology and Aging*, 37(5): 649–666. https://doi.org/10.1037/pag0000692.
20. Job 12:12 NLT.
21. For more information on a "Wisdom Model" for decision making, read Friesen, Garry, & Maxson, J. Robin. (2004). *Decision making and the will of God: A biblical alternative to the traditional view*. Multnomah.
22. HSBC. *The value of education: Learning for life* [Global report]. *Wall Street Journal*. https://www.wsj.com/public/resources/documents/HSBCSurvey.pdf, accessed 12-2-22.
23. Wolfgang Lutz of the International Institute for Applied Systems Analysis in Vienna. Mackenzie, Debora. (2018, April 18). More education is what makes people live longer, not more money. *New Scientist*. https://www.newscientist.com/article/2166833-more-education-is-what-makes-people-live-longer-not-more-money/, accessed 12-2-22.
24. Center on Society and Health. (2015, February 13). *Why education matters to health: Exploring the causes*. https://societyhealth.vcu.edu/work/the-projects/why-education-matters-to-health-exploring-the-causes.html, accessed 12-2-22.
25. University of Western Australia and Edith Cowan University. (2019, December 13). Study finds educated people more likely to help a stranger. Phys.org. https://phys.org/news/2019-12-people-stranger.html, accessed 12-2-22.
26. Deuteronomy 11:19; Proverbs 22:6.
27. John 14:26; Romans 12:2.
28. Vocabulary.com, s.v. "disciple." https://www.vocabulary.com/dictionary/disciple, accessed 12-2-22.
29. Lewis, C. S. (2001). *The great divorce*. HarperSanFrancisco, 41. (Original work published 1946)

Lead #2: Fake IDs and a Stolen Identity

1. Keith Morrison (News Correspondent, Dateline, NBC) in his endorsement of my book *God's Crime Scene* (David C. Cook, 2015.
2. As defined by Dictionary.com, s.v. "identity." https://www.dictionary.com/browse/identity, accessed 12-8-22.
3. Ragelienė, Tija. (2016, Spring). Links of adolescents identity development and relationship with peers: A systematic literature review. *Journal of the Canadian Academy of Child and Adolescent Psychiatry*, 25(2): 97–105. https://www.ncbi.nlm.nih.gov/pmc/articles/PMC4879949/, accessed 12-8-22.
4. Taylor, Charles. (2018). *The ethics of authenticity*. Harvard University Press, 112–113.
5. Barna Research Group. (2016, May 25). *The end of absolutes: America's new moral code*. https://www.barna.com/research/the-end-of-absolutes-americas-new-moral-code/, accessed 12-8-22.
6. For more in this typically overlooked area of identity formation, see Verplanken, Bas, & Sui, Jie. (2019, July 10). Habit and identity: Behavioral, cognitive, affective, and motivational facets of an integrated self. *Frontiers in Psychology, Section of Cognitive Science*, 10. https://www.frontiersin.org/articles/10.3389/fpsyg.2019.01504/full, accessed 12-8-22.
7. Matthew 16:18 ESV.
8. Hollmann, Joshua. (2018, Fall). Christian identity in a secular age: Charles Taylor and Martin Luther on the authenticity of the self in society. *Concordia Theological Journal*, 6(1). https://www.cuw.edu/academics/schools/arts-and-sciences/_assets/theological-journal/2018_v6i1-Fall/Article-Hollmann.pdf, accessed 12-10-22.
9. Psalm 139:13–14, Genesis 1:27, 1 Peter 2:9.
10. Rothfuss, Patrick. (2007). *The name of the wind*. Astra Publishing House, 658.
11. Philippians 2:3, Luke 6:35.
12. Galatians 3:27–29.
13. 1 Corinthians 12:25–28, 1 Corinthians 12:4–6.
14. John 1:12.

15. Ephesians 4:20–24.
16. 1 John 4:9; Isaiah 44:2.
17. Ephesians 1:3–5; Ephesians 1:7.
18. Ephesians 4:4–6; 2 Timothy 3:16–17.
19. Epictetus. (1920). *The moral discourses of Epictetus* (Elizabeth Carter, Trans.). J. M. Dent & Sons, Limited, 134.
20. *The Core Need* as described here: Henriques, Gregg. (2014, June 25). The core need. *Psychology Today.* https://www.psychologytoday.com/us/blog/theory-knowledge/201406/the-core-need, accessed 12-11-22.
21. Genesis 2:19–20.
22. John 17:12; Hebrews 2:14–18.
23. John 20:30–31 ESV.
24. Acts 4:12 ESV.

Lead #3: A Target, a Bull's-Eye, and a Circle of Concern

1. Demir, M., Özen, A., & Procsal, A. D. (2014). Friendship and happiness. In A. C. Michalos (Eds.), *Encyclopedia of quality of life and wellbeing research.* Springer. https://doi.org/10.1007/978-94-007-0753-5_3895, accessed 12-20-22.
2. Cacioppo, J. T., Hughes, M. E., Waite, L. J., Hawkley, L. C., & Thisted, R. A. (2006). Loneliness as a specific risk factor for depressive symptoms: Cross-sectional and longitudinal analyses. *Psychology and Aging,* 21(1): 140–151. https://doi.org/10.1037/0882-7974.21.1.140, accessed 12-20-22.
3. *Nature Reviews Neuroscience,* 13(6): 421–34. https://doi.org/10.1038/nrn3231, accessed 12-20-22.
4. Cohen, S., Doyle, W. J., Turner, R., Alper, C. M., & Skoner, D. P. (2003). Sociability and susceptibility to the common cold. *Psychological Science,* 14(5): 389–395. https://doi.org/10.1111/1467-9280.01452, accessed 12-20-22; American Psychological Association. (2005, May 2). First-year college students who feel lonely have a weaker immune response to the flu shot. ScienceDaily. https://www.sciencedaily.com/releases/2005/05/050502101113.htm, accessed 12-20-22.
5. Holt-Lunstad, J., Smith, T. B., & Layton, J. B. (2010). Social relationships and mortality risk: A meta-analytic review. *PLOS MEDICINE,* 7(7): e1000316. https://doi.org/10.1371/journal.pmed.1000316, accessed 12-20-22.
6. Holt-Lunstad, J., Smith, T. B., & Layton, J. B. Social relationships. https://doi.org/10.1371/journal.pmed.1000316; Yang, Claire Yang, Boen, Courtney, Gerken, Karen, Li, Ting, Schorpp, Kristen, & Harris, Kathleen Mullan. (2016, January 19). Social relationships and physiological determinants of longevity across the human life span. *Proceedings of the National Academy of Sciences,* 113(3). https://doi.org/10.1073/pnas.1511085112, accessed 12-20-22; Shankar, A., Hamer, M., McMunn, A., & Steptoe, A. (2013, February/March). Social isolation and loneliness: Relationships with cognitive function during 4 years of follow-up in the English longitudinal study of ageing. *Psychosomatic Medicine,* 75(2): 161–70. https://doi.org/10.1097/PSY.0b013e31827f09cd, accessed 12-20-22; Sutin, A. R., Stephan, Y., Luchetti, M., & Terracciano, A. (2020, August 13). Loneliness and risk of dementia. *Journals of Gerontology: Series B Psychological Sciences and Social Sciences,* 75(7): 1414–1422. https://doi.org/10.1093/geronb/gby112, accessed 12-20-22; Crooks, V. C., Lubben, J., Petitti, D. B., Little, D., & Chiu, V. (2008, July). Social network, cognitive function, and dementia incidence among elderly women. *American Journal of Public Health,* 98(7): 1221–7. https://doi.org/10.2105/AJPH.2007.115923, accessed 12-20-22; Holwerda, T. J., Deeg, D. J. H., & Beekman, A. T. F., et al. (2014). Feelings of loneliness, but not social isolation, predict dementia onset: Results from the Amsterdam Study of the Elderly (AMSTEL). *Journal of Neurology, Neurosurgery & Psychiatry,* 85: 135–142. https://jnnp.bmj.com/content/85/2/135.long, accessed 12-20-22.
7. From the definition offered by the 1828 Edition of Webster's Dictionary as seen here: WebstersDictionary1828.com, s.v. "friend." https://webstersdictionary1828.com/Dictionary/friend, accessed 12-20-22.
8. For more on this study, see: https://www.adultdevelopmentstudy.org/grantandglueckstudy, accessed 12-20-22.

212 The Truth in True Crime

9. Amati, V., Meggiolaro, S., Rivellini, G., & Zaccarin, S. (2018). Social relations and life satisfaction: The role of friends. *Genus*, 74(1): 7. https://doi.org/10.1186/s41118-018-0032-z, accessed 12-20-22; Demir, M., & Özdemir, M. (2010). Friendship, need satisfaction and happiness. *Journal of Happiness Studies*, 11: 243–259. https://doi.org/10.1007/s10902-009-9138-5, accessed 12-20-22.
10. Demır, M., and Weitekamp, L. A. (2007). I am so happy 'cause today I found my friend: Friendship and personality as predictors of happiness. *Journal of Happiness Studies*, 8: 181–211. https://doi.org/10.1007/s10902-006-9012-7, accessed 12-20-22.
11. Giles, L. C., Glonek, G. F. V., & Luszcz, M. A., et al. (2005). Effect of social networks on 10 year survival in very old Australians: The Australian longitudinal study of aging. *Journal of Epidemiology & Community Health*, 59: 574–579. https://jech.bmj.com/content/59/7/574.abstract, accessed 12-22-22.
12. Demır, M. and Weitekamp, L. A. I am so happy. https://doi.org/10.1007/s10902-006-9012-7.
13. Long, E., Gardani, M., McCann, M., Sweeting, H., Tranmer, M., & Moore, L. (2020, May). Mental health disorders and adolescent peer relationships. *Social Science & Medicine*, 253: 112973. https://doi.org/10.1016/j.socscimed.2020.112973, accessed 12-22-22.
14. Fowler J. H., & Christakis, N. A. (2008). Dynamic spread of happiness in a large social network: Longitudinal analysis over 20 years in the Framingham Heart Study. *BMJ*, 337: a2338. https://doi.org/10.1136/bmj.a2338, accessed 12-22-22.
15. Nezlek, J. B., Imbrie, M., & Shean, G. D. (1994). Depression and everyday social interaction. *Journal of Personality and Social Psychology*, 67(6): 1101–1111. https://doi.org/10.1037/0022-3514.67.6.1101, accessed 12-27-22; Bearman, Peter S., & Moody, James. (2004, January 1). Suicide and friendships among American adolescents. *American Journal of Public Health*, 94(1): 89–95. https://ajph.aphapublications.org/doi/10.2105/AJPH.94.1.89, accessed 1-27-22.
16. Urberg, K. A., Değirmencioğlu, S. M., & Pilgrim, C. (1997). Close friend and group influence on adolescent cigarette smoking and alcohol use. *Developmental Psychology*, 33(5): 834–844. https://doi.org/10.1037/0012-1649.33.5.834, accessed 12-27-22; Andrews, J. A., Tildesley, E., Hops, H., & Li, F. (2002). The influence of peers on young adult substance use. *Health Psychology*, 21(4): 349–357. https://doi.org/10.1037/0278-6133.21.4.349, accessed 12-27-22.
17. Lowe, Michael L., Haws, Kelly L. (2014, August 1). (Im)moral support: The social outcomes of parallel self-control decisions. *Journal of Consumer Research*, 41(2): 489–505. https://doi.org/10.1086/676688, accessed 12-22-22.
18. Wilcox, Keith, & Stephen, Andrew T. (2013, June 1). Are close friends the enemy? Online social networks, self-esteem, and self-control. *Journal of Consumer Research*, 40(1): 90–103. https://doi.org/10.1086/668794, accessed 12-22-22.
19. Cicero, Marcus. *On friendship (De amicitia)*. Little, Brown, and Company, -44. https://oll.libertyfund.org/title/cicero-on-friendship-de-amicitia, accessed 12-27-22.
20. Aristotle. *Nicomachean Ethics* (W. D. Ross, Trans.). http://classics.mit.edu/Aristotle/nicomachaen.8.viii.html, accessed 12-27-22.
21. Proverbs 14:7; Proverbs 18:24; Proverbs 12:26–27; Proverbs 13:20.
22. Proverbs 27:17; 2 Corinthians 6:14.
23. Hebrews 3:13; James 5:16.
24. Colossians 3:12–13.
25. 1 John 3:17–18.
26. Proverbs 21:13 ESV.
27. Ezekiel 34:3–4.
28. Galatians 6:2 ESV. See also 1 Thessalonians 5:11.
29. Colossians 3:12; Romans 12:15.
30. Galatians 6:1; Matthew 18:15–16; Ephesians 4:25.
31. Attributed earliest to Emanuel James Rohn (Jim Rohn), an entrepreneur, author and motivational speaker, in Canfield, Jack, & Switzer, Janet. (2005). Drop out of the "ain't it awful" club . . . and surround yourself with successful people. In *The Success Principles (TM): How to Get from Where You Are to Where You Want to Be*. William Morrow, 189.
32. 1 Corinthians 15:33 ESV.

Lead #4: Trajectory Decisions (for Better or Worse)

1. Citing the definition offered by the American Scientific Affiliation. What is a worldview?—Definition & introduction. https://www.asa3.org/ASA/education/views/index.html, accessed 1-06-23.

2. Wang, Wendy. (2020, September). *More than one-third of prime-age Americans have never married* [Research brief]. Institute for Family Studies. https://ifstudies.org/ifs-admin/resources/final2-ifs-single-americansbrief2020.pdf, accessed 2-19-23.

3. United States Census Bureau. *Figure MS-2: Median age at first marriage: 1890 to present.* https://www.census.gov/content/dam/Census/library/visualizations/time-series/demo/families-and-households/ms-2.pdf, accessed 12-29-23; Henig, Robin Marantz. (2010, August 18). What is it about twenty somethings? *New York Times.* Page MM28. https://www.nytimes.com/2010/08/22/magazine/22Adulthood-t.html, accessed 12-29-22.

4. Hawkins, A. J., Carroll, J. S., Jones, A. M. W., & James, S. L. (2022). *Capstones vs. cornerstones: Is marrying later always better? State of Our Unions: 2022.* The National Marriage Project. http://nationalmarriageproject.org/wp-content/uploads/2022/02/Wheatley_StateofUnions_020222_v1.pdf, accessed 12-29-22; Ortiz-Ospina, Esteban, & Roser, Max. (2020). *Marriages and divorces.* Our World in Data. https://ourworldindata.org/marriages-and-divorces#marriages-are-becoming-less-common, accessed 12-29-22.

5. https://www.jec.senate.gov/public/index.cfm/republicans/2020/4/marriage-rate-blog-test, accessed 12-29-23; *Marriage rate in the United States from 1990 to 2020.* https://www.statista.com/statistics/195951/marriage-rate-in-the-united-states-since-1990/, accessed 12-29-22; National Marriage Project. *Knot yet.* http://nationalmarriageproject.org/wp-content/uploads/2013/03/KnotYet-FinalForWeb.pdf, accessed 12-29-22.

6. Wilcox, W. Bradford, & Lerman, Robert I. *For richer, for poorer: How family structures economic success in America.* AEI & Institute for Family Studies. https://web.archive.org/web/20190317025422/http://www.aei.org/publication/for-richer-for-poorer-how-family-structures-economic-success-in-america/, accessed 12-29-22; Witherspoon Institute. (2008, August). *Marriage and the public good: Ten principles.* https://www.bigskyworldview.org/content/docs/links/MarriageandThePublicGoodTenPrinciples.pdf, accessed 12-29-22, citing Wilcox, W. Bradford, et al. (2005.) *Why marriage matters: Twenty-six conclusions from the social sciences* (2nd ed.). Institute for American Values; Wilcox and Lerman, *For richer, for poorer.* https://web.archive.org/web/20190317025422/http://www.aei.org/publication/for-richer-for-poorer-how-family-structures-economic-success-in-america/; Ahituv, Avner, & Lerman, Robert I. (2007, August). How do marital status, labor supply, and wage rates interact? *Demography,* 44(3): 623–47; Lerman, Robert I. (2011). Economic perspectives on marriage: Causes, consequences, and public policy. In Lloyd R. Cohen & Joshua D. Wright (Eds.), *Research handbook on the economics of family law.* Edward Elgar, p. 72, and Wilcox, W. Bradford, et al. (2005.) *Why marriage matters;* Wilcox and Lerman, *For richer, for poorer.* https://web.archive.org/web/20190317025422/http://www.aei.org/publication/for-richer-for-poorer-how-family-structures-economic-success-in-america/.

7. Wilcox and Lerman, *For richer, for poorer.* https://web.archive.org/web/20190317025422/http://www.aei.org/publication/for-richer-for-poorer-how-family-structures-economic-success-in-america/; Gorman, Elizabeth H. (1999, February); Refer also to *Journal of Marriage and Family,* 61(1): 110–122.

8. June, Patricia Lee. (2014, July). *Cohabitation: Effects of parental cohabitation and other non-marital sexual activity on children.* American College of Pediatricians. https://acpeds.org/position-statements/cohabitation-effects-of-parental-cohabitation-and-other-non-marital-sexual-activity-on-children-part-2-of-2, accessed 12-30-22, citing Lichter, D. T., Qian, Z., & Mellott, L. M. (2006). Marriage or dissolution? Union transitions among poor cohabiting women. *Demography,* 43(2): 223–240; Zissimopoulos, Julie, Karney, Benjamin, & Rauer, Amy. (2008, November). *Marital histories and economic wellbeing.* RAND; Witherspoon, *Marriage and the public good.* https://www.bigskyworldview.org/content/docs/links/MarriageandThePublicGoodTenPrinciples.pdf, citing Wilcox, W. Bradford, et al. (2005). *Why marriage matters;* Wilcox, W. Bradford, et al. (2005). *Why marriage matters;* Marquardt, Elizabeth. (2005). *Between two worlds: The inner lives*

of children of divorce. Crown. And McLanahan, Sara, & Sandefur, Gary. (1994). *Growing up with a single parent*. Harvard University Press.

9. Gardner, Jonathan, & Oswald, Andrew. (2004). How is mortality affected by money, marriage and stress? *Journal of Health Economics*, 23: 1181–1207; Coombs, Robert. (1991). Marital status and personal wellbeing: A literature review. *Family Relations*, 40: 97–102; Kiecolt-Glaser, Janice K., & Newton, Tamara L. (2001). Marriage and health: His and hers. *Psychological Bulletin*, 127: 472–503; Manzoli, Lamberto, et al. (2007, January). Marital status and mortality in the elderly: A systematic review and meta-analysis. *Social Science & Medicine*, 64(1): 77–94; Dupre, Matthew E., Beck, Audry N., & Meadows, Sarah O. (2009, September). Marital trajectories and mortality among US adults. *American Journal of Epidemiology*, 170(5): 546–55; Also, Kaplan, Robert M., & Kronick, Richard G. (2006). Marital status and longevity in the United States population. *Journal of Epidemiology and Community Health*, 60: 763; Hu, Yuaureng, & Goldman, Noreen. (1990). Mortality differentials by marital status: An international comparison. *Demography*, 27: 233–50.

10. Witherspoon, *Marriage and the public good*. https://www.bigskyworldview.org/content/docs/links/MarriageandThePublicGoodTenPrinciples.pdf, citing Wilcox, W. Bradford, et al. (2005). *Why marriage matters*; Hawkins, Daniel N., & Booth, Alan. (2005). Unhappily ever after: Effects of long-term low-quality marriages on wellbeing. *Social Forces*, 84: 451–472; Cohen, Sheldon, Doyle, William J., Skoner, David P., Rabin, Bruce S., & Gwaltney Jr., Jack M. (1997). Social ties and susceptibility to the common cold. *Journal of the American Medical Association*, 277: 1940–44; Stimpson, Jim P., & Lackan, Nuha A. (2007, September). Serum carotenoid levels vary by marital status. *Journal of the American Dietetic Association*, 107(9): 1581–85.

11. *Marriage could improve heart attack survival and reduce hospital stay* [News release]. British Cardiovascular Society Conference. https://www.eurekalert.org/news-releases/852882 and https://www.sciencedaily.com/releases/2016/06/160608100133.htm, accessed 12-31-22; Martínez, María Elena, Anderson, Kristin, Murphy, James D., Hurley, Susan, Canchola, Alison J., Keegan, Theresa H. M., Cheng, Iona, Clarke, Christina A., Glaser, Sally L., & Gomez, Scarlett L. (2016, May 15); *Cancer*, 122(10): 1570–1578. https://doi.org/10.1002/cncr.29886, accessed 1-02-23; Aizer, Ayal A., et al. (2013, September). Marital status and survival in patients with cancer. *Journal of Clinical Oncology*, 31(31): 3869–3876.

12. Bachman et al. (1997). *Smoking, drinking and drug use in young adulthood*. Lawrence Erlbaum; Miller-Tutzauer et al. (1987, December). The effect of marital status on stage, treatment, and survival of cancer patients. *Journal of the American Medical Association*, 258(21): 3125–30; Stanton, Glenn T. The health benefits of marriage. Focus on the Family. https://www.focusonthefamily.com/marriage/the-health-benefits-of-marriage/, accessed 1-03-23, referencing his book: Stanton, Glenn T. (2011). *The ring makes all the difference: The hidden consequences of cohabitation and the strong benefits of marriage*. Moody Publishers, 98–99; Stack, Steven, & Eshleman, J. Ross. (1998). Marital status and happiness: A 17-nation study. *Journal of Marriage and Family*, 60: 528; Waite, Linda, & Gallagher, Maggie. (2000). *The case for marriage*. Doubleday, 55; Waite, Linda, & Gallagher, Maggie. (2000). *The case for marriage*. Doubleday; Witherspoon, *Marriage and the public good*. https://www.bigskyworldview.org/content/docs/links/MarriageandThePublicGoodTenPrinciples.pdf, citing Waite, Linda, & Gallagher, Maggie. (2000). *The case for marriage*. Doubleday.

13. Mahdi, Rezapour. (2022). The interactive factors contributing to fear of death. *Frontiers in Psychology*, 13. https://doi.org/10.3389/fpsyg.2022.905594, accessed 3-30-23.

14. Robins, Lee, & Regier, Darrel. (1991). *Psychiatric disorders in America: The Epidemiologic Catchment Area Study*. Free Press, 64, 334; Stack and Eshleman, Marital status and happiness, 527–36; National Marriage Project. *Knot yet*. http://nationalmarriageproject.org/wp-content/uploads/2013/03/KnotYet-FinalForWeb.pdf, accessed 12-29-22; Grover, S., & Helliwell, J. F. (2019). How's life at home? New evidence on marriage and the set point for happiness. *Journal of Happiness Studies*, 20(2): 373–390. https://doi.org/10.1007/s10902-017-9941-3.

15. Waite, Linda J. (1995, November). Does marriage matter? *Demography*, 32(4): 483–507; Ross, Catherine E., Mirowsky, John, & Goldsteen, Karen. (1990). The impact of family on health: Decade in review. *Journal of Marriage and the Family*, 52: 1064; Witherspoon, *Marriage and the public good*.

https://www.bigskyworldview.org/content/docs/links/MarriageandThePublicGoodTenPrinciples
.pdf, citing Waite, Linda, & Gallagher, Maggie. (2000). *The case for marriage*. Doubleday.
16. Kim, Hyoun K., & McKenry, Patrick C. (2002). The relationship between marriage and psychological wellbeing: A longitudinal analysis. *Journal of Family Issues*, 23: 905.
17. Moore, Kristin Anderson, Jekielek, Susan M., & Emig, Carol. (2002, June). *Marriage from a child's
perspective: How does family structure affect children, and what can be done about it?* [Research
brief]. Child Trends, p. 6, and summaries from Brookings and Princeton in McLanahan, Sara,
Donahue, Elisabeth, & Haskins, Ron. (2005). Introducing the issue. *The Future of Children*, 15:
3–12; Parke, Mary. (2003). *Are married parents really better for children?* Center for Law and
Social Policy. And the Institute for American Values' statement: Wilcox, W. Bradford, et al.
(2005). *Why marriage matters*.
18. Wilcox and Lerman, *For richer, for poorer*. https://web.archive.org/web/20190317025422/http://
www.aei.org/publication/for-richer-for-poorer-how-family-structures-economic-success-in
-america/; BrightCourse. Cohabitation for men. https://www.brightcourse.com/LessonFiles
/Factsheets/0222.pdf, accessed 12-29-22, citing Bennett, William J. (2003). *The broken hearth:
Reversing the moral collapse of the American family*. Broadway Books; June, *Cohabitation*. https://
acpeds.org/position-statements/cohabitation-effects-of-parental-cohabitation-and-other-non
-marital-sexual-activity-on-children-part-2-of-2, citing Manning, W. D., & Brown, S. (2006).
Children's economic well being in married and cohabiting parent families. *Journal of Marriage
and Family*, 68: 345–362; June, *Cohabitation*. https://acpeds.org/position-statements/cohabitation
-effects-of-parental-cohabitation-and-other-non-marital-sexual-activity-on-children-part-2-of
-2, citing Brown, S. L. (2004). Family structure and child wellbeing: The significance of parental
cohabitation. *Journal of Marriage and Family*, 66(2): 362; June, *Cohabitation*. https://acpeds
.org/position-statements/cohabitation-effects-of-parental-cohabitation-and-other-non-marital
-sexual-activity-on-children-part-2-of-2, citing Manning, W., & Lichter, D. (1996). Parental
cohabitation and children's economic wellbeing. *Journal of Marriage and Family*, 58(4): 1003;
Hofferth, Sandra, & Anderson, Kermyt. (2003). Are all dads equal? Biology versus marriage as
a basis for paternal involvement. *Journal of Marriage and Family*, 65: 213–232, also, see Wilcox,
W. Bradford, et al. (2005). *Why marriage matters*; Witherspoon, *Marriage and the public good*.
https://www.bigskyworldview.org/content/docs/links/MarriageandThePublicGoodTenPrinciples
.pdf, citing Wilcox, W. Bradford, et al. (2005). *Why marriage matters*; Marquardt, *Between two
worlds*; And Norval Glenn. (1996). Values, attitudes, and the state of American marriages. In D.
Popenoe, J. Elshtain, & D. Blankenhorn (Eds.) (1996). *Promises to keep*. Rowman and Littlefield,
145; Witherspoon, *Marriage and the public good*. https://www.bigskyworldview.org/content/docs
/links/MarriageandThePublicGoodTenPrinciples.pdf, citing Horn, Wade, and Sylvester, Tom.
(2002). *Father facts*. National Fatherhood Initiative, 153; Powers, Thomas G., et al. (1994). Compliance and self-assertion: Young children's responses to mothers versus fathers. *Developmental
Psychology*, 30: 980–989.
19. Hofferth, Sandra, & Anderson, Kermyt. (2003). Are all dads equal? Biology versus marriage as a
basis for paternal involvement. *Journal of Marriage and Family*, 65: 213–232. Wilcox, W. Bradford,
et al. (2005). *Why marriage matters*; Witherspoon, *Marriage and the public good*. https://www
.bigskyworldview.org/content/docs/links/MarriageandThePublicGoodTenPrinciples.pdf, citing
Amato, Paul. (1998). More than money? Men's contributions to their children's lives. In Booth,
Alan, & A. C. Crouter (Eds.), *Men in families: When do they get involved? What difference does
it make?* Lawrence Erlbaum Associates. Belsky, J., Youngblade, L., Rovine, M., & Volling, B.
(1991). Patterns of marital change and parent-child interaction. *Journal of Marriage and the
Family*, 53: 487–498. Wilcox, W. Bradford, et al. (2005). *Why marriage matters*; King, Valarie, &
Heard, Holly. (1999). Nonresident father visitation, parental conflict, and mother's satisfaction:
What's best for child wellbeing? *Journal of Marriage and the Family*, 61: 385–396. Sorenson,
Elaine, & Zibman, Chava. (2000). *To what extent do children benefit from child support?* The
Urban Institute.
20. Marquardt, Elizabeth. (2005). *Family structure and children's educational outcomes*. Institute for
American Values. https://kipdf.com/acomprehensive-review-of-recent-academic-research-shows

-that-family-structure-wh_5ab18b921723dd349c80f763.html, accessed 1-03-23; Zill, Nicholas. (2020, April 6). *Family still matters for key indicators of student performance* [Research brief]. Institute for Family Studies. https://ifstudies.org/blog/family-still-matters-for-key-indicators-of -student-performance, accessed 12-29-22, citing Zill & Wilcox. (2017, June 8); *What happens at home doesn't stay there: It goes to school.* Institute for Family Studies. https://ifstudies.org/blog /what-happens-at-home-doesnt-stay-there-it-goes-to-school; Zill, *Family still matters.* https:// ifstudies.org/blog/family-still-matters-for-key-indicators-of-student-performance, citing Zill & Wilcox. (2016, September 8). To strengthen Florida schools, start with the family. Institute for Family Studies. https://ifstudies.org/blog/to-strengthen-florida-schools-start-with-the-family, accessed 12-30-22; Zill & Wilcox. (2016, September 9). Married-parent families predict grad-uation rates in Florida. Institute for Family Studies. https://ifstudies.org/blog/married-parent -families-predict-graduation-rates-in-florida, accessed 12-30-22; Wilcox, W. Bradford, & Zill, Nicholas. (2016, September 27). *Stronger families, better schools: Families and high school grad-uation across Arizona* [Research brief]. Institute for Family Studies. https://ifstudies.org/ifs -admin/resources/arizona-research-brief-final.pdf, accessed 12-30-22; Wilcox, W. Bradford, & Zill, Nicholas. (2016, December 14). Married-parent families boost student performance in Ohio. Institute for Family Studies. https://ifstudies.org/blog/married-parent-families-boost-student -performance-in-ohio, accessed 12-30-22.

21. Zill, *Family still matters.* https://ifstudies.org/blog/family-still-matters-for-key-indicators-of -student-performance; June, *Cohabitation.* https://acpeds.org/position-statements/cohabitation -effects-of-parental-cohabitation-and-other-non-marital-sexual-activity-on-children-part-2-of -2, citing Halpern-Meekin, S., & Tach, L. (2008). Heterogenity in two-parent families and ado-lescent wellbeing. *Journal of Marriage and Family,* 70(2): 445; June, *Cohabitation.* https://acpeds .org/position-statements/cohabitation-effects-of-parental-cohabitation-and-other-non-marital -sexual-activity-on-children-part-2-of-2, citing Eckenrode, J., Marcynyszyn, L. A., Evans, G. W. (2008). Family instability during early and middle adolescence. *Journal of Applied Develop-mental Psychology,* 29(5): 380–392; June, *Cohabitation.* https://acpeds.org/position-statements /cohabitation-effects-of-parental-cohabitation-and-other-non-marital-sexual-activity-on -children-part-2-of-2, citing Sun, Y., Li Y. (2002). Children's wellbeing during parents' marital disruption process: A pooled time-series analysis. *Journal of Marriage and Family,* 64: 472–488; Zill, *Family still matters.* https://ifstudies.org/blog/family-still-matters-for-key-indicators-of -student-performance, citing Coleman, James, et al. (1966). *Equality of educational opportunity.* U.S. Government Printing Office; McLanahan, Sara, & Sandefur, Gary. (1994). *Growing up with a single parent: What hurts, what helps.* Harvard; Zill, Nicholas, & Nord, Christine Winquist. (1994). *Running in place: How American families are faring in a changing economy and an individ-ualistic society.* Child Trends. Schneider, Barbara, & Coleman, James (Eds.). (1996). *Parents, their children, and schools.* Westview. Zill, Nicholas. (1996). Family change and student achievement: What we have learned, what it means for schools. In Alan Booth & Judith F. Dunn (Eds.), *Family-school links: How do they affect educational outcomes?* Erlbaum; Amato, Paul R., & Booth, Alan. (2000). *A generation at risk: Growing up in an era of family upheaval.* Harvard University Press. Amato, Paul. (2005). The impact of family formation change on the cognitive, social, and emo-tional wellbeing of the next generation. *Future of Children,* 15(2): 75–96; Emery, Robert. (2006). *The truth about children and divorce.* Plume. Kalil, Ariel, Ryan, Rebecca, & Corey, Michael. (2012). Diverging destinies: Maternal education and the developmental gradient in time with children. *Demography,* 49(4): 1361–1383; Zill, Nicholas, & Wilcox, W. Bradford. (2016). *Strong families, successful students: Family structure and student performance in Ohio.* Institute for Fam-ily Studies. Égalité, Anna J. (2016). How family background influences student achievement. *Edu-cationNext,* 16(2): 71–78; June, *Cohabitation.* https://acpeds.org/position-statements/cohabitation -effects-of-parental-cohabitation-and-other-non-marital-sexual-activity-on-children-part-2-of -2, citing Blackwell, Debra L. (2010). *Family structure and children's health in the United States: Findings from The National Health Interview Survey, 2001–2007* (Vital and Health Statistics Series 10, Issue 246). Centers for Disease Control and Prevention & National Center for Health Statis-tics; June, *Cohabitation.* https://acpeds.org/position-statements/cohabitation-effects-of-parental

-cohabitation-and-other-non-marital-sexual-activity-on-children-part-2-of-2, citing Thompson, M. S., Alexander, K. L., & Entwisle, D. R. (1988). Household composition, parental expectations and school achievement. *Social Forces*, 67: 424–451; Witherspoon, *Marriage and the public good.* https://www.bigskyworldview.org/content/docs/links/MarriageandThePublicGoodTenPrinciples .pdf, citing McLanahan, Sara, & Sandefur, Gary. (1994.) *Growing up with a single parent.* Harvard University Press; June, *Cohabitation.* https://acpeds.org/position-statements/cohabitation-effects -of-parental-cohabitation-and-other-non-marital-sexual-activity-on-children-part-2-of-2, citing Astone, N. M., & McLanahan, S. S. (1991). Family structure, parental practices and high school completion. *American Sociological Review*, 56: 309–320.

22. June, *Cohabitation.* https://acpeds.org/position-statements/cohabitation-effects-of-parental -cohabitation-and-other-non-marital-sexual-activity-on-children-part-2-of-2, citing George, R. M., Harden, A., & Lee, B. J. (2008). Consequences of teen childbearing for child abuse, neglect, and foster care placement. In S. D. Hoffman & R. A. Maynard (Eds.), *Kids having kids: Economic costs and social consequences of teen pregnancy* (2nd ed.). The Urban Institute Press, 276–278; Zill, *Family still matters.* https://ifstudies.org/blog/family-still-matters-for-key-indicators-of-student -performance, citing Zill, Nicholas. (2015, October 29). *How family transitions affect students' achievement.* Institute for Family Studies. https://ifstudies.org/blog/how-family-transitions-affect -students-achievement, accessed 12-30-22.

23. June, *Cohabitation.* https://acpeds.org/position-statements/cohabitation-effects-of-parental -cohabitation-and-other-non-marital-sexual-activity-on-children-part-2-of-2, citing Osborne, C., & Palmo, N. (2009). *Do children benefit if their unmarried parents marry? A focus on young children's behavior.* Population Research Center, University of Texas at Austin; BrightCourse. Cohabitation for men. https://www.brightcourse.com/LessonFiles/Factsheets/0222.pdf, accessed 12-29-22, citing Booth, Alan, et al. (2002). *Just living together: Implications of cohabitation on families, children, and social policy.* Routledge. And Manning, Wendy D., & Lamb, Kathleen A. (2003, November). Adolescent wellbeing in cohabiting, married, and single-parent families. *Journal of Marriage and Family*, 65(4): 876–893. https://doi.org/10.1111/j.1741-3737.2003.00876 .x; Zill, *Family still matters.* https://ifstudies.org/blog/family-still-matters-for-key-indicators-of -student-performance; June, *Cohabitation.* https://acpeds.org/position-statements/cohabitation -effects-of-parental-cohabitation-and-other-non-marital-sexual-activity-on-children-part-2-of -2, citing Cavanagh, S. E., Huston, A. C. (2006). Family instability and children's early problem behavior. *Social Forces*, 85(1): 551–581; June, *Cohabitation.* https://acpeds.org/position-statements /cohabitation-effects-of-parental-cohabitation-and-other-non-marital-sexual-activity-on -children-part-2-of-2, citing Cavanagh, S. E., & Huston, A. C. (2008). The timing of family instability and children's social development. *Journal of Marriage and Family*, 70(5): 1258–1270; June, *Cohabitation.* https://acpeds.org/position-statements/cohabitation-effects-of-parental -cohabitation-and-other-non-marital-sexual-activity-on-children-part-2-of-2, citing Eckenrode, J., Marcynyszyn, L. A., & Evans, G. W. (2008). Family instability during early and middle ado-lescence. *Journal of Applied Developmental Psychology*, 29(5): 380–392; Zill, *Family still matters.* https://ifstudies.org/blog/family-still-matters-for-key-indicators-of-student-performance, citing Zill, Nicholas. (2015, March 24). *Substance abuse, mental illness, and crime more common in disrupted families.* Institute for Family Studies. https://ifstudies.org/blog/substance-abuse-mental -illness-and-crime-more-common-in-disrupted-families; McCord, W., McCord, J., & Howard, A. (1963). Familial correlates of aggression in nondelinquent male children. *Journal of Abnormal and Social Psychology*, 62: 72–93; Loeber, R., & Dishion, T. J. (1983). Early predictors of male delinquency: A review. *Psychological Bulletin*, 94: 68–99; Zill, *Family still matters.* https://ifstudies .org/blog/family-still-matters-for-key-indicators-of-student-performance.

24. June, *Cohabitation.* https://acpeds.org/position-statements/cohabitation-effects-of-parental -cohabitation-and-other-non-marital-sexual-activity-on-children-part-2-of-2, citing Sedlak, A., Mettenburg, J., Li, S., Basena, M., Greene, A., McPherson, K., & Petta, I. (2010). *Fourth National Incidence Study of Child Abuse and Neglect (NIS-4): Report to Congress.* U.S. Depart-ment of Health and Human Services & Administration for Children and Families, 5–19; June, *Cohabitation.* https://acpeds.org/position-statements/cohabitation-effects-of-parental

-cohabitation-and-other-non-marital-sexual-activity-on-children-part-2-of-2, citing George, R. M., Harden, A., & Lee, B. J. (2008). Consequences of teen childbearing for child abuse, neglect, and foster care placement. In Hoffman and Maynard (Eds.), *Kids having kids*, 276–278; Witherspoon, *Marriage and the public good*. https://www.bigskyworldview.org/content/docs/links/MarriageandThePublicGoodTenPrinciples.pdf, citing Wilcox, W. Bradford, et al. (2005). *Why marriage matters*; Marquardt, *Between two worlds*; June, *Cohabitation*. https://acpeds.org/position-statements/effects-of-parental-cohabitation-and-other-non-marital-sexual-activity-on-children-part-2-of-2, citing Kleinsorge, C., & Covitz, L. M. (2013). Impact of divorce on children: Developmental considerations. *Pediatrics in Review*, 33(4): 147–154; Hoffmann, John P. (2002, May). The community context of family structure and adolescent drug use. *Journal of Marriage and Family*, 64(2): 314–330. https://doi.org/10.1111/j.1741-3737.2002.00314.x, accessed 1-02-23; June, *Cohabitation*. https://acpeds.org/position-statements/cohabitation-effects-of-parental-cohabitation-and-other-non-marital-sexual-activity-on-children-part-2-of-2, citing Demuth, S., & Brown, S. L. (2004). Family structure, family processes, and adolescent delinquency: The significance of parental absence versus parental gender. *Journal of Research in Crime and Delinquency*, 41(1): 58–81; Bush, C. A., Mullis, R. L., & Mullis, A. K. (2000). Differences in empathy between offender and nonoffender youth. *Journal of Youth and Adolescence*, 29: 467–478. https://doi.org/10.1023/A:1005162526769, accessed 1-02-23; Witherspoon, *Marriage and the public good*. https://www.bigskyworldview.org/content/docs/links/MarriageandThePublicGoodTenPrinciples.pdf, citing Harper, Cynthia, & McLanahan, Sara. (2004). Father absence and youth incarceration. *Journal of Research on Adolescence*, 14: 369–397.

25. McLanahan, Sara, & Sandefur, Gary. (1994). *Growing up with a single parent*. Harvard University Press, 38.

26. Witherspoon, *Marriage and the public good*. https://www.bigskyworldview.org/content/docs/links/MarriageandThePublicGoodTenPrinciples.pdf, citing Akerlof, George A. (1998). Men without children. *The Economic Journal*, 108: 287–309; Nock, Steven L. (1998). The consequences of premarital fatherhood. *American Sociological Review*, 63: 250–263; Waite, Linda, & Gallagher, Maggie. (2000). *The case for marriage*. Doubleday.

27. Cited from Mencken, H. L. (1982). *A Mencken Chrestomathy*. Vintage. (Original work published 1949)

28. Parke, Ross. (1996). *Fatherhood*. Harvard University Press, 101.

29. Witherspoon, *Marriage and the public good*. https://www.bigskyworldview.org/content/docs/links/MarriageandThePublicGoodTenPrinciples.pdf, citing Akerlof, George A. (1998). Men without children. *The Economic Journal*, 108: 287–309; Nock, Steven L. (1998). The consequences of premarital fatherhood. *American Sociological Review*, 63: 250–263; Waite, Linda, & Gallagher, Maggie. (2000). *The case for marriage*. Doubleday; Wilcox, W. Bradford, et al. (2005). *Why marriage matters*; also Wilcox, W. Bradford, et al. (2011). *Why marriage matters: Thirty conclusions from the social sciences* (3rd ed.). Institute for American Values; Dabbs, James. (2000). *Heroes, rogues, and lovers: Testosterone and behavior*. McGraw-Hill.

30. Waite, Linda, & Gallagher, Maggie. (2000). *The case for marriage*. Doubleday, 54–55.

31. Lehrer, Evelyn L., & Chen, Yu. (2013, September 20). Delayed entry into first marriage and marital stability: Further evidence on the Becker-Landes-Michael hypothesis. *Demographic Research*, 29: 521–542. https://www.demographic-research.org/volumes/vol29/20/29-20.pdf, accessed 12-29-22; Glenn N. D., Uecker J. E., & Love R. W. Jr. (2010, September). Later first marriage and marital success. *Social Science Research*, 39(5): 787–800. https://doi.org/10.1016/j.ssresearch.2010.06.002, accessed 12-29-22.

32. Lupton, Joseph, & Smith, James P. (1999). Marriage, assets, and savings. *Labor and Population Working Paper Series* 99–12. RAND.

33. Uecker, J. E. (2012, March). Marriage and mental health among young adults. *Journal of Health and Social Behavior*, 53(1): 67–83. https://doi.org/10.1177/0022146511419206, accessed 12-29-22; Hawkins et al. (2002). *Capstones vs. cornerstones*. http://nationalmarriageproject.org/wp-content/uploads/2022/02/Wheatley_StateofUnions_020222_v1.pdf; Stone, Lyman, & Wilcox, W. Bradford. *The religious marriage paradox: Younger marriage, less divorce*. Institute for

Family Studies. https://ifstudies.org/blog/the-religious-marriage-paradox-younger-marriage
-less-divorce, accessed 12-29-22; Larson, Lyle E., & Goltz, J. Walter. (1989). Religious participation
and marital commitment. *Review of Religious Research*, 30(4): 387–400. https://doi.org/10.2307
/3511299, accessed 12-29-2022.

34. Khandwala Y. S., Baker V. L., Shaw G. M., Stevenson D. K., Lu, Y., & Eisenberg, M. L., et al. (2018).
Association of paternal age with perinatal outcomes between 2007 and 2016 in the United States:
Population based cohort study. *BMJ*, 363: k4372. https://doi.org/10.1136/bmj.k4372, accessed
12-29-22; Cooke, C.-L. M., Shah, A., Kirschenman, R. D., Quon, A. L., Morton, J. S., Care, A. S.
& Davidge, S. T. (2018). Increased susceptibility to cardiovascular disease in offspring born from
dams of advanced maternal age. *Journal of Physiology*, 596: 5807–5821. https://doi.org/10.1113
/JP275472; For more information on the risks of pregnancies over the age of 30, see the Stanford
Medicine resource: https://www.stanfordchildrens.org/en/topic/default?id=pregnancy-over-age
-30-90-P02481, accessed 8-28-23.

35. Glenn, Uecker, and Love, Later first marriage and marital success. https://doi.org/10.1016/j.ss
research.2010.06.002.

36. Reiner, Rob (Director). (1989). *When Harry met Sally . . .* [Film]. Silvercup Studios.

37. As referenced in this article: Dr. Laura. (2020, July 28). For that successful marriage: Choose
wisely, treat kindly. Newsmax. https://www.newsmax.com/drlaura/counseling-covid-internet
-premarital/2020/07/28/id/979431/, accessed 1-07-23.

38. Dollahite, David C., & Lambert, Nathaniel M. (2007). Forsaking all others: How religious involvement promotes marital fidelity in Christian, Jewish, and Muslim couples. *Review of Religious
Research*, 48(3): 290–307. http://www.jstor.org/stable/20447445, accessed 12-29-22.

39. Barna Group. (2008, March 31). *New marriage and divorce statistics released.* https://www.barna
.com/research/new-marriage-and-divorce-statistics-released/, accessed 1-02-23; Barna Group.
(2008, March 31). *New marriage and divorce statistics released.* https://www.barna.com/research
/new-marriage-and-divorce-statistics-released/, accessed 1-02-23; VanderWeele, Tyler J. Religious
service attendance, marriage, and health. Institute for Family Studies. https://ifstudies.org/
blog/religious-service-attendance-marriage-and-health/, accessed 12-29-22; Stanton, Glenn.
(2018, March 22). Does faith reduce divorce risk? *The Public Discourse.* https://www.thepublic
discourse.com/2018/03/20935/, accessed 8-28-23, citing the following study Li, S., Kubzansky,
L. D., & VanderWeele T. J. (2018). Religious service attendance, divorce, and remarriage among
U.S. nurses in mid and late life. *PLOS ONE*, 13(12): e0207778. https://doi.org/10.1371/journal.
pone.0207778; Wilcox, W. Bradford, & Wolfinger, Nicholas H. (2016). A path to wedded bliss?
In *Soul mates: Religion, sex, love, and marriage among African Americans and Latinos.* Oxford
Academic; Olson, Jonathan R., Marshall, James P., Goddard, H. Wallace, & Schramm, David
G. (2015). Shared religious beliefs, prayer, and forgiveness as predictors of marital satisfaction.
Family Relations, 64(4): 519–533.

40. Boxer, C. F., Noonan, M. C., & Whelan, C. B. (2015). Measuring mate preferences: A replication
and extension. *Journal of Family Issues*, 36(2): 163–187. https://doi.org/10.1177/0192513X13490404,
accessed 1-08-23.

41. Ephesians 5:28–30 ESV.

42. June, *Cohabitation.* https://acpeds.org/position-statements/cohabitation-effects-of-parental
-cohabitation-and-other-non-marital-sexual-activity-on-children-part-2-of-2, citing Mosher,
W., Chandra, A., & Jones, J. (2005). *Sexual behavior and selected health measures: Men and women
15-44 years of age, United States, 2002. Advance Data*, 362: 1–54. http://www.cdc.gov/nchs/data
/ad/ad362.pdf, accessed 12-29-22; June, *Cohabitation.* https://acpeds.org/position-statements
/cohabitation-effects-of-parental-cohabitation-and-other-non-marital-sexual-activity-on
-children-part-2-of-2, citing Goodwin, P. Y., Mosher, W. D., & Chandra, A. (2010, February).
*Marriage and cohabitation in the United States: A statistical portrait based on Cycle 6 (2002)
of the National Survey of Family Growth* (Vital and Health Statistics Series 23, Number 28).
National Center for Health Statistics & Centers for Disease Control and Prevention. http://www
.cdc.gov/nchs/data/series/sr_23/sr23_028.pdf, accessed 12-30-22; BrightCourse. Cohabitation for
men. https://www.brightcourse.com/LessonFiles/Factsheets/0222.pdf, accessed 12-29-22, citing

Manning, Wendy D., et al. (2004). The relative stability of cohabiting and marital unions for children. *Population Research and Policy Review*, 23(2): 135–159. https://doi.org/10.1023/b:popu .0000019916.29156.a7; June, *Cohabitation.* https://acpeds.org/position-statements/cohabitation -effects-of-parental-cohabitation-and-other-non-marital-sexual-activity-on-children-part-2 -of-2, citing Osborne, C., Manning, W. D., & Stock, P. J. (2007). Married and cohabiting parents' relationship stability: A focus on race and ethnicity. *Journal of Marriage and Family*, 69: 1345–1366; June, *Cohabitation.* https://acpeds.org/position-statements/cohabitation-effects-of -parental-cohabitation-and-other-non-marital-sexual-activity-on-children-part-2-of-2, citing Osborne, Manning, and Stock, Married and cohabiting parents' relationship stability: 1345–1366; National Marriage Project. *Knot yet.* http://nationalmarriageproject.org/wp-content/uploads /2013/03/KnotYet-FinalForWeb.pdf, accessed 12-29-22.

43. June, *Cohabitation.* https://acpeds.org/position-statements/cohabitation-effects-of-parental -cohabitation-and-other-non-marital-sexual-activity-on-children-part-2-of-2, citing Brown, S. L. (2000). The effect of union type on psychological wellbeing: Depression among cohabiters versus marrieds. *Journal of Health and Social Behavior*, 41: 241–255; Stanton, Glenn. (2012, October 8). The health benefits of marriage. Focus on the Family. https://www.focusonthefamily.com /marriage/the-health-benefits-of-marriage/, citing the work of Stack and Eshleman, Marital status and happiness, 535; June, *Cohabitation.* https://acpeds.org/position-statements/cohabitation -effects-of-parental-cohabitation-and-other-non-marital-sexual-activity-on-children-part-2-of -2, citing Kenney, C. T., & McLanahan, S. S. (2006). Why are cohabiting relationships more violent than marriages? *Demography*, 43(1): 127–40.

44. June, *Cohabitation.* https://acpeds.org/position-statements/cohabitation-effects-of-parental -cohabitation-and-other-non-marital-sexual-activity-on-children-part-2-of-2, citing Yllo, Kersti, & Straus, Murray A. (1981). Interpersonal violence among married and cohabiting couples. *Family Relations*, 30; June, *Cohabitation.* https://acpeds.org/position-statements/cohabitation -effects-of-parental-cohabitation-and-other-non-marital-sexual-activity-on-children-part-2 -of-2, citing Shackelford, T. K. (2001). Cohabitation, marriage, and murder: Woman-killing by male romantic partners. *Aggressive Behavior*, 27: 284–291. http://www.toddkshackelford .com/downloads/Shackelford-AB-2001.pdf, accessed 12-30-22, Heaton, T. B. (2002). Factors contributing to increasing marital stability in the United States. *Journal of Family Issues*, 23: 392–409; June, *Cohabitation.* https://acpeds.org/position-statements/cohabitation-effects-of -parental-cohabitation-and-other-non-marital-sexual-activity-on-children-part-2-of-2, citing Kenney and McLanahan, Why are cohabiting relationships more violent?: 127–40.

45. June, *Cohabitation.* https://acpeds.org/position-statements/cohabitation-effects-of-parental -cohabitation-and-other-non-marital-sexual-activity-on-children-part-2-of-2, citing Clarkberg, Marin, Stolzenberg, Ross M., & Waite, Linda J. (1995). Attitudes, values and entrance in to cohabitational versus marital unions. *Social Forces*, 4: 609–32; June, *Cohabitation.* https://acpeds .org/position-statements/cohabitation-effects-of-parental-cohabitation-and-other-non-marital -sexual-activity-on-children-part-2-of-2, citing Klausli, J. F., & Owen, M. T. (2009). Stable maternal cohabitation, couple relationship quality, and characteristics of the home environment in the child's first two years. *Journal of Family Psychology*, 23(1): 103–106. https://doi.org/10.1037 /a0014588; BrightCourse. Cohabitation for men. https://www.brightcourse.com/LessonFiles /Factsheets/0222.pdf, accessed 12-29-22, citing Horn, Wade F. (2006). Fatherhood, cohabitation, and marriage. *Gender Issues*, 23(4): 21–35. https://doi.org/10.1007/bf03186787; June, *Cohabitation.* https://acpeds.org/position-statements/cohabitation-effects-of-parental-cohabitation-and-other -non-marital-sexual-activity-on-children-part-2-of-2, citing data from *The fragile families and child wellbeing study (Fragile families)* reported in Osborne and Palmo, *Do children benefit?*; June, *Cohabitation.* https://acpeds.org/position-statements/cohabitation-effects-of-parental -cohabitation-and-other-non-marital-sexual-activity-on-children-part-2-of-2, citing Abma, J. C., Chandra, A., & Mosher, W. D., et al. (1997). *Fertility, family planning, and women's health: New data from the 1995 National Survey of Family Growth* (Vital and Health Statistics, Series 23, Number 19). National Center for Health Statistics & Centers for Disease Control and Prevention. http://www.cdc.gov/nchs/data/series/sr_23/sr23_019.pdf, accessed 12-30-22; June, *Cohabitation.*

https://acpeds.org/position-statements/cohabitation-effects-of-parental-cohabitation-and-other
-non-marital-sexual-activity-on-children-part-2-of-2, citing Chen, X. K., Wen, S. W., Fleming,
N., Demissie, K., Rhoads, G. G., & Walker, M. (2007). Teenage pregnancy and adverse birth
outcomes: A large population based retrospective cohort study. *International Journal of Epidemiology*, 36: 368–373. Cunnington, A. J. (2001). What's so bad about teenage pregnancy? *Journal
of Family Planning and Reproductive Health Care*, 27: 36–41.

46. June, *Cohabitation*. https://acpeds.org/position-statements/cohabitation-effects-of-parental
-cohabitation-and-other-non-marital-sexual-activity-on-children-part-2-of-2, citing Rhoades,
G. K., Stanley, S. M., & Markman, H. J. (2009). The pre-engagement cohabitation effect:
A replication and extension of previous findings. *Journal of Family Psychology*, 23: 107–111;
June, *Cohabitation*. https://acpeds.org/position-statements/cohabitation-effects-of-parental
-cohabitation-and-other-non-marital-sexual-activity-on-children-part-2-of-2, citing Cherlin, Andrew. (2004, November). The deinstitutionalization of American marriage. *Journal of
Marriage and Family*, 66: 849; Teachman, J. D. (2004). The childhood living arrangements
of children and the characteristics of their marriages. *Journal of Family Issues*, 25(1): 86–111.
https://doi.org/10.1177/0192513X03255346, accessed 1-02-23; June, *Cohabitation*. https://acpeds
.org/position-statements/cohabitation-effects-of-parental-cohabitation-and-other-non-marital
-sexual-activity-on-children-part-2-of-2, citing Kenney and McLanahan, Why are cohabitating
relationships more violent?: 127–40; June, Patricia Lee. (2015, March). *Cohabitation: Effects of
cohabitation on the men and women involved*. American College of Pediatricians. https://acpeds
.org/press/cohabitation-effects-of-cohabitation-on-the-men-and-women-involved-part-1-of
-2, accessed 12-29-22, citing Kamp Dush, Claire M., et al. (2003). The relationship between
cohabitation and marital quality and stability: Change across cohorts? *Journal of Marriage and
Family*, 65: 539–549.

47. June, *Cohabitation*. https://acpeds.org/position-statements/cohabitation-effects-of-parental
-cohabitation-and-other-non-marital-sexual-activity-on-children-part-2-of-2, citing Osborne,
Manning, and Stock, Married and cohabiting parents' relationship stability: 1345–1366.

48. Witherspoon, *Marriage and the public good*. https://www.bigskyworldview.org/content/docs
/links/MarriageandThePublicGoodTenPrinciples.pdf, citing Wilcox, W. Bradford, & Nock,
Steven L. (2006). What's love got to do with it? Ideology, equity, gender, and women's marital
happiness. *Social Forces*, 84: 1321–1345; Stanley, Scott, et al. (2004). Maybe I do: Interpersonal
commitment and premarital or nonmarital cohabitation. *Journal of Family Issues*, 25: 496–519;
Wilcox, W. Bradford, et al. (2005). *Why marriage matters*; Amato, Paul, & Rogers, Stacy. (1999).
Do attitudes toward divorce affect marital quality? *Journal of Family Issues*, 20: 69–86.

49. This version of this oft quoted expression is quoted from the Family Life South Africa website:
https://familylife.org.za/embracing-gods-purposes-for-marriage/, accessed 5-28-23.

50. Friedrich Nietzsche, quoted in Safire, William, & Safir, Leonard. (1990). *Words of Wisdom*. Simon
and Schuster, 237.

51. Attributed to Ruth Graham Bell in a number of places, including Lluch, Alex. (2008). *Simple
Principles for a Happy and Healthy Marriage*. WS Publishing Group, 141.

52. 1 Corinthians 7:25–27, 32–35 ESV.

53. Genesis 2:22–24 ESV; Revelation 19:7 ESV.

54. Deuteronomy 22:13–21; 22:28–29; 25:5–10; Exodus 21:10; 20:14; and Deuteronomy 21:10–14;
22:1–27.

55. Ephesians 5:21–33; Colossians 3:18–19; and 1 Peter 3:1–7.

56. Matthew 5:27–28; 5:31–32 and 19:3–8; Matthew 9:14–15; 22:1–14; and 25:1–13.

57. Hosea 1:2–3:5; Jeremiah 2:1–4:4; John 3:28–30; 2 Corinthians 11:1–3; Ephesians 5:28–32; and
Revelation 19:7–9; 21:2; and 22:17–20.

58. Matthew 19:4–6 ESV.

59. 1 Corinthians 11:11–12.

60. Ephesians 5:28.

61. Malachi 2:15.

62. Proverbs 14:26; Proverbs 14:34.

Lead #5: Santa Claus and Misplaced Devotion

1. Many studies confirm this truth, including: Bowling, Ann. (1995). What things are important in people's lives? A survey of the public's judgements to inform scales of health related quality of life. *Social Science & Medicine*, 41(10): 1447–1462. https://doi.org/10.1016/0277-9536(95)00113-L, accessed 1-12-23; Silver, Laura, Van Kessel, Patrick, Huang, Christine, Clancy, Laura, & Gubbala, Sneha. (2021, November 18). *What makes life meaningful? Views from 17 advanced economies.* Pew Research Center. https://www.pewresearch.org/global/2021/11/18/what-makes-life-meaningful -views-from-17-advanced-economies/, accessed 1-12-23; Gervis, Zoya. (2021, September 6). These are the top 20 goals Americans want to achieve in 2020. SWNS Digital. https://swnsdigital.com /us/2020/01/these-are-the-top-20-goals-americans-want-to-achieve-in-2020/, accessed 1-15-23; Survey reveals what's on America's bucket list. https://www.provisionliving.com/survey-reveals -whats-on-americas-bucket-list/, accessed 1-12-23.

2. Quoted by Peterson, David. *Engaging with God: A biblical theology of worship.* Page 66.

3. Online Etymology Dictionary, s.v. "worship." https://www.etymonline.com/word/worship, accessed 1-15-23.

4. From the *Cambridge Dictionary*, s.v. "worship." https://dictionary.cambridge.org/us/dictionary /english/worship, accessed 1-15-23.

5. From David Foster Wallace's 2005 Commencement Address at Kenyon University. Posted now on their archive site under the title, This is water. http://bulletin-archive.kenyon.edu/x4280.html, accessed 1-15-23.

6. Bronk, K. C., Hill, P., Lapsley, D., Talib, T., & Finch, W. H. (2009). Purpose, hope, and life satisfaction in three age groups. *Journal of Positive Psychology*, 4(6): 500–510; Bigler, M., Neimeyer, G. J., & Brown, E. (2001). The divided self revisited: Effects of self-concept clarity and self-concept differentiation on psychological adjustment. *Journal of Social and Clinical Psychology*, 20: 396–415.

7. Strecher, Victor J., & Ryff, Carol D. (2014, November 3). Purpose in life and use of preventive health care services. *Psychological and Cognitive Sciences*, 111(46): 16331–16336. https://doi.org /10.1073/pnas.1414826111, accessed 1-16-23; Boehm, J. K., & Kubzansky, L. D. (2012). The heart's content: The association between positive psychological wellbeing and cardiovascular health. *Psychological Bulletin*, 138(4): 655; Hill, P. L., & Turiano, N. A. (2014, July). Purpose in life as a predictor of mortality across adulthood. *Psychological Science*, 25(7): 1482–6. https://doi.org/10 .1177/0956797614531799, accessed 1-16-23; Owen, R., Berry, K., & Brown, L. J. E. (2021). "I like to feel needed, you know?": A qualitative examination of sense of purpose in older care home residents. *Aging & Mental Health*, 27(2): 236–242. https://www.tandfonline.com/doi/citedby/10.1080 /13607863.2021.2017849, accessed 1-16-23; Boyle, P. A., Buchman, A. S., Barnes, L. L., & Bennett, D. A. (2010). Effect of a purpose in life on risk incident Alzheimer disease and mild cognitive impairment in community-dwelling older adults. *Archives of General Psychiatry*, 67: 304–310.

8. Examination of purpose commitment and positive affect as predictors of grit. *Journal of Happiness Studies*, 1–13; Harlow, L. L., Newcomb, M. D., & Bentler, P. M. (1986). Depression, self-derogation, substance use, and suicide ideation: Lack of purpose in life as a mediational factor. *Journal of Clinical Psychology*, 42: 5–21; Hedberg, Pia, Gustafson, Yngve, Alèx, Lena, & Brulin, Christine. (2010). Depression in relation to purpose in life among a very old population: A five-year follow-up study. *Aging & Mental Health*, 14(6): 757–763. https://doi.org/10 .1080/13607861003713216, accessed 1-16-23; Padelford, B. L. (1974). Relationship between drug involvement and purpose in life. *Journal of Clinical Psychology*, 30: 303–305; Roos, C. R., Kirouac, M., Pearson, M. R., Fink, B. C., & Witkiewitz, K. (2015). Examining temptation to drink from an existential perspective: Associations among temptation, purpose in life, and drinking outcomes. *Psychology of Addictive Behaviors*, 29: 716–724.

9. Black, W. A. M., & Gregson, R. A. M. (1973). Time perspectives, purpose in life, extroversion, and neuroticism in New Zealand prisoners. *British Journal of Social and Clinical Psychology*, 12(1): 50–60.

10. From David Foster Wallace's 2005 Commencement Address at Kenyon University. Posted now on their archive site under the title, This is water. http://bulletin-archive.kenyon.edu/x4280.html, accessed 1-15-23.

11. Cited by Hillerbrand, Hans J. (2004). *Encyclopedia of Protestantism: 4-volume set.* Taylor & Francis, 788.
12. Parker, Theodore. (1859). *The critical and miscellaneous writings of Theodore Parker.* Rufus Leighton, Jr., 24.
13. Lifeway Research. (2022, August 9). *Pastors' views on modern day idols: A survey of 1,000 protestant pastors.* Described here: https://research.lifeway.com/2022/08/09/pastors-identify-modern -day-idols-comfort-tops-list/, and downloadable here: https://research.lifeway.com/wp-content /uploads/2022/08/Pastors-Sept-2021-Idols-Report.pdf, accessed 1-15-23.
14. Pew Research Center. (2018, November 18). *Where Americans find meaning in life.* https://www .pewresearch.org/religion/2018/11/20/where-americans-find-meaning-in-life/, accessed 1-16-23.
15. Spurgeon, Charles H. (2007). *Evening by evening: A new edition of the classic devotional based on the Holy Bible, English Standard Version* (Alistair Begg, Ed.). Crossway, 339.
16. Ball, John T., et al. (2004). *Sermons on the First Readings: Cycle A.* CSS Publications, 350.
17. Simpson, Albert B. (1897). *Days of heaven upon earth.* Christian Alliance Publishing Company, 285.
18. From the definition offered at Dictionary.com, s.v. "fanatic." https://www.dictionary.com/browse /fanatic, accessed 1-17-23.
19. Giglio, Louie. (2003). *The air I breathe: Worship as a way of life.* Multnomah, 2.
20. Pippert, Rebecca Manley. (2021). *Out of the saltshaker and into the world: Evangelism as a way of life.* InterVarsity Press, 47.
21. Giglio, Louie. (2003). *The air I breathe: Worship as a way of life.* Multnomah, 10–11.
22. Wickert, Dan. (2012). *Counseling the hard cases* (Stuart Scott & Health Lambert, Eds.). B&H Publishing, 130.
23. 1 John 2:15–16 ESV.
24. Philippians 3:17–19.
25. Quoted in Luther, Martin. (2022). *The collected works of Martin Luther* (A. T. W. Steinhaeuser et al., Trans.). Digicat.
26. The Bible describes our inclination toward idolatry: Ezekiel 16:17; Romans 1:22–23; Galatians 4:8; Romans 1:25 ESV; 1 Chronicles 16:26; Psalms 135:15–18. The Bible also describes the danger in offering worship to lesser gods: Matthew 6:24; Jonah 2:8; Judges 10:14. Finally, the Bible instructs us to flee from this kind of idolatry: 1 Corinthians 10:14; 1 John 5:21; Colossians 3:5; Leviticus 19:4.
27. Ruskin, John, & Burgess, William. (1907). *The religion of Ruskin: The life and works of John Ruskin; a biographical and anthological study.* Fleming H. Revell Company, 270.

Lead #6: Legends, Liars, and Liabilities

1. Ault, Susanne. (2014, August 5). Survey: YouTube stars more popular than mainstream celebs among U.S. teens. *Variety.* https://variety.com/2014/digital/news/survey-youtube-stars-more -popular-than-mainstream-celebs-among-u-s-teens-1201275245/, accessed 1-23-23; Nouri, Melody. (2018). The power of influence: Traditional celebrity vs social media influencer. *Pop Culture Intersections,* 32. https://scholarcommons.scu.edu/engl_176/32, accessed 5-23-23; Influence Hunter. (2022, March 30). https://influencehunter.com/2022/03/30/how-influencers-have -replaced-traditional-celebrities-in-the-minds-of-consumers/, accessed 5-23-23.
2. Kenya Buzz. (2017, February 7). Would you trade family for fame? A millennial probably would. https://www.kenyabuzz.com/lifestyle/would-you-trade-family-for-fame-a-millennial-probably -would/, accessed 1-23-23.
3. Jayson, Sharon. (2013, April 18). Survey: Young people who use social media seek fame. *USA Today.* https://www.usatoday.com/story/news/nation/2013/04/18/social-media-tweens-fame /2091199/, accessed 1-23-23.
4. Kohut, Andrew, Parker, Kim, Keeter, Scott, Doherty, Carroll, & Dimock, Michael. (2007, January 9). *How young people view their lives, futures and politics: A portrait of "Generation Next."* Pew Research Center. https://www.pewresearch.org/wp-content/uploads/sites/4/legacy-pdf/300.pdf, accessed 1-23-23.

5. Cited by several online sources: Young, Sarah. (2017, January 26). Millennials will go to extreme lengths for celebrity fame including disowning their family, finds social media report. *The Independent*. https://www.independent.co.uk/life-style/millenials-extreme-lengths-celebrity-fame -disowning-family-give-up-marriage-break-up-not-have-children-kids-social-media-a7547041 .html, accessed 1-23-23; Kenya Buzz, Would you trade family for fame? https://www.kenyabuzz .com/lifestyle/would-you-trade-family-for-fame-a-millennial-probably-would/; Henderson, J. Maureen. (2017, January 24). One in four millennials would quit their job to be famous. *Forbes*. https://www.forbes.com/sites/jmaureenhenderson/2017/01/24/one-in-four-millennials-would -quit-their-job-to-be-famous/?sh=20bffee2c438, accessed 1-23-23.

6. Cited from On the desire for fame. The School of Life. https://www.theschooloflife.com/article /your-desire-to-be-famous-and-the-problems-it-will-bring-you/, accessed 1-25-23.

7. Cited from On the desire for fame. https://www.theschooloflife.com/article/your-desire-to-be -famous-and-the-problems-it-will-bring-you.

8. *Merriam-Webster*, s.v. "legend." https://www.merriam-webster.com/dictionary/legend, accessed 1-25-23.

9. Rockwell, Donna, & Giles, David. (2009). Being a celebrity: A phenomenology of fame. *Journal of Phenomenological Psychology*, 40: 178–210. https://doi.org/10.1163/004726609X12482630041889, accessed 1-23-23.

10. Rockwell and Giles, Being a celebrity, https://doi.org/10.1163/004726609X12482630041889.

11. Beaty, Katelyn. (2022). *Celebrities for Jesus: How personas, platforms, and profits are hurting the church*. Brazos Press, 7.

12. Proverbs 27:5–6 ESV.

13. Bhogal, G. S. (2022, June 30). The perils of audience capture. https://gurwinder.substack.com/p /the-perils-of-audience-capture, accessed 1-25-23.

14. Rockwell and Giles, Being a celebrity, https://doi.org/10.1163/004726609X12482630041889.

15. Rockwell and Giles, Being a celebrity, https://doi.org/10.1163/004726609X12482630041889.

16. Rockwell and Giles, Being a celebrity, https://doi.org/10.1163/004726609X12482630041889.

17. Dictionary.com, s.v. "pride." https://www.dictionary.com/browse/pride, accessed 1-27-23.

18. *Merriam-Webster*, s.v. "humility." https://www.merriam-webster.com/dictionary/humility, accessed 1-27-23.

19. Merton, Thomas. (1955). *No man is an island*. Shambhala, 119.

20. Saint Augustine. *The city of God*. Chapter XIV, section 13. https://www.newadvent.org/fathers /120114.htm, accessed 1-25-23.

21. Van Tongeren, D. R. The transformative power of humility. The John Templeton Foundation. https://www.templeton.org/news/the-transformative-power-of-humility, accessed 1-23-23, citing his work: Van Tongeren, D. R., Davis, D. E., Hook, J. N., & Witvliet, C. vanOyen. (2019). Humility. *Current Directions in Psychological Science*, 28(5): 463–468. https://doi.org/10.1177 /0963721419850153; Davis, Jr., Don Emerson, & Hook, Joshua N. (2013, September 30). Measuring humility and its positive effects. The Association for Psychological Science. https:// www.psychologicalscience.org/observer/measuring-humility-and-its-positive-effects, accessed 1-23-23; Porter, T., Elnakouri, A., & Meyers, E. A., et al. (2022). Predictors and consequences of intellectual humility. *Nature Reviews Psychology*, 1: 524–536. https://doi.org/10.1038/s44159 -022-00081-9, accessed 1-24-23; Carey, Benedict. (2019, October 21). Be humble, and proudly, psychologists say. *New York Times*. https://www.nytimes.com/2019/10/21/health/psychology -humility-pride-behavior.html%20rel=, accessed 1-23-23; Rowatt, Wade C., Powers, Christie, Targhetta, Valerie, Comer, Jessamy, Kennedy, Stephanie, & Labouff, Jordan. (2006). Development and initial validation of an implicit measure of humility relative to arrogance. *Journal of Positive Psychology*, 1(4): 198–211. https://doi.org/10.1080/17439760600885671, accessed 1-23-23; Nielsen, R., & Marrone, J. A. (2018). Humility: Our current understanding of the construct and its role in organizations. *International Journal of Management Reviews*, 20: 805–824. https://doi.org/10 .1111/ijmr.12160, accessed 1-23-23.

22. Schaffner, Anna Katharina. (2020, June 8). The art of humility: Why it is time for an urgent revival of spiritual modesty. *Psychology Today*. https://www.psychologytoday.com/us/blog/the

-art-self-improvement/202006/the-art-humility, accessed 1-23-23, citing Owens, Bradley P., et al. (2013). Expressed humility in organizations: Implications for performance, teams, and leadership. *Organization Science*, 24(5); Rowatt et al., Development and initial validation, 198–211. https:// doi.org/10.1080/17439760600885671, accessed 1-23-23; Nielsen and Marrone, Humility. https:// doi.org/10.1111/ijmr.12160; Porter et al., Predictors and consequences. https://doi.org/10.1038 /s44159-022-00081-9; Carey, Benedict. (2019, October 21). Be humble, and proudly, psychologists say. *New York Times*. https://www.nytimes.com/2019/10/21/health/psychology-humility-pride -behavior.html%20rel= accessed 1-23-23.

23. Johnson, Megan K., Rowatt, Wade C., & Petrini, Leo. (2011). A new trait on the market: Honesty–Humility as a unique predictor of job performance ratings. *Personality and Individual Differences*, 50(6): 857–862. https://doi.org/10.1016/j.paid.2011.01.011, accessed 1-23-23; Van Tongeren, The transformative power of humility. https://www.templeton.org/news/the-transformative -power-of-humility, citing his work: Van Tongeren et al., Humility. https://doi.org/10.1177 /0963721419850153; Schaffner, The art of humility. https://www.psychologytoday.com/us/blog /the-art-self-improvement/202006/the-art-humility, citing Rego, Arménio, et al. (2017). How leader humility helps teams to be humbler, psychologically stronger, and more effective: A moderated mediation model. *The Leadership Quarterly*, 28(5): 639–58.

24. Van Tongeren, The transformative power of humility. https://www.templeton.org/news/the -transformative-power-of-humility, citing his work: Van Tongeren et al., Humility. https://doi .org/10.1177/0963721419850153; Davis and Hook, Measuring humility and its positive effects. https://www.psychologicalscience.org/observer/measuring-humility-and-its-positive-effects; Davis, Don E., Worthington Jr., Everett L., Hook, Joshua N., Emmons, Robert A., Hill, Peter C., Bollinger, Richard A., & Van Tongeren, Daryl R. (2013). Humility and the development and repair of social bonds: Two longitudinal studies. *Self and Identity*, 12(1): 58–77. https://doi.org /10.1080/15298868.2011.636509, accessed 1-23-23; Nielsen and Marrone, Humility. https://doi .org/10.1111/ijmr.12160.

25. Porter et al., Predictors and consequences. https://doi.org/10.1038/s44159-022-00081-9; Carey, Benedict. (2019, October 21). Be humble, and proudly, psychologists say. *New York Times*. https://www.nytimes.com/2019/10/21/health/psychology-humility-pride-behavior.html%20 rel=, accessed 1-23-23; Nielsen and Marrone, Humility. https://doi.org/10.1111/ijmr.12160; Davis and Hook, Measuring humility and its positive effects. https://www.psychologicalscience.org /observer/measuring-humility-and-its-positive-effects.

26. Nielsen and Marrone, Humility. https://doi.org/10.1111/ijmr.12160; LaBouff, Jordan Paul, Rowatt, Wade C., Johnson, Megan K., Tsang, Jo-Ann, & McCullough Willerton, Grace. (2012). Humble persons are more helpful than less humble persons: Evidence from three studies. *Journal of Positive Psychology*, 7(1): 16–29. https://doi.org/10.1080/17439760.2011.626787, accessed 1-23-23.

27. Mother Teresa, from *Jesus, the Word to Be Spoken*, as cited by Manser, Martin H. (Ed.). (2001). *The Westminster collection of Christian quotations*. Westminster John Knox Press, 182.

28. Choukas-Bradley, Sophia. (2021, July 6). Do social media "likes" matter for teens' wellbeing? What psychological science reveals about "likes" and adolescent development. *Psychology Today*. https://www.psychologytoday.com/us/blog/psychology-adolescence/202107/do-social-media -likes-matter-teens-wellbeing, accessed 1-28-23; Lee, Hae Yeon, Jamieson, Jeremy, Reis, Harry, Beevers, Christopher G. (2020, September). Getting fewer "likes" than others on social media elicits emotional distress among victimized adolescents. *Child Development*, 91(6). https://doi.org /10.1111/cdev.13422, accessed 1-28-23.

29. Charles Spurgeon as cited in several places, most notably in Murray, Andrew. (2001). *Humility: The journey toward holiness*. Baker Publishing Group, 13. (Original work published 1884)

30. *Cambridge Dictionary*, s.v. "humility." https://dictionary.cambridge.org/us/dictionary/english /humility, accessed 1-27-23.

31. Rockwell and Giles, Being a celebrity. https://doi.org/10.1163/004726609X12482630041889.

32. Margaret Thatcher, as quoted in Smith, David, & Freeman, Thomas S. (Eds.). (2019). *Biography and history in film*. Springer International Publishing, 302.

33. Wooden, John, with Tobin, Jack. (2003). *They call me coach*. McGraw-Hill Education, 50.

34. Stamps, R. Lucas. (2022, November 30). Pursue obscurity. *Mere Orthodoxy*. https://mereorthodoxy .com/pursue-obscurity/, accessed 1-25-23.
35. Lewis, C. S. (2007). *The complete C. S. Lewis signature classics*. HarperCollins, 105.
36. Matthew 18:1–4 ESV, Luke 22:24–30 ESV, Mark 10:42–44 ESV.
37. Philippians 2:5–11.
38. John Newton, from Newton, John, & Bull, Josiah. (1869). *Letters by the Rev. John Newton of Olney and St. Mary Woolnoth*. Religious Tract Society, 39.
39. Psalm 131:1; 2 Chronicles 7:14; Micah 6:8.
40. Psalm 25:9; Proverbs 11:2; Proverbs 15:33; Proverbs 22:4; Proverbs 3:34; Psalm 37:11; Isaiah 57:15; Psalm 147:6.
41. Matthew 23:5–7; Luke 14:10–14.
42. Matthew 18:1–4.
43. 1 Peter 5:5–6 ESV.
44. James 1:21.
45. 1 Thessalonians 4:10–12.
46. Jeremiah 1:5; Psalm 139:13–16.
47. Psalm 139:14 ESV. See also Romans 5:8.
48. 1 Timothy 6:16; Romans 6:23.

Lead #7: Felons, Fugitives, and Financial Freedom

1. Charles Spurgeon, cited in several reliable sources, including Spurgeon, Charles H. (2015). *The complete works of C. H. Spurgeon, volume 5: Sermons 225–285*. Delmarva Publications, Inc. And Spurgeon, Charles H. (2012). *The Spurgeon series 1859 & 1860: Unabridged sermons in modern language*. New Leaf Publishing Group, Incorporated.
2. Lammers, J., Stoker, J. I., Rink, F., & Galinsky, A. D. (2016). To have control over or to be free from others? The desire for power reflects a need for autonomy. *Personality and Social Psychology Bulletin*, 42(4): 498–512. https://doi.org/10.1177/0146167216634064, accessed 1-30-23.
3. Epictetus, as cited in Epictetus. (2017). *The philosophy of Epictetus: Golden sayings and fragments*. Dover Publications, 87.
4. Oscar Wilde, as cited by Sreechinth, C. (2016). *Oscar Wilde and his wildest quotes*. UB Tech, 109.
5. Online Etymology Dictionary, s.v. "contentment." https://www.etymonline.com/word/content ment, accessed 1-29-23.
6. *Collins Dictionary*, s.v. "contented." https://www.collinsdictionary.com/us/dictionary/english /contented, accessed 1-29-23.
7. Spurgeon, Charles & Needham, George Carter. (1883). *The life and labors of Charles H. Spurgeon: The faithful preacher, the devoted pastor, the noble philanthropist, the beloved college president, and the voluminous writer*. D. L. Guernsey, 394.
8. Cordaro, Daniel. (2020, May 27). What if you pursued contentment rather than happiness? *Greater Good Magazine*. https://wisdomcenter.uchicago.edu/news/wisdom-news/what-if-you -pursued-contentment-rather-happiness, accessed 1-29-23.
9. Cordaro, D. T., Brackett, M., Glass, L., & Anderson, C. L. (2016). Contentment: Perceived completeness across cultures and traditions. *Review of General Psychology*, 20(3): 221–235. https:// doi.org/10.1037/gpr0000082, accessed 1-29-23; Rojas, Mariano, & Veenhoven, Ruut. (2011). Contentment and affect in the estimation of happiness. *Social Indicators Research*, 110: 415–431. https://doi.org/10.1007/s11205-011-9952-0, accessed 1-29-23.
10. Exodus 20:17.
11. Online Etymology Dictionary, s.v. "envy." https://www.etymonline.com/word/envy, accessed 1-29-23.
12. *Merriam-Webster*, s.v. "evil eye." https://www.merriam-webster.com/dictionary/evil%20eye, accessed 1-30-23.
13. Crusius, J., Gonzalez, M. F., Lange, J., & Cohen-Charash, Y. (2020). Envy: An adversarial review and comparison of two competing views. *Emotion Review*, 12(1): 3–21. https://doi.org/10.1177 /1754073919873131, accessed 1-29-23.

14. Smith, Richard H., Combs, David J. Y., & Thielke, Stephen M. (2008). Envy and the challenges to good health. In Richard Smith (Ed.), *Envy: Theory and research*. Oxford Academic. https://doi .org/10.1093/acprof:oso/9780195327953.003.0016, accessed 1-29-23.
15. Xiang, Y., Dong, X., & Zhao, J. (2020, June). Effects of envy on depression: The mediating roles of psychological resilience and social support. *Psychiatry Investigation*, 17(6): 547–555. https:// doi.org/10.30773/pi.2019.0266, accessed 1-29-23; Reiss, Natalie Staats. (2007, January 18). The nature of envy: A mental health reader. MentalHelp.net. https://www.mentalhelp.net/blogs/the -nature-of-envy/, accessed 1-29-23.
16. Reiss, The nature of envy. https://www.mentalhelp.net/blogs/the-nature-of-envy/.
17. Moran, Simone, Schweitzer, Maurice E. (2008, February). When better is worse: Envy and the use of deception. University of Pennsylvania ScholarlyCommons Management Papers. https:// repository.upenn.edu/cgi/viewcontent.cgi?article=1350&context=mgmt_papers, accessed 1-29-23; Morgan, R., Locke, A., & Arnocky, S. (2022). Envy mediates the relationship between physical appearance comparison and women's intrasexual gossip. *Evolutionary Psychological Science*, 8: 148–157. https://doi.org/10.1007/s40806-021-00298-6, accessed 1-29-23.
18. Langman, Peter. (2009, May 27). Murderous envy: What is the role of envy in school shootings? *Psychology Today*. https://www.psychologytoday.com/us/blog/keeping-kids-safe/200905 /murderous-envy, accessed 1-30-23.
19. Mujcic, R., & Oswald, A. J. (2018, February). Is envy harmful to a society's psychological health and wellbeing? A longitudinal study of 18,000 adults. *Social Science & Medicine*, 198: 103–111. https://doi.org/10.1016/j.socscimed.2017.12.030, accessed 1-29-23.
20. Wu, Jiao, & Srite, Mark. (2021). Envy on social media: The good, the bad and the ugly. *International Journal of Information Management*, 56: 102255. https://doi.org/10.1016/j.ijinfomgt .2020.102255, accessed 1-29-23; Hurst, Nathan. (2015, February 3). *If Facebook use causes envy, depression could follow: Users should be aware of why people use Facebook to avoid feelings of envy* [News release]. University of Missouri News Bureau. https://munewsarchives.missouri .edu/news-releases/2015/0203-if-facebook-use-causes-envy-depression-could-follow/, accessed 1-29-23; Boers, E., Afzali, M. H., Newton, N., & Conrod, P. (2019). Association of screen time and depression in adolescence. *JAMA Pediatrics*, 173(9): 853–859. https:doi.org/10.1001/jama pediatrics.2019.1759, accessed 1-30-23.
21. Sass, Erik. (2014, July 28). Social media makes users feel ugly. MediaPost. https://www.mediapost .com/publications/article/230900/social-media-makes-users-feel-ugly-inadequate.html, accessed 1-29-23.
22. Kelly, Yvonne, Zilanawala, Afshin, Booker, Cara, & Sacker, Amanda. (2018, December). Social media use and adolescent mental health: Findings from the UK Millennium Cohort Study. *eClinicalMedicine Research Paper*, 6: 59–68. https://doi.org/10.1016/j.eclinm.2018.12.005, accessed 1-30-23; Verduyn, Philippe, Lee, David Seungjae, Park, Jiyoung, Shablack, Holly, Orvell, Ariana, Bayer, Joseph, Ybarra, Oscar, Jonides, John, & Kross, Ethan. (2015, April). Passive Facebook usage undermines affective wellbeing: Experimental and longitudinal evidence. *Journal of Experimental Psychology: General*, 144(2): 480–488.
23. Epstein, Joseph. (2003). *Envy: The seven deadly sins*. Oxford University Press, 1.
24. This quote is attributed to Thomas Edison in many books and publications, including its reference in a speech on the floor of the United States Senate as recorded in Government Printing Office. (2012). *United States Congressional Serial Set, Serial No. 14997, Senate Documents Nos. 15–16*. Page 69.
25. Faragher, E. B., Cass, M., & Cooper, C. L. (2005). The relationship between job satisfaction and health: A meta-analysis. *Occupational & Environmental Medicine*, 62: 105–112. https://doi .org/10.1136/oem.2002.006734; van der Noordt, M., IJzelenberg, H., Droomers, M., & Proper, K. I. (2014, October). Health effects of employment: A systematic review of prospective studies. *Occupational & Environmental Medicine*, 71(10): 730–6. https://doi.org/10.1136/oemed-2013 –101891, accessed 1-29-23.
26. Krekel, Christian, Ward, George, Neve, Jan-Emmanuel, Blankson, Amy, Clark, Andrew, Cooper, Cary, Harter, James, Lim, Jenn, Litchfield, Paul, McKinnon, Ewen, Moss, Jennifer, Norton,

Michael, Rojas, Mariano, & Whillans, Ashley. (2018). Work and wellbeing: A global perspective. https://www.researchgate.net/publication/324830283_Work_and_Wellbeing_A_Global _Perspective/citation/download, accessed 1-29-23; Weziak-Bialowolska, Dorota, Bialowolski, Piotr, Sacco, Pier Luigi, VanderWeele, Tyler J., & McNeely, Eileen. (2020). Wellbeing in life and wellbeing at work: Which comes first? Evidence from a longitudinal study. *Frontiers in Public Health*, 8. https://www.frontiersin.org/articles/10.3389/fpubh.2020.00103, accessed 1-29-23; Whittington, J. Lee, Meskelis, Simone, Asare, Enoch, Beldona, Sri. (2017). *Enhancing employee engagement: An evidence-based approach.* Springer International Publishing. Quoted here: https://www.palgrave.com/gp/campaigns/happiness-and-wellbeing/meaningful-work-and -wellbeing, accessed 1-29-23.

27. Krekel et al., Work and wellbeing, https://www.researchgate.net/publication/324830283_Work _and_Wellbeing_A_Global_Perspective/citation/download; Waddell, Gordon, A Kim Burton. (2006). Is work good for your health and wellbeing? The Stationery Office. https://assets .publishing.service.gov.uk/government/uploads/system/uploads/attachment_data/file/209510 /hwwb-is-work-good-for-you-exec-summ.pdf, accessed 1-29-23; Gafner, Jocelyne. (2022, August 17). The impact of workplace wellbeing and how to foster it. Indeed.com. https://www .indeed.com/career-advice/career-development/workplace-wellbeing, accessed 1-29-23.

28. Franklin, Benjamin. (2012). *Wit and wisdom from Poor Richard's Almanack.* Dover Publications, 4.

29. Epicurus, as cited by Dimitriadis, Haris. (2018). *Epicurus and the pleasant life.* Lulu.com, 257.

30. Medvec, V. H., Madey, S. F., & Gilovich, T. (1995). When less is more: Counterfactual thinking and satisfaction among Olympic medalists. *Journal of Personality and Social Psychology*, 69(4): 603–610. https://doi.org/10.1037/0022-3514.69.4.603, accessed 1-30-23.

31. Attributed to Clergyman Henry Ward Beecher in many publications, perhaps earliest in *Freemason's Monthly, Volume 1, 1870*, printed digitally by the University of Michigan, October 5, 2007, p. 499.

32. Prelec, D., & Simester, D. (2001). Always leave home without it: A further investigation of the credit-card effect on willingness to pay. *Marketing Letters*, 12: 5–12. https://doi.org/10.1023 /A:1008196717017, accessed 1-31-23; Also see Peterson, Bailey. (2018, March 22). Credit card spending studies (2018 report): Why you spend more when you pay with a credit card. Value Penguin. https://www.valuepenguin.com/credit-cards/credit-card-spending-studies, accessed 1-31-23.

33. Schultz, Matt. (2023, January 20). 2023 credit card debt statistics. Lending Tree. https://www .lendingtree.com/credit-cards/credit-card-debt-statistics/#carry-balance, accessed 1-31-23; Hiilamo, A. (2020, August 22). Debt matters? Mental wellbeing of older adults with household debt in England. *SSM Population Health*, 12: 100658. https://doi.org/10.1016/j.ssmph.2020 .100658, accessed 1-31-23; Garforth-Bles, Simon, Warner, Christoher, & Keohane, Kieran. (2020, November 6). The wellbeing effects of debt and debt-related factors. https://www.fca.org.uk /publication/research/simetrica-jacobs-wellbeing-impacts-debt-related-factors.pdf, accessed 1-31-23; American Public Health Association. (2021, October 26). *The impacts of individual and household debt on health and wellbeing* [Policy statement]. https://www.apha.org/Policies -and-Advocacy/Public-Health-Policy-Statements/Policy-Database/2022/01/07/The-Impacts-of -Individual-and-Household-Debt-on-Health-and-Well-Being, accessed 1-31-23.

34. Thoreau, Henry David. (2012). *The green Thoreau: America's first environmentalist on technology, possessions, livelihood, and more.* New World Library, 61.

35. Attributed to Sir Walter Scott, perhaps earliest in Southgate, Henry (Ed.). (2006). *Many thoughts of many minds.* Oxford University, 561. (Original work published 1862)

36. Dunn, E. W., Aknin, L. B., Norton, M. I. (2008, March 21). Spending money on others promotes happiness. *Science*, 319(5870): 1687–8. https://doi.org/10.1126/science.1150952. Erratum: (2009, May 29). *Science*, 324(5931): 1143. https://pubmed.ncbi.nlm.nih.gov/18356530/, accessed 1-29-23.

37. Gervais, Sarah. (2015, November 11). Three psychological principles to consider before you make your next purchase. University of Nebraska Department of Psychology. https://psychology.unl .edu/can-money-buy-happiness, accessed 1-29-23.

38. Weir, Kirsten. (2013, December). More than job satisfaction: Psychologists are discovering what

makes work meaningful—and how to create value in any job. American Psychological Association. https://www.apa.org/monitor/2013/12/job-satisfaction, accessed 1-29-23.

39. Tidball, Jennifer. (2014, December 17). Employees who are open about religion are happier, study suggests. ScienceDaily. https://www.sciencedaily.com/releases/2014/12/141217113524.htm, accessed 1-31-23.

40. Ephesians 4:28 NRSV.

41. Genesis 1:1–15.

42. John 5:17; John 10:25.

43. Genesis 2:15 ESV, Genesis 3:17–19 ESV.

44. Ecclesiastes 3:12–13; Ecclesiastes 5:18–20.

45. Revelation 22:9; Isaiah 65:17–18a, 21–23a.

46. Ecclesiastes 5:19; Philippians 4:11–12.

47. 1 Timothy 6:6–7; Hebrews 13:5–6.

48. Ecclesiastes 4:4; Psalm 73:2–3, 16–17, 28.

49. Proverbs 23:17; 1 Peter 2:1–2.

50. Luke 12:15; 2 Corinthians 10:12; Galatians 6:4; 1 Thessalonians 5:18; Psalm 118:24; James 1:17; Colossians 3:17; Ecclesiastes 5:11; Romans 13:8; Psalm 37:21; Titus 2:11–12; Ecclesiastes 5:11; Timothy 6:8; Proverbs 11:24; Luke 6:38; 1 Timothy 6:17–19; Proverbs 10:4; Proverbs 10:5; 2 Thessalonians 3:10–13; Proverbs 12:11; Proverbs 21:5; Proverbs 28:20; Proverbs 13:11; Proverbs 18:9, Proverbs 13:4; Hebrews 4:9–10; Colossians 3:23; 1 Corinthians 10:31.

Lead #8: Sense and Suffering

1. Tyson appears to have said this on more than one occasion, the earliest of which is this version of the statement: "Everybody has plans until they get hit for the first time"–recorded here: (1987, August 19). Biggs has plans for Tyson. *Oroville Mercury-Register*. Page 1B, column 2. Newspapers .com.

2. CAMH. Trauma. https://www.camh.ca/en/health-info/mental-illness-and-addiction-index /trauma, accessed 2-02-23.

3. *Cambridge Dictionary*, s.v. "trauma." https://dictionary.cambridge.org/us/dictionary/english /trauma, accessed 2-02-23.

4. https://www.camh.ca/en/health-info/mental-illness-and-addiction-index/trauma, accessed 2-02-23.

5. American Psychological Association. Trauma. https://www.apa.org/topics/trauma, accessed 2-02-23.

6. Park, C. L. (2017). Meaning making and resilience. In U. Kumar (Ed.), *The Routledge international handbook of psychosocial resilience* (pp. 162–172). Routledge/Taylor & Francis Group. https://psycnet.apa.org/record/2016-07493-014, accessed 2-02-23.

7. Ramos, Catarina, & Leal, Isabel. (2013). Posttraumatic growth in the aftermath of trauma: A literature review about related factors and application contexts. *Psychology, Community & Health*, 2: 43–54. https://doi.org/10.5964/pch.v2i1.39, accessed 2-02-23.

8. Park, C. L. (2017). Meaning making and resilience. In U. Kumar (Ed.), *The Routledge international handbook of psychosocial resilience* (pp. 162–172). Routledge/Taylor & Francis Group. https://psycnet.apa.org/record/2016-07493-014, accessed 2-02-23.

9. Rocky Balboa, from Stallone, Sylvester. (Director). (2006). *Rocky Balboa* [Film]. United Artists. https://www.imdb.com/title/tt0479143/characters/nm0000230, accessed 2-06-23.

10. Buch, Joshua. (2019). *Mindfulness, meaning-making, and resilience among recently returned veterans: Development of a workshop and preliminary manual.* Theses and Dissertations, 1103. https://digitalcommons.pepperdine.edu/etd/1103, accessed 2-02-23.

11. Collier, Lorna. (2016, November). Growth after trauma: Why are some people more resilient than others—and can it be taught? American Psychological Association, 47(10). https://www.apa.org /monitor/2016/11/growth-trauma, accessed 2-02-23; Post-traumatic growth. *Psychology Today*. https://www.psychologytoday.com/us/basics/post-traumatic-growth, accessed 2-02-23; PTSD

Association of Canada. What is post-traumatic growth? http://www.ptsdassociation.com/post-traumatic-growth, accessed 2-02-23.

12. Tedeschi, Richard G., & Calhoun, Lawrence G. (1996). The posttraumatic growth inventory: Measuring the positive legacy of trauma. https://doi.org/10.1002/jts.2490090305, accessed 2-02-23; McDermott, Nicole, & Courtney, Deborah. (2023, February 2). Post-traumatic growth: Everything you need to know. Forbes Health. https://www.forbes.com/health/mind/post-traumatic-growth/, accessed 2-02-23.

13. Frankl, Viktor Emil. (1992). *Man's search for meaning: An introduction to logotherapy.* Beacon Press, 9.

14. Park, Crystal L. (2022, March 23). Meaning making following trauma. *Frontiers in Psychology, Section of Theoretical and Philosophical Psychology*, 13. https://doi.org/10.3389/fpsyg.2022.844891, accessed 2-02-23.

15. Routledge, Clay, & FioRito, Taylor A. (2021, January 14). Why meaning in life matters for societal flourishing. *Frontiers in Psycholology, Section of Personality and Social Psychology*, 11. https://doi.org/10.3389/fpsyg.2020.601899, accessed 2-02-23; Vail, K., & Routledge, C. (2020). *The science of religion, spirituality, and existentialism.* Elsevier; Steger, M. F., & Frazier, P. (2005). Meaning in life: One chain from religiousness to wellbeing. *Journal of Counseling Psychology*, 52: 574–582. https://doi.org/10.1037/0022-0167.52.4.574; Disabato, D. J., Kashdan, T. B., Short, J. L., & Jarden, A. (2017). What predicts positive life events that influence the course of depression? A longitudinal examination of gratitude and meaning in life. *Cognitive Therapy and Research*, 41: 444–458. https://doi.org/10.1007/s10608-016-9785-x; Routledge, Clay. (2014, November 3). To feel meaningful is to feel immortal. *Scientific American.* https://blogs.scientificamerican.com/mind-guest-blog/to-feel-meaningful-is-to-feel-immortal/, accessed 2-02-23; Routledge, C., Arndt, J., Wildschut, T., Sedikides, C., Hart, C. M., Juhl, J., Vingerhoets, A. J. J. M., & Schlotz, W. (2011). The past makes the present meaningful: Nostalgia as an existential resource. *Journal of Personality and Social Psychology*, 101(3): 638–652. https://doi.org/10.1037/a0024292, accessed 2-02-23; Debats, Dominique Louis. (1996, November). Meaning in life: Clinical relevance and predictive power. *British Journal of Clinical Psychology.* https://doi.org/10.1111/j.2044-8260.1996.tb01207.x, accessed 2-02-23; Buch, Joshua. (2019). *Mindfulness, meaning-making, and resilience among recently returned veterans: Development of a workshop and preliminary manual.* Theses and Dissertations, 1103. https://digitalcommons.pepperdine.edu/etd/1103, accessed 2-02-23; Stokes, Victoria. Post-traumatic growth: How to start healing. Healthline. https://www.healthline.com/health/what-is-post-traumatic-growth, accessed 2-07-23; Gerson, Marylie W. Psychoanalysis, resilience, and meaning-making. Institute of Advanced Psychological Studies. https://www.psychstudies.net/psychoanalysis-resilience-meaning-making/, accessed 2-02-23.

16. Routledge and FioRito, Why meaning in life matters. https://doi.org/10.3389/fpsyg.2020.601899; Kinnier, R. T., Metha, A. T., Keim, J. S., Okey, J. L., Adler-Tabia, R. L., & Berry, M. A., et al. (1994). Depression, meaninglessness, and substance abuse in "normal" and hospitalized adolescents. *Journal of Alcohol and Drug Education*, 39: 101–111; Edwards, M. J., & Holden, R. R. (2001). Coping, meaning in life, and suicidal manifestations: Examining gender differences. *Journal of Clinical Psychology*, 57: 1517–1534. https://doi.org/10.1002/jclp.1114.

17. Routledge, To feel meaningful is to feel immortal. https://blogs.scientificamerican.com/mind-guest-blog/to-feel-meaningful-is-to-feel-immortal/; Greenberg, Jeff, Koole, Sander L., & Pyszczynski, Tom (Eds.). (2004). *Handbook of experimental existential psychology.* The Guilford Press; Routledge and FioRito, Why meaning in life matters. https://doi.org/10.3389/fpsyg.2020.601899; Park, C. L., & Folkman, S. (1997). Meaning in the context of stress and coping. *Review of General Psychology*, 1: 115–144. https://doi.org/10.1037/1089-2680.1.2.115.

18. Routledge and FioRito, Why meaning in life matters. https://doi.org/10.3389/fpsyg.2020.601899; Heintzelman, S., & King, L. A. (2014). Life is pretty meaningful. *American Psychologist*, 69: 561–574. https://doi.org/10.1037/a0035049; Routledge, C. (2018). *Supernatural: Death, meaning, and the power of the invisible world.* Oxford University Press.

19. Routledge and FioRito, Why meaning in life matters. https://doi.org/10.3389/fpsyg.2020.601899; Hill, P. L., Turiano, N. A., Mroczek, D. K., & Burrow, A. L. (2016). The value of a purposeful life:

Sense of purpose predicts greater income and net worth. *Journal of Research in Personality*, 65: 38–42. https://doi.org/10.1016/j.jrp.2016.07.003; FioRito, T. A., Routledge, C., & Jackson, J. (in press). Meaning-motivated community action: the need for meaning and prosocial goals and behavior. *Personality and Individual Differences*, Substance Abuse and Mental Health Services Administration. (2014). Understanding the impact of trauma. *Trauma-informed care in behavioral health services*. Treatment Improvement Protocol (TIP) Series, 57. https://www.ncbi.nlm.nih.gov/books/NBK207191/, accessed 2-02-23.

20. Routledge and FioRito, Why meaning in life matters. https://doi.org/10.3389/fpsyg.2020.601899; Hooker, S. A., & Masters, K. S. (2016). Purpose in life is associated with physical activity measured by accelerometer. *Journal of Health Psychology*, 21: 962–971. https://doi.org/10.1177/1359105314542822; Hooker, S. A., & Masters, K. S. (2018). Daily meaning salience and physical activity in previously inactive exercise initiates. *Journal of Health Psychology*, 37: 344–354. https://doi.org/10.1037/hea0000599.

21. Routledge, To feel meaningful is to feel immortal. https://blogs.scientificamerican.com/mind-guest-blog/to-feel-meaningful-is-to-feel-immortal/; Krause, Neal. (2009, July). Meaning in life and mortality. *The Journals of Gerontology: Series B*, 64B(4): 517–527. https://doi.org/10.1093/geronb/gbp047, accessed 2-02-23; Routledge and FioRito, Why meaning in life matters. https://doi.org/10.3389/fpsyg.2020.601899; Routledge, C., & Vess, M. (2018). *The handbook of terror management theory*. Academic Press; Czekierda, K., Banik, A., Park, C. L., & Luszczynska, A. (2017). Meaning in life and physical health: Systematic review and meta-analysis. *Health Psychology Review*, 11: 387–418. https://doi.org/10.1080/17437199.2017.1327325; Schaefer, S. M., Morozink Boylan, J., van Reekum, C. M., Lapate, R. C., Norris, C. J., Ryff, C. D., & Davidson, R. J. (2013, November 13). Purpose in life predicts better emotional recovery from negative stimuli. *PLOS ONE*, 8(11): e80329. https://doi.org/10.1371/journal.pone.0080329, accessed 1-16-23.

22. For more information on my journey from atheism to Christian theism, please read *Cold-case Christianity: A homicide detective investigates the claims of the gospels*, David C. Cook Publishing (2013), and *Person of interest: Why Jesus still matters in a world that rejects the Bible*, Zondervan (2021).

23. "The epistemic question posed by evil is whether the world contains undesirable states of affairs that provide the basis for an argument that makes it unreasonable to believe in the existence of God." - (2015, March 3). The problem of evil. *Stanford Encyclopedia of Philosophy*. https://plato.stanford.edu/entries/evil/, accessed 2-08-23.

24. For more information on why the existence of evil is actually evidence *for* the existence of God, please read my book, *God's crime scene: A cold-case detective examines the evidence for a divinely created universe*, David C. Cook Publishers (2015), chapter eight, The evidence of evil: Can God and evil coexist?

25. 1 John 4:7–8 ESV.

26. Lewis, C. S. (2007). *The complete C. S. Lewis signature classics*. HarperCollins, 565.

27. Ramos and Leal, Posttraumatic growth in the aftermath of trauma. https://doi.org/10.5964/pch.v2i1.39.

28. Lewis, C. S. (1962). *The problem of pain*. Macmillan Publishing, 93.

29. Tada, Joni Eareckson. (1987). *Is God really in control*. Joni and Friends, 9.

30. Gerson, Marylie W. (2018). Spirituality, social support, pride, and contentment as differential predictors of resilience and life satisfaction in emerging adulthood. *Psychology*, 9(3). https://doi.org/10.4236/psych.2018.93030, accessed 2-01-23.

31. Pastwa-Wojciechowska, Beata, Grzegorzewska, Iwona, & Wojciechowska, Mirella. (2021). The role of religious values and beliefs in shaping mental health and disorders. *Religions*, 12: 840. https://doi.org/10.3390/rel12100840, accessed 2-01-23.

32. Pastwa-Wojciechowska, Grzegorzewska, and Wojciechowska, The role of religious values https://doi.org/10.3390/rel12100840.

33. Pastwa-Wojciechowska, Grzegorzewska, and Wojciechowska, The role of religious values https://doi.org/10.3390/rel12100840; Greenberg, Jeff, & Kosloff, Spee. (2008, September 20). Terror management theory: Implications for understanding prejudice, stereotyping, intergroup conflict, and political attitudes. https://doi.org/10.1111/j.1751-9004.2008.00144.x, accessed 2-02-23.

34. Tedeschi, Richard G. (2020, July–August). Growth after trauma. *Harvard Business Review Magazine.* https://hbr.org/2020/07/growth-after-trauma, accessed 2-02-23.
35. Tedeschi, Growth after trauma. https://hbr.org/2020/07/growth-after-trauma.
36. Tedeschi, Growth after trauma. https://hbr.org/2020/07/growth-after-trauma.
37. Tedeschi, Growth after trauma. https://hbr.org/2020/07/growth-after-trauma.
38. Stokes, Post-traumatic growth. https://www.healthline.com/health/what-is-post-traumatic-growth#Takeaway.
39. Viscott, David S. (1993). *Finding your strength in difficult times: A book of meditations by life.* Contemporary Books, 87.
40. John 16:33 ESV, 1 Peter 2:19–21 ESV.
41. 1 Peter 4:12–17.
42. Hebrews 4:15 ESV.
43. Proverbs 1:5 ESV, Proverbs 18:15 ESV, Proverbs 4:13 ESV.
44. Romans 12:17–21 ESV, Galatians 5:16–24 ESV, Proverbs 16:32 ESV, Matthew 6:25–33 ESV, Romans 8:18 ESV, Philippians 4:4–8 ESV, 1 Thessalonians 5:16–19 ESV.
45. James 5:16 ESV, Proverbs 11:14 NASB1995, Deuteronomy 26:7 ESV, Psalm 88:1–5 ESV, Psalm 57:2 ESV, Psalm 34:17 ESV.
46. Romans 5:3–5 ESV.
47. 2 Corinthians 1:3–7.
48. Acts 3:15 ESV.
49. Romans 8:29 ESV.

Lead #9: Prejudice, Injustice, and the Father of All "Isms"

1. Fernandez, Manny, Pérez-Peña, Richard, & Bromwich, Jonah Engel. (2016, July 8). Five Dallas officers were killed as payback, police chief says. *New York Times.* https://www.nytimes.com/2016/07/09/us/dallas-police-shooting.html, accessed 2-13-23.
2. The White House Office of the Press Secretary. (2016, July 12). Remarks by the president at memorial service for fallen Dallas police officers. https://obamawhitehouse.archives.gov/the-press-office/2016/07/12/remarks-president-memorial-service-fallen-dallas-police-officers, accessed 2-13-23.
3. *APA Dictionary of Psychology,* s.v. "prejudice." https://dictionary.apa.org/prejudice, accessed 2-13-23.
4. *Collins Dictionary,* s.v. "prejudice." https://www.collinsdictionary.com/us/dictionary/english/prejudice, accessed 2-13-23.
5. *Merriam-Webster,* s.v. "prejudice." https://www.merriam-webster.com/dictionary/prejudice, accessed 2-13-23.
6. *APA Dictionary of Psychology,* s.v. "prejudice." https://dictionary.apa.org/prejudice, accessed 2-13-23.
7. Greville, Fulke, & Greville, Frances. (1768). *Maxims, characters, and reflections, critical, satirical, and moral. The third edition, with alterations, additions, and explanatory notes.* T. Cadell, 175.
8. *Collins Dictionary,* s.v. "prejudice." https://www.collinsdictionary.com/us/dictionary/english/prejudice, accessed 2-13-23; *Open Education Sociology Dictionary,* s.v. "prejudice." https://sociologydictionary.org/prejudice/, accessed 2-13-23.
9. Ben-Ner, Avner, McCall, Brian P., Stephane, Massoud, & Wang, Hua. (2006, August). Identity and self-other differentiation in work and giving behaviors: Experimental evidence. University of Minnesota. https://sciencecheerleaders.org/wp-content/uploads/2017/07/PaperBen-NerKramer.pdf, accessed 2-12-23; Bahns, A. J., Pickett, K. M., & Crandall, C. S. (2012). Social ecology of similarity: Big schools, small schools and social relationships. *Group Processes & Intergroup Relations,* 15(1): 119–131. https://doi.org/10.1177/1368430211410751, accessed 2-12-23; Lynch, Brendan M. (2016, February 23). Study finds our desire for "like-minded others" is hard-wired. University of Kansas. https://news.ku.edu/2016/02/19/new-study-finds-our-desire-minded-others-hard-wired-controls-friend-and-partner, citing Bahns, A. J., Crandall, C. S., Gillath, O., & Preacher, K. J.

(2017). Similarity in relationships as niche construction: Choice, stability, and influence within dyads in a free choice environment. *Journal of Personality and Social Psychology*, 112(2): 329–355. https://doi.org/10.1037/pspp0000088, accessed 2-12-23.

10. Laeng, B., Vermeer, O., & Sulutvedt U. (2013). Is beauty in the face of the beholder? *PLOS ONE*, 8(7): e68395. https://doi.org/10.1371/journal.pone.0068395, accessed 2-12-23; Tea-makorn, P. P., & Kosinski, M. (2020). Spouses' faces are similar but do not become more similar with time. *Scientific Reports*, 10: 17001. https://doi.org/10.1038/s41598-020-73971-8, accessed 2-12-23; Fraley, R. C., & Marks, M. J. (2010). Westermarck, Freud, and the incest taboo: Does familial resemblance activate sexual attraction? *Personality and Social Psychology Bulletin*, 36(9): 1202–1212. https://doi.org/10.1177/0146167210377180, accessed 2-12-23.

11. Dribe, M., & Lundh, C. (2009, October). Status homogamy in the preindustrial marriage market: Partner selection according to age, social origin, and place of birth in nineteenth-century rural Sweden. *Journal of Family History*, 34(4): 387–406; Schmidt, H. D., Glavce, C., & Hartog, J. (1987, September). Influences on assortative mating. *Anthropologischer Anzeiger*, 45(3): 261–7; Sanchez-Andres, A., & Mesa, M. S. (1994, October). Assortative mating in a Spanish population: Effects of social factors and cohabitation time. *Journal of Biosocial Science*, 26(4): 441–50; Hur, Y. M. (2003, December). Assortative mating for personality traits, educational level, religious affiliation, height, weight, and body mass index in parents of Korean twin sample. *Twin Research*, 6(6): 467–70; Salces, I., Rebato, E., & Susanne, C. (2004, March). Evidence of phenotypic and social assortative mating for anthropometric and physiological traits in couples from the Basque country (Spain). *Journal of Biosocial Science*, 36(2): 235–50.

12. Cox, Daniel, Navarro-Rivera, Juhem, & Jones, Robert P. (2016, August 3). *Race, religion, and political affiliation of Americans' core social networks*. Public Religion Research Institute. https://www.prri.org/research/poll-race-religion-politics-americans-social-networks/, accessed 2-12-23; Sebro, R., Peloso G. M., Dupuis, J., & Risch N. J. (2017). Structured mating: Patterns and implications. *PLOS GENETICS*, 13(4): e1006655. https://doi.org/10.1371/journal.pgen.1006655, accessed 2-12-23, citing Baldwin J. C., & Damon, A. (1973, September). Some genetic traits in Solomon Island populations. V. Assortative mating, with special reference to skin color. *American Journal of Physical Anthropology*, 39(2): 195–201.

13. Anders, Silke, de Jong, Roos, Beck, Christian, Haynes, John-Dylan, & Ethofer, Thomas. (2016). A neural link between affective understanding and interpersonal attraction. *Proceedings of the National Academy of Sciences*, 113(16): E2248–E2257. https://doi.org/10.1073/pnas.1516191113, accessed 2-12-23.

14. Youyou, W., Stillwell, D., Schwartz, H. A., & Kosinski, M. (2017). Birds of a feather do flock together: Behavior-based personality-assessment method reveals personality similarity among couples and friends. *Psychological Science*, 28(3): 276–284. https://doi.org/10.1177/095679761 6678187, accessed 2-12-23; Selfhout, M., Denissen, J., Branje, S., & Meeus, W. (2009). In the eye of the beholder: Perceived, actual, and peer-rated similarity in personality, communication, and friendship intensity during the acquaintanceship process. *Journal of Personality and Social Psychology*, 96(6): 1152–1165. https://doi.org/10.1037/a0014468, accessed 2-12-23.

15. Cox, Navarro-Rivera, and Jones, *Race, religion, and political affiliation*. https://www.prri.org /research/poll-race-religion-politics-americans-social-networks/.

16. Montoya, R. M., Horton, R. S., & Kirchner, J. (2008). Is actual similarity necessary for attraction? A meta-analysis of actual and perceived similarity. *Journal of Social and Personal Relationships*, 25(6): 889–922. https://doi.org/10.1177/0265407508096700, accessed 2-12-23; DiLonardo, Mary Jo. (2014, April 7). Do opposites really attract? CNN. https://www.cnn.com/2014/04/07/living /opposites-attract-upwave-relate, accessed 2-12-23, referring to Ickes, William. (2013). *Strangers in a strange lab: How personality shapes our initial encounters with others*. Oxford University Press; Byrne, D., & Nelson, D. (1965). Attraction as a linear function of proportion of positive reinforcements. *Journal of Personality and Social Psychology*, 1(6): 659–663. https://doi.org/10 .1037/h0022073, accessed 2-12-23.

17. Bahns et al., Similarity in relationships as niche. https://doi.org/10.1037/pspp0000088; Pepper, Margaret. (2013, December 10). How opposites don't attract in long-term relationships - because

conflicting personalities ultimately clash. Daily Mail. https://www.dailymail.co.uk/femail/article
-2521447/EXCLUSIVE-How-opposites-DONT-attract-long-term-relationships--conflicting
-personalities-ultimately-clash.html, accessed 2-12-23.

18. Buss, D. M. (1985). Human mate selection: Opposites are sometimes said to attract, but in fact we
are likely to marry someone similar to us in almost every variable. *American Scientist*, 73: 47–51;
Tea-makorn and Kosinski, Spouses' faces are similar. https://doi.org/10.1038/s41598-020-73971
-8, citing Luo, S. (2017). Assortative mating and couple similarity: Patterns, mechanisms, and
consequences. *Social and Personality Psychology Compass*, 11: e12337; Watson, D., et al. (2004).
Match makers and deal breakers: Analyses of assortative mating in newlywed couples. *Journal of
Personality*, 72: 1029–1068; Buss, D. M. (1984). Marital assortment for personality dispositions:
Assessment with three different data sources. *Behavior Genetics*, 14: 111–123; Schwartz, C., & Graff,
N. (2009). Assortative matching among same-sex and different-sex couples in the United States,
1990–2000. *Demographic Research*, 21: 843–878; Robinson, M. R., et al. (2017). Genetic evidence
of assortative mating in humans. *Nature Human Behaviour*, 1: 16; Vandenberg, S. G. (1972). Assortative mating, or who marries whom? *Behavior Genetics*, 2: 127–157; Epstein, E., & Guttman, R.
(1984). Mate selection in man: Evidence, theory, and outcome. *Biodemography and Social Biology*,
31: 243–278; Tea-makorn and Kosinski, Spouses' faces are similar. https://doi.org/10.1038/s41598
-020-73971-8, citing Gonzaga, G. C., Carter, S., & Galen Buckwater, J. (2010). Assortative mating,
convergence, and satisfaction in married couples. *Personal Relationships*, 17: 634–644.

19. Greenwood, Jeremy, Guner, Nezih, Kocharkov, Georgi, & Santos, Cezar. (2014, May). Marry your
like: Assortative mating and income inequality. *American Economic Review*, 104(5): 348–53. http://
pareto.uab.es/nguner/ggksPandP-December2013.pdf, accessed 2-12-23; Sanchez-Andres and
Mesa, Assortative mating in a Spanish population: 441–50; Hur, Assortative mating for personality
traits: 467–70; Esteve, A., & Cortina, C. (2006). Changes in educational assortative mating in
contemporary Spain. *Demographic Research*, 14: 405–428; Dribe and Lundh, Status homogamy:
387–406; Hugh-Jones, David, Verweij, Karin J. H., St. Pourcain, Beate, & Abdellaoui, Abdel. (2016).
Assortative mating on educational attainment leads to genetic spousal resemblance for polygenic
scores. *Intelligence*, 59: 103–108. https://doi.org/10.1016/j.intell.2016.08.005, accessed 2-15-23.

20. Di Castelnuovo, A., Quacquaruccio, G., Donati, M. B., de Gaetano, G., & Iacoviello, L. (2009,
January 1). Spousal concordance for major coronary risk factors: A systematic review and meta-
analysis. *American Journal of Epidemiology*, 169(1): 1–8; Grant, J. D., Heath, A. C., Bucholz, K. K.,
Madden, P. A., Agrawal, A., & Statham D. J., et al. (2007, May). Spousal concordance for alcohol
dependence: Evidence for assortative mating or spousal interaction effects? *Alcoholism: Clinical
and Experimental Research*, 31(5): 717–28; Merikangas, K. R. (1982, October). Assortative mating
for psychiatric disorders and psychological traits. *Archives of General Psychiatry*, 39(10): 1173–80.

21. Nagoshi, C. T., Johnson, R. C., & Danko, G. P. (1990, January). Assortative mating for cultural
identification as indicated by language use. *Behavior Genetics*, 20(1): 23–31.

22. Domingue, Benjamin W., Fletcher, Jason, Conley, Dalton, & Boardman, Jason D. (2014, May 19).
Genetic and educational assortative mating among US adults, *Social Sciences*, 111(22): 7996–8000.
https://doi.org/10.1073/pnas.1321426111, accessed 2-12-23; Sebro, Peloso, Dupuis, and Risch,
Structured mating. https://doi.org/10.1371/journal.pgen.1006655.

23. *Merriam-Webster*, s.v. "pride." https://www.merriam-webster.com/dictionary/pride, accessed
2-15-23; *Cambridge Dictionary*, s.v. "pride." https://dictionary.cambridge.org/us/dictionary
/english/pride, accessed 2-15-23.

24. AV1611, KJV Dictionary, s.v. "pride." https://av1611.com/kjbp/kjv-dictionary/pride.html,
accessed 2-15-23; Bible Study Tools, s.v. "pride." https://www.biblestudytools.com/dictionary
/pride/, accessed 2-15-23; *Holman Bible Dictionary*, s.v. "pride." Studylight.org. https://www
.studylight.org/dictionaries/eng/hbd/p/pride.html, accessed 2-15-23.

25. Serling, Rod, from his 1967 *Los Angeles Times* interview, as recorded in Serling, Anne. (2014). *As
I knew him: My dad, Rod Serling*. Citadel Press, 71.

26. Carnegie, Dale. (2010). *The 5 essential people skills: How to assert yourself, listen to others, and
resolve conflicts*. Simon & Schuster UK, 105.

27. Bible Hub, s.v. "prejudice." https://biblehub.com/greek/4299.htm, accessed 2-16-23.

28. Online Etymology Dictionary, s.v. "prejudice." https://www.etymonline.com/word/prejudice, accessed 2-13-23.

29. Cited by King, Alveda C., & Howard, Ginger. (2020). *We're not colorblind*. Stanton Publishing House, 147.

30. Dictionary.com, s.v. "tolerance." https://www.dictionary.com/browse/tolerance, accessed 2-18-23.

31. Romans 12:16 ESV. See also Proverbs 18:12 ESV; https://www.etymonline.com/word/haughtiness, accessed 2-18-23.

32. Philippians 2:3; Romans 12:3; Romans 12:3; Ephesians 5:29; Philippians 2:3; 2 Timothy 3:1–5.

33. Corinthians 10:24; Ephesians 4:32; Matthew 22:37–39; James 2:1–4, 9; 1 Timothy 5:21; John 7:24.

34. Micah 6:8.

35. Deyoung, Kevin. (2018, September 11). Is social justice a gospel issue? The Gospel Coalition. https://www.thegospelcoalition.org/blogs/kevin-deyoung/social-justice-gospel-issue/, accessed 5-25-23.

36. Genesis 1:26–28.

37. Romans 12:4–5; 1 Corinthians 12:12.

38. Acts 17:26.

39. Revelation 7:9; Revelation 5:9.

40. Acts 10:34–35 ESV.

41. 1 Samuel 16:7; Galatians 3:28; Colossians 3:11; Romans 2:11.

42. Ephesians 1:10 ESV.

43. Isaiah 9:7.

44. 1 Corinthians 1:10; 1 Peter 3:8; Philippians 2:2; Romans 14:19.

Lead #10: Tough Love and a Tale of Two Brothers

1. The Free Dictionary by Farlex, s.v. "Three Strikes Laws." https://legal-dictionary.thefreedictionary.com/Three+Strikes+Laws, accessed 2-28-23.

2. For more on the discussion about justice between Socrates, Cephalus, Polymarchus, Thrasymachus and Glaucon, refer to the Republic, book 1. https://www.perseus.tufts.edu/hopper/text?doc=Perseus%3Atext%3A1999.01.0168%3Abook%3D1, accessed 2-23-23.

3. Chesterton, G. K. (1938). On household gods and goblins. In *The Coloured Lands*. Sheed and Ward, 195.

4. Nucci, Larry P., & Nucci, Maria Santiago. (1982). Children's social interactions in the context of moral and conventional transgressions. *Child Development*, 53(2): 403–12. https://doi.org/10.2307/1128983, accessed 2-21-23; Hamlin, J. Kiley, Wynn, Karen, Bloom, Paul, & Mahajan, Neha. (2011, November 28). How infants and toddlers react to antisocial others. *Psychological and Cognitive Sciences*, 108(50): 19931–19936. https://doi.org/10.1073/pnas.1110306108, accessed 2-20-23.

5. Taylor, A. J. W. (2009). Justice as a basic human need. *New Zealand Journal of Psychology*, 38(2). https://www.psychology.org.nz/journal-archive/NZJP-Vol382-2009-1-Taylor.pdf, accessed 2-20-23.

6. Sznycer, D., & Patrick, C. (2020). The origins of criminal law. *Nature Human Behaviour*, 4: 506–516. https://doi.org/10.1038/s41562-020-0827-8, accessed 2-20-23; Sznycer, Daniel. (2022, November 2). Intuitions about justice are a consistent part of human nature across cultures and millenia. Salon. https://www.salon.com/2022/11/02/intuitions-about-justice-are-a-consistent-part-of-human-nature-across-cultures-and-millennia_partner/, citing Stylianou, Stelios. (2003). Measuring crime seriousness perceptions: What have we learned and what else do we want to know. *Journal of Criminal Justice*, 31(1): 37–56. https://doi.org/10.1016/S0047-2352(02)00198-8. And Awad, Edmond, Dsouza, Sohan, Shariff, Azim, & Bonnefon, Jean-François. (2020, January 21). Universals and variations in moral decisions made in 42 countries by 70,000 participants. *Psychological and Cognitive Sciences*, 117(5): 2332–2337. https://doi.org/10.1073/pnas.1911517117, accessed 2-20-23.

7. Ingmire, Jann. (2014, April 9). The brain's need for justice is based in reason, not emotion. Furity. https://www.futurity.org/need-justice-based-reason-emotion/, accessed 2-20-23, citing this study: Yoder, Keith J., & Decety, Jean. (2014, March 19). The good, the bad, and the just: Justice

sensitivity predicts neural response during moral evaluation of actions performed by others. *Journal of Neuroscience*, 34(12): 4161–4166. https://doi.org/10.1523/JNEUROSCI.4648-13.2014, accessed 2-20-23; Monash University. (2015, June 18). Emotional brains "physically different" from rational ones. Science News. https://www.sciencedaily.com/releases/2015/06/150618104153 .htm, citing Eres, Robert, Decety, Jean, Louis, Winnifred R., & Molenberghs, Pascal. (2015). Individual differences in local gray matter density are associated with differences in affective and cognitive empathy. *NeuroImage*, 117: 305. https://doi.org/10.1016/j.neuroimage.2015.05.038, accessed 2-28-23.

8. Similar to an oft quoted expression, sometimes attributed originally to Chip Ingram.

9. Cited as a remark to Joseph Gillespie, in a letter from Gillespie to Herald and Torch Light (Hagerstown, MD) on March 15, 1876, quoted by Ratcliffe, Susan (Ed.). (2017). *Oxford Essential Quotations* (5th ed.). Oxford University Press. Posted here: https://www.oxfordreference.com /display/10.1093/acref/9780191843730.001.0001/q-oro-ed5-00006699;jsessionid=932C5D44E 17C8A86FAD7778C126471C4, accessed 2-25-23.

10. SSM Health. (2022, November 8). The science behind kindness and how it's good for your health. https://www.ssmhealth.com/blogs/ssm-health-matters/november-2022/the-science-behind -kindness, accessed 2-25-23; Pace, T. W., Negi, L. T., Adame, D. D., Cole, S. P., Sivilli, T. I., Brown, T. D., Issa, M. J., & Raison, C. L. (2009, January). Effect of compassion meditation on neuroendocrine, innate immune and behavioral responses to psychosocial stress. *Psychoneuroendocrinology*, 34(1): 87–98. https://doi.org/10.1016/j.psyneuen.2008.08.011; Nelson-Coffey, S. K., Fritz, M. M., Lyubomirsky, S., & Cole, S. W. (2017, July). Kindness in the blood: A randomized controlled trial of the gene regulatory impact of prosocial behavior. *Psychoneuroendocrinology*, 81: 8–13. https://doi.org/10.1016/j.psyneuen.2017.03.025, accessed 2-22-23; Whillans, Ashley V., Dunn, Elizabeth W., Sandstrom, Gillian M., Dickerson, Sally S., & Madden, Kenneth M. (2016, June). Is spending money on others good for your heart? *Health Psychology*, 35(6): 574–583; Kim, Seoyoun, & Ferraro, Kenneth F. (2014, October). Do productive activities reduce inflammation in later life? Multiple roles, frequency of activities, and C-reactive protein. *The Gerontologist*, 54(5): 830–839. https://doi.org/10.1093/geront/gnt090, accessed 2-22-23; Post, Stephen. (2005). Altruism, happiness, and health: It's good to be good. *International Journal of Behavioral Medicine*, 12: 66–77. https://doi.org/10.1207/s15327558ijbm1202_4; Midlarsky, Elizabeth, Kahana, Eva, & Belser, Alexander. (2014). Prosocial behavior in late life. https://doi.org/10.1093/oxfordhb /9780195399813.013.030.

11. Rowland, L., & Curry, O. S. (2019). A range of kindness activities boost happiness. *Journal of Social Psychology*, 159(3): 340–343. https://doi.org/10.1080/00224545.2018.1469461; Dunn, Elizabeth W., Aknin, Lara B., & Norton, Michael I. (2008). Spending money on others promotes happiness. *Science*, 319(5870): 1687–1688. https://doi.org/10.1126/science.1150952, accessed 2-22-23; Kumar, A., & Epley, N. (2023). A little good goes an unexpectedly long way: Underestimating the positive impact of kindness on recipients. *Journal of Experimental Psychology: General*, 152(1): 236–252. https://doi.org/10.1037/xge0001271, accessed 2-22-23; Ko, Kellon, Margolis, Seth, Revord, Julia, & Lyubomirsky, Sonja. (2021). Comparing the effects of performing and recalling acts of kindness. *The Journal of Positive Psychology*, 16(1): 73–81. https://doi.org/10 .1080/17439760.2019.1663252; Hui, B. P. H., Ng, J. C. K., Berzaghi, E., Cunningham-Amos, L. A., & Kogan, A. (2020). Rewards of kindness? A meta-analysis of the link between prosociality and wellbeing. *Psychological Bulletin*, 146(12): 1084–1116. https://doi.org/10.1037/bul0000298, accessed 2-22-23; Dunn, Aknin, and Norton, Spending money on others promotes happiness. https://doi.org/10.1126/science.1150952. Erratum: (2009, May 29). *Science*, 324(5931): 1143; Curry, O. S., Rowland, L. A., Van Lissa, C. J., Zlotowitz, S., McAlaney, J., & Whitehouse, H. (2018). Happy to help? A systematic review and meta-analysis of the effects of performing acts of kindness on the wellbeing of the actor. *Journal of Experimental Social Psychology*, 76: 320–329. https://doi .org/10.1016/j.jesp.2018.02.014, accessed 2-22-23; Alden, L. E., Trew, J. L. (2013, February). If it makes you happy: Engaging in kind acts increases positive affect in socially anxious individuals. *Emotion*, 13(1): 64–75. https://doi.org/10.1037/a0027761; Aknin, L. B., & Whillans, A. V. (2021). Helping and happiness: A review and guide for public policy. *Social Issues and Policy Review*,

15: 3–34. https://doi.org/10.1111/sipr.12069, accessed 2-22-23; Nelson, S. K., Layous, K., Cole, S. W., & Lyubomirsky, S. (2016). Do unto others or treat yourself? The effects of prosocial and self-focused behavior on psychological flourishing. *Emotion*, 16(6): 850–861. https://doi.org/10.1037 /emo0000178, accessed 2-22-23; Trew, J. L., & Alden, L. E. (2015). Kindness reduces avoidance goals in socially anxious individuals. *Motivation and Emotion*, 39: 892–907. https://doi.org/10 .1007/s11031-015-9499-5, accessed 2-22-23; Raposa, E. B., Laws, H. B., & Ansell, E. B. (2016). Prosocial behavior mitigates the negative effects of stress in everyday life. *Clinical Psychological Science*, 4(4): 691–698. https://doi.org/10.1177/2167702615611073, accessed 2-22-23; Buchanan, K. E., & Bardi, A. (2010, May–June). Acts of kindness and acts of novelty affect life satisfaction. *Journal of Social Psychology*, 150(3): 235–7. https://doi.org/10.1080/00224540903365554.

12. Chancellor, J., Margolis, S., Jacobs Bao, K., & Lyubomirsky, S. (2018). Everyday prosociality in the workplace: The reinforcing benefits of giving, getting, and glimpsing. *Emotion*, 18(4): 507–517. https://doi.org/10.1037/emo0000321, accessed 2-22-23; Hepach, R., Vaish, A., & Tomasello, M. (2017, January). The fulfillment of others' needs elevates children's body posture. *Developmental Psychology*, 53(1): 100–113. https://doi.org/10.1037/dev0000173; Aknin, L. B., Broesch, T., Hamlin, J. K., & Van de Vondervoort, J. W. (2015). Prosocial behavior leads to happiness in a small-scale rural society. *Journal of Experimental Psychology: General*, 144(4): 788–795. https://doi.org/10 .1037/xge0000082, accessed 2-22-23.

13. Thomas Aquinas, Super Mattheum, Cap. V, l. 2., as quoted by Solimeo, Luiz Sergio. (2011, June 2). Mercy without justice is the mother of dissolution; justice without mercy is cruelty. The American Society for the Defense of Tradition, Family and Property. https://www.tfp.org/mercy -without-justice-is-the-mother-of-dissolution-justice-without-mercy-is-cruelty/#easy-footnote -3-27739, accessed 2-25-23.

14. *Merriam-Webster*, s.v. "tough love." https://www.merriam-webster.com/dictionary/tough%20 love, accessed 2-19-23.

15. Clark, Allison. (2013, August 20). Does tough love parenting work? Educational Connections. https://ectutoring.com/does-tough-love-parenting-work, accessed 2-19-23.

16. Lexmond, Jen, & Reeves, Richard. (2009). Building character. DEMOS. https://www.demos.co .uk/files/Building_Character_Web.pdf, accessed 2-19-23.

17. Trautner, Tracy. (2017, January 19). Authoritative parenting style. Michigan State University Extension. https://www.canr.msu.edu/news/authoritative_parenting_style, accessed 2-20-23; Faw, Meara H., Sonne, Jennifer, & Leustek, John. (2019). Exploring tough love communication in parents' relationships with their young adult children. *Communication Studies*. https://doi .org/10.1080/10510974.2019.1642220, accessed 2-20-23; McVittie, Jody. (2003, April 7). Research supporting positive discipline. Positive Discipline. https://positivediscipline.org/resources /Documents/ResearchSupportingPositiveDisciplineinHomesSchoolsandCommunities.pdf, accessed 2-22-23.

18. Nieman, P., & Shea, S. (2004, January). Effective discipline for children. *Paediatrics & Child Health*, 9(1): 37–50. https://doi.org/10.1093/pch/9.1.37, accessed 2-22-23; Wasserman, J. (2016). *Compassionate discipline: A study of research and practice.* Bank Street College of Education. https://educate.bankstreet.edu/independent-studies/165 and https://educate.bankstreet.edu/cgi /viewcontent.cgi?article=1164&context=independent-studies, accessed 2-22-23; Watson, Jennifer Lisa Moradian. (2014, October). Alternative discipline structures: A comprehensive approach to changing behavior. *CLEARvoz Journal*, 1(2): 9–14. http://www.fixschooldiscipline.org/wp -content/uploads/2020/09/2.Alternative_Discipline_Structures.2014.pdf, accessed 2-22-23.

19. Flett, M. Ryan, Gould, Daniel, Griffes, Katherine R., & Lauer, Larry. Tough love for underserved youth: A comparison of more and less effective coaching. *The Sport Psychologist*, 27(4): 325–337. https://doi.org/10.1123/tsp.27.4.325, accessed 2-20-23; Taylor, J., Ashford, M., & Collins, D. (2022, May 25). Tough love—Impactful, caring coaching in psychologically unsafe environments. *Sports (Basel)*, 10(6): 83. https://doi.org/10.3390/sports10060083; Flett, M. Ryan, & Brown, Rene. (2016). A balancing act: Benefits and concerns of a tough-love approach to coaching inner-city females. *Canadian Society for Psychomotor Learning and Sport Psychology*, 48(1). https://www.scapps.org /jems/index.php/1/article/view/1339, accessed 2-20-23.

20. Polcin, Douglas L., Mulia, Nina, & Jones, Laura. (2012). Substance users' perspectives on helpful and unhelpful confrontation: Implications for recovery. *Journal of Psychoactive Drugs*, 44(2): 144–152. https://doi.org/10.1080/02791072.2012.684626; Roozen, Hendrik G., De Waart, Ranne, & Van Der Kroft, Petra. (2010, September 15). Community reinforcement and family training: An effective option to engage treatment-resistant substance-abusing individuals in treatment. https://doi.org/10.1111/j.1360-0443.2010.03016.x, accessed 2-23-23; Meyers, R. J., Villanueva, M., & Smith, J. E. (2005). The community reinforcement approach: History and new directions. *Journal of Cognitive Psychotherapy*, 19(3): 247–260. https://doi.org/10.1891/jcop.2005.19.3.247, accessed 2-23-23; Chang, L. H., & Wang J. (2009, September). A tough-love pedagogy in rehabilitation: Integration of rehabilitation ideology with local cultures. *International Journal of Rehabilitation Research*, 32(3): 219–27. https://doi.org/10.1097/MRR.0b013e328329823a, accessed 2-23-23.

21. Loeffler, Charles E., & Nagin, Daniel S. (2022). The impact of incarceration on recidivism. *Annual Review of Criminology*, 5(1): 133–152. https://doi.org/10.1146/annurev-criminol-030920 -112506, accessed 2-21-23. For examples of studies arguing for a mercy/grace dominant criminal justice system for youth over a truth/justice model, see: Bonnie, Richard J., Johnson, Robert L., Chemers, Betty M., & Schuck, Julie (Eds.). (2012). *Reforming juvenile justice: A developmental approach*. National Research Council of the National Academies. https://www.njjn .org/uploads/digital-library/Reforming_JuvJustice_NationalAcademySciences.pdf, accessed 2-21-23; McCarthy, Patrick, Schiraldi, Vincent, & Shark, Miriam. (2016, October). *The future of youth justice: A community-based alternative to the youth prison model*. New Thinking in Community Corrections, No. 2. Harvard Kennedy School, Program in Criminal Justice Policy and Management. https://www.ojp.gov/pdffiles1/nij/250142.pdf, accessed 2-21-23; Mendel, Richard A. *No place for kids: The case for reducing juvenile incarceration*. The Annie E. Casey Foundation. https://files.eric.ed.gov/fulltext/ED527944.pdf, accessed 2-21-23; Kelman, Steven, & Hong, Sounman. (2012, February). "Hard," "soft," or "tough love": What kinds of organizational culture promote successful performance in cross-organizational collaborations? HKS Faculty Research Working Paper Series RWP12-005. Harvard University, John F. Kennedy School of Government.

22. Cited in Jeffreys, Mary Ann. Colorful sayings of colorful Luther: A sample of the reformer's wit and wisdom. *Christianity Today*. https://www.christianitytoday.com/history/issues/issue -34/colorful-sayings-of-colorful-luther.html, accessed 2-21-23; this quote (or a similar variation) may originally have been recorded by Veit Dietrich in 1533, as seen in the German text here: https://archive.org/details/werketischreden10201luthuoft/page/298/mode/1up, translated literally as "The world is like a drunken peasant. If you lift him into the saddle on one side, he will fall off on the other side. One can't help him, no matter how one tries. He wants to be the devil's."

23. Alcorn, Randy. (2009). *The grace and truth paradox: Responding with Christlike balance*. Crown Publishing Group, 21.

24. Nohria, Nitin, & Gurtler, Bridget. (2004, February). Note on human behavior: Reason and emotion. Harvard Business School Case 404–104.

25. Saint Thomas (Aquinas), & Newman, Saint John Henry (Beato). (2007). *Catena Aurea: The Gospel of St. Matthew. 1*. Cosimo Classics, 152.

26. Baucham, Voddie. Fault lines–Critical social justice. Speech given at TPUSA, transcribed here: https://docplayer.net/234769015-Fault-lines-critical-social-justice-by-voddie-baucham.html, accessed 8-31-23.

27. This quote from Tom Landry is not well sourced although it is attributed to him in several places, such as http://www.goodreads.com/author/quotes/108209.Tom_Landry, http://www.brainyquote .com/quotes/authors/t/tom_landry.html#ixzz1l3iBUHr3, accessed 3-02-23.

28. Clore, G. L. (2011, April 1). Psychology and the rationality of emotion. *Modern Theology*, 27(2): 325–338. https://doi.org/10.1111/j.1468-0025.2010.01679.x; Lamia, Mary C. (2010, December 31). Like it or not, emotions will drive the decisions you make today. *Psychology Today*. https:// www.psychologytoday.com/us/blog/intense-emotions-and-strong-feelings/201101/like-it-or-not

-emotions-will-drive-the-decisions, accessed 2-28-23; Trettenero, Scott. (2017, April 13). Human beings are first and foremost emotional creatures. Psychreg. https://www.psychreg.org/human-beings-are-first-foremost-emotional-creatures/#, accessed 2-28-23, referencing Gu, S., Wang, F., Patel, N. P., Bourgeois, J. A., & Huang, J. H. (2019, April 24). A model for basic emotions using observations of behavior in drosophila. *Frontiers in Psychology*, 10: 781. https://doi.org/10.3389/fpsyg.2019.00781.

29. Carlson, Richard (quoting Dr. Wayne Dyer). (2002). *Don't sweat the small stuff . . . and it's all small stuff: Simple ways to keep the little things from taking over your life.* Hachette Books.

30. Lu, D., & Hong, D. (2022, July 15). Emotional contagion: Research on the influencing factors of social media users' negative emotional communication during the COVID-19 pandemic. *Frontiers in Psychology*, 13: 931835. https://doi.org/10.3389/fpsyg.2022.931835; Ferrara, E., & Yang, Z. (2015). Measuring emotional contagion in social media. *PLOS ONE*, 10(11): e0142390. https://doi.org/10.1371/journal.pone.0142390, accessed 3-01-23; Wollebæk, D., Karlsen, R., Steen-Johnsen, K., & Enjolras, B. (2019). Anger, fear, and echo chambers: The emotional basis for online behavior. *Social Media + Society*, 5(2). https://doi.org/10.1177/2056305119829859, accessed 3-01-23; Brady, William J., McLoughlin, Killian, Doan, Tuan, N., & Crockett, Molly J. (2021). How social learning amplifies moral outrage expression in online social networks. *Science Advances*, 7(33): eabe5641. https://doi.org/10.1126/sciadv.abe5641, accessed 3-01-23.

31. Matthew 7:12.

32. Genesis 3:15.

33. Genesis 24:27 ASV.

34. This quote is attributed to the late R. C. Sproul in many places, including his Twitter page (https://twitter.com/RCSproul/status/666585908691496960, 11-17-15), the Ligonier Ministries Facebook page (https://www.facebook.com/Ligonier/photos/a-god-who-is-all-love-all-grace-all-mercy-no-sovereignty-no-justice-no-holiness-/10157758333398115/?paipv=0&eav=AfYhlvWF2NXqMmm h5QX284B2cqWm2W7A0knbNZ0k4ku6IqwIdkYoznhOkDx06FAkrGg&_rdr, 5-20-19), and on the Gospel Coalition website article, 40 quotes from R. C. Sproul (https://www.thegospelcoalition.org/article/40-quotes-rc-sproul/, 12-14-17), all accessed 3-02-23.

35. Psalm 89:14; Isaiah 30:18; Hosea 2:19; Psalm 103:17; Psalm 33:5; Jeremiah 9:24; Deuteronomy 10:18; Psalm 119:149.

36. Psalm 85:10 ESV.

37. Isaiah 16:5 ESV.

38. John 1:14 NIV, John 1:16–18 NKJV, Colossians 1:6 ESV.

39. This quote has been widely attributed to Lesslie Newbigin on websites collecting his quotes, such as: https://quotefancy.com/quote/1762200/Lesslie-Newbigin-The-living-God-is-a-God-of-justice-and-mercy-and-He-will-be-satisfied; https://loveexpands.com/quotes/lesslie-newbigin-1239204/; https://quotlr.com/author/lesslie-newbigin; https://quotestats.com/topic/lesslie-newbigin-quotes/; but no citation is offered in any of these locations (all accessed 3-03-23).

40. James 2:13; Luke 6:37.

41. Exodus 20:6; Amos 5:15; Hosea 12:6; Micah 6:8.

42. Romans 6:23 ESV.

43. Romans 5:8.

44. Romans 10:9–10; John 3:16–17; 2 John 3.

45. Stott, John. (2021). *The cross of Christ.* InterVarsity Press, 221.

46. Emmons, R. A., Hill, P. C., Barrett, J. L., & Kapic, K. M. (2017). Psychological and theological reflections on grace and its relevance for science and practice. *Psychology of Religion and Spirituality*, 9(3): 276–284. https://doi.org/10.1037/rel0000136, accessed 2-22-23; Hodge, Adam S., Hook, Joshua N., Davis, Don E., Van Tongeren, Daryl R., Bufford, Rodger K., Bassett, Rodney L., & McMinn, Mark R. (2022). Experiencing grace: A review of the empirical literature. *The Journal of Positive Psychology*, 17(3): 375–388. https://doi.org/10.1080/17439760.2020.1858943; Thangbiakching, & Soreng, Eric. (2019). Grace of God: A phenomenological inquiry. *The International Journal of Indian Psychology*, 4: 142. https://doi.org/10.25215/0404.035.

47. Psalm 57:3 NASB1995.

Lead #11: The Killer Inside

1. Schopenhauer, A. (2004). *Essays and aphorisms*. Penguin Books Limited.
2. Jung, C. G. (1972). On the psychology of the unconscious. In *The collected works of C. G. Jung* (Vol. 7). Princeton University Press, 35; Jung, C. G. (1970). Psychology and religion. In *The collected works of C. G. Jung* (Vol. 11). Princeton University Press, 131.
3. Harris, Thomas A. (2004). *I'm OK—You're OK* (Quill ed.). HarperCollins, 233. (Original work published 1968).
4. Hobbes, Thomas. (1909–14). Of the natural condition of mankind as concerning their felicity and misery. *Of man, being the first part of Leviathan*. The Harvard Classics. https://www.bartleby.com/34/5/13.html, accessed 3-05-23.
5. Mcleod, Saul. (2023, February 20). The Milgram shock experiment: Summary, results, & ethics. Simply Psychology. https://simplypsychology.org/milgram.html, accessed 3-04-23.
6. Burger, J. M. (2009, January). Replicating Milgram: Would people still obey today? *American Psychologist*, 64(1): 1–11. https://doi.org/10.1037/a0010932, accessed 3-06-23.
7. www.prisonexp.org, and Haney, C., Banks, W. C., & Zimbardo, P. G. (1973). Study of prisoners and guards in a simulated prison. *Naval Research Reviews*, 9 (1–17). Office of Naval Research.
8. Zak, Paul J. (2011, February 10). Are humans good or evil? Chemistry can provide the answer. *Psychology Today*. https://www.psychologytoday.com/us/blog/the-moral-molecule/201102/are-humans-good-or-evil, citing his work: Zak, Paul J. (2009, June 12). The physiology of moral sentiments. *Journal of Economic Behavior and Organization*. CELS 2009 4th Annual Conference on Empirical Legal Studies Paper. https://ssrn.com/abstract=1418753, and Zak, Paul J. (2009, May 19). The moral molecule. Gruter Institute Squaw Valley Conference 2009: Law, Behavior & the Brain. https://ssrn.com/abstract=1405393, both accessed 3-04-23; Hardin, Garrett. (1968). The Tragedy of the Commons. *Science*, 162(3859): 1243–1248. https://doi.org/10.1126/science.162.3859.1243, accessed 3-06-23; Aksoy, Billur, & Palma, Marco A. (2019). The effects of scarcity on cheating and in-group favoritism. *Journal of Economic Behavior & Organization*, 165: 100–117. https://doi.org/10.1016/j.jebo.2019.06.024, accessed 3-06-23; Winking, J., & Mizer, N. (2013). Natural-field dictator game shows no altruistic giving. *Evolution and Human Behavior*, 34(4): 288–293. https://doi.org/10.1016/j.evolhumbehav.2013.04.002, accessed 3-05-23.
9. Bryner, Jeanna. (2006, November 16). Mere thought of money makes people selfish. Live Science. https://www.livescience.com/1128-mere-thought-money-people-selfish.html, accessed 3-05-23, citing the work of Kathleen Vohs of the Carlson School of Management at the University of Minnesota. Money priming can change people's thoughts, feelings, motivations, and behaviors: An update on 10 years of experiments. https://carlsonschool.umn.edu/sites/carlsonschool.umn.edu/files/2019-04/vohs_2015_money_priming_review_replications_jepg.pdf, accessed 3-05-23; Vohs, K. D., Mead, N. L., & Goode, M. R. (2008). Merely activating the concept of money changes personal and interpersonal behavior. *Current Directions in Psychological Science*, 17(3): 208–212. https://doi.org/10.1111/j.1467-8721.2008.00576.x, accessed 3-05-23; Piff, Paul K., Stancato, Daniel M., Côté, Stéphane, & Keltner, Dacher, (2012, February 27). Higher social class predicts increased unethical behavior. *Psychological and Cognitive Sciences*, 109(11): 4086–4091. https://doi.org/10.1073/pnas.1118373109, accessed 3-05-23; Crocker, Jennifer, Canevello, Amy, & Brown, Ashley A. (2017). Social motivation: Costs and benefits of selfishness and otherishness. *Annual Review of Psychology*, 68(1): 299–325. https://doi.org/10.1146/annurev-psych-010416-044145, accessed 3-05-23; Pappas, Stephanie. Conflicts of interest: Are humans inherently selfish? https://www.livescience.com/57991-conflicts-of-interest-science-humans-selfish-cooperation.html, accessed 3-05-23.
10. Harris, L. T., & Fiske, S. T. (2006). Dehumanising the lowest of the low. Neuroimaging responses to extreme out-groups. *Psychological Science*, 17: 847–853; Kteily, N., Bruneau, E., Waytz, A., & Cotterill, S. (2015, November). The ascent of man: Theoretical and empirical evidence for blatant dehumanization. *Journal of Personality and Social Psychology*, 109(5): 901–31. https://doi.org/10.1037/pspp0000048; Boudjemadi, V., Demoulin, S., & Bastart, J. (2017). Animalistic dehumanization of older people by younger ones: Variations of humanness perceptions as a function of a target's age. *Psychology and Aging*, 32(3): 293–306. https://doi.org/10.1037/pag0000161, accessed 3-03-23.

11. McLoughlin, Niamh Caitriona, Tipper, Steven Paul, & Over, Harriet. (2018). Young children perceive less humanness in outgroup faces. *Developmental Science*, 21(2): e12539. https://doi.org/10.1111/desc.12539, accessed 3-04-23.

12. Kunst, Jennifer. (2011, August 17). Are we good? Or bad? Or both? *Psychology Today*. https://www.psychologytoday.com/us/blog/headshrinkers-guide-the-galaxy/201108/are-we-good-or-bad-or-both, accessed 3-04-23.

13. Valdesolo, Piercarlo, & DeSteno, David. (2008). The duality of virtue: Deconstructing the moral hypocrite. *Journal of Experimental Social Psychology*, 44(5): 1334–1338. https://doi.org/10.1016/j.jesp.2008.03.010, accessed 3-04-23.

14. Klein, N., & Epley, N. (2017). Less evil than you: Bounded self-righteousness in character inferences, emotional reactions, and behavioral extremes. *Personality and Social Psychology Bulletin*, 43(8): 1202–1212. https://doi.org/10.1177/0146167217711918, accessed 3-04-23; Thompson, Ashley E., & O'Sullivan, Lucia F. (2017). Understanding variations in judgments of infidelity: An application of attribution theory. *Basic and Applied Social Psychology*, 39(5): 262–276. https://doi.org/10.1080/01973533.2017.1350578; Hess, U., Cossette, M., Hareli S. (2016, February 29). I and my friends are good people: The perception of incivility by self, friends and strangers. *Europe's Journal of Psychology*, 12(1): 99–114. https://doi.org/10.5964/ejop.v12i1.937.

15. Lerner, M. J., & Simmons, C. H. (1966). Observer's reaction to the "innocent victim": Compassion or rejection? *Journal of Personality and Social Psychology*, 4(2): 203–210. https://doi.org/10.1037/h0023562, accessed 3-04-23; Montada, L. (1998). Belief in a just world: A hybrid of justice motive and self-interest? In L. Montada & M. J. Lerner (Eds.), *Responses to victimizations and belief in a just world*. Springer. https://doi.org/10.1007/978-1-4757-6418-5_12, accessed 3-04-23.

16. Baumeister, R. F., Bratslavsky, E., Finkenauer, C., & Vohs, K. D. (2001). Bad is stronger than good. *Review of General Psychology*, 5(4): 323–370. https://doi.org/10.1037/1089-2680.5.4.323, accessed 3-06-23.

17. Lord, C. G., Ross, L., & Lepper, M. R. (1979). Biased assimilation and attitude polarization: The effects of prior theories on subsequently considered evidence. *Journal of Personality and Social Psychology*, 37(11): 2098–2109. https://doi.org/10.1037/0022-3514.37.11.2098, accessed 3-04-23; Trevors, Gregory J., Muis, Krista R., Pekrun, Reinhard, Sinatra, Gale M., & Winne, Philip H. (2016). Identity and epistemic emotions during knowledge revision: A potential account for the backfire effect. *Discourse Processes*, 53(5–6): 339–370. https://doi.org/10.1080/0163853X.2015.1136507; Johnson, D. R., Murphy, M. P., & Messer, R. M. (2016, May). Reflecting on explanatory ability: A mechanism for detecting gaps in causal knowledge. *Journal of Experimental Psychology: General*, 145(5): 573–588. https://doi.org/10.1037/xge0000161; Hall, Michael P., & Raimi, Kaitlin T. (2018). Is belief superiority justified by superior knowledge? *Journal of Experimental Social Psychology*, 76: 290–306. https://doi.org/10.1016/j.jesp.2018.03.001, accessed 3-04-23.

18. Dufner, M., Rauthmann, J. F., Czarna, A. Z., & Denissen, J. J. A. (2013). Are narcissists sexy? Zeroing in on the effect of narcissism on short-term mate appeal. *Personality and Social Psychology Bulletin*, 39(7): 870–882. https://doi.org/10.1177/0146167213483580, accessed 3-04-23; Jauk, E., Neubauer, A. C., Mairunteregger, T., Pemp, S., Sieber, K. P., & Rauthmann, J. F. (2016). How alluring are dark personalities? The Dark Triad and attractiveness in speed dating. *Europe's Journal of Psychology*, 30: 125–138. https://doi.org/10.1002/per.2040; Carter, Gregory Louis, Campbell, Anne C., & Muncer, Steven. (2014). The Dark Triad personality: Attractiveness to women. *Personality and Individual Differences*, 56: 57–61. https://doi.org/10.1016/j.paid.2013.08.021, accessed 3-04-23; Marcinkowska, Urszula M., Lyons, Minna T., & Helle, Samuli. (2016). Women's reproductive success and the preference for Dark Triad in men's faces. *Evolution and Human Behavior*, 37(4): 287–292. https://doi.org/10.1016/j.evolhumbehav.2016.01.004, accessed 3-04-23.

19. Howe, Jacqueline, Falkenbach, Diana, & Massey, Christina. (2014). The relationship among psychopathy, emotional intelligence, and professional success in finance. *International Journal of Forensic Mental Health*, 13(4): 337–347. https://doi.org/10.1080/14999013.2014.951103.

20. Bowles, S. (2008, June 20). Policies designed for self-interested citizens may undermine "the moral sentiments": Evidence from economic experiments. *Science*, 320(5883): 1605–9. https://doi.org/10.1126/science.1152110.

21. Luke 6:31 ESV.
22. Batson, Dan. (1999, October 3). Addressing the altruism question experimentally [Abstract of talk]. EAA Conference, Boston, MA, United States.
23. Zaki, Jamil. (2020, August). Catastrophe compassion: Understanding and extending prosociality under crisis. *Science & Society*, 24(8): 587–589. https://doi.org/10.1016/j.tics.2020.05.006, accessed 3-04-23.
24. Strudler, Are humans good or evil? https://harpers.org/2014/10/are-humans-good-or-evil/, citing Isen, A. M., & Levin, P. F. (1972). Effect of feeling good on helping: Cookies and kindness. *Journal of Personality and Social Psychology*, 21(3): 384–388. https://doi.org/10.1037/h0032317, also: Levin, Paula F., & Isen, Alice M. (1975). Further studies on the effect of feeling good on helping. *Sociometry*, 38(1): 141–47. https://doi.org/10.2307/2786238, accessed 3-04-23.
25. Plato's *The republic*, Chapter II, viewable at The Project Gutenberg. https://www.gutenberg.org/files/1497/1497-h/1497-h.htm#link2H_4_0005, accessed 8-31-23.
26. Smith, A. (1937). *The wealth of nations*. Pages 1, ii. (Original work published 1776)
27. Dawkins, Richard. (2006). *The selfish gene: 30th anniversary edition*. OUP Oxford, xxi; Campbell, D. T. (1975a). The conflict between social and biological evolution and the concept of original sin. *Zygon*, 10: 234–249; Campbell, D. T. (1975b). On the conflicts between biological and social evolution and between psychology and moral tradition. *American Psychologist*, 30(12): 1103–1126.
28. Dawkins, Richard. (1989). *The selfish gene* (2nd ed.). Oxford University Press, 2–3.
29. Dawkins, Richard. (2006). *The selfish gene: 30th anniversary edition*. OUP Oxford, 2; Campbell, D. T. (1975a). The conflict between social and biological evolution and the concept of original sin. *Zygon*, 10: 234–249; Campbell, On the conflicts: 1103–1126.
30. MacKinnon, Barbara, & Fiala, Andrew. (2014). *Ethics: Theory and contemporary issues*. Cengage Learning, 71.
31. Dawkins, Richard. (1989). *The selfish gene*. Oxford University Press, 3.
32. Yoder, Keith. (2021, March 17). Selfish or selfless? Human nature means you're both. Neuroscience News. https://neurosciencenews.com/human-nature-selfish-selfless-18057/, describing his study: Yoder, Keith J., & Decety, Jean. (2020). Me first: Neural representations of fairness during three-party interactions. *Neuropsychologia*, 147: 107576. https://doi.org/10.1016/j.neuropsychologia.2020.107576, accessed 3-05-23.
33. Fehr, E., & Gächter, S. (2002, January 10). Altruistic punishment in humans. *Nature*, 415(6868): 137–40. https://doi.org/10.1038/415137a; Henrich, J., McElreath, R., Barr, A., Ensminger, J., Barrett, C., Bolyanatz, A., Cardenas, J. C., Gurven, M., Gwako, E., Henrich, N., Lesorogol, C., Marlowe, F., Tracer, D., & Ziker, J. (2006, June 23). Costly punishment across human societies. *Science*, 312(5781): 1767–70. https://doi.org/10.1126/science.1127333.
34. Stewart, A., & Plotkin, J. (2016). Small groups and long memories promote cooperation. *Scientific Reports*, 6: 26889. https://doi.org/10.1038/srep26889, accessed 3-06-23.
35. Stevenson, Robert Louis. (1886). *Strange case of Dr. Jekyll and Mr. Hyde*. Longmans, Green, and Company, 108.
36. Plato. (1972). *Plato: Phaedrus* (R. Hackforth, Ed.). Cambridge University Press. https://doi.org/10.1017/CBO9781316036396.
37. Psalm 51:1–2 ESV.
38. Smith, Adam. (2009). *The theory of moral sentiments*. GRIN-Verlag, 21.
39. Fyodor Dostoevsky, from a letter to his brother, Mikhail, (*Pisma*, 2: p. 549, August 16, 1839), cited by Santayana, George. (2017). *Dostoevsky: The author as psychoanalyst*. Taylor & Francis, 99.
40. Expression similar to this have been quoted many times, including the script from the *BoJack Horseman* television series (2015 episode, "Yes And") in which the character Wanda Pierce says, "When you look at someone through rose-colored glasses, all the red flags just look like flags." https://www.imdb.com/title/tt4835746/characters/nm0001435, accessed 3-09-23.
41. This story has been repeated in many books and articles, including Baum, Steven K. (2008). *The psychology of genocide: Perpetrators, bystanders, and rescuer*. Cambridge University Press, 237.
42. Gandhi, Mahatma. (2005). *All men are brothers*. Bloomsbury Academic, 166.
43. Dawkins, Richard. (2008). *River out of Eden: A Darwinian view of life*. Basic Books, 133.

44. Bavinck, Herman. (1956). *Our reasonable faith.* Eerdmans, 22–23.
45. Genesis 1:4, 10, 12, 18, 21, 25, 31.
46. Psalm 139:14 ESV, Genesis 1:26–27 ESV.
47. Romans 5:12 ESV.
48. Jeremiah 17:9 ESV, Matthew 15:19 ESV, Mark 7:21–23 ESV, Galatians 5:19–21 ESV.
49. Romans 3:10; Romans 3:23; 1 John 1:8.
50. Romans 6:23 ESV. See also Romans 5:9–12; 1 Corinthians 15:20–22.

Lead #12: A Good Guilt Trip

1. Hare, Robert D. (2003). *The Hare psychopathy checklist revised* (2nd ed.). Multi-Health Systems; Cleckley, H. M. (1982). *Mask of sanity: An attempt to clarify some issues about the so-called psychopathic personality* (6th ed.). CV Mosby Co; Hare, R. D., Harpur, T. J., & Hakstian, A. R., et al. (1990). The revised psychopathy checklist: descriptive statistics, reliability, and factor structure. *Psychological Assessment*, 2: 338–341, and Campbell, J. S., & Elison, J. (2005). Shame coping styles and psychopathic personality traits. *Journal of Personality Assessment*, 84(1): 96–104. https:// doi.org/10.1207/s15327752jpa8401_16, accessed 3-12-23, and Gregory, S., ffytche, D., Simmons, A., Kumari, V., Howard, M., Hodgins, S., & Blackwood, N. (2012, September). The antisocial brain: Psychopathy matters. *Archives of General Psychiatry*, 69(9): 962–72. https://doi.org/10 .1001/archgenpsychiatry.2012.222, accessed 3-12-23. However, some modern researchers are challenging this notion about psychopathic shamelessness. For more, refer to Baskin-Sommers, Arielle, Stuppy-Sullivan, Allison M., & Buckholtz, Joshua W. (2016, November 28). Psychopathic individuals exhibit but do not avoid regret during counterfactual decision making. *Biological Sciences* 113(50): 14438–14443. https://doi.org/10.1073/pnas.1609985113, accessed 3-12-23.
2. *Cambridge Dictionary*, s.v. "guilt." https://dictionary.cambridge.org/us/dictionary/english/guilt, accessed 3-12-23.
3. *Collins Dictionary*, s.v. "shame." https://www.collinsdictionary.com/us/dictionary/english/shame, accessed 3-12-23.
4. *APA Dictionary of Psychology*, s.v. "guilt." https://dictionary.apa.org/guilt, accessed 7-26-23.
5. *APA Dictionary of Psychology*, s.v. "shame." https://dictionary.apa.org/shame, accessed 7-26-23.
6. To be clear, I am using modern western definitions of "guilt" and "shame" as the foundation for this chapter and distinguishing them from non-western notions of shame connected with dishonor. For a differing view about the definition and value of shame as a potentially adaptive emotion, read Elshof, Gregg Ten. (2021). *For shame: Rediscovering the virtues of a maligned emotion.* Zondervan.
7. Ekman, Paul. (2009). *Telling lies: Clues to deceit in the marketplace, politics, and marriage* (Revised Edition). W. W. Norton, 65.
8. Lewis, H. B. (1971). Shame and guilt in neurosis. *Psychoanalytic Review*, 58(3): 419–438. https:// pep-web.org/browse/document/psar.058.0419a?index=40&page=P0419, accessed 3-12-23.
9. Bradshaw, John. (1988). *Healing the shame that binds you* (International Edition, 1st ed.). HCI, 15.
10. Bastin, C., Harrison, B. J., Davey, C. G., Moll, J., & Whittle, S. (2016, December). Feelings of shame, embarrassment and guilt and their neural correlates: A systematic review. *Neuroscience & Biobehavioral Reviews*, 71: 455–471. https://doi.org/10.1016/j.neubiorev.2016.09.019, accessed 3-12-23; Michl, Petra, Meindl, Thomas, Meister, Franziska, Born, Christine, Engel, Rolf R., Reiser, Maximilian, & Hennig-Fast, Kristina. (2014, February). Neurobiological underpinnings of shame and guilt: A pilot fMRI study. *Social Cognitive and Affective Neuroscience*, 9(2): 150–157. https:// doi.org/10.1093/scan/nss114, accessed 3-12-23; Federor, F. (2022). Effect of shame and guilt on mental health. *Journal of Forensic Psychology*, 7: 224. https://www.walshmedicalmedia.com/open -access/effect-of-shame-and-guilt-on-mental-health-111897.html, accessed 3-12-23.
11. Tangney, J. P., Stuewig, J., & Hafez, L. (2011, September 1). Shame, guilt and remorse: Implications for offender populations. *Journal of Forensic Psychiatry & Psychology*, 22(5): 706–723. https://doi .org/10.1080/14789949.2011.617541, accessed 3-12-23.
12. Pivetti, M., Camodeca, M., & Rapino, M. (2016). Shame, guilt, and anger: Their cognitive,

physiological, and behavioral correlates. *Current Psychology: A Journal for Diverse Perspectives on Diverse Psychological Issues*, 35(4): 690–699. https://doi.org/10.1007/s12144-015-9339-5, accessed 3-12-23; Corrigan, Frank M. (2014). Shame and the vestigial midbrain urge to withdraw. In *Neurobiology and treatment of traumatic dissociation*. Springer Publishing Company, 173–191. https://doi.org/10.1891/9780826106322.0009, https://connect.springerpub.com/content/book/978-0-8261-0632-2/part/part01/chapter/ch09, accessed 3-12-23.

13. Budiarto, Y., & Helmi, A. F. (2021, May 31). Shame and self-esteem: A meta-analysis. *Europe's Journal of Psychology*, 17(2): 131–145. https://doi.org/10.5964/ejop.2115, accessed 3-12-23; Andrews, B., Qian, M., & Valentine, J. D. (2002, March). Predicting depressive symptoms with a new measure of shame: The experience of shame scale. British Journal of Clinical Psychology, 41(1): 29–42. https://doi.org/10.1348/014466502163778, accessed 3-12-23; Garofalo, C., Holden, C. J., Zeigler-Hill, V., & Velotti, P. (2016, January–February). Understanding the connection between self-esteem and aggression: The mediating role of emotion dysregulation. *Aggressive Behavior*, 42(1): 3–15. https://doi.org/10.1002/ab.21601, accessed 3-12-23; Selva, Joaquín. (2018, January 22). Why shame and guilt are functional for mental health. Positive Psychology. https://positivepsychology.com/shame-guilt/, accessed 3-12-23, citing Patock-Peckham, J. A., Canning, J. R., & Leeman, R. F. (2018, January 15). Shame is bad and guilt is good: An examination of the impaired control over drinking pathway to alcohol use and related problems. *Personality and Individual Differences*, 121: 62–66. https://doi.org/10.1016/j.paid.2017.09.023, accessed 3-12-23.

14. See, for example, Ross, Evan, Crijns, Tom J., Ring, David, & Coopwood, Ben. (2021). Social factors and injury characteristics associated with the development of perceived injury stigma among burn survivors. *Burns*, 47(3): 692–697. https://doi.org/10.1016/j.burns.2020.07.022.

15. Tilghman-Osborne, C., Cole, D. A., Felton, J. W., & Ciesla, J. A. (2008). Relation of guilt, shame, behavioral and characterological self-blame to depressive symptoms in adolescents over time. *Journal of Social and Clinical Psychology*, 27(8): 809–842. https://doi.org/10.1521/jscp.2008.27.8.809, accessed 3-12-23; Arimitsu, Kohki. (2001). The relationship of guilt and shame to mental health. *The Japanese Journal of Health Psychology*, 14: 24–31. https://doi.org/10.11560/jahp.14.2_24, accessed 3-12-23; Nechita, Diana, & Szentagotai-Tatar, Aurora. (2018). Shame-proneness, guilt-proneness and anxiety symptoms: A meta-analysis. *Journal of Anxiety Disorders*, 58. https://doi.org/10.1016/j.janxdis.2018.07.005, accessed 3-12-23.

16. Shen, L. (2018, July 11). The evolution of shame and guilt. *PLOS ONE*, 13(7): e0199448. https://doi.org/10.1371/journal.pone.0199448; Harder, D. W., Cutler, L., & Rockart, L. (1992, December). Assessment of shame and guilt and their relationships to psychopathology. *Journal of Personality Assessment*, 59(3): 584–604. https://doi.org/10.1207/s15327752jpa5903_12, accessed 3-12-23; Hallsworth, L., Wade, T., & Tiggemann, M. (2005, September). Individual differences in male body-image: An examination of self-objectification in recreational body builders. *British Journal of Health Psychology*, 10(3): 453–65. https://doi.org/10.1348/135910705X26966, accessed 3-12-23; Schoenleber, M., Berenbaum, H., & Motl, R. (2014, April). Shame-related functions of and motivations for self-injurious behavior. *Personality Disorders*, 5(2): 204–11. https://doi.org/10.1037/per0000035, accessed 3-12-23; Tangney, J. P., Stuewig, J., & Mashek, D. J. (2007). Moral emotions and moral behavior. *Annual Review of Psychology*, 58: 345–72. https://doi.org/10.1146/annurev.psych.56.091103.070145, accessed 3-12-23; Miller-Prieve, Vienna. (2016). *Women, shame, and mental health: A systematic review of approaches in psychotherapy*. Sophia, the St. Catherine University repository. https://sophia.stkate.edu/msw_papers/630, accessed 3-12-23; Velotti, Patrizia, Garofalo, Carlo, Bottazzi, Federica, & Caretti, Vincenzo. (2017). Faces of shame: Implications for self-esteem, emotion regulation, aggression, and wellbeing. *The Journal of Psychology*, 151(2): 171–184. https://doi.org/10.1080/00223980.2016.1248809, accessed 3-12-23; Wright, Kim, Gudjonsson, Gisli H., & Young, Susan. (2008). An investigation of the relationship between anger and offence-related shame and guilt. *Psychology, Crime & Law*, 14(5): 415–423. https://doi.org/10.1080/10683160701770369, accessed 3-12-23; Tangney, Stuewig, and Hafez, Shame, guilt and remorse: https://doi.org/10.1080/14789949.2011.617541; Bennett, D. S., Sullivan, M. W., & Lewis, M. (2005, November). Young children's adjustment as a function of maltreatment, shame, and anger. *Child Maltreatment*, 10(4): 311–23. https://doi.org/10.1177/1077559505278619, accessed 3-12-23; Luyten,

Patrick, Fontaine, Johnny R. J., & Corveleyn, Jozef. (2002). Does the Test of Self-Conscious Affect (TOSCA) measure maladaptive aspects of guilt and adaptive aspects of shame? An empirical investigation. *Personality and Individual Differences*, 33(8): 1373–1387. https://doi.org/10.1016 /S0191-8869(02)00197-6, accessed 3-12-23; Paulhus, D. L., Robins, R. W., Trzesniewski, K. H., & Tracy, J. L. (2004, April 1). Two replicable suppressor situations in personality research. *Multivariate Behavior Research*, 39(2): 303–28. https://doi.org/10.1207/s15327906mbr3902_7, accessed 3-12-23; Bear, G. G., Uribe-Zarain, X., & Manning, M. A., et al. (2009). Shame, guilt, blaming, and anger: Differences between children in Japan and the US. *Motivation and Emotion*, 33: 229–238. https://doi.org/10.1007/s11031-009-9130-8, accessed 3-12-23.

17. Selva, Why shame and guilt are functional. https://positivepsychology.com/shame-guilt/, citing Hofseth, E., Toering, T., & Jordet, G. (2015). Shame proneness, guilt proneness, behavioral self-handicapping, and skill level: A mediational analysis. *Journal of Applied Sport Psychology*, 27(3): 359–370. https://doi.org/10.1080/10413200.2015.1014974, accessed 3-12-23.

18. Stuewig, Jeffrey, Tangney, June, Kendall, Stephanie, Folk, Johanna, Meyer, Candace, & Dearing, Ronda. (2014). Children's proneness to shame and guilt predict risky and illegal behaviors in young adulthood. *Child Psychiatry and Human Development*, 46. https://doi.org/10.1007/s10578 -014-0467-1, accessed 3-12-23; Morrison, David, & Gilbert, Paul. (2001). Social rank, shame and anger in primary and secondary psychopaths. *The Journal of Forensic Psychiatry*, 12(2): 330–356. https://doi.org/10.1080/09585180110056867, accessed 3-12-23.

19. Classically attributed to Carl Jung in many places, including Sanderson, Christiane. (2015). *Counselling skills for working with shame (essential skills for counselling)* (1st ed.). Jessica Kingsley Publishers, 11.

20. Sewell, Jacqueline. (2017). *Detachments: If it is not by loving, it will be by hurting.* BalboaPressAU, facepage of chapter 21.

21. Crilly, Lynn. (2012). *Hope with eating disorders.* Hay House, 5.

22. Whelchel, Mary. (2007). *Why do I always feel guilty?* Harvest House Publishers, 11.

23. Nayeri, Daniel and Denise. (2010). *Another Faust.* Candlewick Press, 294.

24. Tangney, J. P. (1995). Recent advances in the empirical study of shame and guilt. *American Behavioral Scientist*, 38(8): 1132–1145. https://doi.org/10.1177/0002764295038008008, accessed 3-12-23.

25. Rubin, Gretchen. (2013, November 6). Feeling lonely? Consider these 7 strategies. https:// gretchenrubin.com/articles/feeling-lonely-consider-these-7-strategies/, accessed 3-14-23.

26. Selva, Why shame and guilt are functional. https://positivepsychology.com/shame-guilt/, citing Drummond, J. D. K., Hammond, S. I., Satlof-Bedrick, E., Waugh, W. E., & Brownell, C. A. (2017, July). Helping the one you hurt: Toddlers' rudimentary guilt, shame, and prosocial behavior after harming another. *Child Development*, 88(4): 1382–1397. https://doi.org/10.1111/cdev.12653, accessed 3-12-23.

27. Dr. Willard Gaylin, a New York psychotherapist, quoted by Brody, Jane E. (1983, November 29). Guilt: Or why it's good to feel bad. *New York Times.* https://www.nytimes.com/1983/11/29/science /guilt-or-why-it-s-good-to-feel-bad.html, accessed 3-12-23.

28. Tangney, Stuewig, and Hafez, Shame, guilt and remorse: https://doi.org/10.1080/14789949.2011 .617541; Stuewig, J., & McCloskey, L. A. (2005, November). The relation of child maltreatment to shame and guilt among adolescents: Psychological routes to depression and delinquency. *Child Maltreatment*, 10(4): 324–36. https://doi.org/10.1177/1077559505279308, accessed 3-12-23.

29. Selva, Why shame and guilt are functional. https://positivepsychology.com/shame-guilt/, citing Zhang, H., Chen, S., Wang, R., Jiang, J., Xu, Y., & Zhao, H. (2017, September 12). How upward moral comparison influences prosocial behavioral intention: Examining the mediating role of guilt and the moderating role of moral identity. *Frontiers in Psychology*, 8: 1554. https://doi.org /10.3389/fpsyg.2017.01554. Erratum: (2017, October 17). *Frontiers in Psychology*, 8: 1815, accessed 3-12-23.

30. Tangney, Stuewig, and Hafez, Shame, guilt and remorse: https://doi.org/10.1080/14789949.2011 .617541; Ahmed, E., & Braithwaite, V. (2004). "What, me ashamed?" Shame management and school bullying. *Journal of Research in Crime and Delinquency*, 41(3): 269–294. https://doi.org/10 .1177/0022427804266547, accessed 3-12-23; Lutwak, N., Panish, J. B., Ferrari, J. R., & Razzino,

B. E. (2001, Winter). Shame and guilt and their relationship to positive expectations and anger expressiveness. *Adolescence*, 36(144): 641–53. https://pubmed.ncbi.nlm.nih.gov/11928873/, accessed 3-12-23; Paulhus et al., Two replicable suppressor situations. https://doi.org/10.1207 /s15327906mbr3902_7; Stuewig, J., Tangney, J. P., Heigel, C., Harty, L., & McCloskey, L. (2010, February 1). Shaming, blaming, and maiming: Functional links among the moral emotions, externalization of blame, and aggression. *Journal of Research in Personality*, 44(1): 91–102. https:// doi.org/10.1016/j.jrp.2009.12.005, accessed 3-12-23; Tangney, J. P., Wagner, P. E., Hill-Barlow, D., Marschall, D. E., & Gramzow, R. (1996, April). Relation of shame and guilt to constructive versus destructive responses to anger across the lifespan. *Journal of Personality and Social Psychology*, 70(4): 797–809. https://doi.org/10.1037//0022-3514.70.4.797, accessed 3-12-23.

31. Selva, Why shame and guilt are functional. https://positivepsychology.com/shame-guilt/, citing Graton, A., & Ric, F. (2017). How guilt leads to reparation? Exploring the processes underlying the effects of guilt. *Motivation and Emotion*, 41(3): 343–352. https://doi.org/10.1007/s11031-017-9612 -z, accessed 3-12-23; Baumeister, R. F., Stillwell, A. M., & Heatherton, T. F. (1994, March). Guilt: An interpersonal approach. *Psychological Bulletin*, 115(2): 243–67. https://doi.org/10.1037/0033 -2909.115.2.243, accessed 3-12-23; Cryder, C. E., Springer, S., & Morewedge, C. K. (2012, May). Guilty feelings, targeted actions. *Personality and Social Psychology Bulletin*, 38(5): 607–18. https:// doi.org/10.1177/0146167211435796, accessed 3-12-23; Tangney, Stuewig, and Hafez, Shame, guilt and remorse: https://doi.org/10.1080/14789949.2011.617541; Pivetti, Camodeca, and Rapino, Shame, guilt, and anger. https://doi.org/10.1007/s12144-015-9339-5; Dr. Helen Block Lewis, a psychoanalyst and psychologist at Yale University, quoted by Brody, Jane E. (1983, November 29). Guilt: Or why it's good to feel bad. *New York Times*. https://www.nytimes.com/1983/11/29 /science/guilt-or-why-it-s-good-to-feel-bad.html, accessed 3-12-23.

32. Julle-Danière, Eglantine, Whitehouse, Jamie, Vrij, Aldert, Gustafsson, Erik, & Waller, Bridget M. (2020). The social function of the feeling and expression of guilt. *Royal Society Open Science*, 7(12): 200617. https://royalsocietypublishing.org/doi/10.1098/rsos.200617, accessed 3-12-23.

33. Tangney, Stuewig, and Hafez, Shame, guilt and remorse: https://doi.org/10.1080/14789949.2011 .617541.

34. Copeland, Libby. (2008, April). When guilt is good. *Atlantic Magazine*. https://www.theatlantic .com/magazine/archive/2018/04/how-to-guilt-trip-your-kids/554102/, accessed 3-12-23, citing Malti, T., & Ongley, S. F. (2014). The development of moral emotions and moral reasoning. In M. Killen & J. G. Smetana (Eds.), *Handbook of moral development* (pp. 163–183). Psychology Press. https://doi.org/10.4324/9780203581957.ch8, accessed 3-12-23; Dr. Tina Malti, professor of psychology at the University of Toronto, quoted by Copeland, When guilt is good. https://www .theatlantic.com/magazine/archive/2018/04/how-to-guilt-trip-your-kids/554102/.

35. Gandhi, Mahatma. (1958). *Collected works: Volume 26*. Publications Division, Ministry of Information and Broadcasting, Government of India, 448.

36. Mandeville, Bernard de. (2017). *The fable of the bees, or Private vices, public benefits*. Jonathan Bennett, 64. https://www.earlymoderntexts.com/assets/pdfs/mandeville1732.pdf, accessed 3-15-23. (Original work published 1732)

37. Maxwell, John C. (2007). *Talent is never enough: Discover the choices that will take you beyond your talent*. HarperCollins Leadership, 10.

38. Federor, Effect of shame and guilt. https://www.walshmedicalmedia.com/open-access/effect-of -shame-and-guilt-on-mental-health-111897.html.

39. 2 Corinthians 5:17.

40. Leviticus 19:2.

41. Romans 3:23 ESV.

42. James 2:10; Leviticus 5:17.

43. Widely attributed to Voltaire online and in publication, i.e., Sreechinth, C. (2018). *The laughing lion quotes: Quotes of Voltaire*. UB Tech, 7; Alexander, James. (2017). *Best Voltaire quotes*. Crombie Jardine Publishing Limited; Seka, M. I. (2014). *Life lessons of wisdom & motivation - volume IV: Insightful, enlightened and inspirational quotations and proverbs*. CreateSpace Independent Publishing Platform, 235; Taylor, Michael. (2006). *Musings: The philosophy of God*. Lulu.com, 52.

44. Philippians 3:19.
45. Romans 6:21.
46. Psalm 32:3–4.
47. Jeremiah 51:5.
48. Psalm 103:8–12 ESV.
49. Revelation 12:10.
50. Isaiah 43:25 ESV.
51. Hebrews 10:17 ESV. See also Hebrews 8:12; Psalm 103:12; Jeremiah 31:34.
52. Hebrews 10:22; Psalm 51:12; Psalm 139:23–24.
53. 1 John 1:9; Proverbs 28:13; Psalm 32:5.
54. Colossians 1:13–14.
55. Romans 8:1; Romans 3:21–22; Romans 10:11; Isaiah 54:4; Isaiah 61:7.
56. 2 Corinthians 5:17.
57. Galatians 2:20; 1 Peter 2:9; Ephesians 2:10; 1 John 1:7.

Lead #13: What Gangsters Have in Common

1. Singleton, John (Director). (1991). *Boyz n the Hood* [Film]. Columbia Pictures. For more info, visit the Internet Movie Database page: https://www.imdb.com/title/tt0101507/, accessed 3-21-23.
2. Quote from the movie cited here: Shad3487. (2016, July 12). "Boyz to men: How furious styles raised an entire generation." All Hip Hop. https://allhiphop.com/features/furious-styles/, accessed 3-22-23.
3. Modified slightly for clarity from "Damn, your Daddy mean. He worse than the bogeyman himself. You got to do all these leaves. Who do he think you is? Kunta Kinte? Later, Tre." Quote available here: https://www.imdb.com/title/tt0101507/quotes/?item=qt3763747&ref_=ext_shr_lnk, accessed 3-24-23.
4. Quote from the movie again cited here: Shad3487. "Boyz to men": https://allhiphop.com/features/furious-styles/.
5. Kramer, Stephanie. (2019, December 12). *U.S. has world's highest rate of children living in single-parent households.* Pew Research Center. https://www.pewresearch.org/fact-tank/2019/12/12/u-s-children-more-likely-than-children-in-other-countries-to-live-with-just-one-parent/, accessed 3-23-23.
6. U.S. Census Bureau. (2022). *Living arrangements of children under 18 years old: 1960 to present.*
7. U.S. Census Bureau. *Table FG10. Family groups: 2021.* https://www.census.gov/data/tables/2022/demo/families/cps-2022.html, accessed 3-19-23.
8. U.S. Census Bureau. *Table FG6. One-parent unmarried family groups with own children under 18.* https://www2.census.gov/programs-surveys/demo/tables/families/2022/cps-2022/tabfg6-all_one.xls, accessed 3-19-23.
9. National Center for Fathering. *Fathering in America poll, January, 1999.* https://fathers.com/wp-content/uploads/2021/08/1999-NCF-Poll-Fathering-in-America.pdf, accessed 3-19-23.
10. President Obama in his speech at Apostolic Church of God, Chicago, IL, June 15, 2008. https://www.realclearpolitics.com/articles/2008/06/obamas_speech_on_fatherhood.html, accessed 3-18-23.
11. Bozick, R. (2023). An increasing disinterest in fatherhood among childless men in the United States: A brief report. *Journal of Marriage and Family,* 85(1): 293–304. https://doi.org/10.1111/jomf.12874, accessed 3-19-23.
12. McLanahan, Sara, Tach, Laura, & Schneider, Daniel. (2013). The causal effects of father absence. *Annual Review of Sociology,* 39(1): 399–427. https://www.annualreviews.org/doi/abs/10.1146/annurev-soc-071312-145704, accessed 3-23-23.
13. Glenn, Norval, & Sylvester, Thomas. (2008, February). *The shift and the denial: Scholarly attitudes toward family change, 1977–2002* (Research Brief No. 8). Institute for American Values & Center for Marriage and Families. https://www.apfn.com.pt/Noticias/Mar2008/the_shift_and_the_denial_fev08.pdf, accessed 3-18-23.

14. Witherspoon Institute. (2008, August). *Marriage and the public good: Ten principles*. https://www.bigskyworldview.org/content/docs/links/MarriageandThePublicGoodTenPrinciples.pdf, accessed 12-29-22, citing Maccoby, Eleanor. (1998). *The two sexes: Growing up apart, coming together*. Harvard University; Witherspoon, *Marriage and the public good*. https://www.bigskyworldview.org/content/docs/links/MarriageandThePublicGoodTenPrinciples.pdf, citing Geary, David. (1998). *Male, female: The evolution of human sex differences*. American Psychological Association, 104, 142.

15. Popenoe, David. (1996). *Life without father*. The Free Press, 163; Rohner, Ronald P., & Veneziano, A. (2001). The importance of father love: History and contemporary evidence. *Review of General Psychology*, 5(4): 382–405; Amato, Paul R., & Rivera, Fernando. (1999). Paternal involvement and children's behavior problems. *Journal of Marriage and the Family*, 61: 375–384; *Psychology Today* Staff. (July/August 1993). Shuttle diplomacy. *Psychology Today*. Page 15; McLanahan, Tach, and Schneider, The causal effects of father absence: 399–427; Buswell, Lydia, Zabriskie, Ramon, Lundberg, Neil, & Hawkins, Alan. (2012). The relationship between father involvement in family leisure and family functioning: The importance of daily family leisure. *Leisure Sciences*, 34: 172–190. https://doi.org/10.1080/01490400.2012.652510, https://www.researchgate.net/publication/254316963_The_Relationship_Between_Father_Involvement_in_Family_Leisure_and_Family_Functioning_The_Importance_of_Daily_Family_Leisure, accessed 3-19-23.

16. Goldberg, J. S. (2015). Identity and involvement among resident and nonresident fathers. *Journal of Family Issues*, 36(7): 852–879. https://doi.org/10.1177/0192513X13500963, accessed 3-20-23.

17. Pew Research Center. (2013, March 14). *Modern parenthood: Roles of moms and dads converge as they balance work and family*. http://www.pewsocialtrends.org/2013/03/14/modern-parenthood-roles-of-moms-and-dads-converge-as-they-balance-work-and-family/, accessed 3-19-23; Livingston, Gretchen, & Parker, Kim. (2019, June 12). *8 facts about American dads*. Pew Research Center. https://www.pewresearch.org/fact-tank/2019/06/12/fathers-day-facts/, accessed 3-19-23.

18. Brown, Jerrod. *Father-absent homes: Implications for criminal justice and mental health professionals*. Minnesota Psychological Association. https://www.mnpsych.org/index.php?option=com_dailyplanetblog&view=entry&category=industry%20news&id=54:father-absent-homes-implications-for-criminal-justice-and-mental-health-professionals, accessed 3-19-23, citing McLanahan, S., & Casper, L. (1995). The American family in 1990: Growing diversity and inequality. In R. Farley (Ed.), *State of the union, II* (pp. 1–45). Russell Sage Foundation.

19. Brown, *Father-absent homes*. https://www.mnpsych.org/index.php?option=com_dailyplanetblog&view=entry&category=industry%20news&id=54:father-absent-homes-implications-for-criminal-justice-and-mental-health-professionals, citing Steinberg, L. (1987). Single parents, stepparents, and the susceptibility of adolescents to antisocial peer pressure. *Child Development*, 58: 269–275; Allen, Sarah, & Daly, Kerry. (2007). The effects of father involvement: An updated research summary of the evidence. Father Involvement Research Alliance: 10; Brown, *Father-absent homes*. https://www.mnpsych.org/index.php?option=com_dailyplanetblog&view=entry&category=industry%20news&id=54:father-absent-homes-implications-for-criminal-justice-and-mental-health-professionals, citing Davidson, N. (1990). Life without father. *Policy Review*, 51: 40.

20. Brown, *Father-absent homes*. https://www.mnpsych.org/index.php?option=com_dailyplanetblog&view=entry&category=industry%20news&id=54:father-absent-homes-implications-for-criminal-justice-and-mental-health-professionals, citing Leving, J. (2009, March 5). Absent fathers & youth violence. *Leving's Divorce Magazine*. http://divorcemagazine.wordpress.com/2009/03/05/absent-fathers-youth-violence.

21. Brown, *Father-absent homes*. https://www.mnpsych.org/index.php?option=com_dailyplanetblog&view=entry&category=industry%20news&id=54:father-absent-homes-implications-for-criminal-justice-and-mental-health-professionals, citing Leving, Absent fathers & youth violence. http://divorcemagazine.wordpress.com/2009/03/05/absent-fathers-youth-violence; Brown, *Father-absent homes*. https://www.mnpsych.org/index.php?option=com_dailyplanetblog&view=entry&category=industry%20news&id=54:father-absent-homes-implications-for-criminal-justice-and-mental-health-professionals, citing Coley, R. L., & Medeiros, B. L. (2007).

Reciprocal longitudinal relations between nonresident father involvement and adolescent delinquency. *Child Development*, 78: 132–147.

22. Brown, *Father-absent homes*. https://www.mnpsych.org/index.php?option=com_dailyplanet-blog&view=entry&category=industry%20news&id=54:father-absent-homes-implications-for-criminal-justice-and-mental-health-professionals, citing Manning, W. D., & Lamb, K. A. (2003). Adolescent wellbeing in cohabiting, married, and single-parent families. *Journal of Marriage & Family*, 65: 876–893.

23. Allen, A. N., & Lo, C. C. (2012). Drugs, guns, and disadvantaged youths: Co-occurring behavior and the code of the street. *Crime & Delinquency*, 58(6): 932–953. https://journals.sagepub.com/doi/10.1177/0011128709359652, accessed 3-23-23.

24. Harper, C. C., & McLanahan, S. S. (2004). Father absence and youth incarceration. *Journal of Research on Adolescence*, 14: 369–397. https://doi.org/10.1111/j.1532-7795.2004.00079.x, accessed 3-19-23; Pruett, K. D. (2000). *Fatherneed: Why father care is as essential as mother care for your child*. Free Press; Brown, *Father-absent homes*. https://www.mnpsych.org/index.php?option=com_dailyplanetblog&view=entry&category=industry%20news&id=54:father-absent-homes-implications-for-criminal-justice-and-mental-health-professionals, citing Snell, T. L., & Morton, D. C. (1994). *Women in prison: Survey of prison inmates, 1991*; Brown, *Father-absent homes*. https://www.mnpsych.org/index.php?option=com_dailyplanetblog&view=entry&category=industry%20news&id=54:father-absent-homes-implications-for-criminal-justice-and-mental-health-professionals, citing Hill, M. A., & O'Neill, J. (1993). *Underclass behaviors in the United States: Measurement and analysis of determinants*. City University of New York; Brown, *Father-absent homes*. https://www.mnpsych.org/index.php?option=com_dailyplan-etblog&view=entry&category=industry%20news&id=54:father-absent-homes-implications-for-criminal-justice-and-mental-health-professionals, citing Harper and McLanahan, Father absence and youth incarceration.

25. Sarkadi, Anna, Kristiansson, Robert, Oberklaid, Frank, & Bremberg, Sven. (2008). Fathers' involvement and children's developmental outcomes: A systematic review of longitudinal studies. *Acta Paediatrica*, 97: 153–8. https://doi.org/10.1111/j.1651-2227.2007.00572.x, accessed 3-18-23; Demuth, Stephen, & Brown, Susan L. (2004, February). Family structure, family processes, and adolescent delinquency: The significance of parental absence versus parental gender. *Journal of Research in Crime and Delinquency*, 41(1): 58–81; Bush, Connee, Mullis, Ronald L., & Mullis, Ann K. (2000, August). Differences in empathy between offender and nonoffender youth. *Journal of Youth and Adolescence*, 29: 467–478. https://link.springer.com/article/10.1023/A:1005162526769, accessed 3-23-23; Flouri, Eirini, & Buchanan, Ann. (2002, March). *Involved fathers key for children* [News Release]. Economic & Social Research Council. https://www.eurekalert.org/news-releases/611401, accessed 3-19-23; Father involvement using a tough love approach leads to better behavioral outcomes for kids. Marsiglio, W., Amato, P., Day, R. D., & Lamb, M. E. (2000). Scholarship on fatherhood in the 1990s and beyond. *Journal of Marriage and Family*, 62(4): 1173–1191; This study involved 1,977 children age 3 and older living with a residential father or father figure. Kids raised with fathers exhibit fewer externalizing and internalizing behavioral problems. See Hofferth, S. L. (2006). Residential father family type and child wellbeing: Investment versus selection. *Demography*, 43: 53–78; Adamsons, K., & Johnson, S. K. (2013). An updated and expanded meta-analysis of nonresident fathering and child wellbeing. *Journal of Family Psychology*, 27: 589–599, https://doi.org/10.1037/a0033786; In many additional studies, positive father involvement results in kids exhibiting fewer behavioral problems. Flouri, E., & Buchanan, A. (2003). The role of father involvement in children's later mental health. *Journal of Adolescence*, 26: 63–78; Mosley, J., & Thomson, E. Fathering behavior and child outcomes: The role of race and poverty. In W. Marsiglio (Ed.), *Research on men and masculinities series 7, fatherhood: Contemporary theory, research and social policy* (148–165); Volling, B. L., & Belsky, J. (1992). The contribution of mother-child and father-child relationships to the quality of sibling interaction: A longitudinal study. *Child Development*, 63: 1209–1222; Yeung, W. J., Duncan, G. J., & Hill, M. S. (2000). Putting fathers back in the picture: Parental activities and children's adult outcomes. *Marriage & Family Review*, 29(2–3): 97–113. http://dx.doi.org/10.1300/J002v29n02_07,

accessed 3-19-23; Magnuson, K., & Berger, L. M. (2009). Family structure states and transi-tions: Associations with children's wellbeing during middle childhood. *Journal of Marriage and Family*, 71: 575–591. https://minds.wisconsin.edu/bitstream/handle/1793/38560/EllisCory .pdf?sequence=4&isAllowed=y, accessed 3-19-23; Redding, Richard E. (2008). It's really about sex: Same-sex marriage, lesbigay parenting, and the psychology of disgust. *Duke Journal of Gender Law & Policy*, 15: 127–194. https://scholarship.law.duke.edu/djglp/vol15/iss2/4, accessed 3-23-23; For more related to the relationship between absent fathers, peer delinquency, and socioeconomic status, see Ellis, Cory. (2009). *Growing up without father: The effects on African American boys*. University of Wisconsin-Platteville; Also, delinquency scores were much higher from teens who said their parent was in jail at some point while they were growing up. Swisher, R. R., & Shaw-Smith, U. (2015). Paternal incarceration and adolescent wellbeing: Life course contingencies and other moderators. *Journal of Criminal Law & Criminology*, 104(4): 929–959. https://pubmed.ncbi.nlm.nih.gov/27239076/, accessed 3-23-23.

26. Kids born to single mothers showed higher levels of aggression than kids born to married mothers. See Osborne, C., & McLanahan, S. (2007). Partnership instability and child wellbeing. *Journal of Marriage and Family*, 69: 1065–1083. https://psycnet.apa.org/record/2007-14907-012, accessed 3-23-23; When the number of fathers is low in a neighborhood, there are more acts of teen violence. Knoester, C., & Hayne, D. A. (2005). Community context, social integration into family, and youth violence. *Journal of Marriage and Family*, 67: 767–780. https://onlinelibrary .wiley.com/doi/abs/10.1111/j.1741-3737.2005.00168.x, accessed 3-03-23; Fatherless sons lacking discipline are more likely to disrespect authority, become rebellious, and act aggressively. Cross, Tambra. (2021). *The impact of the absent African American father: Findings and implications*. Dissertations, 1065. https://irl.umsl.edu/dissertation/1065, accessed 3-19-23.

27. Witherspoon, *Marriage and the public good*. https://www.bigskyworldview.org/content/docs /links/MarriageandThePublicGoodTenPrinciples.pdf, citing Horn, Wade, & Sylvester, Tom. (2002). *Father facts*. National Fatherhood Initiative, 153. Popenoe, David. (1996). *Life without father*. Harvard University Press, 145. Powers, Thomas G., et al. (1994). Compliance and self-assertion: Young children's responses to mothers versus fathers. *Developmental Psychology*, 30: 980–989.

28. "Positive father care is associated with more pro-social and positive moral behavior in boys and girls." For more, Pruett, Kyle D. (2000). *Fatherneed: Why father care is as essential as mother care for your child*. The Free Press, 41–42, 52; Arlinghaus, K. R., & Johnston, C. A. (2017, February 8). Engaging fathers in the promotion of healthy lifestyle behaviors. *American Journal of Lifestyle Medicine*, 11(3): 216–219. https://doi.org/10.1177/1559827617690724, accessed 3-19-23; St George, J., Fletcher, R., & Palazzi, K. (2017). Comparing fathers' physical and toy play and links to child behaviour: An exploratory study. *Infant and Child Development*, 26: e1958. https://doi.org/10 .1002/icd.1958, accessed 3-19-23; Snarey, John. (1993). *How fathers care for the next generation: A four decade study*. Harvard University Press, 35–36; Paquette, D. (2012). The father-child activation relationship: A new theory to understand the development of infant mental health. *The Signal, Newsletter of the World Association for Infant Mental Health* 20(1); Paquette, D. (2004). Theorizing the father-child relationship: Mechanisms and developmental outcomes. *Human Development*, 47(4): 193–219; Paquette, D. (2004). La relation père-enfant et l'ouverture au monde. *Enfance*, 2: 205–225; Paquette, D., Eugène, M. M., Dubeau, D., & Gagnon, M.-N. (2009). Les pères ont-ils une influence spécifique sur le développement des enfants? In D. Dubeau, A. Devault, and G. Forget (Eds.), *La paternité au 21e siècle* (pp. 99–122). PUL.

29. Witherspoon, *Marriage and the public good*. https://www.bigskyworldview.org/content/docs /links/MarriageandThePublicGoodTenPrinciples.pdf, citing Pruett, Kyle. (2000). *Fatherneed*. Broadway, 30–31, Horn, Wade, & Sylvester, Tom. (2002). *Father facts*. National Fatherhood Initiative, 153. Popenoe, David. (1996). *Life without father*. Harvard University Press, 144–145; Clarke-Stewart, K. A. (1978). And Daddy makes three: The father's impact on mother and young child. *Child Development*, 49(2): 466–478. http://dx.doi.org/10.2307/1128712, accessed 3-19-23; Crawley, S. B., & Sherrod, K. B. (1984). Parent-infant play the first year of life. *Infant Behavior and Development*, 7(1): 65–75. https://doi.org/10.1016/S0163-6383(84)80023-5; Kazura, K. (2000).

Fathers' qualitative and quantitative involvement: An investigation of attachment, play, and social interactions. *The Journal of Men's Studies*, 9(1): 41–57. https://doi.org/10.3149/jms.0901.41; Kotelchuck, M. (1976). The infant's relationship to the father: Experimental evidence. In M. E. Lamb (Ed.), *The role of the father in child development*. John Wiley; Yeung, W. J., Sandberg, J. F., Davis-Kean, P. E., & Hofferth, S. L. (2001). Children's time with fathers in intact families. *Journal of Marriage and Family*, 63: 136–154.

30. Jeynes, William. (2018, June). Acknowledging the unique role of fathers. Institute for Family Studies. https://ifstudies.org/blog/acknowledging-the-unique-role-of-fathers, accessed 3-24-23; Jeynes, William H. (2016). Meta-analysis on the roles of fathers in parenting: Are they unique? *Marriage & Family Review*, 52(7): 665–688. https://doi.org/10.1080/01494929.2016.1157121, accessed 3-19-23.

31. Koestner, R., Franz, C., & Weinberger, J. (1990, April). The family origins of empathic concern: A 26-year longitudinal study. *Journal of Personality and Social Psychology*, 58(4): 709–17. https://doi.org/10.1037//0022-3514.58.4.709, accessed 3-24-23.

32. Committee of Ministers. (1994, November 24). The demographic characteristics of linguistic and religious groups in Switzerland. Council of Europe. https://rm.coe.int/CoERM Public CommonSearchServices/DisplayDCTMContent?documentId=0900001 6804 fb7b1, accessed 3-18-23; Raley, Billy Gage, & Felver, Troy B. Implications of Vitz's "Defective Father" hypothesis for the intergenerational transmission of religious belief in South Asia. *Man in India*, 97(23): 811–819. Publisher's version. https://scholar.harvard.edu/files/gageraley/files/raley_-_implications_of_vitzs_22defective_father22_hypothesis.pdf, accessed 3-18-23; Vitz, Paul C. The psychology of atheism. https://www.leaderu.com/truth/1truth12.html, accessed 3-18-23.

33. National Center for Education Statistics. (1998, April). *Students do better when their fathers are involved at school* [Issue Brief]. U.S. Department of Education, Office of Educational Research and Improvement. https://nces.ed.gov/pubs98/98121.pdf, accessed 3-18-23; Nord, Christine Winquist, & West, Jerry. (2001). *Fathers' and mothers' involvement in their children's schools by family type and resident status*. (NCES 2001-032). U.S. Department of Education, National Center for Education Statistics; Brown, *Father-absent homes*. https://www.mnpsych.org/index.php?option=com_dailyplanetblog&view=entry&category=industry%20news&id=54:father-absent-homes-implications-for-criminal-justice-and-mental-health-professionals, citing Bryant, A. L. (2003). Role models and psychosocial outcomes among African-American adolescents. *Journal of Adolescent Research*, 18: 36–87; Flouri and Buchanan, The role of father involvement: 63–78; Mosley and Thomson, Fathering behavior and child outcomes. In Marsiglio, *Research on men and masculinities*. 148–165; Sarkadi et al., Fathers' involvement: 153–158; Volling and Belsky, The contribution of mother-child: 1209–1222; Yeung, Duncan, and Hill, Putting fathers back in the picture. http://dx.doi.org/10.1300/J002v29n02_07; Allen and Daly, *The effects of father involvement*. 8; Fathers who employ tough love raise kids with better academic outcomes. Marsiglio et al., Scholarship on fatherhood: 1173–1191; Adamsons and Johnson, An updated and expanded meta-analysis of nonresident fathering. https://doi.org/10.1037/a0033786; Osborne and McLanahan, Partnership instability and child wellbeing: 1065–1083; U.S. Census Bureau. (2021). *Living arrangements of children under 18 years old: 1960 to present*. https://www.census.gov/data/tables/time-series/demo/families/children.html, accessed 3-19-23; U.S. Department of Education. (2010, February 19). *A call to commitment: Fathers' involvement in children's learning*. https://mentalhealthce.com/courses/contentSI/SI-Special-About-Fathers-Involvement.pdf, accessed 3-19-23.

34. Kruk, Edward. (2012, May 23). The vital importance of paternal presence in children's lives. *Psychology Today*. http://www.psychologytoday.com/blog/co-parenting-after-divorce/201205/father-absence-father-deficit-father-hunger, accessed 3-18-23; Brown, *Father-absent homes*. https://www.mnpsych.org/index.php?option=com_dailyplanetblog&view=entry&category=industry%20news&id=54:father-absent-homes-implications-for-criminal-justice-and-mental-health-professionals, citing Whitehead, M., & Holland, P. (2003). What puts children of lone parents at a health disadvantage? *Lancet*, 361: 271; Popenoe, D. (1996). *Life without a father*. Harvard University Press; Blankenhorn, D. (1995). *Fatherless America: Confronting our most urgent social*

problem. Basic Books; McLanahan and Casper, The American family in 1990. In R. Farley (Ed.), *State of the union, II* (pp. 1–45). Russell Sage Foundation; Sampson, R. J. (1987). Urban Black violence: The effect of male joblessness and family disruption. *American Journal of Sociology*, 93: 348–405; National Institute of Justice and the Executive Office for Weed and Seed. (1998). What can the federal government do to decrease crime and revitalize communities? National Institute of Justice Research Forum. https://www.ncjrs.gov/pdffiles/172210.pdf, accessed 3-19-23; McLanahan, Tach, and Schneider, The causal effects of father absence. https://doi.org/10.1146/annurev-soc-071312-145704; Sutherland, Anna. (2014, February). Yes, father absence causes the problems it's associated with. Institute for Family Studies. https://ifstudies.org/blog/yes-father-absence-causes-the-problems-its-associated-with, accessed 3-24-23, citing McLanahan, Tach, and Schneider, The causal effects of father absence. https://doi.org/10.1146/annurev-soc-071312-145704; Whitney, S., Prewett, S., Wang, Ze, & Haigin C. (2017). Fathers' importance in adolescents' academic achievement. *International Journal of Child, Youth and Family Studies*, 8(3–4): 101–126; Pruett, K. D. (2000). *Fatherneed: Why father care is as essential as mother care for your child*. Free Press;'Brown, *Father-absent homes*. https://www.mnpsych.org/index.php?option=com_dailyplanetblog&view=entry&category=industry%20news&id=54:father-absent-homes-implications-for-criminal-justice-and-mental-health-professionals, citing Keith, V. M., & Finlay, B. (1988). The impact of parental divorce on children's educational attainment, marital timing, and likelihood of divorce. *Journal of Marriage & the Family*, 50: 797–809; Furstenberg, Frank, & Harris, Kathleen. (1993). When and why fathers matter: Impacts of father involvement on children of adolescent mothers. In R. Lerman and T. Ooms (Eds.), *Young unwed fathers: Changing roles and emerging policies*. Temple University Press; Kruk, The vital importance of paternal presence. https://www.psychologytoday.com/us/blog/co-parenting-after-divorce/201205/father-absence-father-deficit-father-hunger.

35. U.S. Census Bureau. (2011). *Children's living arrangements and characteristics: March 2011, Table C8*; ASPE. (2012, September 11). *Information on poverty and income statistics: A summary of 2012 current population survey data* [Issue Brief]. https://aspe.hhs.gov/reports/information-poverty-income-statistics-summary-2012-current-population-survey-data-0, accessed 3-19-23; U.S. Census Bureau. *Children's living arrangements and characteristics: 2020, Table C8*. https://www.census.gov/data/tables/2020/demo/families/cps-2020.html, accessed 3-19-23; Fatherlessness is also a primary contributor to poverty involving African-American adolescents. Cross, Tambra. (2021). *The impact of the absent African American father: Findings and implications*. Dissertations, 1065. https://irl.umsl.edu/dissertation/1065, accessed 3-19-23; Brown, *Father-absent homes*. https://www.mnpsych.org/index.php?option=com_dailyplanetblog&view=entry&category=industry%20news&id=54:father-absent-homes-implications-for-criminal-justice-and-mental-health-professionals, citing Coleman, J. (1988). Social capital and the creation of human capital. *American Journal of Sociology*, 94: S95–S120.

36. Yogman, Michael. (2021, September 8). The role of fathers in child and family health. In *Engaged fatherhood for men, families and gender equality* (pp. 15–30). https://link.springer.com/chapter/10.1007/978-3-030-75645-1_2, accessed 3-19-23; Leach, Anna. (2014, June 26). Recognizing the importance of fathers [Presidential Statement]. Department of Education. https://obamawhitehouse.archives.gov/blog/2014/06/26/recognizing-importance-fathers, accessed 3-18-23, referring to the *Promoting responsible fatherhood* report. https://obamawhitehouse.archives.gov/sites/default/files/docs/fatherhood_report_6.13.12_final.pdf, accessed 3-18-23.

37. Garfield, C. F., & Isacco, A. (2006). Fathers and the well-child visit. *Pediatrics*, 117: 637–645; Lamb, M. E. (1977). Father-infant and mother-infant interaction in the first year of life. *Child Development*, 167–181; Matthews, T. J., Curtin, Sally C., & MacDorman, Marian F. (2000). Infant mortality statistics from the 1998 period linked birth/infant death data set. *National Vital Statistics Reports*, 48(12). National Center for Health Statistics; Shah, M., Gee, R., & Theall, K. (2014). Partner support and impact on birth outcomes among teen pregnancies in the United States. *Journal of Pediatric and Adolescent Gynecology*, 27: 14–19; Anthes, E. (2010, May/June). Family guy. *Scientific American Mind*.

38. Figueroa-Colon, R., Arani, R. B., Goran, M. I., & Weinsier, R. L. (2000, March). Paternal body

fat is a longitudinal predictor of changes in body fat in premenarcheal girls. *American Journal of Clinical Nutrition*, 71(3): 829–34. https://doi.org/10.1093/ajcn/71.3.829, accessed 3-19-23; Brown, *Father-absent homes.* https://www.mnpsych.org/index.php?option=com_dailyplanet-blog&view=entry&category=industry%20news&id=54:father-absent-homes-implications-for-criminal-justice-and-mental-health-professionals, citing Wake, M., Nicholson, J. M., Hardy, P., & Smith, K. (2007). Preschooler obesity and parenting styles of mothers and fathers: Australian national population study. *Pediatrics*, 12: 1520–1527.

39. Brown, *Father-absent homes.* https://www.mnpsych.org/index.php?option=com_dailyplanet blog&view=entry&category=industry%20news&id=54:father-absent-homes-implications-for-criminal-justice-and-mental-health-professionals, citing Finn, K., Johannsen, N., & Specker, B. (2002). Factors associated with physical activity in preschool children. *Journal of Pediatrics*, 140: 81–85. https://pubmed.ncbi.nlm.nih.gov/11815768/, accessed 3-24-23; Strauss, R. S., & Knight, J. (1999, June). Influence of the home environment on the development of obesity in children. *Pediatrics*, 103(6): e85. https://doi.org/10.1542/peds.103.6.e85, accessed 3-24-23.

40. Mitchell, Colter, McLanahan, Sara, Schneper, Lisa, Garfinkel, Irv, Brooks-Gunn, Jeanne, & Notterman, Daniel. (2017, August). Father loss and child telomere length. *Pediatrics*, 140 (2): e20163245. https://doi.org/10.1542/peds.2016-3245, https://publications.aap.org/pediatrics/article-abstract/140/2/e20163245/38629/Father-Loss-and-Child-Telomere-Length?redirectedFrom=fulltext, accessed 3-19-23.

41. Harknett, Kristen. (2005). *Children's elevated risk of asthma in unmarried families: Underlying structural and behavioral mechanisms.* Working Papers, 943. Princeton University, School of Public and International Affairs, Center for Research on Child Wellbeing. https://ideas.repec.org/p/pri/crcwel/wp05-01-ff-harknett.pdf.html, accessed 3-24-23.

42. McMunn, A., Martin, P., Kelly, Y., & Sacker, A. (2017, June). Fathers' involvement: Correlates and consequences for child socioemotional behavior in the United Kingdom. *Journal of Family Issues*, 38(8): 1109–1131. https://doi.org/10.1177/0192513X15622415, accessed 3-18-23; Adamsons and Johnson, An updated and expanded meta-analysis of nonresident fathering. https://doi.org/10.1037/a0033786; Marsiglio et al., Scholarship on fatherhood: 1173–1191.

43. Flouri and Buchanan, The role of father involvement: 63–78; Mosley and Thomson, Fathering behavior and child outcomes. In Marsiglio, *Research on men and masculinities.* 148–165; Sarkadi et al., Fathers' involvement: 153–158; Volling and Belsky, The contribution of mother-child: 1209–1222; Yeung, Duncan, and Hill, Putting fathers back in the picture. http://dx.doi.org/10.1300/J002v29n02_07; Flouri, Eirini, & Buchanan, Ann. (2002, March). *Involved fathers key for children.* Economic & Social Research Council. https://www.eurekalert.org/news-releases/611401, accessed 3-19-23; Sarkadi et al., Fathers' involvement https://doi.org/10.1111/j.1651-2227.2007.00572.x.

44. Batty, David. (2006, February 21). Single-parent families double likelihood of child mental illness. *The Guardian.* https://www.theguardian.com/society/2006/feb/21/mentalhealth.childrensservices, accessed 3-19-23; Teel, K. S., Verdeli, H., Wickramaratne, P., Warner, V., Vousoura, E., Haroz, E. E., & Talati, A. (2016, February). Impact of a father figure's presence in the household on children's psychiatric diagnoses and functioning in families at high risk for depression. *Journal of Child and Family Studies*, 25(2): 588–597. https://doi.org/10.1007/s10826-015-0239-y, accessed 3-19-23; Sarkadi et al., Fathers' involvement https://doi.org/10.1111/j.1651-2227.2007.00572.x; Pruett, K. D. (2000). *Fatherneed: Why father care is as essential as mother care for your child.* Free Press; Swisher and Shaw-Smith, Paternal incarceration and adolescent wellbeing: 929–959; Weitoft, Gunilla Ringbäck. (2003, January 25). Mortality, severe morbidity, and injury in children living with single parents in Sweden: A population-based study. *The Lancet*, 361(9354): 289–295; Martinez, Ken, et al. (2011, February). A guide for father involvement in systems of care. Technical Assistance Partnership for Child and Family Mental Health. https://www.air.org/sites/default/files/FatherhoodInvolvementGuide.pdf, accessed 3-19-23; Brown, *Father-absent homes.* https://www.mnpsych.org/index.php?option=com_dailyplanetblog&view=entry&category=industry%20news&id=54:father-absent-homes-implications-for-criminal-justice-and-mental-health-professionals, citing Osborne and McLanahan, Partnership instability

and child wellbeing: 1065–1083; Brown, *Father-absent homes.* https://www.mnpsych.org/index
.php?option=com_dailyplanetblog&view=entry&category=industry%20news&id=54:father
-absent-homes-implications-for-criminal-justice-and-mental-health-professionals, citing Flouri,
E. (2007). Fathering and adolescents' psychological adjustment: The role of fathers' involvement,
residence and biology status. *Childcare, Health & Development*, 34: 152–161; McLanahan, Tach,
and Schneider, The causal effects of father absence. https://doi.org/10.1146/annurev-soc-071312
-145704; Sarkadi et al., Fathers' involvement https://doi.org/10.1111/j.1651-2227.2007.00572.x.

45. Brown, *Father-absent homes.* https://www.mnpsych.org/index.php?option=com_dailyplan-
etblog&view=entry&category=industry%20news&id=54:father-absent-homes-implications
-for-criminal-justice-and-mental-health-professionals, citing America's Children. (1997). *Key
national indicators of wellbeing.* Federal Interagency Forum on Child and Family Statistics;
Bendheim-Thomas Center for Research on Child Wellbeing and Social Indicators Survey Center. (2010). *CPS involvement in families with social fathers.* Fragile Families Research Brief, 46.
Bendheim-Thomas Center for Research on Child Wellbeing and Social Indicators Survey Center;
Also: (2010). CPS involvement in families with social fathers. Fragile Families Research Brief,
46. Bendheim-Thomas Center for Research on Child Wellbeing and Social Indicators Survey
Center. https://ffcws.princeton.edu/sites/g/files/toruqf4356/files/documents/researchbrief46
.pdf, accessed 3-24-23; Brown, *Father-absent homes.* https://www.mnpsych.org/index.php?option
=com_dailyplanetblog&view=entry&category=industry%20news&id=54:father-absent-homes
-implications-for-criminal-justice-and-mental-health-professionals, citing Smith, S. M, Hanson,
R, & Nobel, S. (1980). Social aspects of the battered baby syndrome. In J. V. Cook & R. T. Bowles
(Eds.), *Child abuse: Commission and omission.* Butterworths; Waldfogel, J., Craigie, T. A., Brooks-
Gunn, J. (2010, Fall). Fragile families and child wellbeing. *Future of Children*, 20(2): 87–112.
https://doi.org/10.1353/foc.2010.0002, accessed 3-19-23; Turner, Heather A. (2006, January). The
effect of lifetime victimization on the mental health of children and adolescents. *Social Science
& Medicine*, 62(1): 13–27.

46. Brown, *Father-absent homes.* https://www.mnpsych.org/index.php?option=com_dailyplanet-
blog&view=entry&category=industry%20news&id=54:father-absent-homes-implications-for
-criminal-justice-and-mental-health-professionals, citing Bronte-Tinkew, J., Moore, K. A., Capps,
R. C., & Zaff, J. (2004). The influence of father involvement on youth risk behaviors among
adolescents: A comparison of native-born and immigrant families. *Social Science Research*, 35:
181–209; U.S. Department of Health and Human Services & National Center for Health Statistics.
(1993). *Survey on Child Health*; Hoffmann, John P. (May 2002). The community context of family
structure and adolescent drug use. *Journal of Marriage and Family*, 64: 314–330; Hemovich, V., &
Crano, W. D. (2009). Family structure and adolescent drug use: An exploration of single-parent
families. *Substance Use & Misuse*, 44(14): 2099–113. https://doi.org/10.3109/10826080902858375,
accessed 3-19-23; Brown, *Father-absent homes.* https://www.mnpsych.org/index.php?option=com
_dailyplanetblog&view=entry&category=industry%20news&id=54:father-absent-homes
-implications-for-criminal-justice-and-mental-health-professionals, citing Mandara, J., & Murray, C. B. (2006). Father's absence and African American adolescent drug use. *Journal of Divorce
& Remarriage*, 46: 1–12; National Center for Fathering. *Fatherlessness epidemic.* https://fathers
.com/wp39/wp-content/uploads/2015/07/fatherlessInfographic.pdf, accessed 3-19-23.

47. Allen and Daly, *The effects of father involvement.* 9.

48. DelPriore, D. J., Schlomer, G. L., & Ellis, B. J. (2017). Impact of fathers on parental monitoring of
daughters and their affiliation with sexually promiscuous peers: A genetically and environmentally controlled sibling study. *Developmental Psychology*, 53(7): 1330–1343. https://doi.org/10.1037
/dev0000327, accessed 3-19-23; Ellis, B. J., Bates, J. E., Dodge, K. A., Fergusson, D. M., Horwood,
L. J., Pettit, G. S., & Woodward, L. (2003 May–Jun). Does father absence place daughters at special
risk for early sexual activity and teenage pregnancy? *Child Development*, 74(3): 801–21. https://doi
.org/10.1111/1467-8624.00569, accessed 3-19-23; Jordahl, T., & Lohman, B. J. (2009, December 1).
A bioecological analysis of risk and protective factors associated with early sexual intercourse of
young adolescents. *Children and Youth Services Review*, 31(12): 1272–1282. https://doi.org/10.1016
/j.childyouth.2009.05.014, accessed 3-19-23; Biglan, Anthony, Metzler, Carol W., Wirt, Roger, Ary,

Dennis, Noell, John, Ochs, Linda, French, Christine, & Hood, Don. (1990). Social and behavioral factors associated with high-risk sexual behavior among adolescents. *Journal of Behavioral Medicine*, 13: 245–261; Billy, John O. G., Brewster, Karin L., & Grady, William R. (1994). Contextual effects of the sexual behavior of adolescent women. *Journal of Marriage and the Family*, 56: 387–404; Flewelling, Robert L., & Bauman, Karl E. (1990). Family structure as a predictor of initial substance use and sexual intercourse in early adolescence. *Journal of Marriage and the Family*, 52: 171–181; Meschke, Laurie L., Zweig, Janine M., Barber, Bonnie L., & Eccles, Jacquelynne S. (2000). Demographic, biological, social, and psychological correlates of the timing of first intercourse. *Journal of Research on Adolescence*, 10: 315–338; Simons, Ronald L., and Associates, Understanding differences between divorced and intact families (Thousand Oaks, CA: Sage, 1996). As cited in McGuire, Jenifer K., & Barber, Bonnie L. (2010). A person-centered approach to the multifaceted nature of young adult sexual behavior. *Journal of Sex Research*, 47(4): 308, 310. As cited in Fagan, Patrick F. & Churchill, Aaron. (2012, January). *The effects of divorce on children*. MARRI Research. http://downloads.frc.org/EF/EF12A22.pdf, accessed 3-19-23; Day, Robert. (1992). The transition to first intercourse among racially and culturally diverse youth. *Journal of Marriage and Family*, 54: 749–762; Allen and Daly, *The effects of father involvement*. 11; Jablonska, B., & Lindberg, L. (2007). Risk behaviours, victimization and mental distress among adolescents in different family structures. *Social Psychiatry & Psychiatric Epidemiology*, 42: 656–663; Ellis, B. J., Schlomer, G. L., Tilley, E. H., & Butler, E. A. (2012, February) Impact of fathers on risky sexual in daughters: a genetically and environmentally controlled sibling study. *Development and Psychopathology*, 24(1): 317–32, https://pubmed.ncbi.nlm.nih.gov/22293012/; Teachman, Jay D. (2004, January). The childhood living arrangements of children and the characteristics of their marriages. *Journal of Family Issues*, 25: 86–111; Beckwith, Andrew. (2019, June 14). No dad, no baby: Abortion in the age of fatherlessness. *New Boston Post*. https://newbostonpost.com/2019/06 /14/no-dad-no-baby-abortion-in-the-age-of-fatherlessness/, accessed 3-19-23.

49. Hendricks, C. S., Cesario, S. K., Murdaugh, C., Gibbons, M. E., Servonsky, E. J., Bobadilla, R. V., Hendricks, D. L., Spencer-Morgan, B., & Tavakoli, A. (2005, Nov–Dec). The influence of father absence on the self-esteem and self-reported sexual activity of rural southern adolescents. *ABNF Journal*, 16(6): 124–31. https://pubmed.ncbi.nlm.nih.gov/16382796/, accessed 3-24-23; Schwarzwalder, Rob, & Tax, Natasha. *How fatherlessness impacts early sexual activity, teen pregnancy, and sexual abuse*. Family Research Council. https://downloads.frc.org/EF/EF15L32.pdf, accessed 3-19-23; Anthes, E. (2010, May/June). Family guy. *Scientific American Mind*.

50. Brown, *Father-absent homes*. https://www.mnpsych.org/index.php?option=com_dailyplanet-blog&view=entry&category=industry%20news&id=54:father-absent-homes-implications-for -criminal-justice-and-mental-health-professionals, citing Poehlmann, J. (2005). Representations of attachment relationships in children of incarcerated mothers. *Child Development*, 76: 679–696; Also: Flouri and Buchanan, *Involved fathers key for children*. https://www.eurekalert.org /news-releases/611401; Brown, *Father-absent homes*. https://www.mnpsych.org/index.php?option=com_dailyplanetblog&view=entry&category=industry%20news&id=54:father-absent -homes-implications-for-criminal-justice-and-mental-health-professionals, citing Hirschi, T. (1969). *Causes of delinquency*. University of California Press; Jensen, G. F. (1972). Parents, peers, and delinquency action: A test of the differential association perspective. *American Journal of Sociology*, 78: 562–575; Johnson, R. E. (1987). Mothers' versus fathers' role in causing delinquency. *Adolescence*, 22: 305–315; Webster, P. S., Orbuch, T. L., & House, J. S. (1995). Effects of childhood family background on adult marital quality and perceived stability. *American Journal of Sociology*, 101(2): 404–432. https://doi.org/10.1086/230729, accessed 3-24-23.

51. Risch, Sharon, Jodl, Kathleen, & Eccles, Jacquelynne. (2004). Role of the father-adolescent relationship in shaping adolescents' attitudes toward divorce. *Journal of Marriage and Family*, 66. https://doi.org/10.1111/j.1741-3737.2004.00004.x, https://www.researchgate.net/publication /264717822_Role_of_the_Father-Adolescent_Relationship_in_Shaping_Adolescents'_Attitudes _Toward_Divorce, accessed 3-24-23.

52. Furstenberg Jr., F. F. (1988). Good dads-bad dads: Two faces of fatherhood. In A. J. Cherlin (Ed.), *The changing domestic priorities series: The changing American family and public policy*

(pp. 193–218). Urban Institute Press; Horn, W. F. (2006). Fatherhood, cohabitation, and marriage. *Gender Issues* 23: 21–35. https://doi.org/10.1007/BF03186787, accessed 3-24-23; Pougnet, E., Serbin, L. A., Stack, D. M., Ledingham, J. E., & Schwartzman, A. E. (2012). The intergenerational continuity of fathers' absence in a socioeconomically disadvantaged sample. *Journal of Marriage and Family*, 74(3): 540–555. https://doi.org/10.1111/j.1741-3737.2012.00962.x, accessed 3-24-23.

53. Billy Graham quoted from the Billy Graham Evangelistic Association. (2019, June 13). 10 quotes from Billy Graham on fatherhood. https://billygraham.org/story/10-quotes-from-billy-graham-on-fatherhood/, accessed 3-21-23.

54. Science News, regarding a study from Dr. Lynda Boothroyd and a team of psychologists from Durham University, published in the July 2007 issue of *Evolution and Human Behaviour*. https://www.sciencedaily.com/releases/2007/06/070613071240.htm#:~:text=Summary%3A,resemble%20their%20dads%2C%20research%20suggests, accessed 3-28-23.

55. John Green, from his video, Fatherhood. Vlogbrothers channel. https://www.youtube.com/watch?v=bgOtnLmJxno, accessed 3-21-23.

56. Eco, Umberto. (2007). *Foucault's pendulum*. Houghton Mifflin Harcourt. Also quoted here: https://gist.github.com/fasiha/283ede0d78abd059df43e2332aaa61fa, accessed 3-21-23.

57. Freud, Sigmund. (2005). *Civilization and its discontents*. Norton, 47.

58. Harmon Killebrew at his 1984 Hall of Fame induction ceremony in Cooperstown, New York and cited in Brackin, Dennis, Reusse, Patrick, & Star Tribune. (2010). *Minnesota Twins: The complete illustrated history*. Quarto Publishing Group USA, 32.

59. Hurd, N., Varner, F., & Rowley, S. (2013). Involved-vigilant parenting and socio-emotional wellbeing among Black youth: The moderating influence of natural mentoring relationships. *Journal of Youth and Adolescence*, 42(10): 1583–1595. https://doi.org/10.1007/s10964-012-9819-y, accessed 3-29-23.

60. Hebrews 13:4; Matthew 5:32; Luke 16:18; Proverbs 23:23–24; Proverbs 15:5.

61. Luke 15:20–24; Proverbs 17:25; Proverbs 19:13; Proverbs 23:24; Proverbs 17:21.

62. Luke 15:20–24.

63. 1 Timothy 5:8; Deuteronomy 6:6–9.

64. 1 Thessalonians 2:11–12; Proverbs 22:6; Deuteronomy 4:9; Psalm 78:2–8; Deuteronomy 6:6–7.

65. Proverbs 15:5; Proverbs 19:18; Proverbs 13:1; Proverbs 13:24; Ephesians 6:4; Colossians 3:21.

66. Malachi 4:6; Luke 6:36.

67. Psalm 103:13; Deuteronomy 8:5; Proverbs 3:11–12; Hebrews 12:7–11; 2 Corinthians 6:18; Matthew 7:11; Deuteronomy 1:31; Malachi 4:6; Luke 11:11–13.

Lead #14: Death Sentences and Life without Parole

1. Lehto, Rebecca Helen, & Stein, Karen Farchaus. (2009). Death anxiety: An analysis of an evolving concept. *Research and Theory for Nursing Practice*, 23(1). https://deepblue.lib.umich.edu/bitstream/handle/2027.42/66464/Death+Anxiety+An+Analysis+of+an+Evolving+Concept.pdf?sequence=1, accessed 3-30-23, citing Tomer, A., & Eliason, G. (1996). Toward a comprehensive model of death anxiety. *Death Studies*, 20: 345.

2. Pandya, Apurva-kumar, & Kathuria, Tripti. (2021, January). Death anxiety, religiosity and culture: Implications for therapeutic process and future research. *Religions*. https://doi.org/10.3390/rel12010061, accessed 3-30-23; Zhang, Jiaxi, Peng, Jiaxi, Gao, Pan, Huang, He, Cao, Yunfei, Zheng, Lulu, & Miao, Danmin. (2019). Relationship between meaning in life and death anxiety in the elderly: Self-esteem as a mediator. *BMC Geriatrics*, 19: 308; Mahdi, Rezapour. (2022). The interactive factors contributing to fear of death. *Frontiers in Psychology*, 13. https://doi.org/10.3389/fpsyg.2022.905594, accessed 3-30-23, citing Lester, D. (1967). Experimental and correlational studies of the fear of death. *Psychological Bulletin*, 67(1): 27–36. https://doi.org/10.1037/h0024068, accessed 3-30-23; Gegieckaite, G., & Kazlauskas, E. (2022). Fear of death and death acceptance among bereaved adults: Associations with prolonged grief. *OMEGA - Journal of Death and Dying*, 84(3): 884–898. https://doi.org/10.1177/0030222820921045, accessed 3-30-23; Pandya and

Kathuria, Death anxiety, religiosity and culture. https://doi.org/10.3390/rel12010061, citing Lehto and Stein, Death anxiety. https://doi.org/10.1891/1541-6577.23.1.23.

3. Lehto and Stein, Death anxiety. https://doi.org/10.1891/1541-6577.23.1.23, citing Becker, E. (1973). *The denial of death*. Free Press; Lonetto, R., & Templer, D. I. (1986). *Death anxiety*. Hemisphere Publishing; Neimeyer, R. A. (1994). *Death anxiety handbook: Research, instrumentation, and application*. Taylor & Francis; Panksepp, J. (1998). *Affective neuroscience: The foundations of human and animal emotions*. Oxford University Press; Yalom, I. D. (1980). *Existential psychotherapy*. Basic Books.

4. Kashdan, Todd B., DeWall, C. Nathan, Schurtz, David R., Deckman, Timothy, Lykins, Emily L. B., Evans, Daniel R., McKenzie, Jessica, Segerstrom, Suzanne C., Gailliot, Matthew T., Brown, & Kirk Warren. (2014). More than words: Contemplating death enhances positive emotional word use. *Personality and Individual Differences*, 71: 171–175. https://doi.org/10.1016/j.paid.2014.07.035, accessed 3-30-23.

5. Pandya and Kathuria, Death anxiety, religiosity and culture. https://doi.org/10.3390/rel12010061; Langs, Robert. (2004). Death anxiety and the emotion-processing mind. *Psychoanalytic Psychology*, 21: 31–53.

6. *APA Dictionary of Psychology* definition of Terror Management Theory. https://dictionary.apa.org/terror-management-theory, accessed 4-02-23.

7. Becker, *The denial of death*.

8. Lehto and Stein, Death anxiety. https://doi.org/10.1891/1541-6577.23.1.23, citing Pyszczynski, T., Greenberg, J., Solomon, S., Arndt, J., & Schimel, J. (2004). Why do people need self-esteem? A theoretical and empirical overview. *Psychological Bulletin*, 130: 435–468; Solomon, S., Greenberg, J., & Pyszczynski, T. (2000). Pride and prejudice: Fear of death and social behavior. *Current Directions in Psychological Science*, 9(6): 200–204. https://doi.org/10.1111/1467-8721.00094, accessed 3-30-23; Jong, Jonathan, Halberstadt, Jamin, & Bluemke, Matthias. (2012). Foxhole atheism, revisited: The effects of mortality salience on explicit and implicit religious belief. *Journal of Experimental Social Psychology*, 48(5): 983–989. https://doi.org/10.1016/j.jesp.2012.03.005, accessed 3-30-23; Goleman, Daniel. (1989, December 5). Fear of death intensifies moral code, scientists find. *New York Times*. https://www.nytimes.com/1989/12/05/science/fear-of-death-intensifies-moral-code-scientists-find.html, accessed 3-30-23, citing Maxfield, M., Pyszczynski, T., Kluck, B., Cox, C. R., Greenberg, J., Solomon, S., & Weise, D. (2007, June). Age-related differences in responses to thoughts of one's own death: Mortality salience and judgments of moral transgressions. *Psychology and Aging*, 22(2): 341–53. https://doi.org/10.1037/0882-7974.22.2.341, accessed 3-30-23; Hirschberger, Gilad, Pyszczynski, Tom, Ein-Dor, Tsachi, Shani Sherman, Tal, Kadah, Eihab, Kesebir, Pelin, & Park, Young Chin. (2016, February). Fear of death amplifies retributive justice motivations and encourages political violence, *Peace and Conflict: Journal of Peace Psychology*, 22(1): 67–74. https://psycnet.apa.org/buy/2015-40874-001, accessed 3-30-23; Lehto and Stein, Death anxiety. https://doi.org/10.1891/1541-6577.23.1.23, citing Bassett, J. F. (2007). Psychological defenses against death anxiety: Integrating terror management theory and Firestone's separation theory. *Death Studies*, 31: 727–750; Landau, M. J., Greenberg, J., Solomon, S., Pyszczynski, T., & Martens, A. (2006). Windows into nothingness: Terror management, meaninglessness, and negative reactions to art. *Journal of Personality and Social Psychology*, 90: 879–892.

9. Greenberg, J., Pyszczynski, T., Solomon, S., Rosenblatt, A., Veeder, M., Kirkland, S., & Lyon, D. (1990). Evidence for terror management theory II: The effects of mortality salience on reactions to those who threaten or bolster the cultural worldview. *Journal of Personality and Social Psychology*, 58(2): 308–318. https://doi.org/10.1037/0022-3514.58.2.308, accessed 3-30-23.

10. Quoted from the English version of the study: https://scielo.isciii.es/pdf/eg/v19n58/en_1695-6141-eg-19-58-287.pdf, accessed 3-30-23, citing Duran-Badillo, T., Maldonado Vidales, M. A., Martínez Aguilar, M. de la L., Gutierrez Sánchez, G. y Ávila Alpirez, H. (2020, March). Miedo ante la muerte y calidad de vida en adultos mayores. *Enfermería Global*, 19(2): 287–304. https://doi.org/10.6018/eglobal.364291, accessed 3-30-23; Brewer, Kenneth Grant. (2002, August). *Differing death scenarios: Self esteem and death anxiety*. East Tennessee State University School of Graduate

Studies. https://dc.etsu.edu/cgi/viewcontent.cgi?article=1841&context=etd, accessed 3-31-23, citing Harmon-Jones, E., Simon, L., Greenberg, J., Pyszczynski, T., Solomon, S., & McGregor, H. (1997). Terror management theory and self-esteem: Evidence that increased self-esteem reduces morality salience effects. *Journal of Personality and Social Psychology*, 72: 24–36; Greenberg, J., Pyszczynski, T., & Solomon, S. (1986). The causes and consequences of the need for self-esteem: A terror management theory. In R. F. Baumeister (Ed.), *Public self and private self* (pp. 189–212). Springer-Verlag; Solomon, S., Greenberg, J., & Pyszczynski, T. (1991). Terror management theory of self-esteem. In C. Synder & D. Forsyth (Eds.), *Handbook for social and clinical psychology: The health perspective* (pp. 21–40). Pergamon Press; Brewer, *Differing death scenarios*. https://dc.etsu .edu/cgi/viewcontent.cgi?article=1841&context=etd, citing Buzzanga, V., Miller, H., Perne, S., Sander, J., & Davis, S. (1989). The relationship between death anxiety and level of self-esteem: A reassessment. *Bulletin of the Psychonomic Society*, 27: 570–572; Davis, S., Bremer, S., Anderson, B., & Tramill, J. (1983). The interrelationships of ego strength, self-esteem, death anxiety, and gender in undergraduate students. *The Journal of General Psychology*, 108: 55–59; Davis, S., Martin, D., Wilee, C., & Voorhees, J. (1978). Relationship of fear of death and level of self-esteem in college students. *Psychological Reports*, 42: 419–422.

11. Gegieckaite and Kazlauskas, Fear of death and death acceptance. https://doi.org/10.1177/0030222 820921045; Dolan, Eric W. (2019, October 6). New psychology research has linked death anxiety to bedtime procrastination. PsyPost. https://www.psypost.org/2019/10/new-psychology-research-has -linked-death-anxiety-to-bedtime-procrastination-54598, accessed 3-30-23, citing Türkarslan, Kutlu Kağan, Okay, Deniz, Çevrim, Mustafa, & Bozo, Özlem. (2020). Life is short, stay awake: Death anxiety and bedtime procrastination. *The Journal of General Psychology*, 147(1): 43–61. https://doi.org/10.1080/00221309.2019.1633994, accessed 3-30-23; Lehto and Stein, Death anxiety. https://doi.org/10.1891/1541-6577.23.1.23, citing Martz, E. (2004). Death anxiety as a predictor of posttraumatic stress levels among individuals with spinal cord injuries. *Death Studies*, 28: 1–17.

12. Menzies, R., Sharpe, L., Helgadóttir, F., & Dar-Nimrod, I. (2021). Overcome death anxiety: The development of an online cognitive behaviour therapy programme for fears of death. *Behaviour Change*, 38(4): 235–249. https://doi.org/10.1017/bec.2021.14, accessed 3-30-23; Lehto and Stein, Death anxiety. https://doi.org/10.1891/1541-6577.23.1.23, citing DePaola, S. J., Neimeyer, R. A., Lupfer, M. B., & Fiedler, J. (1992). Death concern and attitudes toward the elderly in nursing home personnel. *Death Studies*, 16: 537–555; Pandya and Kathuria, Death anxiety, religiosity and culture. https://doi.org/10.3390/rel12010061, citing Galek, K., Krause, N., & Ellison, C. G., et al. (2007). Religious doubt and mental health across the lifespan. *Journal of Adult Development*, 14: 16–25. https://doi.org/10.1007/s10804-007-9027-2, accessed 3-30-23; Sherman, Deborah Witt, Norman, Robert, & McSherry, Christina Beyer. (2010). A comparison of death anxiety and quality of life of patients with advanced cancer or AIDS and their family caregivers. *Journal of the Association of Nurses in AIDS Care*, 21(2): 99–112. https://doi.org/10.1016/j.jana.2009.07.007, accessed 3-30-23; Bahrami, N., Moradi, M., Soleimani, M. A., Kalantari, Z., & Hosseini, F. Death anxiety and its relationship with quality of life in women with cancer. *IJN*, 26(82). http://ijn.iums.ac.ir /article-1-1562-en.html, accessed 3-30-23; Iverach, Lisa, Menzies, Ross G., & Menzies, Rachel E. (2014). Death anxiety and its role in psychopathology: Reviewing the status of a transdiagnostic construct. *Clinical Psychology Review*, 34(7): 580–593. https://doi.org/10.1016/j.cpr.2014.09.002, accessed 3-30-23; Willis, Kelcie D., Nelson, Tamara, & Moreno, Oswaldo. (2019). Death anxiety, religious doubt, and depressive symptoms across race in older adults. *International Journal of Environmental Research and Public Health*, 16(19): 3645. https://doi.org/10.3390/ijerph16193645, accessed 3-30-23; Pandya and Kathuria, Death anxiety, religiosity and culture. https://doi.org/10 .3390/rel12010061, citing Menzies, R. E., Sharpe, L., & Dar-Nimrod, I. (2019). The relationship between death anxiety and severity of mental illnesses. *British Journal of Clinical Psychology*, 58: 452–467. https://doi.org/10.1111/bjc.12229, accessed 3-30-23; Le Marne, K., & Harris, L. (2016). Death anxiety, perfectionism and disordered eating. *Behaviour Change*, 33(4): 193–211. https:// doi.org/10.1017/bec.2016.11, accessed 3-30-23; Menzies, R. E., & Dar-Nimrod, I. (2017). Death anxiety and its relationship with obsessive-compulsive disorder. *Journal of Abnormal Psychology*, 126(4): 367–377. https://doi.org/10.1037/abn0000263, accessed 3-30-23; Öngider, Nilgün, & Özışık

Notes   259

Eyüboğlu, Suna. (2013). Investigation of death anxiety among depressive patients. *Journal of Clinical Psychiatry*, 16(1): 34–46. https://klinikpsikiyatri.org/jvi.aspx?pdir=kpd&plng=eng&un=KPD -86635&look4=, accessed 3-30-23; Lehto and Stein, Death anxiety. https://doi.org/10.1891/1541 -6577.23.1.23, citing Abdel-Khalek, A. M. (1991). Death anxiety among Lebanese samples. *Psychological Reports*, 68: 924–926; Hoelter, J. W., & Hoelter, J. A. (1978, July). The relationship between fear and death and anxiety. *Journal of Psychology*, 99(2): 225–6. https://doi.org/10.1080 /00223980.1978.9921462; Maxfield, Molly, John, Samantha, & Pyszczynski, Tom. (2014). A terror management perspective on the role of death-related anxiety in psychological dysfunction. *The Humanistic Psychologist*, 42(1): 35–53. https://doi.org/10.1080/08873267.2012.732155, accessed 3-30-23; Vaccaro, Lisa D., Jones, Mairwen, K., Menzies, Ross G., & St Clare, Tamsen. (2010). *DIRT [Danger Ideation Reduction Therapy] for obsessive compulsive checkers: A comprehensive guide to treatment* (General ed.). Australian Academic Press; Menzies, Ross, Menzies, Rachel, & Iverach, Lisa. (2015). The role of death fears in obsessive compulsive disorder. *Australian Clinical Psychologist*, 1: 6–11. https://www.researchgate.net/publication/280142510_Menzies _R_G_Menzies_R_E_Iverach_L_2015_The_role_of_death_fears_in_Obsessive_Compulsive _Disorder_Australian_Clinical_Psychologist_1_6-11, accessed 3-30-23; Fleet, Richard P., & Beitman, Bernard D. (1998). Cardiovascular death from panic disorder and panic-like anxiety: A critical review of the literature. *Journal of Psychosomatic Research*, 44(1): 71–80. https://doi.org /10.1016/S0022-3999(97)00135-9, accessed 3-30-23; Strachan, E., Schimel, J., Arndt, J., Williams, T., Solomon, S., Pyszczynski, T., & Greenberg, J. (2007). Terror mismanagement: Evidence that mortality salience exacerbates phobic and compulsive behaviors. *Personality and Social Psychology Bulletin*, 33(8): 1137–1151. https://doi.org/10.1177/0146167207303018, accessed 3-30-23; Lehto and Stein, Death anxiety. https://doi.org/10.1891/1541-6577.23.1.23, citing Farber, S. K., Jackson, C., Tabin, J. K., & Bachar, E. (2007). Death and annihilation anxieties in anorexia nervosa, bulimia, and self-mutilation. *Psychoanalytic Psychology*, 24: 289–305; Jackson, C., Davidson, G., Russell, J., & Vandereycken, W. (1990). Ellen West revisited: The theme of death in eating disorders. *International Journal of Eating Disorders*, 9: 529–536.

13. Lehto and Stein, Death anxiety. https://doi.org/10.1891/1541-6577.23.1.23, citing Hirschberger, G., Florian, V., & Mikulincer, M. (2005). Fear and compassion: A terror management analysis of emotional reactions to physical disability. *Rehabilitation Psychology*, 50: 246–257; Lehto and Stein, Death anxiety. https://doi.org/10.1891/1541-6577.23.1.23, citing Bassett, Psychological defenses against death anxiety: 727–750; Goldenberg, J. L., Hart, J., Pyszczynski, T., Warnica, G. M., Landau, M., & Thomas, L. (2006). Ambivalence toward the body: Death, neuroticism, and the flight from physical sensation. *Personality and Social Psychology Bulletin*, 32: 1264–1277.

14. Lehto and Stein, Death anxiety. https://doi.org/10.1891/1541-6577.23.1.23, citing Becker, *The denial of death*; Landau et al., Windows into nothingness: 879–892; Lehto and Stein, Death anxiety. https://doi.org/10.1891/1541-6577.23.1.23, citing Momeyer, R. W. (1988). *Confronting death*. Indianapolis: Indiana University Press.

15. Lehto and Stein, Death anxiety. https://doi.org/10.1891/1541-6577.23.1.23, citing Arndt, J., Solomon, S., Kasser, T., & Sheldon, K. (2004). The urge to splurge: A terror management account of materialism and consumer behavior. *Journal of Consumer Psychology*, 14: 198–212; Zaleskiewicz, Tomasz, Gasiorowska, Agata, Kesebir, Pelin, Luszczynska, Aleksandra, & Pyszczynski, Tom. (2013). Money and the fear of death: The symbolic power of money as an existential anxiety buffer. *Journal of Economic Psychology*, 36: 55–67. https://doi.org/10.1016/j.joep.2013.02.008, accessed 3-30-23; Lehto and Stein, Death anxiety. https://doi.org/10.1891/1541-6577.23.1.23, citing Rindfleisch, A., & Burroughs, J. E. (2004). Terrifying thoughts, terrible materialism? Contemplations on a terror management account of materialism and consumer behavior. *Journal of Consumer Psychology*, 14: 219–224.

16. Pascal, Blaise, & Eliot, T. S. (1958). *Pascal's Pensées*. E. P. Dutton, 139.

17. Zhang et al., Relationship between meaning in life. https://doi.org/10.1186/s12877-019-1316 -7; Mahdi, The interactive factors. https://doi.org/10.3389/fpsyg.2022.905594, citing Snyder, C. R., & Forsyth, D. R. (1991). *Handbook of social and clinical psychology: The health perspective*. Pergamon Press.

18. Fritsche, Immo, Jonas, Eva, Fischer, Peter, Koranyi, Nicolas, Berger, Nicole, & Fleischmann, Beatrice. (2007). Mortality salience and the desire for offspring. *Journal of Experimental Social Psychology*, 43(5): 753–762. https://doi.org/10.1016/j.jesp.2006.10.003, accessed 3-30-23; Vicary, Amanda M. (2011). Mortality salience and namesaking: Does thinking about death make people want to name their children after themselves? *Journal of Research in Personality*, 45(1): 138–141. https://doi.org/10.1016/j.jrp.2010.11.016, accessed 3-30-23.

19. Pandya and Kathuria, Death anxiety, religiosity and culture. https://doi.org/10.3390/rel12010061, citing Hart, Joshua, & Goldenberg, Jamie L. (2008). A terror management perspective on spirituality and the problem of the body. In Adrian Tomer, Grafton T. Eliason, & Paul T. P. Wong (Eds.), *Existential and spiritual issues in death attitudes* (pp. 91–113). Lawrence Erlbaum.

20. Greenberg, Jeff, Kosloff, Spee, Solomon, Sheldon, Cohen, Florette, & Landau, Mark. (2010). Toward understanding the fame game: The effect of mortality salience on the appeal of fame. *Self and Identity*, 9(1): 1–18. https://doi.org/10.1080/15298860802391546, accessed 3-30-23.

21. Wu, Jade. (2020, September 2). Why we fear death and how to overcome it. *Psychology Today*. https://www.psychologytoday.com/us/blog/the-savvy-psychologist/202009/why-we-fear-death -and-how-overcome-it, accessed 4-03-23, citing Griffith, J. D., Gassem, M., Hart, C. L., Adams, L. T., & Sargent, R. (2018). A cross-sectional view of fear of death and dying among skydivers. *OMEGA - Journal of Death and Dying*, 77(2): 173–187. https://doi.org/10.1177/0030222815600178, accessed 3-30-23.

22. Pascal, Blaise, & Eliot, T. S. (1958). *Pascal's Pensées*. E. P. Dutton, 169.

23. Popham, Lauren E., Kennison, Shelia M., & Bradley, Kristopher I. (2011). Ageism and risk-taking in young adults: Evidence for a link between death anxiety and ageism. *Death Studies*, 35(8): 751–763. https://doi.org/10.1080/07481187.2011.573176, accessed 3-30-23.

24. George Mason University. (2011, February 28). Being "mindful" can neutralize fears of death and dying. ScienceDaily. https://www.sciencedaily.com/releases/2011/02/110228151800.htm, accessed 3-30-23, citing this study: Niemiec, Christopher, Brown, Kirk, Kashdan, Todd, Cozzolino, Philip, Breen, William, Levesque-Bristol, Chantal, & Ryan, Richard. (2010). Being present in the face of existential threat: The role of trait mindfulness in reducing defensive responses to mortality salience. *Journal of Personality and Social Psychology*. 99: 344–65. https://doi.org/10 .1037/a0019388, accessed 3-30-23; Sullivan, M. J., Wood, L., Terry, J., Brantley, J., Charles, A., & McGee, V., et al. (2009). The Support, Education, and Research in Chronic Heart Failure Study (SEARCH): A mindfulness-based psychoeducational intervention improves depression and clinical symptoms in patients with chronic heart failure. *American Heart Journal*, 157: 84–90. https://doi.org/10.1016/j.ahj.2008.08.033, accessed 3-30-23.

25. Epicurus. (1994). Letter to Menoeceus. In *The Epicurus Reader: Selected writings and testimonia translated and edited, with notes* (Brad Inwood and L. P. Gerson, Eds.). Hackett, 125.

26. Seneca. (1953). On taking one's own life. In *Epistulae Morales II* (R. M. Gummere, Trans.). Harvard University Press, 175.

27. Pandya, Apurva-kumar, & Kathuria, Tripti. (2021, January). Death anxiety religiosity and culture: Implications for therapeutic process and future research. *Religions*. https://doi.org/10.3390 /rel12010061, accessed 3-30-23, citing Kastenbaum, Robert. (2000). *The psychology of death* (3rd ed.). Springer.

28. Kass, Leon. (1985). *Toward a more natural science: Biology and human affairs*. Free Press, 309.

29. For a more robust collection of academic papers related to "mind uploading" refer to the Mind Uploading page at Philosophy of Cognitive Science website. https://philpapers.org/browse/mind -uploading, accessed 4-04-23.

30. Mahdi, The interactive factors. https://doi.org/10.3389/fpsyg.2022.905594, citing Minsky, R. (2013). *Psychoanalysis and culture: Contemporary states of mind*. John Wiley and Sons.

31. Sagan, Carl. (2011). *Billions & billions: Thoughts on life and death at the brink of the millennium*. Random House Publishing Group, 258.

32. Ipsos Global. (2011, April). Ipsos Global @dvisory: Supreme being(s), the afterlife and evolution. https://www.ipsos.com/en-us/news-polls/ipsos-global-dvisory-supreme-beings-afterlife-and -evolution, accessed 3-30-23, fuller report here: https://www.ipsos.com/sites/default/files/news

_and_polls/2011-04/5217-ppt.pdf, accessed 3-30-23; Gallup International Center for Public and Political Studies. (2023, March 23). More prone to believe in God than identify as religious. https://www.gallup-international.bg/en/46964/more-prone-to-believe-in-god-than-identify-as-religious/, accessed 3-30-23.

33. Pew Research Center. (2021, November 23). *Few Americans blame God or say faith has been shaken amid pandemic, other tragedies.* https://www.pewresearch.org/religion/2021/11/23/views-on-the-afterlife/, accessed 3-30-23; Roper Center for Public Opinion Research. (2005, June 15). *Paradise polled: Americans and the afterlife.* https://ropercenter.cornell.edu/paradise-polled-americans-and-afterlife, accessed 3-30-23; Barna Research. (2003, October 21). Americans describe their views about life after death. https://www.barna.com/research/americans-describe-their-views-about-life-after-death/, accessed 3-30-23; Statista. (2016, November 1). Do you believe in survival of the soul after death? https://www.statista.com/statistics/632117/united-states-belief-in-survival-of-the-soul-after-death/, accessed 3-30-23.

34. Twenge, J. M., Sherman, R. A., Exline, J. J., & Grubbs, J. B. (2016). Declines in American adults' religious participation and beliefs, 1972–2014. *SAGE Open*, 6(1). https://doi.org/10.1177/2158244016638133, accessed 4-01-23.

35. Kurt Cobain, quoted by Roy Trakin in his interview. Trakin, Roy. (2004, April 14). In utero: Kurt Cobain speaks. Hits Daily Double. https://hitsdailydouble.com/news&id=278335&title=IN-UTERO:-KURT-COBAIN-SPEAKS, accessed 4-04-23.

36. Lehto and Stein, Death anxiety. https://doi.org/10.1891/1541-6577.23.1.23, citing Fortner, B. V., & Neimeyer, R. A. (1999). Death anxiety in older adults: A quantitative review. *Death Studies*, 23: 387–411; Ellis, Lee, Wahab, Eshah A., & Ratnasingan, Malini. (2013). Religiosity and fear of death: A three-nation comparison. *Mental Health, Religion & Culture*, 16(2): 179–199. https://doi.org/10.1080/13674676.2011.652606, accessed 3-30-23.

37. Brewer, *Differing death scenarios.* https://dc.etsu.edu/cgi/viewcontent.cgi?article=1841&context=etd, citing Rasmussen, C., & Johnson, M. (1994). Spirituality and religiosity: Relative relationships to death anxiety. *Omega*, 29, 313–318; Pandya and Kathuria, Death anxiety, religiosity and culture. https://doi.org/10.3390/rel12010061, citing Alvarado, K. A., Templer, D. I., Bresler, C., & Thomas-Dobson, S. (1995). The relationship of religious variables to death depression and death anxiety. *Journal of Clinical Psychology* 51: 202–204. https://doi.org/10.1002/1097-4679(199503)51:2<202::AID-JCLP2270510209>3.0.CO;2-M, accessed 3-30-23; Mohammadzadeh, A., & Najafi, M. (2020). The comparison of death anxiety, obsession, and depression between Muslim population with positive and negative religious coping. *Journal of Religious Health*, 59: 1055–1064. https://doi.org/10.1007/s10943-018-0679-y, accessed 3-30-23; Moore, Gavin. (2013). The relationship between religious orientation, coping style, and psychological health on death anxiety and life satisfaction. Dublin Business School. http://hdl.handle.net/10788/1605, accessed 3-30-23; Saini, Prabhjot, Patidar, Anurag B., Kaur, Ravneet, Kaur, Mandeep, & Kaur, Jasbir. (2016). Death anxiety and its associated factors among elderly population of Ludhiana City, Punjab. *Indian Journal of Gerontology*, 30(1): 101–110. http://www.gerontologyindia.com/pdf/Vol-30-1.pdf#page=107, accessed 3-30-23; Taghiabadi, Mina, Kavosi, Ali, Mirhafez, Seyed Reza, Keshvari, Mahrokh, & Mehrabi, Tayebe. (2017). The association between death anxiety with spiritual experiences and life satisfaction in elderly people. *Electronic Physician*, 9: 3980. https://www.ncbi.nlm.nih.gov/pmc/articles/PMC5407231/, accessed 3-30-23; Mahdi, The interactive factors. https://doi.org/10.3389/fpsyg.2022.905594, citing Harding, Stephen R., Flannelly, Kevin J., Weaver, Andrew J., & Costa, Karen G. (2005). The influence of religion on death anxiety and death acceptance. *Mental Health, Religion & Culture*, 8(4): 253–261. https://doi.org/10.1080/13674670412331304311, accessed 3-30-23; Lehto and Stein, Death anxiety. https://doi.org/10.1891/1541-6577.23.1.23, citing Knight, K. H., & Elfenbein, M. H. (1993). Relationship of death education to the anxiety, fear, and meaning associated with death. *Death Studies*, 17: 411–425.

38. Pandya and Kathuria, Death anxiety, religiosity and culture. https://doi.org/10.3390/rel12010061, citing Lewis, Adam M. (2014). Terror management theory applied clinically: Implications for existential-integrative psychotherapy. *Death Studies*, 38(6): 412–417. https://doi.org/10.1080/07481187.2012.753557, accessed 3-30-23.

39. Lehto and Stein, Death anxiety. https://doi.org/10.1891/1541-6577.23.1.23, citing Alvarado et al., The relationship of religious variables: 202–204; Lehto and Stein, Death anxiety. https://doi.org /10.1891/1541-6577.23.1.23, citing Smith, D. K., Nehemkis, A. M., & Charter, R. A. (1983–1984). Fear of death, death attitudes, and religious conviction in the terminally ill. *International Journal of Psychiatric Medicine*, 13: 221–232; Glas, G. (2007). Anxiety, anxiety disorders, religion, and spirituality. *Southern Medical Journal*, 100: 621–625; Kraft, W. A., Litwin, W. J., & Barber, S. E. (1987). Religious orientation and assertiveness: Relationship to death anxiety. *Journal of Social Psychology*, 127: 93–95; Pierce, J. D. (2007). Gender differences in death anxiety and religious orientation among U.S. high school and college students. *Mental Health, Religion, and Culture*, 10: 143–150; Pandya and Kathuria, Death anxiety, religiosity and culture. https://doi.org/10.3390 /rel12010061, citing Allport, Gordon W., & Ross, James M. (1967). Personal religious orientation and prejudice. *Journal of Personality and Social Psychology*, 5: 432–43; Ardelt, Monika, & Koenig, Cynthia S. (2006). The role of religion for hospice patients and relatively healthy older adults. *Research on Aging*, 28: 184–215; Arrowood, Robert Britton, Cox, Cathy R., Weinstock, Maddie, & Hoffman, Jill. (2018). Intrinsic religiosity protects believers from the existential fear of a human Jesus. *Mental Health, Religion and Culture*, 21: 534–45; Cohen, Adam B., Pierce Jr., John D., Chambers, Jacqueline, Meade, Rachel, Gorvine, Benjamin J., & Koenig, Harold G. (2005). Intrinsic and extrinsic religiosity, belief in the afterlife, death anxiety, and life satisfaction in young Catholics and Protestants. *Journal of Research in Personality*, 39: 307–24; Hui, Victoria Ka-Ying, & Fung, Helene H. (2008). Mortality anxiety as a function of intrinsic religiosity and perceived purpose in life. *Death Studies*, 33: 30–50; Saleem, T., & Saleem, S. (2020). Religiosity and death anxiety: A study of Muslim Dars attendees. *Journal of Religion and Health*, 59: 309–317. https://doi.org/10.1007/s10943-019-00783-0, accessed 3-30-23; Pandya and Kathuria, Death anxiety, religiosity and culture. https://doi.org/10.3390/rel12010061, citing Wen, Y. H. (2010). Religiosity and death anxiety. *Journal of Human Resource and Adult Learning*, 6: 31–37; Brewer, *Differing death scenarios*. https://dc.etsu.edu/cgi/viewcontent.cgi?article=1841&context=etd, citing Alvarado et al., The relationship of religious variables: 202–204; Brewer, *Differing death scenarios*. https://dc.etsu.edu/cgi/viewcontent.cgi?article=1841&context=etd, citing Templer, D. (1970). The construction and validation of the death anxiety scale. *Journal of General Psychology*, 82: 165–177.
40. Florian, V., & Snowden, L. R. (1989). Fear of personal death and positive life regard: A study of different ethnic and religious-affiliated American college students. *Journal of Cross-Cultural Psychology*, 20(1): 64–79. https://doi.org/10.1177/0022022189201004, accessed 3-30-23; Brewer, *Differing death scenarios*. https://dc.etsu.edu/cgi/viewcontent.cgi?article=1841&context=etd.
41. Nichols, S., Strohminger, N., Rai, A., & Garfield, J. (2018). Death and the self. *Cognitive Science*, 42: 314–332. https://doi.org/10.1111/cogs.12590, accessed 4-01-23; Allmond, Joy. (2018, July 3). What religious group fears death the most? Lifeway Research. https://research.lifeway .com/2018/07/03/what-religious-group-fears-death-most/, accessed 3-30-23, citing Nichols, Shaun, Strohminger, Nina, Rai, Arun, & Garfield, Jay. Supplemental material for death and the self. https://onlinelibrary.wiley.com/action/downloadSupplement?doi=10.1111%2Fcogs .12590&file=cogs12590-sup-0001-supInfo.pdf, accessed 3-30-23; Florian, V., & Kravetz, S. (1983). Fear of personal death: Attribution, structure, and relation to religious belief. *Journal of Personality and Social Psychology*, 44(3): 600–607. https://doi.org/10.1037/0022-3514.44.3.600, accessed 3-30-23.
42. Nichols et al., Death and the self. https://doi.org/10.1111/cogs.12590.
43. Clements, R. (1998). Intrinsic religious motivation and attitudes toward death among the elderly. *Current Psychology*, 17: 237–248. https://doi.org/10.1007/s12144-998-1009-4, accessed 3-30-23; Nienke, P. M. Fortuin, Johannes, Schilderman, B. A. M., & Venbrux, Eric. (2019). Religion and fear of death among older Dutch adults. *Journal of Religion, Spirituality & Aging*, 31(3): 236–254. https://doi.org/10.1080/15528030.2018.1446068, accessed 3-30-23; Mahdi, The interactive factors. https://doi.org/10.3389/fpsyg.2022.905594, citing Henrie, J., & Patrick, J. H. (2014). Religiousness, religious doubt, and death anxiety. *The International Journal of Aging and Human Development*, 78(3): 203–227. https://doi.org/10.2190/AG.78.3.a, accessed 3-30-23.

44. Flew, Antony, & Varghese, Roy Abraham. (2007). *There is a God: How the world's most notorious atheist changed his mind.* HarperCollins, 93.
45. Wallace, J. Warner. (2015). *God's crime scene: A cold-case detective examines the evidence for a divinely created universe.* David C. Cook.
46. For more information about the evidence for mind and soul, see my article: Wallace, J. Warner. (2018, May 23). A very brief review of arguments for the existence of the soul. Cold-Case Christianity. https://coldcasechristianity.com/writings/a-very-brief-review-of-arguments-for-the-existence-of-the-soul-bible-insert/, accessed 4-06-23.
47. Baker, Mark C., & Goetz, Stewart. (2010). *The soul hypothesis: Investigations into the existence of the soul.* Bloomsbury Academic, 7.
48. Sanders, E. P. (1995). *The historical figure of Jesus.* Penguin Books, 10–11, 280.
49. Matthew 10:28 ESV.
50. 1 Corinthians 15:20 ESV.
51. 1 Corinthians 15:12–14.
52. Wallace, J. Warner. (2013). *Cold-case Christianity: A homicide detective investigates the claims of the gospels.* David C. Cook. And Wallace, J. Warner. (2021). *Person of interest: Why Jesus still matters in a world that rejects the Bible.* Zondervan.
53. Wallace, J. Warner. (2017). *Forensic faith: A homicide detective makes the case for a more reasonable, evidential Christian faith.* David C. Cook.
54. Billy Graham, quoted from Graham, Franklin, & Toney, Donna Lee. (2011). *Billy Graham in quotes.* Thomas Nelson, 201.
55. Arendt, Hannah. (1996). *Love and Saint Augustine.* University of Chicago Press, 10–11.
56. Romans 5:12.
57. Romans 5:14–17.
58. John 3:16; John 11:25; John 5:24; 1 Corinthians 15:22; Matthew 26:29.
59. Lewis, C. S., from *Miracles*, as published in (2007). *The Complete C. S. Lewis Signature Classics.* HarperCollins, 413.
60. Matthew 6:34, John 14:27; Matthew 6:25; 1 Corinthians 15:55.
61. 1 Corinthians 15:26 ESV. See also Ecclesiastes 12:7; Romans 6:23; Matthew 25:46; Philippians 3:20; Philippians 1:22–24; Luke 23:43; John 14:1–5; 1 Thessalonians 4:13–17; 2 Corinthians 5:8; Philippians 1:21; 1 Peter 1:4.
62. Revelation 21:4.
63. Ephesians 2:7 ESV.
64. Colossians 3:2 ESV. See also James 1:12; Luke 6:22–23.
65. Romans 8:18 ESV. See also Matthew 5:12; 2 Timothy 4:8; Philippians 3:14; Colossians 3:24.
66. Hebrews 2:14–15 ESV.

Lead #15: Every Kind of Stupid

1. *Collins Dictionary*, s.v. "hopeless." https://www.collinsdictionary.com/us/dictionary/english/hopeless, accessed 4-10-23; Vocabulary.com, s.v. "hopeless." https://www.vocabulary.com/dictionary/hopeless, accessed 4-10-23.
2. World Health Organization. (2017). *Depression and other common mental disorders: Global health estimates.* License: CC BY-NC-SA 3.0 IGO. https://apps.who.int/iris/handle/10665/254610, https://apps.who.int/iris/bitstream/handle/10665/254610/WHO-MSD-MER-2017.2-eng.pdf, accessed 4-10-23; Lim, G. Y., Tam, W. W., & Lu, Y., et al. (2018). Prevalence of depression in the community from 30 countries between 1994 and 2014. *Scientific Reports*, 8: 2861. https://doi.org/10.1038/s41598-018-21243-x, accessed 4-10-23; World Health Organization. (2023, March 31). Depressive disorder (depression) fact sheet. https://www.who.int/news-room/fact-sheets/detail/depression, accessed 4-10-23.
3. Kessler, R. C., et al. (2005, June). Prevalence, severity, and comorbidity of twelve-month DSM-IV disorders in the National Comorbidity Survey Replication (NCS-R). *Archives of General Psychiatry*, 62: 617–627.

4. Bitsko, R. H., Claussen, A. H., Lichtstein, J., Black, L. J., Everett Jones, S., Danielson, M. D., Hoenig, J. M., Davis, Jack S. P., Brody, D. J., Gyawali, S., Maenner, M. M., Warner, M., Holland, K. M., Perou, R., Crosby, A. E., Blumberg, S. J., Avenevoli, S., Kaminski, J. W., & Ghandour, R. M. (2022). Surveillance of children's mental health–United States, 2013–2019. *Morbidity and Mortality Weekly Report Supplements*, 71(2): 1–42. https://www.cdc.gov/mmwr/volumes/71/su /su7102a1.htm, accessed 4-10-23.

5. Harvard Kennedy School Institute of Politics. (2021, April 23). *Harvard youth poll*. https://iop .harvard.edu/youth-poll/spring-2021-harvard-youth-poll, accessed 4-10-23; Geiger, A. W., & Davis, Leslie. (2019, July 12). *A growing number of American teenagers–particularly girls–are facing depression*. Pew Research Center. https://www.pewresearch.org/fact-tank/2019/07/12/a -growing-number-of-american-teenagers-particularly-girls-are-facing-depression/, accessed 4-10-23; Mojtabai, R., Olfson, M., & Han, B. (2016, December). National trends in the prevalence and treatment of depression in adolescents and young adults. *Pediatrics*, 138(6): e20161878. https://doi.org/10.1542/peds.2016-1878, accessed 4-10-23; Twenge, J. M., Cooper, A. B., Joiner, T. E., Duffy, M. E., & Binau, S. G. (2019, April). Age, period, and cohort trends in mood disorder indicators and suicide-related outcomes in a nationally representative dataset, 2005–2017. *Journal of Abnormal Psychology*, 128(3): 185–199. https://doi.org/10.1037/abn0000410, accessed 4-10-23; Jones, Sherry, Ethier, Kathleen, Hertz, Marci, DeGue, Sarah, Le, Vi, Thornton, Jemekia, Lim, Connie, Dittus, Patricia, & Geda, Sindhura. (2022). Mental health, suicidality, and connectedness among high school students during the COVID-19 pandemic - Adolescent Behaviors and Experiences Survey, United States, January-June 2021. *Morbidity and Mortality Weekly Report Supplements*, 71: 16–21. https://doi.org/10.15585/mmwr.su7103a3, accessed 4-10-23; Goodwin, Renee D., Dierker, Lisa C., Wu, Melody, Galea, Sandro, Hoven, Christina W., & Weinberger, Andrea H. (2022, September 19). Trends in U.S. depression prevalence from 2015 to 2020: The widening treatment gap. *American Journal of Preventive Medicine*, 63(5): 726–733. https://doi.org /10.1016/j.amepre.2022.05.014, accessed 4-10-23.

6. Bitsko et al., Surveillance of children's mental health. https://www.cdc.gov/mmwr/volumes/71 /su/su7102a1.htm.

7. Peterson, C., Stone, D. M., Marsh, & S. M., et al. (2018). Suicide rates by major occupational group—17 states, 2012 and 2015. *Morbidity and Mortality Weekly Report*, 67: 1253–1260. http:// dx.doi.org/10.15585/mmwr.mm6745a1, accessed 4-10-23.

8. Öztürk, Meral, Türk, Ahmet, Gonultas, Burak, & Aydemir, Ishak. (2022). Mediator role of social media use on the effect of negative emotional state of young adults on hopelessness during COVID-19 outbreak. *Archives of Health Science and Research*. https://doi.org/10.5152 /ArcHealthSciRes.2022.22096, accessed 4-11-23; Aalbers, George, McNally, Richard J., Heeren, Alexandre, de Wit, Sanne, & Fried, Eiko I. (2019, August). Social media and depression symptoms: A network perspective. *Journal of Experimental Psychology: General*, 148(8): 1454–1462. https://www.researchgate.net/publication/365047344_Mediator_Role_of_Social_Media_Use _on_the_Effect_of_Negative_Emotional_State_of_Young_Adults_on_Hopelessness_During _COVID-19_Outbreak, accessed 4-11-23; Fioravanti, Giulia, Flett, Gordon, Hewitt, Paul, Rugai, Laura, & Casale, Silvia. (2020). How maladaptive cognitions contribute to the development of problematic social media use. *Addictive Behaviors Reports*, 11: 100267. https://doi.org/10.1016/j .abrep.2020.100267, accessed 4-11-23.

9. Melore, Chris. (2022, July 9). Hopeless nation: 2 in 3 Americans don't think they'll ever see positive social change. StudyFinds. https://studyfinds.org/americans-positive-social-change/, accessed 4-10-23.

10. Murphy, Elijah R. (2023). Hope and wellbeing. *Current Opinion in Psychology*, 50: 101558. https:// doi.org/10.1016/j.copsyc.2023.101558, accessed 4-09-23; Scogin, F., Morthland, M., DiNapoli, E. A., LaRocca, M., & Chaplin, W. (2016). Pleasant events, hopelessness, and quality of life in rural older adults. *The Journal of Rural Health*, 32: 102–109. https://doi.org/10.1111/jrh.12130, accessed 4-09-23.

11. Gum, A., Shiovitz-Ezra, S., & Ayalon, L. (2017). Longitudinal associations of hopelessness and loneliness in older adults: Results from the US health and retirement study. *International Psychogeriatrics*, 29(9): 1451–1459. https://doi.org10.1017/S1041610217000904, accessed 4-09-23.

12. Hill, R. D., Gallagher, D., Thompson, L. W., & Ishida, T. (1988). Hopelessness as a measure of suicidal intent in the depressed elderly. *Psychology and Aging*, 3(3): 230–232. https://doi.org/10.1037/0882-7974.3.3.230, accessed 4-09-23; Brothers, B. M., & Andersen, B. L. (2009). Hopelessness as a predictor of depressive symptoms for breast cancer patients coping with recurrence. *Psycho-Oncology*, 18: 267–275. https://doi.org/10.1002/pon.1394, accessed 4-09-23; Karatas, Zeynep, & Cakar, Firdevs Savi. (2011, November). Self-esteem and hopelessness, and resiliency: An exploratory study of adolescents in Turkey. *International Education Studies*, 4(4): 84–91. https://eric.ed.gov/?id=EJ1066570, accessed 4-09-23; Dixson, Dante D. (2023). Promoting hope in minoritized and economically disadvantaged students. *Current Opinion in Psychology*, 49: 101519. https://doi.org/10.1016/j.copsyc.2022.101519, accessed 4-09-23; Serafini, Gianluca, Lamis, Dorian A., Aguglia, Andrea, Amerio, Andrea, Nebbia, Jacopo, Geoffroy, Pierre Alexis, Pompili, Maurizio, & Amore, Mario. (2020). Hopelessness and its correlates with clinical outcomes in an outpatient setting. *Journal of Affective Disorders*, 263: 472–479. https://doi.org/10.1016/j.jad.2019.11.144, accessed 4-08-23; Long, Laura J. (2022). Hope and PTSD. *Current Opinion in Psychology*, 48: 101472. https://doi.org/10.1016/j.copsyc.2022.101472, accessed 4-09-23; Senger, Amy R. (2023). Hope's relationship with resilience and mental health during the COVID-19 pandemic. *Current Opinion in Psychology*, 50: 101559. https://doi.org/10.1016/j.copsyc.2023.101559, accessed 4-09-23.
13. Serafini et al., Hopelessness and its correlates. https://doi.org/10.1016/j.jad.2019.11.144; Long, Hope and PTSD. https://doi.org/10.1016/j.copsyc.2022.101472.
14. Beck, Aaron T., Brown, Gary, Berchick, Robert J., Stewart, Bonnie L., & Steer, Robert A. (2006). Relationship between hopelessness and ultimate suicide: A replication with psychiatric outpatients. *FOCUS*, 4(2): 291–296. https://doi.org/10.1176/foc.4.2.291, accessed 4-08-23; Czeisler, Mark É., Lane, Rashon I., Petrosky, Emiko, Wiley, Joshua F., Christensen, Aleta, Njai, Rashid, Weaver, Matthew D., Robbins, Rebecca, Facer-Childs, Elise R., Barger, Laura K., Czeisler, Charles A., Howard, Mark E., & Rajaratnam, Shantha M. W. (2020, August 14). Mental health, substance use, and suicidal ideation during the COVID-19 pandemic—United States, June 24–30, 2020. *Morbidity and Mortality Weekly Report*, 69(32): 1049–1057. https://www.cdc.gov/mmwr/volumes/69/wr/mm6932a1.htm, accessed 4-10-23; Mental Health America. The state of mental health in America. https://mhanational.org/issues/state-mental-health-america, accessed 4-10-23; Also: Centers for Disease Control and Prevention. (2013, 2011). Web-based Injury Statistics Query and Reporting System (WISQARS) [Online]. http://www.cdc.gov/injury/wisqars/index.html, accessed 4-10-23; Hirsch, Jameson K., Hall, Benjamin B., Wise, Haley A., Brooks, Byron D., Chang, Edward C., & Sirois, Fuschia M. (2021). Negative life events and suicide risk in college students: Conditional indirect effects of hopelessness and self-compassion. *Journal of American College Health*, 69(5): 546–553. https://doi.org/10.1080/07448481.2019.1692023, accessed 4-08-23; Christodoulou, Christos, Efstathiou, Vasiliki, Michopoulos, Ioannis, Ferentinos, Panagiotis, Korkoliakou, Panagiota, Gkerekou, Maria, Bouras, Georgios, Papadopoulou, Athanasia, Papageorgiou, Charalabos, & Douzenis, Athanassios. (2017). A case-control study of hopelessness and suicidal behavior in the city of Athens, Greece. The role of the financial crisis. *Psychology, Health & Medicine*, 22(7): 772–777. https://doi.org/10.1080/13548506.2016.1164872, accessed 4-08-23; Hirsch, Jameson K., Visser, Preston L., Chang, Edward C., & Jeglic, Elizabeth L. (2012). Race and ethnic differences in hope and hopelessness as moderators of the association between depressive symptoms and suicidal behavior. *Journal of American College Health*, 60(2): 115–125. https://doi.org/10.1080/07448481.2011.567402, accessed 4-08-23; Petrie, K., & Brook, R. (1992). Sense of coherence, self-esteem, depression and hopelessness as correlates of reattempting suicide. *British Journal of Clinical Psychology*, 31: 293–300. https://doi.org/10.1111/j.2044-8260.1992.tb00996.x, accessed 4-08-23; Chang, Edward C. (2017). Hope and hopelessness as predictors of suicide ideation in Hungarian college students, *Death Studies*, 41(7): 455–460. https://doi.org/10.1080/07481187.2017.1299255, accessed 4-08-23; Steeg, Sarah, Haigh, Matthew, Webb, Roger T., Kapur, Nav, Awenat, Yvonne, Gooding, Patricia, Pratt, Daniel, & Cooper, Jayne. (2016). The exacerbating influence of hopelessness on other known risk factors for repeat self-harm and suicide. *Journal of Affective Disorders*, 190: 522–528. https://doi.org/10.1016/j.jad.2015.09.050, accessed 4-09-23; Ropaj, Esmira. (2023). Hope and suicidal ideation and behaviour. *Current Opinion in Psychology*,

49: 101491. https://doi.org/10.1016/j.copsyc.2022.101491, accessed 4-09-23; Grafiadeli, Raphaela, Glaesmer, Heide, Hofmann, Laura, Schäfer, Thomas, & Wagner, Birgit. (2021). Suicide risk after suicide bereavement: The role of loss-related characteristics, mental health, and hopelessness. *Journal of Psychiatric Research*, 144: 184–189. https://doi.org/10.1016/j.jpsychires.2021.09.056, accessed 4-09-23; Tan Dat, Nguyen, Mitsui, Nobuyuki, Asakura, Satoshi, Watanabe, Shinya, Takanobu, Keisuke, Fujii, Yutaka, Toyoshima, Kuniyoshi, Kako, Yuki, & Kusumi, Ichiro. (2021). The mediating role of hopelessness in the relationship between self-esteem, social anxiety, and suicidal ideation among Japanese university students who visited a university health care center. *Journal of Affective Disorders Reports*, 6: 100192, accessed 4-09-23.

15. Ejdemyr, I., Hedström, F., Gruber, M., & Nordin, S. (2021). Somatic symptoms of helplessness and hopelessness. *Scandinavian Journal of Psychology*. https://onlinelibrary.wiley.com/doi/abs/10.1111/sjop.12713, accessed 4-08-23.

16. Whipple, Mary O., Lewis, Ten T., Sutton-Tyrrell, Kim, Matthews, Karen A., Barinas-Mitchell, Emma, Powell, Lynda H., & Everson-Rose, Susan A. (2009). Hopelessness, depressive symptoms, and carotid atherosclerosis in women. *Stroke*, 40(10): 3166–3172. https://doi.org/10.1161/STROKEAHA.109.554519, accessed 4-09-23; Everson, Susan A., Kaplan, George A., Goldberg, Debbie E., Salonen, Riitta, & Salonen, Jukka T. (1997). Hopelessness and 4-year progression of carotid atherosclerosis. *Arteriosclerosis, Thrombosis, and Vascular Biology*, 17(8): 1490–1495. https://doi.org/10.1161/01.ATV.17.8.1490, accessed 4-09-23; Savasan, Aysegul, et al. (2013, January). Hopelessness and healthy life style behaviors in patients with coronary artery disorder/ Koroner arter hastalarinda saglikli yasam bicimi davranislari ve umutsuzluk. *Journal of Psychiatric Nursing*, 4(1): 1+. Gale OneFile: Health and Medicine, https://go.gale.com/ps/i.do?id=-GALE%7CA365982224&sid=googleScholar&v=2.1&it=r&linkaccess=abs&issn=13093568&p=HRCA&sw=w&userGroupName=anon%7Ed06a5705, accessed 4-09-23; Do, D. P., Dowd, J. B., Ranjit, N., House, J. S., & Kaplan, G. A. (2010, September). Hopelessness, depression, and early markers of endothelial dysfunction in U.S. adults. *Psychosomatic Medicine*, 72(7): 613–9. https://doi.org/10.1097/PSY.0b013e3181e2cca5, accessed 4-09-23; Eslami, Bahareh, Kovacs, Adrienne H., Moons, Philip, Abbasi, Kyomars, & Jackson, Jamie L. (2017). Hopelessness among adults with congenital heart disease: Cause for despair or hope? *International Journal of Cardiology*, 230: 64–69. https://doi.org/10.1016/j.ijcard.2016.12.090, accessed 4-09-23; Everson, Susan A., Kaplan, George A., Goldberg, Debbie E., & Salonen, Jukka T. (2000). Hypertension incidence is predicted by high levels of hopelessness in Finnish men. *Hypertension*, 35(2): 561–567. https://doi.org/10.1161/01.HYP.35.2.561, accessed 4-09-23; DeVon, Holli A., Tintle, Nathan, Bronas, Ulf G., Mirzaei, Sahereh, Rivera, Eleanor, Gutierrez-Kapheim, Melissa, Alonso, Windy W., Keteyian, Steven J., Goodyke, Madison, & Dunn, Susan L. (2023). Comorbidities are associated with state hopelessness in adults with ischemic heart disease. *Heart & Lung*, 60: 28–34. https://doi.org/10.1016/j.hrtlng.2023.02.025, accessed 4-10-23.

17. Lindholm, Lisbet, Holmberg, Maria, & Mäkelä, Carita. (2005, June 1). Hope and hopelessness—Nourishment for the patient's vitality. *International Journal of Human Caring*, 9(4): 33–38. https://doi.org/10.20467/1091-5710.9.4.33, accessed 4-08-23; Kurita, N., Wakita, T., & Fujimoto, S., et al. (2021). Hopelessness and depression predict sarcopenia in advanced CKD and dialysis: A multicenter cohort study. *Journal of Nutrition, Health, & Aging*, 25: 593–599. https://doi.org/10.1007/s12603-020-1556-4, accessed 4-08-23; Rasmussen, Heather N., England, Elisabeth, & Cole, Brian P. (2023). Hope and physical health. *Current Opinion in Psychology*, 49: 101549. https://doi.org/10.1016/j.copsyc.2022.101549, accessed 4-09-23; Schmale, A. H., Iker, H. (1971). Hopelessness as a predictor of cervical cancer. *Social Science & Medicine (1967)*, 5(2): 95–100. https://doi.org/10.1016/0037-7856(71)90090-4, accessed 4-09-23.

18. Mystakidou, K., Tsilika, E., Parpa, E., Pathiaki, M., Galanos, A. & Vlahos, L. (2008). The relationship between quality of life and levels of hopelessness and depression in palliative care. *Depression and Anxiety*, 25: 730–736. https://doi.org/10.1002/da.20319, accessed 4-08-23; Feldman, David B., & Corn, Benjamin W. (2023). Hope and cancer. *Current Opinion in Psychology*, 49: 101506. https://doi.org/10.1016/j.copsyc.2022.101506, accessed 4-09-23.

19. Orwelius, Lotti, Kristenson, Margareta, Fredrikson, Mats, Walther, Sten, & Sjöberg, Folke. (2017).

Hopelessness: Independent associations with health-related quality of life and short-term mortality after critical illness: A prospective, multicentre trial. *Journal of Critical Care*, 41: 58–63. https://doi.org/10.1016/j.jcrc.2017.04.044, accessed 4-09-23; Dunn, Susan L., Stommel, Manfred, Corser, William D., & Holmes-Rovner, Margaret. (2009, January). Hopelessness and its effect on cardiac rehabilitation exercise participation following hospitalization for acute coronary syndrome. *Journal of Cardiopulmonary Rehabilitation and Prevention*, 29(1): 32–39. https://doi.org/10.1097/HCR.0b013e31819276ba, accessed 4-09-23; Burke, A. (2008). Could anxiety, hopelessness and health locus of control contribute to the outcome of a kidney transplant? *South African Journal of Psychology*, 38(3): 527–540. https:doi.org/10.1177/008124630803800307, accessed 4-09-23.

20. Anastasiades, Maria, Gupton, Olivia, Fritz, Yvonne, Calzada, Pablo, & Stillman, Mark. (2016). Diabetes, depression, and nonadherence: Exploring hopelessness as a mediating factor: A preliminary study. *Mental Health in Family Medicine*, 12: 241. https://www.researchgate.net/profile/Mark-Stillman/publication/306167436_Diabetes_Depression_and_Nonadherence_Exploring_Hopelessness_as_a_Mediating_Factor_A_Preliminary_Study/links/5ab108d6458515ecebe-be6a9/Diabetes-Depression-and-Nonadherence-Exploring-Hopelessness-as-a-Mediating-Factor-A-Preliminary-Study.pdf, accessed 4-10-23.

21. Lancaster, Brittany D., & Van Allen, Jason. (2023). Hope and pediatric health. *Current Opinion in Psychology*, 49: 101500. https://doi.org/10.1016/j.copsyc.2022.101500, accessed 4-09-23; Stern, Stephen L., Dhanda, Rahul, & Hazuda, Helen P. (2001, May). Hopelessness predicts mortality in older Mexican and European Americans. *Psychosomatic Medicine*, 63(3): 344–351. https://journals.lww.com/psychosomaticmedicine/Abstract/2001/05000/Hopelessness_Predicts_Mortality_in_Older_Mexican.3.aspx, accessed 4-09-23; Mitchell, Uchechi A., Gutierrez-Kapheim, Melissa, Nguyen, Ann W., & Al-Amin, Nadia. (2020). Hopelessness among middle-aged and older blacks: The negative impact of discrimination and protecting power of social and religious resources. *Innovation in Aging*, 4(5): igaa044. https://doi.org/10.1093/geroni/igaa044, accessed 4-08-23; Everson, Susan A., Goldberg, Debbie E. Kaplan, George A., Cohen, Richard D., Pukkala, Eero, Tuomilehto, Jaakko, & Salonen, Jukka T. (1996, March/April). Hopelessness and risk of mortality and incidence of myocardial infarction and cancer. *Psychosomatic Medicine*, 58(2): 113–121. https://journals.lww.com/psychosomaticmedicine/Abstract/1996/03000/Hopelessness_and_Risk_of_Mortality_and_Incidence.3.aspx, accessed 4-09-23; Håkansson, K., Soininen, H., Winblad, B., & Kivipelto M. (2015). Feelings of hopelessness in midlife and cognitive health in later life: A prospective population-based cohort study. *PLOS ONE*, 10(10): e0140261. https://doi.org/10.1371/journal.pone.0140261, accessed 4-09-23; Fortuna, Karen L., Venegas, Maria, Bianco, Cynthia L., Smith, Bret, Batsis, John A., Walker, Robert, Brooks, Jessica, & Umucu, Emre. (2020). The relationship between hopelessness and risk factors for early mortality in people with a lived experience of a serious mental illness. *Social Work in Mental Health*, 18(4): 369–382. https://doi.org/10.1080/15332985.2020.1751772, accessed 4-09-23.

22. Hans-Georg Gadamer in one of his last interviews. Gadamer, Hans-Georg. (2002, February 11). Die Menschen können nicht ohne Hoffnung leben. *Rhein-Neckar-Zeitung*.

23. Serafini et al., Hopelessness and its correlates. https://doi.org/10.1016/j.jad.2019.11.144; Mouton, Angela. (2023). Hope and work: From the pandemic to possibility, purpose, and resilience. *Current Opinion in Psychology*, 49: 101550. https://doi.org/10.1016/j.copsyc.2022.101550, accessed 4-09-23.

24. Cole, Brian P., & Molloy, Sonia. (2023). Hope and parenting. *Current Opinion in Psychology*, 49: 101554. https://doi.org/10.1016/j.copsyc.2022.101554, accessed 4-09-23; Bolland, J. M., McCallum, D. M., & Lian, B., et al. (2001). Hopelessness and violence among inner-city youths. *Maternal and Child Health Journal*, 5: 237–244. https://doi.org/10.1023/A:1013028805470, accessed 4-09-23; Stoddard, S. A., Henly, S. J., & Sieving, R. E., et al. (2011). Social connections, trajectories of hopelessness, and serious violence in impoverished urban youth. *Journal of Youth and Adolescence*, 40: 278–295. https://doi.org/10.1007/s10964-010-9580-z, accessed 4-09-23; James, Shamagonam, Reddy, Sasiragha Priscilla, Ellahebokus, Afzal, Sewpaul, Ronel, & Naidoo, Pamela. (2017). The association between adolescent risk behaviours and feelings of sadness or hopelessness:

A cross-sectional survey of South African secondary school learners. *Psychology, Health & Medicine*, 22(7): 778–789. https://doi.org/10.1080/13548506.2017.1300669, accessed 4-09-23; Fedorowicz, Anna R., Hellerstedt, Wendy L., Schreiner, Pamela J., & Bolland, John M. (2014). Associations of adolescent hopelessness and self-worth with pregnancy attempts and pregnancy desire. *American Journal of Public Health*, 104: e133_e140. https://doi.org/10.2105/AJPH.2014.301914, accessed 4-09-23; Broccoli, T. L., & Sanchez, D. T. (2009). Implicit hopelessness and condom use frequency: Exploring nonconscious predictors of sexual risk behavior. *Journal of Applied Social Psychology*, 39: 430–448. https://doi.org/10.1111/j.1559-1816.2008.00445.x, accessed 4-08-23; Kagan, S., Deardorff, J., McCright, J., Lightfoot, M., Lahiff, M., & Lippman, S. A. (2012, September). Hopelessness and sexual risk behavior among adolescent African American males in a low-income urban community. *American Journal of Men's Health*, 6(5): 395–9. https://doi.org/10.1177/1557988312439407, accessed 4-09-23; Jalilian, Farzad, Karami Matin, Behzad, Ahmadpanah, Mohammad, Motlagh, F., Mahboubi, Mohammad, & Eslami, Ahmad Ali. (2014). Substance abuse among college students: Investigation the role of hopelessness. *Life Science Journal*, 11: 396–399. https://www.researchgate.net/publication/289850946_Substance_abuse_among_college_students_Investigation_the_role_of_hopelessness, accessed 4-08-23.

25. Keller, Helen. (1903). *Optimism: An essay*. T. Y. Crowell, 67.

26. Game Changers & Ipsos. (2021, August). What worries the world? https://www.ipsos.com/sites/default/files/ct/publication/documents/2021-08/What%20Worries%20the%20World-August_2021.pdf, accessed 4-10-23; Doherty, Carroll, & Gomez, Vianney. (2022, May 12). *By a wide margin, Americans view inflation as the top problem facing the country today*. Pew Research Center. https://www.pewresearch.org/fact-tank/2022/05/12/by-a-wide-margin-americans-view-inflation-as-the-top-problem-facing-the-country-today/, accessed 4-10-23; Statista. (2023, February). What do you think is the most important problem facing this country today? https://www.statista.com/statistics/323380/public-opinion-on-the-most-important-problem-facing-the-us/, accessed 4-10-23; Gallup. (2023). Most important problem. https://news.gallup.com/poll/1675/most-important-problem.aspx, accessed 4-10-23.

27. Global Shapes Community. (2017, August 31). *Global Shapers Annual Survey 2017*. https://www.es.amnesty.org/fileadmin/noticias/ShapersSurvey2017_Full_Report_24Aug__002__01.pdf, accessed 4-10-23; Poushter, Jacob, Fagan, Moira, & Gubbala, Sneha. (2022, August 31). *Climate change remains top global threat across 19-country survey*. Pew Research Center. https://www.pewresearch.org/global/2022/08/31/climate-change-remains-top-global-threat-across-19-country-survey/, accessed 4-10-23; UNESCO. (2020, November 16). *"World in 2030" Public Survey: Climate change and biodiversity loss biggest concern by far, multilateralism and education most important solutions*. https://en.unesco.org/news/world-2030-public-survey-climate-change-and-biodiversity-loss-biggest-concern-far, accessed 4-10-23.

28. Drucker, Peter F. (2010). *Men, ideas & politics*. Harvard Business Review Press, ix.

29. Sun, F.-K., Wu, M.-K., Yao, Y., Chiang, C.-Y., & Lu, C.-Y. (2022). Meaning in life as a mediator of the associations among depression, hopelessness and suicidal ideation: A path analysis. *Journal of Psychiatric and Mental Health Nursing*, 29: 57–66. https://doi.org/10.1111/jpm.12739, accessed 4-09-23; Gülerce, H., & Maraj, H. A. (2021). Resilience and hopelessness in Turkish society: Exploring the role of spirituality in the COVID-19 pandemic. *Journal of Economy Culture and Society*: 1–15. https://dergipark.org.tr/en/pub/jecs/issue/63369/960215, accessed 4-09-23; Hasanshahi, M., Amidi Mazaheri, M., & Baghbanian, A. (2018). Relationship between spiritual health, hopelessness, and self-efficacy in medical sciences students. *Iranian Journal of Psychiatry and Behavioral Sciences*, 12(2): e2071. https://doi.org/10.5812/ijpbs.2071, https://brieflands.com/articles/ijpbs-2071.html, accessed 4-09-23.

30. Murphy, P. E., Ciarrocchi, J. W., Piedmont, R. L., Cheston, S., Peyrot, M., & Fitchett, G. (2000). The relation of religious belief and practices, depression, and hopelessness in persons with clinical depression. *Journal of Consulting and Clinical Psychology*, 68(6): 1102–1106. https://doi.org/10.1037/0022-006X.68.6.1102, accessed 4-09-23; De Berardis, D., Olivieri, L., Rapini, G., Serroni, N., Fornaro, M., Valchera, A., Carano, A., Vellante, F., Bustini, M., Serafini, G., Pompili, M., Ventriglio, A., Perna, G., Fraticelli, S., Martinotti, G., & Di Giannantonio, M. (2020). Religious

coping, hopelessness, and suicide ideation in subjects with first-episode major depression: An exploratory study in the real world clinical practice. *Brain Science* 10: 912. https://doi.org/10.3390/brainsci10120912, accessed 4-09-23; Gençöz, F., Vatan, S., Walker, R. L., & Lester, D. (2007). Hopelessness and suicidality in Turkish and American respondents. *OMEGA - Journal of Death and Dying,* 55(4): 311–319. https://doi.org/10.2190/OM.55.4.e, accessed 4-08-23; Austin, D., & Lennings, C. J. (1993). Grief and religious belief: Does belief moderate depression? *Death Studies,* 17(6): 487–496. https://doi.org/10.1080/07481189308252634, accessed 4-09-23; Simonson, Randy H. (2008). Religiousness and non-hopeless suicide ideation. *Death Studies,* 32(10): 951–960. https://doi.org/10.1080/07481180802440589, accessed 4-09-23; Baird, J. G. (1990). *The relationship between suicide risk, hopelessness, depression, and religious commitment in high school students.* Dissertation Abstracts International, 51(6-B), 3119. https://www.proquest.com/openview/35baf3bd034c5bf3edbaab55afc4104b/1?pq-origsite=gscholar&cbl=18750&diss=y, accessed 4-09-23; Molock, S. D., Puri, R., Matlin, S., & Barksdale, C. (2006). Relationship between religious coping and suicidal behaviors among African American adolescents. *Journal of Black Psychology,* 32(3): 366–389. https://doi.org/10.1177/0095798406290466, accessed 4-09-23; Mitchell et al., Hopelessness among middle-aged. https://doi.org/10.1093/geroni/igaa044.

31. Kavak Budak, F., Özdemir, A., & Gültekin, A., et al. (2021). The effect of religious belief on depression and hopelessness in advanced cancer patients. *Journal of Religion and Health,* 60: 2745–2755. https://doi.org/10.1007/s10943-020-01120-6, accessed 4-09-23.

32. Murphy, P. E., & Fitchett, G. (2009). Belief in a concerned god predicts response to treatment for adults with clinical depression. *Journal of Clinical Psychology,* 65: 1000–1008. https://doi.org/10.1002/jclp.20598, accessed 4-09-23.

33. Cruz, Mario, Schulz, Richard, Pincus, Harold A., Houck, Patricia R., Bensasi, Salem, & Reynolds, Charles F. (2009). The association of public and private religious involvement with severity of depression and hopelessness in older adults treated for major depression. *The American Journal of Geriatric Psychiatry,* 17(6): 503–507. https://doi.org/10.1097/JGP.0b013e31819d37a9, accessed 4-09-23.

34. Sullivan, Mark D. (2003). Hope and hopelessness at the end of life. *The American Journal of Geriatric Psychiatry,* 11(4): 393–405. https://doi.org/10.1097/00019442-200307000-00002, accessed 4-09-23; Mihaljević, S., Aukst-Margetić, B., Vuksan-Ćusa, B., Koić, E., & Milošević, M. (2012, September). Hopelessness, suicidality and religious coping in Croatian war veterans with PTSD. *Psychiatria Danubina,* 24(3): 292–7. https://hrcak.srce.hr/file/156454, accessed 4-08-23.

35. Samuel Johnson, letter of 8 June 1762, in Boswell, James. (1791). *Life of Samuel Johnson* (Vol. 1). Page 103.

36. Romans 3:23 ESV.

37. Romans 6:23 ESV.

38. Romans 5:8 ESV.

39. Romans 10:9–10 ESV.

40. Romans 5:1 ESV.

41. Lewis, C. S. (2001). *The Weight of Glory.* HarperCollins, 140.

42. Romans 1:16 ESV.

43. Mark 2:17 ESV.

44. 2 Corinthians 5:17 ESV.

45. Justin Martyr (103–165), in Claiborne, Shane, Wilson-Hartgrove, Jonathan, & Okoro, Enuma (Eds.). (2010). *Common prayer: A liturgy for ordinary radicals.* Zondervan, 375.

46. Leviticus 25:35.

47. Lactantius of Rome (c. 304–313) served as tutor to Emperor Constantine, in W. 7.177, 178.

48. Eusebius Pamphilius (263–339). Constantine's liberality to the poor. In *The Life of Constantine,* book I, chapter XLIII.

49. Proverbs 22:2; James 2:1–7; Leviticus 19:15.

50. Proverbs 20:10.

51. Ambrose of Milan (c. 339–397) as recounted in Chemnitz, Martin. (2004). *On almsgiving.* LCMS World Relief and Human Care, 5.

52. Romans 15:13.

53. Hebrews 11:1–2 ESV.

54. Titus 1:2 ESV. See also 1 Corinthians 15:19; Ephesians 1:18; 2 Corinthians 4:16–18; 1 Thessalonians 4:13; Colossians 3:1–2.

55. Romans 5:2 ESV. See also 1 Thessalonians 5:8; Titus 3:7; 1 Peter 1:13; Titus 2:13; 1 Timothy 1:1; Hebrews 3:6; Colossians 1:5.

56. Psalm 31:24 ESV. See also Psalm 39:7; Psalm 62:5; Galatians 5:5; Romans 8:25.

57. Romans 12:12 ESV. See also Deuteronomy 31:6; Hebrews 10:23; Psalm 9:18; Romans 15:4; Isaiah 41:10; Hebrews 6:11; Lamentations 3:24; John 14:27.

58. Victor Hugo, oft quoted in this way, is modified from the quote: "That word which God, however, has written on the brow of every man: hope!" Hugo, Victor. (1862). *Les Misérables*. Hurst and Blackett, 79.

Postscript: The Bible Describes You the Way You Really Are

1. For more, see Wallace, J. Warner. (2021). *Person of interest: Why Jesus still matters in a world that rejects the Bible.* Zondervan.

We're Not Always in Igloos

A Book on Different Inuit Homes

3rd Grade Social Studies | Children's Geography & Cultures Books

BABY PROFESSOR
EDUCATION KIDS

First Edition, 2021

Published in the United States by Speedy Publishing LLC, 40 E Main Street, Newark, Delaware 19711 USA.

© 2021 Baby Professor Books, an imprint of Speedy Publishing LLC

Baby Professor Books are available at special discounts when purchased in bulk for industrial and sales-promotional use. For details contact our Special Sales Team at Speedy Publishing LLC, 40 E Main Street, Newark, Delaware 19711 USA. Telephone (888) 248-4521 Fax: (210) 519-4043.

10 9 8 7 6 * 5 4 3 2 1

Print Edition: 9781541978478
Digital Edition: 9781541978614
Hardcover Edition: 9781541983397

See the world in pictures. Build your knowledge in style.
www.speedypublishing.com

Table of Contents

Have you ever thought about the type of material that was used to construct the home in which you live? Was your home made of concrete, brick, wood, or a combination of different materials? Different people live in different types of homes. Moreover, different materials are used to make homes and often the choice of materials is determined by the place in which people live.

Different materials are used to make homes and often the choice of materials is determined by the place in which people live.

Colorful Inuit houses in Ilulissat, North Greenland.

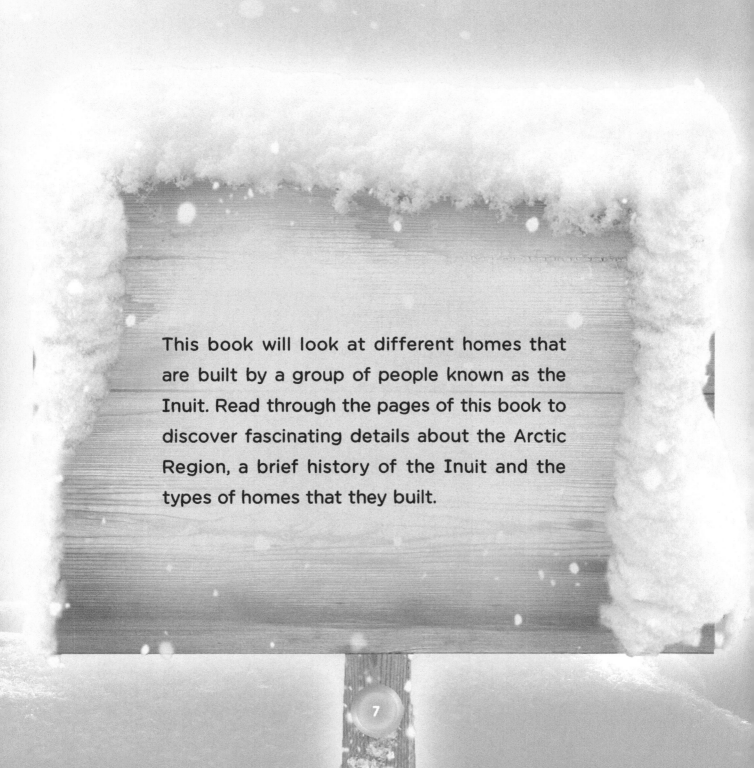

This book will look at different homes that are built by a group of people known as the Inuit. Read through the pages of this book to discover fascinating details about the Arctic Region, a brief history of the Inuit and the types of homes that they built.

Chapter One:

The Inuit and The Arctic Region

Inuit is a word that refers to indigenous people who live in the Arctic region of the Earth. This region consists of parts of northern Canada, the United States, Sweden, Norway, Finland, Iceland, Greenland, and Russia. It is believed that the Inuit are the last indigenous people to have settled in North America.

It is believed that the Inuit are the last indigenous
people to have settled in North America.

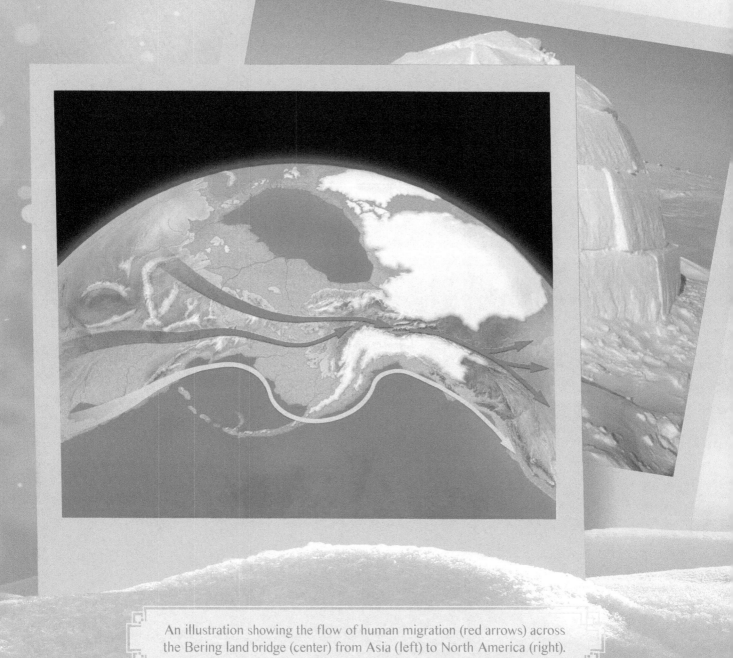

An illustration showing the flow of human migration (red arrows) across
the Bering land bridge (center) from Asia (left) to North America (right).

Some Inuit History

It is thought that the Inuit arrived in what is now the state of Alaska in 6000 B.C. They probably came over from Asia by crossing the Bering Land Bridge. The Bering Land Bridge was a small strip of land that would have connected Alaska to Northeast Asia. However, most of that bridge is now gone due to the shifts in land which can occur.

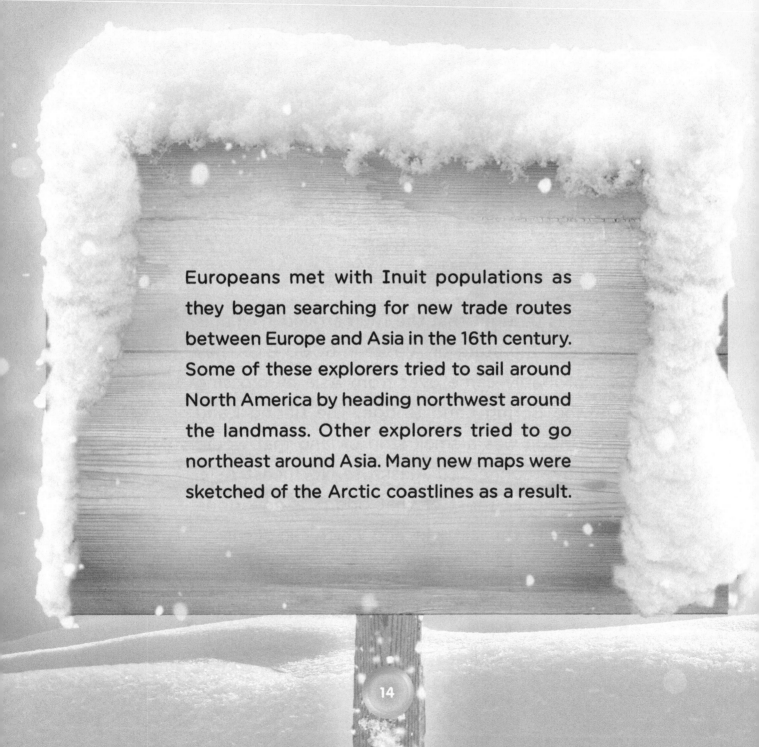

Europeans met with Inuit populations as they began searching for new trade routes between Europe and Asia in the 16th century. Some of these explorers tried to sail around North America by heading northwest around the landmass. Other explorers tried to go northeast around Asia. Many new maps were sketched of the Arctic coastlines as a result.

Europeans met with Inuit populations as they began
searching for new trade routes between Europe and Asia.

Explorers had made it to the North Pole, the northernmost tip of the Earth.

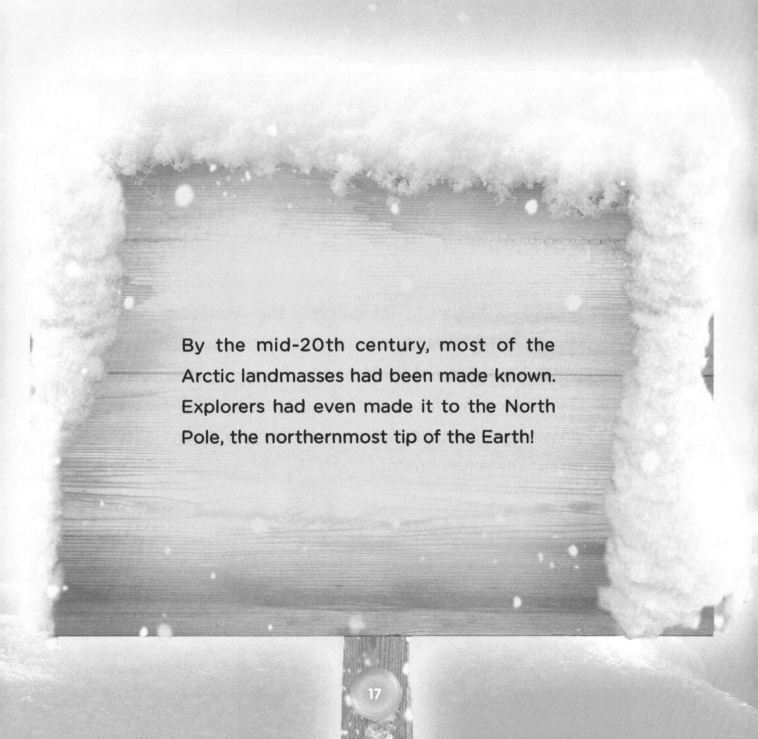

By the mid-20th century, most of the Arctic landmasses had been made known. Explorers had even made it to the North Pole, the northernmost tip of the Earth!

Scientists began to investigate the Arctic to research the local plants, animals, minerals, and other environmental elements. Currently, the big concern with the Artic is to consider how possible influences like global warming might affect the environment.

Scientists began to investigate the Arctic to research the local plants, animals, minerals, and other environmental elements.

Map of the Arctic Region

Where is the Arctic Region?

The Arctic region is the area close to the North Pole. There is an imaginary line called the Arctic Circle which surrounds most of this area. The landmasses have the Arctic Ocean lying between them.

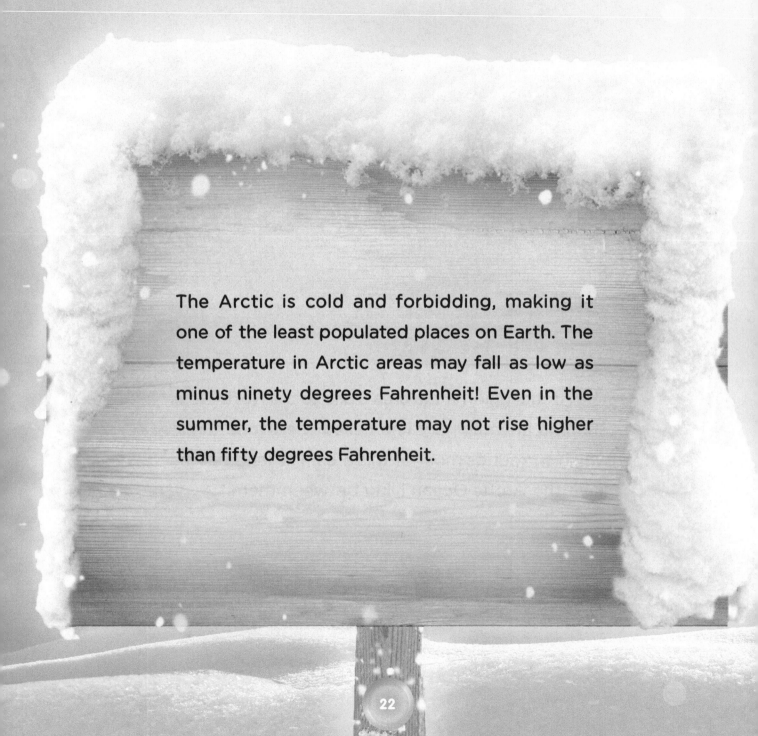

The Arctic is cold and forbidding, making it one of the least populated places on Earth. The temperature in Arctic areas may fall as low as minus ninety degrees Fahrenheit! Even in the summer, the temperature may not rise higher than fifty degrees Fahrenheit.

The Arctic is cold and forbidding, making it
one of the least populated places on Earth.

Land that is found in the Arctic region is typically
flat, treeless, and covered in ice and snow.

Land that is found in the Arctic region is typically flat, treeless, and covered in ice and snow. We call such environments tundra. The ground there is generally frozen permanently, with only a thin layer on top being able to thaw in summer. In fact, Greenland is covered by a large sheet of ice for most of the year!

Areas in the Arctic also have remarkably interesting days and nights. At the North Pole, the Sun will not rise properly for six months of the year, during winter. The other half of the year, the Sun will not properly set! The Arctic areas that are found more towards the south will get some daylight in the winter, but only a few hours. Conversely, they will get some hours of nighttime in the summer, but not many.

At the North Pole, the Sun will not properly set half of the year.

Chapter Two:

Shelters and the Igloo

Igloos are often thought of when people think of Inuit people. An igloo can be pictured as a round house that is made of blocks of snow or ice. However, the word comes from the Inuit word igdlu which means house and the Inuit had more than one kind. They also had summer and spring houses that were not made of snow.

An igloo can be pictured as a round house
that is made of blocks of snow or ice.

Shelter is important for both people and animals so that
they can be protected from the outside environment.

What is Shelter and Why is it Necessary?

Shelter is important for both people and animals so that they can be protected from the outside environment. It is harder to stay alive if you have no protection from rain or snowstorms, for instance. You will probably freeze to death or get sick!

Humans have learned to create different shelters based upon the needs of various environments and climates. For the Inuit population, shelter was critical to offer protection from the harshness of the Arctic weather. A blizzard could easily kill people if they did not have appropriate shelter. Inuit hunters learned how to build shelters quite quickly. They could overturn their dogsleds and pack the area all around with snow, if necessary, to stay warm until the storm was over.

Humans have learned to create different shelters based upon the needs of various environments and climates.

Snow is an excellent insulator to keep in heat when it is cold.

Shelters are built in different regions based upon what is available. For the Inuit peoples, snow was the most easily available resource with which to build. No trees grew in the tundra, and plants were rare in the winter. It may be surprising, but snow is an excellent insulator to keep in heat when it is cold.

Shelter for Nomads:

Inuit people had to be able to build there homes quickly, not only to survive sudden snowstorms when they were far from home, but also due to their nomadic lifestyle. A nomad refers to someone who moves around without one permanent home. Before farms and cities became more common, many people lived nomadic lifestyles as they searched for food, either for themselves or their animals. As they moved, they would need good shelter for themselves and their families.

As nomads moved, they would need good
shelter for themselves and their families.

The Inuit population make tents by shaping
animal skin around wooden poles or bone.

Not only did the Inuit population take advantage of the abundant snow, in the summer, they could make tents by shaping animal skin around wooden poles or bone. These tents could be carried to wherever the Inuit people need to go. If they were going to be somewhere more permanently, they could even build a home out of sod. Hence, the homes of the Inuit people were adapted to both their lifestyle as well as location. Other names for their homes are iglu and aputiak.

Snow Homes:

When the temperature fell, and snow houses were built, the Inuit population had to be careful to make sure that there were no cracks in the walls of the igloo. If there were cracks, the warm air would leak out and the people would not be able to keep very warm. Despite this, the igloos were built quickly. A small house could be built within a couple of hours! A larger house would take longer, but an entire family might live in it throughout the whole winter.

The Inuit population had to be careful to make sure
that there were no cracks in the walls of the igloo.

Tools used by Inuit peoples in the Arctic during the 1920s. Caribou skin was sewn to caribou antler to create a snow shovel, the stick was used to test snow and the knife to cut snow when making blocks for an igloo.

In the modern day, many Inuit people choose to live in more permanent houses. Nevertheless, they still know how to make snow houses. These can be quite useful when hunting. All they need is a snow knife which they can use to cut blocks from hardened snow. Snow that has already been packed by the wind is the best snow with which to build.

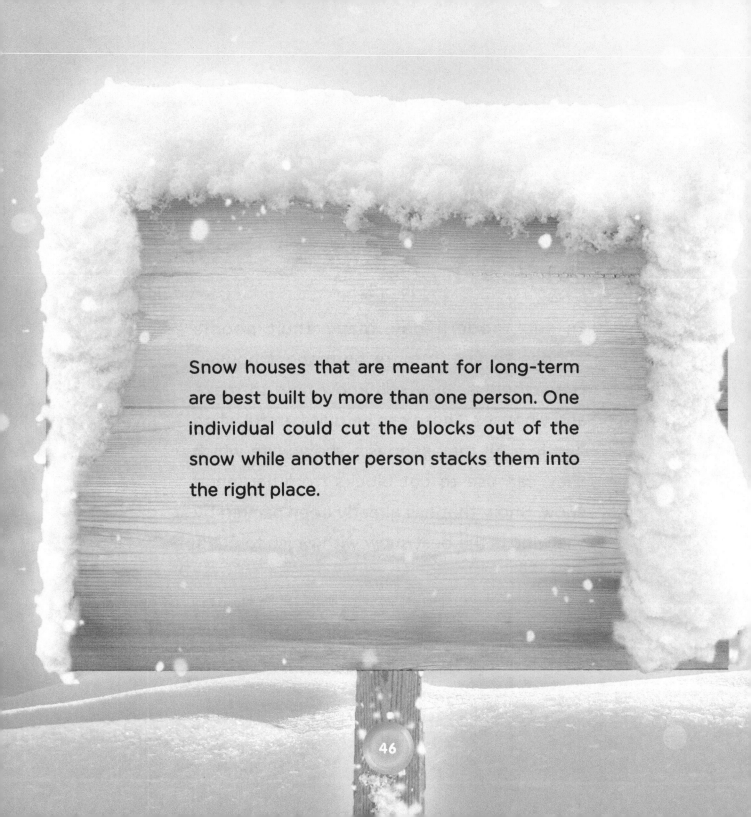

Snow houses that are meant for long-term are best built by more than one person. One individual could cut the blocks out of the snow while another person stacks them into the right place.

Inuit cutting ice blocks with knife and trims
them while building A traditional igloo.

Inuit building an igloo by carving snow blocks and carefully placing them.

As the bricks of snow are being set into place, each row tilts in slightly more to the center.

Where to place the blocks is planned by mapping out a circle that is than stomped into the snow. As the bricks of snow are being set into place, each row tilts in slightly more to the center. In this way, the house becomes round and is less likely to be damaged by the wind.

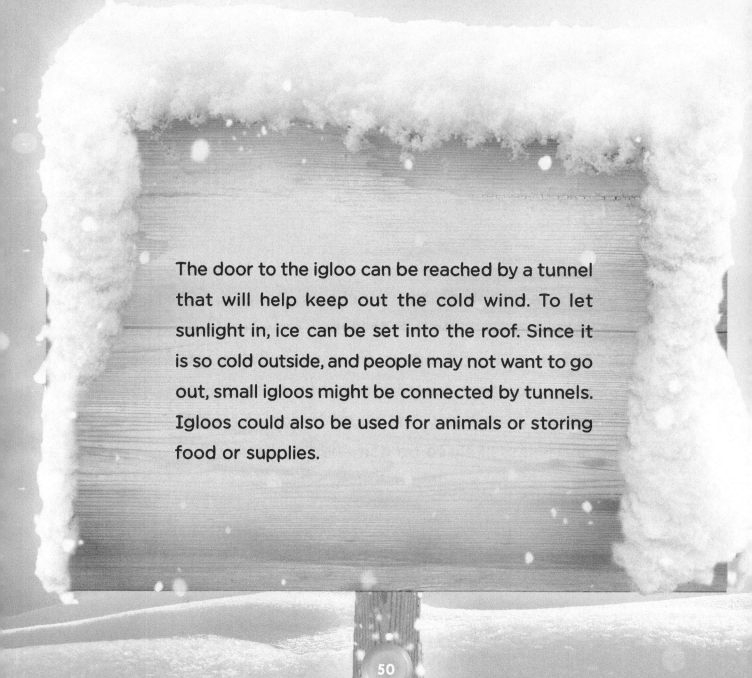

The door to the igloo can be reached by a tunnel that will help keep out the cold wind. To let sunlight in, ice can be set into the roof. Since it is so cold outside, and people may not want to go out, small igloos might be connected by tunnels. Igloos could also be used for animals or storing food or supplies.

The door to the igloo can be reached by a
tunnel that will help keep out the cold wind.

Chapter Three:
The Other Types of Inuit Homes

In the last chapter, we mentioned that houses of snow were not the only houses that the Inuit people built. They built different kinds of homes in the spring and the summer. These homes could also help them maintain their nomadic lifestyle. This chapter will examine those homes in more detail.

The Inuit people built different kinds of
homes in the spring and the summer.

The Inuit people would need to follow
the caribou herds that they hunted.

Houses of the Nomads:

When spring and summer came, the days became much longer. It was time for the Inuit people to take advantage of the exceedingly long days and warmer weather to hunt, fish, gather, and prepare for the next winter. This meant that the Inuit would need to follow the caribou herds that they hunted.

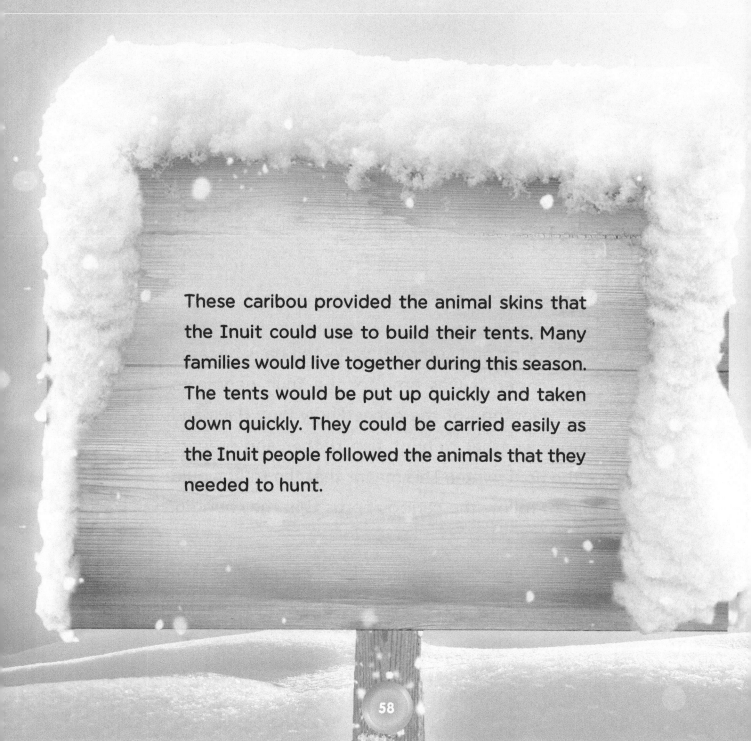

These caribou provided the animal skins that the Inuit could use to build their tents. Many families would live together during this season. The tents would be put up quickly and taken down quickly. They could be carried easily as the Inuit people followed the animals that they needed to hunt.

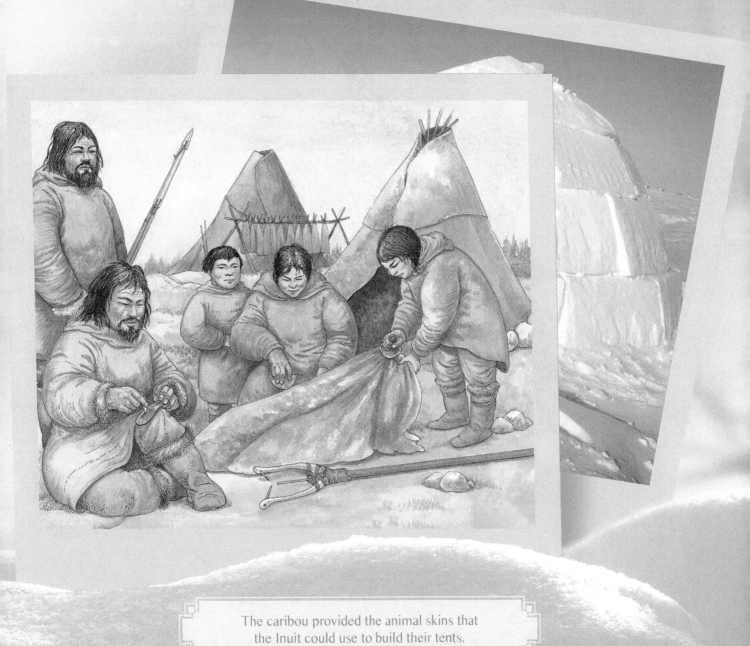

The caribou provided the animal skins that
the Inuit could use to build their tents.

The tents were triangular with a flap that
could be tied shut to keep the wind out.

It is said that the tent villages that sprang up during an Arctic summer looked similar to the teepees of the Native American villages. The tents were triangular with a flap that could be tied shut to keep the wind out. In the modern age, some Inuit people still use the traditional tents. Others use camping tools from the modern day.

The Inuit population used dogsleds in the winter to travel. In the summer, they would use kayaks or umiaks. Umiaks were large boats. These boats were used to hunt large mammals like whales in the ocean.

The Inuit population would use kayaks to hunt whales in the ocean.

The Inuit population used dogsleds in the winter to travel.

Inuit people did not limit themselves to tents made form animal skin, they also make their homes from sod.

Staying Permanently:

Inuit people did not limit themselves to tents made form animal skin. If other materials were available, they might make their homes from sod. Sod is the top layer of Earth that has grass growing on it. The roots of the grass help hold it together. Typically, however, these homes are found when the Inuit people were able to stay in one place for a while.

To build these homes, a foundation was put into the ground about a foot deep. The walls would be made from driftwood or whalebones. Finally, large bits of sod would be taken up from the ground and packed against the sides and top of the structure. Since the ground was so often frozen, these structures could only be built when it was warm, and the ground had thawed. Skylights or windows could be made from the stretched and dried intestines of animals. These intestines could let in light.

Interior of a sod house framed out of whale bones.

The Inuit people moved around a
lot and left behind their houses.

The Inuit people did not think of themselves as owning their own land or houses. They moved around a lot and they left behind their houses. These houses could be used by anyone who found them empty and needed them.

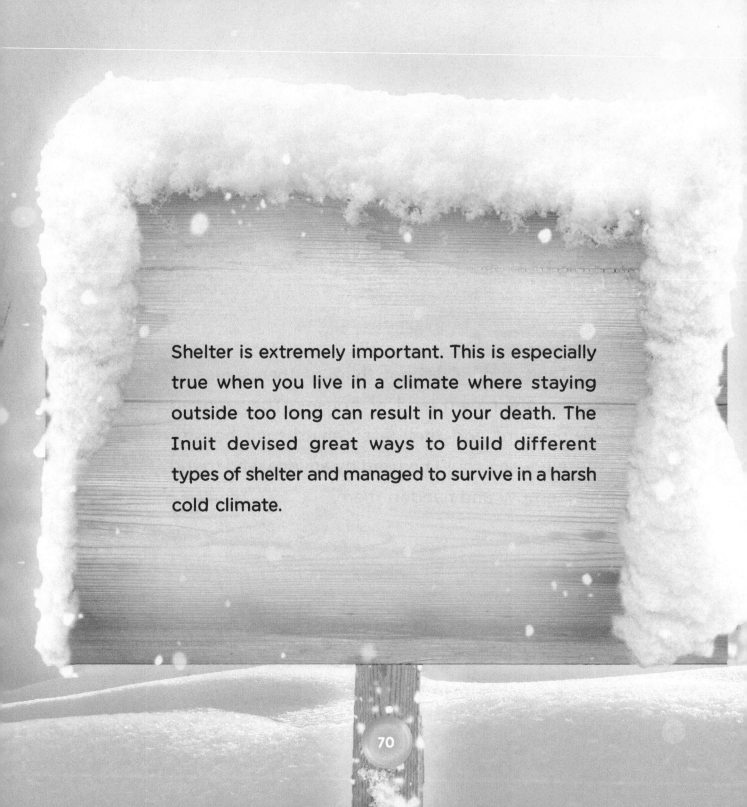

Shelter is extremely important. This is especially true when you live in a climate where staying outside too long can result in your death. The Inuit devised great ways to build different types of shelter and managed to survive in a harsh cold climate.

Visit

www.speedypublishing.com

To view and download free content
on your favorite subject and browse
our catalog of new and exciting
books for readers of all ages.

Made in the USA
Monee, IL
14 April 2022

94755920R00044